Chou Wah-shan

Tongzhi
Politics of Same-Sex Eroticism in Chinese Societies

"**C**hou carefully describes the evolution of homosexual life and culture in various Chinese societies. The reader will learn just how differently Chinese and Western cultures express sexual identity, and how inadequate Western theory and rhetoric are for understanding Chinese sexuality. Most interesting, Chou contrasts the homosexual cultures of Hong Kong, China, and Taiwan. In recent times, under the very different political and social conditions of each place, traditional Chinese sexuality has developed in very different directions. In sum, this book ably conveys the uniqueness and rich diversity of Chinese sexuality."

Bret Hinsch, PhD
Associate Professor,
Department of History,
National Chung Cheng University,
Taiwan

The Haworth Press, Inc.

Tongzhi
Politics of Same-Sex Eroticism in Chinese Societies

THE HAWORTH PRESS
Human Sexuality
Eli Coleman, PhD
Editor

Tonghzi: Politics of Same-Sex Eroticism in Chinese Societies by Chou Wah-shan

Additional titles of related interest:

Male to Male: Sexual Feeling Across the Boundaries of Identity by Edward J. Tejirian

Queer Asian Cinema: Shadows in the Shade edited by Andrew David Grossman

The Sexual Construction of Latino Youth: Implications for the Spread of HIV/AIDS by Jacobo Schifter and Johnny Madrigal

Lady Boys, Tom Boys, Rent Boys: Male and Female Homosexualities in Contemporary Thailand edited by Peter A. Jackson and Gerard Sullivan

One of the Boys: Masculinity, Homophobia, and Modern Manhood by David Plummer

Strategic Sex: Why They Won't Keep It in the Bedroom edited by D. Travers Scott

A Sea of Stories: The Shaping Power of Narrative in Gay and Lesbian Cultures—A Festschrift for John P. De Cecco edited by Sonya L. Jones

The Bear Book II: Further Readings in the History and Evolution of a Gay Male Subculture edited by Les Wright

Tongzhi
Politics of Same-Sex Eroticism in Chinese Societies

Chou Wah-shan

The Haworth Press®
New York • London • Oxford

The Haworth Press, Inc., 10 Alice Street, Binghamton, NY 13904-1580

Cover design by Jennifer M. Gaska.

Cover photos and collage by Stanley Lai.

Library of Congress Cataloging-in-Publication Data

Chou, Hua-shan, 1962-
    Tongzhi: politics of same-sex eroticism in Chinese societies / Chou Wah-shan.
        p.   cm.
    Includes bibliographical references and index.
    ISBN 1-56023-153-X (hard : alk. paper) — ISBN 1-56023-154-8 (soft : alk. paper)
    1. Homosexuality—China. I. Title.

HQ76.3.C2 C48 2000
306.76'6'0951—dc21

                                                00-031912

CONTENTS

ABOUT THE AUTHOR

Dr. Chou Wah-shan taught at the University of Hong Kong. He has published more than twenty Chinese books, mostly on sexuality and gender politics. He is now living in China and doing research on the Mosuo culture, the matrilineal culture located in Southwestern China.

Introduction

The Cultural Politics of *Tongzhi*

This book examines the cultural specificity of same-sex eroticism in Chinese societies, in which the family kinship system, rather than an erotic object choice, is the basis of a person's identity. I will argue for the need to build up indigenous *tongzhi* politics that need not reproduce the Anglo-American experiences and strategies of lesbigay liberation. Throughout this book, I will use "lesbigay" when referring to lesbians, bisexuals, and gay people in the West, "PEPS" when referring to "People who are Erotically attracted to People of the Same sex" in "traditional" (defined as pre-twentieth century) Chinese societies, and *tongzhi* when referring to contemporary Chinese lesbigay people. Although the *tongzhi* perspectives have relevance for Chinese living in different societies, I confine my analysis to *tongzhi* living in Taiwan, mainland China, and Hong Kong. In the context of same-sex eroticism in China, I would use the term homosexuality only as an adjective and not as a noun (i.e., homosexual) because the concept of "homosexual" as a different type of person did not exist in Chinese language and culture until the 1980s, and even now it is rarely used as a noun. The term "gay" will be italicized when it refers to both sexes and includes bisexuals.

Tongzhi is the most popular contemporary Chinese word for lesbians, bisexuals, and gay people. The word, which has very positive historical references, was a Chinese translation from a Soviet communist term, "comrade," which refers to the revolutionaries who shared a comradeship. The term was first adopted by Chinese in Republican China, and then taken both by the Communist and Nationalist Parties to refer to comrades struggling for the communist/nationalist revolution. *Tong* literally means "same/homo," which is the Chinese word for "homo(sexual)," and *zhi* means goal, spirit, or orientation. The most popular association of *tongzhi* is probably the famous statement by the "national father" of modern China, Sun Yat-sen: "The revolution has not succeeded, *tongzhi* still have to fight." After 1949, *tongzhi* (comrade) became a friendly and politically correct term by which to address everyone in China, as it refers to the most sacred ideal of a classless society where sisters and brothers share a self-less vision of fighting for the socialist collective interest. Since the opening up of the market economy of China in 1978, the term has lost its popularity, as it represents the outdated era of communism, which is now giving way to a more capitalistic and individualistic way of using personal names or titles such as Mr./Ms. In the 1990s, *tongzhi* (comrade) is used in China only in an official context and by people of older generations.

The term *tongzhi* was appropriated by a Hong Kong gay activist in 1989 for the first Lesbian and Gay Film Festival in Hong Kong. The Chinese term *tongzhi* was used, as the organizer was keen to employ an indigenous representation of same-sex eroticism. "Homosexual" was dropped as it was a medical term denoting sickness and pathology. Even positive categories such as "gay," "lesbian," and "queer" are Anglo-Saxon constructs with specific histories that fail to capture the indigenous features of Chinese same-sex relationships. The reappropriation is widely accepted by the community for its positive cultural references, gender neutrality, desexualization of the stigma of homosexuality, politics beyond the homo-hetero duality, and use as an indigenous cultural identity for integrating the sexual into the social. Within a few years, it became the most common usage in Hong Kong and Taiwan, though the English term "gay" is still commonly used, sometimes interchangeably with *tongzhi*.

Though *tongzhi* was appropriated by a Hong Kong activist, it has an interesting historical resonance as far back as *Yi Jing* (The Book of Changes) around 3,000 years ago. The thirteenth hexagram (a sort of diagram) in *Yi Jing* is *tongren* (fellowship). This hexagram states, "It is by extending Fellowship even to the fields that one prevails. Thus it is fitting to cross the great river and fitting for the noble man to practice constancy" (Lynn, 1994: 216). The translator of *Yi Jing* made a detailed commentary on *tongren*:

> The exercise of strength here should not be done through military force but through the use of civility and enlightenment . . . so one's heart and mind here should not be bound by particularism. Instead one thoroughly identifies with the great community, so when one goes out of his [sic] gate, he [sic] treats all with fellowship . . . then one who is soft and yielding in substance but abides in the Mean will gain the support of the masses, but one who insists on rigidity and employs inflexible methods will not win a mass following. (Lynn, 1994: 116, 117, 220-221)

While *tongren* refers to the social order of fellowship and the specific mode of attaining social harmony through the transcendence of particularism, this *tongren* could be recontextualized in the sexual politics of *tongzhi*. *Ren* (people) sounds the same as *ren* (benevolence). Thus *tongren* (fellowship, people, benevolence) could be a footnote to and an elaboration of *tongzhi* both in terms of stressing flexibility and going beyond particularism to attain liberation, not only of a sexual minority but the general public.[1]

It is a telling point that as Hong Kong approached 1997, *tongzhi* adopted the most sacred term in communist China as their identity, signifying both a desire to indigenize sexual politics and to reclaim their cultural identity. *Tongzhi* symbolizes a strong sentiment for integrating the sexual (legitimizing same-sex love), political (sharing the goals of combating heterosexism), and cultural (reappropriating Chinese identity). It is in the cultural uniqueness of stressing both *zhi* (subverting heterosexism) and *tong* (sexual differences between *tongzhi* and non-*tongzhi*) that the insights of the *tongzhi* perspective lie, of going beyond the homo-hetero dichotomy without losing the sociopolitical specificity of the sexual minority.

Unlike "homo" or "hetero," *tongzhi* is not defined by the gender of one's erotic object choice but connotes an entire range of alternative sexual practices and sensitivities in a way that "lesbian," "gay," or "bisexual" does not. It rejects essentialism and behaviorism, and it does not require counting the incidence of same-sex sexual acts to qualify an individual's *tongzhi* identity. There is no "sex" in the word itself, thus helping to counteract the pervasive vulgarization of *tongxinglian* (homosexuality) in the mainstream society; yet it also helps to pluralize sexuality, as *tongzhi* refers not only to *tongxinglian* but to all forms of sexual practice that have been marginalized by hegemonic heterosexism. That explains why the category *tongzhi* is most welcome to nonhomosexual *tongzhi,* such as bisexual women, sadomasochists (S/Mers), and all other sexual minorities who cannot be subsumed under the category gay or *tongxinglian.*

Tongzhi is a completely self-proclaimed identity of nonunitary position but not without social and cultural boundaries, as the word *tong* strongly hints at same-sex eroticism. It achieves a political contribution similar to "queer politics," but whereas queer politics confronts the mainstream by taking back a bigoted label, *tongzhi* harmonizes social relationships by taking the most sacred title from the mainstream culture. It is an indigenous strategy of proclaiming one's sexual identity by appropriating rather than denying one's familial-cultural identity. Instead of stigmatizing oneself as a sexual minority, or confronting the mainstream with a homo-hetero duality, *tongzhi* penetrates and appropriates the core of the mainstream to destabilize the imagined duality of homo and hetero. What *tongzhi* resists is not identity politics per se but the universalization of the confrontational and minoritizing identity politics that may not be the best resistance strategy for a cultural tradition that did not divide people into homo or hetero categories. *Tongzhi* subverts the mainstream culture by queering and destabilizing rather than antagonizing and essentializing the supposedly straight world.

Tongzhi is a strategy of inclusion and exclusion—it expresses both the sexual identity of difference and a political identity of sameness. *Tongzhi* asserts its identity not by antagonizing heterosexuals but by inviting them to explore their own homophobia and homoeroticism. It is such tension and integration between the sexual and the political, between sameness and difference, that generates a high level of internal indeterminacy, as the distinction between *tongzhi* and non-*tongzhi* is neither discrete, fixed, nor definitive. There can be no final definition of *tongzhi,* as its meaning and content depend on and require everyday practices of all self-identified *tongzhi* to actualize, define, and redefine. *Tongzhi* identity is a moment-by-moment process of constructing self-identity through everyday practices; thus it sensitizes us to the nature of identity as difference. Every *tongzhi* needs to define, even in the unconscious, the *zhi* (goal, heart, spirit) that she or he is supposed to share with other *tongzhi.* This need pushes *tongzhi* to constantly examine the internal differences and diversities: Who are my *tongzhi?* Are we sharing the same goal and spirit? Who are included and excluded in the "we"? What kinds of voices will be repressed by the *tongzhi* platform?

Tongzhi identity, because of its internal indeterminacy, is an endless process of repeated signifying practices, with different parties competing to define *tongzhi.* By continually assuming but simultaneously calling one's own identity into question, *tongzhi* poses a constant threat to the heterosexual structure—the boundaries that define straightness (non-*tongzhi*) can never be secured if the "otherness of straight" (*tongzhi*) is sexually unstable and politically fluid. As the normalization of heterosexuality is predicated on the pathologization of homosexuality, the highly fluid and unstable self-identity of *tongzhi* helps to challenge the imagined stability of straightness. *Tongzhi* problematizes the idea of identity as fixed, natural, or objective, and destabilizes the automatic acceptance of "being gay." To articulate an unstable and fluid notion of identity by no means destroys politics; it only denies an exclusionary politics that produces an imagined stability and unity of "being gay" by "otherizing" the minorities from within.

Although most *tongzhi* may not be aware of the sociopolitical complexities of the *tongzhi* perspective, and often perceive it merely as a positive representation for homosexuals, this by no means denies the capacity of *tongzhi* discourses for a different scenario of same-sex eroticism.[2] Indeed, it is this capacity for a fluid and relational identity that has generated healthy debates, especially in Taiwan and Hong Kong, concerning the cultural specificity and political strategies of *tongzhi*.

The emergence of the discourses on *tongzhi* signifies an endeavor to integrate the sexual into the social and cultural. In a cultural tradition that has never felt the need to divide people by the gender of their erotic object choice, PEPS may not adopt the identity of *gay* or homosexual, not because of homophobia, but because they do not feel the need to segregate themselves from those who love the opposite sex. Chinese culture has a cosmology in which sexuality is not a separable category of behavior and existence, but an integral force of life. Chinese *tongzhi* who have resisted adopting the category "lesbian" or "gay" to come out have often been criticized as being closeted, dishonest, and self-denying. Although this may be true, it may also be an attempt to resist the imposition of homo-hetero duality upon the Chinese relational and fluid conception of sexuality.

For white, Anglo-Saxon, middle-class gay men, sexuality may be the site of greatest oppression. But for third-world, working-class, female, black, Asian, or, in this case, Chinese people, who love people of the same sex, issues such as race, ethnicity, culture, class, or family may be more important than sexuality. The motto "We are here, we are queer, get used to it!" is predicated upon individualism and confrontational politics in which the right to one's body is of central cultural importance. Asking all people to come out and identify themselves as lesbian or gay because they love people of the same sex is to prioritize and absolutize sexuality at the expense of all other identities and differences. It can be an act of racism, classism, sexism, and cultural imperialism. Therefore, it is crucial to historicize and theorize same-sex eroticism, and to dismantle the presupposed universality of the Anglo-American experiences of lesbigay identity formation.

"Anglo-American" is not a monolithic, fixed, or essentialized category. Neither is "white-West." It covers different places such as Italy, Poland, Denmark, and the United States, which have very different perspectives and strategies of lesbigay liberation. Even in the United States, lesbigay people living in the Midwest may not identify with the confrontational strategy of activists in cosmopolitan cities such as New York and San Francisco. These individuals and groups, including ACT UP, Queer Nation, or Outrage, are actually the minority compared with most U.S. and U.K. lesbigay, who are relatively quiet. Yet, because confrontation makes news, it is usually these confrontational images such as Kiss In, AIDS protests, or the "outrageous" drag queen in the parade that are reported and distorted in the media, and become the images that most Asians know about the so-called Western lesbigay movement. Such a distorted image of the West has often been glamorized and standardized by many Asians themselves as the ideal model of lesbigay liberation, for "being out and proud," without understanding the specific historical context of long-term homophobic violence, together with the AIDS epidemic in the 1980s, that finally generated this empowering confrontational politics.

This book by no means minimizes the immense achievement and contribution of confrontational strategies. Given the extent of homophobia and gay-bashing, which has lasted for centuries in the West, coupled with state hypocrisy and hostility during the AIDS epidemic, confrontational politics is needed to fight for the basic rights of lesbigay people. My only reservation is in the universalizing of the Anglo-American experience and its imposition upon other cultures. My aim is to develop ways to theorize and understand the experiences and categories of same-sex eroticism in different Chinese societies.

I will use the confrontational model of lesbigay liberation as the prototype for the so-called Western model of lesbigay liberation, because it has often been idealized and universalized as such a prototype by many Asian PEPS. Lesbigay confrontational politics are actually generated by a specific socioeconomic and cultural history of possessive individualism, industrial capitalism, urbanization, a framework of psychoanalysis, and a discourse of rights. It is the cultural specificity of lesbigay identity that leads some Chinese *tongzhi* to resist the modern categorization of "homo" and "hetero," rather than a self-denial of their own same-sex sexualities.

The categories of being a homosexual, lesbian, gay, and queer are neither natural nor self-evident but are highly unstable and contestable categories that may not be applicable to non-Western cultures. The fact that one is Chinese living in a Chinese society significantly changes the way one experiences and constructs a same-sex relationship. Not every person who loves others of the same sex needs to prioritize sexuality as the master category of the self. Homo and hetero identity is only one specific way to classify and construct sexual experiences. The naturalization of lesbian and gay identity is predicated on the definition of the experiences of oppression where differences can only be understood as homo-hetero. The insistence on seeing sexuality as a class, race, gender, age, and cultural category would threaten the complacency of lesbians and gays who view differences only in terms of sexuality, and view sexual differences only in terms of the gender of erotic object choice.

If the differences between Chinese and Caucasian or black and white are taken as the starting point for all queer theories and politics, one may realize that queer is often a "white project." A political strategy predicated on an "essential lesbigay identity" may fail to contest the very oppressive structure of compulsory heterosexuality and homo-hetero duality that generates such an identity in the first place. To theorize homosexuality as a discrete essential minority is to dichotomize human beings into two discrete sexual orientations and biological sexes. We need to explore how sexual categories are produced, constructed, and "attached" to different bodies as their natural and essential core self.

All bodies are sexed, raced, classed, aged, and gendered. The mainstream model of sexual identity politics tends to construct all subjects as sexual beings categorized by the rigid scheme of homo-, hetero-, or bisexuality, and may thus take class and race as the presupposed but unclarified foundation of sexual identity. There is a pretense that a homogeneity of experiences is covered by the term *gay/gay liberation*. It is a violence of the sameness that suppresses and denies different cultural constructions of same-sex eroticism.

This book develops perspectives and strategies of *tongzhi* movements in different Chinese communities. The (ir)relevance of confrontational identity politics will be highlighted, thus problematizing the notions of "coming out," "the closet," and "being lesbigay." The politics of coming out is predicated upon the prioritization of sexual identity and a homo-hetero duality. But in a society that denounces confrontational politics, and where sexuality is not segregated from social life to become a discrete identity, how should we contextualize and indigenize "coming out" and "confrontational politics"? How can Chinese *tongzhi* integrate their sexual identity within the cultural and family order? Can *tongzhi* empowerment be generated by "queering" rather than antagonizing the mainstream culture?

However, it is dangerous to romanticize traditional Chinese culture, as the cultural tolerance of same-sex eroticism appeared only within a classist and sexist hierarchy of unequal social relations—it is the male elite who have enjoyed the class-gender privileges of sexually dominating their social inferiors of both sexes. In this book, I will start by rewriting the Chinese history of same-sex eroticism and explain why the category of homosexual and the entire homo-hetero duality is inappropriate to comprehend the Chinese situation. While we should problematize the categories of the "West" and "America" by exposing and exploring their internal tensions, diversities, and differences, we should stress that the traditional Chinese discourses on same-sex eroticism are also a historical construct. It is dangerous to essentialize and universalize the notion of "Chinese culture," which is neither static nor totalizing. Indeed, so-called Western features such as possessive individualism and industrial capitalism are already part of the reality of Hong Kong, Taiwan, Singapore, and even to some extent Shanghai, Beijing, and Guangzhou. Although scholars generally agree on the continuity of Chinese cultural heritage, especially the primacy of the familial-kinship system over individual rights, and harmonious social relationships over confrontational politics, this book also emphasizes the diversities and differences among Taiwan, Hong Kong, mainland China, and other Chinese communities. Indeed, the diversities among the so-called Chinese societies are not necessarily less distinctive than the differences between East and West, or Chinese and Americans. Given the diversities and differences among Chinese societies, it is impossible and undesirable to pursue a unified Chinese *tongzhi* strategy of resistance. *Tongzhi* are as diverse as their heterosexual counterparts. Multifaceted *tongzhi* perspectives of resistance in different localized contexts should be developed.

I have conducted in-depth interviews in Hong Kong and mainland China in the last four years. In 1995, I interviewed forty *nan* (male) *tongzhi* and twenty *nü* (female) *tongzhi* in Hong Kong, and the results were published in the book *Xianggang Tongzhi Gushi* (Hong Kong *Tongzhi* Stories). In 1996, I interviewed around 200 PEPS in Beijing, and the stories were published in *Beijing Tongzhi Gushi*. In 1997, I interviewed eighty Chinese *tongzhi* who have interracial relationships and forty Caucasian lesbigays living in Hong Kong, which were published in *Houzhimin Tongzhi* (Postcolonial *Tongzhi*) (Chou, 1996a, b, 1997).

The interviews were generally informal, for on most occasions we met in a quiet restaurant, public park, or comfortable public area. Before I conducted the research, I had already published seven books about Chinese *tongzhi*. Thus, most interviewees had some trust in me and were willing to share their personal stories. The data presented in this research, even direct quotes from the interviewees, do not directly represent their experiences, as it involves a double interpretation/hermeneutic: the first is the interpretations that the *tongzhi* bring to their own experiences, then, second, I interpret their interpretations into the framework of the research. And I have had to translate the Chinese conversations into English. It is thus dangerous to rely unproblematically on "experience" as the source of knowledge, even though the way people make sense of their lives is a necessary starting point to understand the power relations through which our society is constituted. It is through the personal dynamics of everyday life practices that the wider sociopolitical relationships are explored.

A personal note: I position myself not only as an academic but also an activist who, for the last six years, has been intensely involved in Hong Kong *tongzhi* discourses and also well-connected with the Beijing and

Taipei *tongzhi* communities. I have been deeply enlightened by Western queer theories but also felt the strong need to develop indigenous *tongzhi* perspectives and strategies in the local context. This book is therefore guided by a burning passion to explore, develop, and empower different *tongzhi* perspectives and strategies. Instead of simply describing the *tongzhi* reality, this book articulates the possibilities of *tongzhi* empowerment not by antagonizing but rather by queering the mainstream, and not by segregating but rather by appropriating the family-kin categories into *tongzhi* discourses. Finally, given the background of the author, *tongzhi* experiences in Hong Kong will be given a more detailed analysis.

Several friends need to be mentioned. A few English-speaking friends have most kindly polished the language for me: Raymond Ng, Jeff Liu, Peter Madill, and the Williamsons. Joseph Schneider and Rodney Jones gave very critical and helpful comments on the manuscript. Angelina Chin, Lisa Rofel, Graham Smith, Mark McLelland, Tan Chong-kee, Ben Chan, June Wang, Chung To, and Peggy Lam have also given me comments on specific chapters. I am very grateful for the companionship and unconditional support of David Man, Chung To, and John Loo in the last four years. Finally, I must thank my mother, who helps me to understand that men always have something to learn from women. Despite her persistent objection to my *tongzhi* activism and writing, her love and care have provided me with the very cozy living environment that makes me a "privileged" scholar and activist.

SECTION I:
THE CULTURAL CONSTRUCTION
OF CHINESE SAME-SEX EROTICISM

Chapter 1

A World Without Homo-Hetero Duality: Rewriting the Traditional Chinese History of Same-Sex Eroticism

THE CHINESE CONCEPTION OF SEXUALITY

Same-sex eroticism has never been a serious social, political, or scientific concern in China. In Confucian and Taoist thought, sex is not treated as the central feature of life, but rather is seen as an integral part of life that should not be segregated as an independent sphere of study. Strictly speaking, there were no heterosexuals, bisexuals, or homosexuals in Chinese history. The concept of sexual orientation, i.e., dividing people by the gender of their erotic object choice, did not exist.[1]

The equivalence between the English word "sex" and the Chinese word *xing* has been established only recently in the relentless process of modernization (read Westernization) through which many Western categories have been translated and superimposed on the Chinese language and culture. The concept of sexuality has been imported from the West. Before the twentieth century, there were no corresponding Chinese words for sex or sexuality. There were words for erotic sentiments such as *se* (sensory), *yu* (eroticism), or *qing* (passion or sentiment), but none of them can be reduced to sexual acts, although connotations of sexual activities were sometimes implied. There were specific words for intercourse *(jiao-he, zhougong li)*, but they were used mostly in marital relations within the familial-kinship context, thus differing from the Western notion of sexual intercourse, which postulates two individuals abstracted from social relations. Whereas Western notions of sex, from the Judeo-Christian tradition and Plato and Aristotle's philosophy to the modern Cartesian body-mind duality, all contributed to sentencing sex to an inferior position, there is no such inherent negativity in the Chinese notion of *jiao-he, zhougong li, qing, se, yu,* or *xing.* The current word for sex, *xing,* is a recent translation.

Xing is an important Chinese word meaning nature, thus revealing the Chinese naturalistic paradigm of sex. Authoritative Chinese dictionaries still refer to *xing* not as "sex" but to its original meaning as the "nature of things." The Chinese character *xing* (nature) is composed of two parts: *xin,* which means heart or mind, and *sheng,* which is made up of two components, "grass" and "soil," that when added together mean life or birth. In other words, *xing* (sex) is seen as natural. The most famous saying about sex in Chinese history was the statement made by the philosopher Gaozi in the book *Mencius: "Shi se xing ye"* (Eating and sex are human nature).[2]

Van Gulik's work, *Sexual Life in Ancient China* (1961), has now become the classic authority stating that before the thirteenth century the Chinese had a fairly open attitude toward sexual practices; sex was not something to be afraid of, nor was it regarded as sinful. The association of sin and guilt with sexual activity per se was unheard-of in traditional China. Without the concept of God or any theological orthodoxy, Chinese culture was dictated not by any absolute or sacred order but by the social hierarchy of human relationships, which indeed corresponds to the Mandate of Heaven.

After the thirteenth century, China went through a gradual process of "neo-Confucianization," marked by a turn toward conservative, antisex, antiwoman attitudes, until the nineteenth century, when Westernization brought a new set of discourses on sexuality. In the late nineteenth century, the Chinese intellectuals' outcry for modernization, which always conflates with Westernization, paved the way for the superimposition of the Western discourse of sexuality. The more integrative and relational categories such as *se, yu, qing, jiao,* yin, and yang were gradually replaced by a new set of modern Western discourses of sexology, such as gender, sex, orgasm, perversity, and heterosexuality. These new categories, much like *xing yu* (sexual desire), *xing jiaoyu* (sex education), *xing bie* (gender), and *lang man* (romance), were by no means value-free, but were generated from the specific context of Western industrial-capitalist, positivist, biological determinist, and individualist traditions.

The traditional Chinese cosmology of yin-yang was gradually abandoned in the name of modernity, and replaced by a biological determinism that medicalizes a woman's body as weak and passive, in contrast to the male body, which is said to be active and strong.[3] The imposition of Western categories is well represented in the translation of "gender," a term that has no equivalent in the Chinese language. It is perhaps crucial, though unfortunate, that gender, which in contemporary Western society has a strong sense of social constructionism, was translated into Chinese as *xing bie,* which literally means sexual differences, thus implying a strong biological determinist connotation of a "natural" difference between female and male. When "gender" first appeared in China in the twentieth century, it became an essentialized category constructed as heterosexual, which is said to be based on scientific and biological facts about the sexes—*xing* (sex) *bie* (differences).[4]

What was imported in the twentieth century from the West was not only the concept of sex and sexuality, but also the notion of love. Modern Western discourses have prescribed the ideal (heterosexual) relationship between sex and love as a sequential one, from romantic love to passionate sex via monogamous marriage. Any sexual relations not in that sequence, such as sex outside or before marriage, or sex not based on love, or love between two people of the same sex, would be marginalized. Although such a tripartite sequence from love to sex via marriage has been naturalized and normalized in the contemporary world, it never actually prevailed in traditional Chinese history. Even in the Western world romantic love has been prevalent for less than 150 years. In traditional China, romantic love was never the grounds for marriage or sex. The Chinese word for love *(ai)* originally meant a manner of walking, and later was taken to mean an altruistic consideration (Tsang, 1986); never did *ai* refer to passionate or romantic love between two individuals. Traditional Chinese thinking does not advocate romantic love. The opposite prevails: Confucianists reject passionate love even between a wife and husband, as it would distract them from family obligations. No decent man is supposed to express public affection for his wife, and a woman showing sexual charm in public, even purely for her husband, is committing one of the worst crimes. Francis Hsu reports that as late as 1943 a young man from Hong Kong was punished because he walked hand in hand with his wife in a Chinese village (Hsu, 1953). The traditional Chinese marital system is patriarchal, polygamous, and arranged by parents. This system, which allowed the adoption of concubines, was legally accepted in Hong Kong until 1971.

In Chinese language and culture, the deepest expression of intimacy is not love but *qing* (deep sentiment or passion). Chinese Buddhism rarely talks about love, and when it does, love is always associated with greed and obsession. What Buddhism emphasizes is *ci bei* (kindness or benevolence), which focuses not on any individual or particular relations but on a compassionate sentiment of care and concern for all things. It is only since the May Fourth Movement that Chinese intellectuals have begun to advocate Western conceptions of individual freedom and romantic love. The notion of *qing* still prevails in contemporary Chinese societies. The main reason why many Chinese refuse to say "I love you" in Chinese is not the so-called Chinese characteristic of being shy, subtle, and introverted. Many vocal and expressive Chinese also would not express their deepest affection in terms of a subject-object split by saying "I love you" in Chinese. It is common in Taiwan and mainland China for people to use mixed codes, writing the word "love" in English and "I" and "you" in Chinese, or simply using English to say "I love you" in an otherwise completely Chinese conversation, implying that the expression "I love you" is basically a Western import. Compared to romantic or passionate love, *qing* seems to be culturally more comfortable for many Chinese. To understand the reasons why, we need to explore the basic structural features of *qing*.[5]

1. *Qing* goes beyond the subject-object split. The word *qing*, unlike romantic or passionate love, cannot be used as a transitive verb. *Qing* expresses the intimate sentiment shared by the people involved. Linguistically, we cannot say *"wo* (I) *qing ni* (you)." A sentence using *qing* rarely starts with "I" but rather with "we" without a subject-object split, for example, "we share *qing*."

2. *Qing* is not part of an individualistic tradition but stresses sentiment shared by more than one party. *Qing* appears among friends, between parents and children, and between the self and nature. Indeed, it always starts from the cosmological state of *tiendi you qing* (nature has *qing*). In other words, *qing* always de-emphasizes the centrality of human beings, as it involves the cosmological context in the natural world.

3. Instead of a passionate drive that is often ignited at first sight and ends a short time later, *qing* is usually a long-lasting sentiment that flows continuously.

4. *Qing*, for Confucianists, must reflect and reciprocate propriety *(li)*. *Qing* is generated from within and manifests one's innate humanity.

5. Unlike the Christian notion of love, *qing* is not targeted at marriage. Indeed, many famous Chinese stories of *qing* occur outside the marital context.

6. Unlike the notion of passionate love, sex is not an essential, logical, or necessary element of *qing*. *Qing* is a deep, affectionate sentiment that permeates an intimate relationship, and does not require a sexual encounter to actualize its "climax."

7. *Qing* is not a property or concrete entity that can be possessed; it is a relation and a sentiment that circulates and flows in a specific relational context.

8. To construct a theory of *qing* would be self-defeating, as it is a sentiment to be shared and grasped in an intersubjective context rather than analyzed objectively and conceptually by a third party or analyst.

9. *Qing* emphasizes not the cognitive or rational control of one's feelings but a spontaneous and harmonious flowing of emotions.

10. *Qing* is not judged by the gender of the people experiencing it. In the famous Chinese "homosexual" novel *Pin-hua bao-jian* (A Prized Guidebook for Appraising Flowers), first published in 1849, in depicting same-sex activity among people involved in the theater scene during the Qing dynasty, author Chen Sen does not judge people according to the homo-hetero value system. Instead, he differentiates ten types of *qing*, all of which can apply to both same-sex and different-sex relationships: extreme *qing*, shred *qing*, tasteful *qing*, pure *qing*, virtuous *qing*, impetuous *qing*, straightforward *qing*, drunken *qing*, voluptuous *qing*, and seductive *qing*. Chen Sen also makes an important statement about (male) sexuality: "I do not comprehend why it is acceptable for a man to love a woman, but is unacceptable for a man to love a man. *Qing* is *qing* whether to a man or to a woman. To love a woman but not a man is lust and not *qing*. To lust is to forget *qing*. If one treasures *qing*, s/he is not lewd" (Ruan, 1991:119). Although Chen Sen confines the discourse of *qing* to men, it also applies to women.

A serious understanding of the Chinese conception of *qing* and sexuality requires a discussion of the concept of Tao (The Way). According to Taoism, Tao is the central ordering principle of the cosmos, the organic totality of the eternal order and course of nature that has produced two fundamental principles or forces, yin and yang, which constitute all aspects of life. A key principle of Tao is the holistic and interactive conception of reality, which denies any essentialist conception of things. All particularities, human or otherwise, instead of being independent and discontinuous, are mutually constitutive of each other. John Henderson argues that "correlative thinking is the most basic ingredient of Chinese cosmology":

> Correlative thinking in general draws systematic correspondences among aspects of various orders of reality or realms of the cosmos, such as the human body, the body politic, and the heavenly bodies. It assumes that these related orders as a whole are homologous, that they correspond with one another in some basic aspect. (Henderson, 1984:1)

In Taoist cosmology, yin and yang are the primordial binary forces that create the dynamics for all facets of existence. Yet they are neither antagonistic, fixed, nor mutually exclusive, but interdependent, complementary, and interactive. Although yin is predominant in women and yang in men, every person from birth is a combination of yin and yang. Neither yin nor yang exists in an exclusive or pure form. As Charlotte Furth argues, the actual sexual differentiation of each person depends on the momentary balance of the dynamics between these two forces. Such a natural philosophy opens up a broad and tolerant attitude toward a variety of sexual and gender behaviors. Yin and yang are relativistic and have no fixed meaning (Furth, 1988:3, 1998). For example, a man is yang relative to his wife, but he is yin relative to his mother who would be portrayed as yang. Yin and yang are not ontologically binary, as what they produce are not generic women and men, but persons in specific relations such as mother and father, husband and wife, brother and sister, emperor and favorite.

Taoism regards sexual intercourse primarily as a cosmological and medical category that transcends lust. Yin-yang duality "differs fundamentally from Western dualism which posits a radical separation between a transcendent creative source and a dependent object of creation" (Morris, 1991:105). Sexual activities are beneficial to one's health, and they bring longevity when practiced properly according to the *fang zhong shu* (the art of the bedchamber). Sexual dissipation and the excessive loss of seminal fluid are seen as dangerous sources of illness. In traditional Chinese beliefs, semen is a finite substance containing a man's *chi* (life essence) and should not be wasted through masturbation or an excessive sex life. The way to replenish *chi* is to adopt a sexual technique through which the man can absorb the *chi* of the woman. There are sophisticated guidelines in Taoist sex manuals on the proper ways to conduct sex. According to Chinese alchemical beliefs, two men who share orgasms were exchanging, rather than losing, their yang essence (semen). Sex between two women was even less problematic, as women were supposed to have unlimited yin essence. For the same reason, female masturbation was largely ignored while male masturbation was strictly disapproved of for causing the loss of the limited vital essence. Yet what Taoism developed was not a discourse on sexuality, as neither sexual pleasure nor sexual acts constitute an independent domain of sexuality as they do for the modern Western construct, but rather a wider sociocosmological concern for longevity for the individual and reproduction for the human race.

Taoism proposes the complementarity and unity of softness and hardness, and advocates a life-affirming attitude of flowing and growing in harmony with the natural force of life. There is softness in hardness and hardness in softness. Roger Ames (1981) rejects Joseph Needham's description of Taoism as feminine in orientation. Instead, Ames argues that Taoism proposes an androgynous integration of feminine and masculine traits in harmonious balance. Yin and yang embrace, correlate, and unite each other in this harmonious balance. Laozi says, "The female always vanquishes the male with her tranquillity, and takes the submissive position because of the same tranquillity" (Young and Ames, 1977:61). He goes on, "One who knows masculinity and yet preserves femininity, becomes the river gorge of the world" (p. 33).

Confucian thought, the dominant ideology in China for 2,000 years, rejects an essentialist reading of sex, and makes no judgment on the intrinsic value of sexual behavior. Sex, like any other personal or social activity, has to be regulated by the Five Relations, by which all human relationships and behaviors are organized hierarchically. There are only two major restrictions on sexual activities: follow appropriate family-kinship relationships, and do not partake in indulgence or excess (yin). Within these two guidelines, sex is supposed to be enjoyed freely.

The traditional Chinese concern is not sexuality per se but the social relations in which sex occurs. Never has sex been treated as an independent and isolated subject of discourse abstracted from wider social relations. The absence of the Judeo-Christian tradition in Chinese culture has "exempted" China from the most die-hard opponent of homosexuality. There is no parallel religious guilt and obsession with sexuality in Chinese culture. Buddhism, an Asian religion with a 1,400-year history of prominence in China, treats homosexuality and all worldly reality as just a phase.[6] Buddhism does not even advocate heterosexuality, as it believes that no one should indulge in any form of worldly desire.

Taoism, Confucianism, and Buddhism have gradually mingled since the Tang dynasty (618-907 A.D.) and have permeated popular belief to the degree that it is sometimes difficult to separate them from the people's everyday belief system. Despite complicated historical differences, it is fair to say that all three institutions support a relaxed and naturalistic attitude toward sex, and have no homophobic hostility toward same-sex eroticism, although Neo-Confucianism since the thirteenth century has developed into a more antisex form of conservatism.

Lacking a cultural interest in homosexuality or heterosexuality, the Chinese do not use abstract universal principles similar to those in the Judeo-Christian tradition that define all homosexual acts as sinful. For traditional Chinese, sex is contextual and relational, and cannot be assessed in the abstract by asking "Is sex good?" or "Is homosexuality sinful?" This cultural disinterest in classifying sexual preferences also explains, as the following section will discuss, the absence of a homo-hetero duality.

COMPATIBILITY BETWEEN
HETEROSEXUAL MARRIAGES
AND SAME-SEX EROTICISM

What constitutes a person is culturally specific. In the modern Anglo-American world, each person is an independent being. Privacy is a major principle. The entire legal and social system works upon the harm principle—you can do whatever you like unless you harm someone. In traditional Chinese societies, nobody is a discrete, isolated being; rather anyone is a full person only in the context of family and social relationships. Since everyone, irrespective of sexual orientation, is expected to get married, someone who has an exclusively homosexual lifestyle is culturally inconceivable and definitely intolerable, a nonbeing in society. In other words, nobody can be primarily a lesbian, bisexual, or gay man. Everyone is, first, a daughter or son of her or his parents, which is a role in the social-familial system, before she or he can be anything else. Traditional Chinese culture never felt the need to use medical or scientific terms to produce the dual categories "heterosexual" or "homosexual." What is represented by the concept of sexuality cuts across many aspects of the traditional Chinese domain, such as family, marriage, kinship, sentiment, concern, affection, desire, virility, procreation, yin-yang, *qing*, happiness, and pleasure.

The Chinese have a holistic and relational notion of self and identity. Personal identity is not seen as fixated on a certain psychological or sexual essence; instead, identity is created, altered, and dismantled in particular social relationships. In the Chinese conception of full personhood, there is an important sense in which gender and sex differences are rather irrelevant. In traditional Chinese medical theories, both males and females were correlated to the cosmological order of yin-yang. Everyone, irrespective of gender, is constructed by and contains hundreds of meridians (*jingluo*) through which vital energy (*qi*) and blood (*xue*) circulate with a balanced yin-yang as the ideal state of health (Furth, 1994, 1998).

Rather than using gender or sexuality as an abstract category, the Chinese characterize gender by specific social roles such as wife, husband, daughter, son, mother, or father. One becomes, rather than being born as, a wife or husband, a daughter or son, a *funü* (adult woman) or *nanzihan* (male with macho style). Gender is seen through the lens of class and social roles rather than any essential abstract traits such as appearance or the body. Traditionally, it is *funü* (women, as embedded in familial-kinship networks) rather than *nüren* (women, as independent people) who take precedence, for whom family and class are more important than gender binarism or the representation of an abstract concept of femininity. Unlike the prediscursive category "woman," *funü* is not an abstract or generic category that exists beyond *jia* (family/home). It is through the kinship relationship that *funü* becomes a meaningful social category (Barlow, 1993, 1994). In other words, woman or man does not exist as an essentialized category that goes beyond familial-kin social relationships.

Modern Western gender discourse has fantasized a racially and culturally undivided global subject called "woman." Such a notion of the generic woman rarely appears in Chinese discourse. For example, in the famous Confucian statement that sentences *funü* to be domestic, a *funü* "follows on a father before marriage (daughter), follows on her husband after marriage (wife), and follows on her sons when old (mother)." While women are defined by the patriarchal family-kinship system, it is crucial to note that the generic woman does not exist here. Tani Barlow quotes a statement made by an eighteenth-century scholar, Chen Hongmou, which she translates as "before women are married they are *nü*/female/daughter, when they get married they are *fu*/wives, and when they give birth to children then they are *mu*/mothers." Instead of a generic category, gender exists only in concrete social relations: "What appear as 'gender' are *yin/yang* differentiated positions: not two anatomical 'sexes,' but a profusion of relational, bound, unequal dyads, each signifying difference and positioning difference analogically. A *nü* is a daughter, unequally related to parents and parents-in-law. A *xiaozi*, or filial son, is differentially unequal to mother and father, *yin* to their *yang*" (Barlow, 1994:259).

The notion of male-female gender binarism as accepted by Republican China is very new even in Western history. Laqueur (1990) stated that sexual differences were only a matter of degree in the pre-nineteenth-century Western world: "To be a man or a woman was to hold a social rank, a place in society, to assume a cultural role, not to be organically one or the other of two incommensurable sexes" (p. 8). Trumbach (1989) depicts a cultural transition in eighteenth-century England from two genders (woman and man) and three biological sexes (female, male, and hermaphrodite) to four genders (woman, man, sodomite, and sapphist) and two sexes (female and male). Only in the last years of the eighteenth century was there an essentialist notion of fundamental biological differences between the sexes that went beyond class and kin in constituting masculinity and femininity.

Anthropologists have long reminded us that gender is not always divided into a female-male duality. It is colonialist to assume that this division is always the central organizing principle in all societies. In non-Western societies, sex-linked symbols are often secondary and integral to wider social principles of the family-kinship system. Yin-yang, for example, is not always sexed.

Sexual identity politics first entered China during the May Fourth Movement, at a time when the new urban intellectuals appropriated the newest Western ideology of individualism, democracy, and scientism. Chinese *funü* in the twentieth century appropriated the colonial sign "woman" (*nüxing*) and sexual binarism (masculine versus feminine) to subvert the Confucian patrilineal construction of *funü* who was situated historically in *jia ting* (family). Intellectuals began to use the terms *nüren* (female person) and *nüxing* (women) in a generic sense.

It is in this context of Chinese modernity and the influx of modern Western sexual discourses that the concept of sexual orientation has been imported into China, though even up to the 1990s, none of the categories homo-, hetero-, or bisexual have taken root in the general population. Chinese culture recognizes the differences between same-sex and opposite-sex eroticism, but sex is simply not the grounds on which to classify people. Sexual desire neither signals a master category of identity nor is it the constitutive principle of the self. One does not become "beefman" or "porkwoman" because she or he loves eating beef or pork. One needs such a label only if one is oppressed for eating beef or pork. Same-sex intimacy is not emotionally loaded as it is in the West. Relations between people of the same gender can be very physical and intimate without suspicion of abnormality and perversity. Same-sex and opposite-sex desire are not understood in dichotomous terms. In the Chinese context, sexual desires are seen and constructed as specific social roles rather than as the essential condition of human personality. In other words, homosexuality is seen not as a sexual essence monopolized by a minority group, but as a social practice that everyone can experience in specific classist and sexist relations.

In Chinese history, *tongxinglian* (homosexuality) has never been used as a noun to designate a generic personality possessing a unique psychosexual essence. In modern Chinese, *tongxinglian* is a transitive verb consisting of a present participle and a noun that describes behavior. If one wishes to ascribe identity to the person involved, the suffix *zhe* has to be added, as if to say "homosexuality-er" in English (Pan and Aggleton, 1996). Before the term *tongxinglian* first appeared in Chinese in the early twentieth century, there was no generic term to describe sex between people of same sex. Most of the terms used for same-sex activity are highly gender-specific roles or practices. The notion of the homogeneous, universal and gender-inclusive "*gay* identity" did not exist in China.

In traditional China, same-sex activities are portrayed in predominantly social rather than sexual terms, with social roles such as *xiang gong* (male prostitute), *pi* (favorite), *duan xiu* (cut sleeve), *long yang, fen tao* (shared peach), *hanlu* (the dry canal), *tuzi* (little rabbit); social relations such as *jinlan zimei* (golden orchid sisters), *qidi* and *qixiong* (adopted brothers), and *hanlu yingxiong* (stranded heroes); or a style such as: *nanfeng* (male wind, male custom, male practice, male style), *nanse* (male eroticism, beauty, and seductiveness). Even when sexual activities are categorized, they never refer to a specific minority of people, but to specific behavioral practices that can involve everyone in certain social relations, such as *mo jing* (polishing mirrors), *mo doufu* (grinding bean curd), *hou ting hua* (the backyard flower), *dui shi* (paired eating), or *chui xiao* (to play a vertical bamboo flute). All the terms describing the same-sex sexual acts are rather poetic, with no sense of social or moral condemnation. The first derogatory term for a homosexual act, *jijian* (chicken lewdness, which refers to the belief that domesticated fowls commonly engage in same-sex acts) appears as late as the Tang dynasty, and it implies disparagement rather than hostility (Hinsch, 1992). Most important, all these terms referring to same-sex activities do not denote a fixed or generic personality. That explains the absence of any theory of *tongxinglian,* and a lack of any academic research on the cause or common features of PEPS.

As was acknowledged by the Hong Kong Law Reform Commission in 1983, *tongxinglian* was not regarded in the traditional Chinese world as any more socially undesirable than serious gambling or prostitution, having a social sanction of nothing more than public ridicule (Law Reform Commission of Hong Kong, 1983). Same-sex behavior could be compatible with marriage, without carrying a severe social stigma. The idea of leading two different lives and being unable to reveal one's sexual identity publicly may sound frustrating and painful to openly lesbigay people in the West. Yet it is not necessarily perceived as a double life for traditional Chinese, nor were traditional marriages as oppressive to PEPS as they are today. Traditionally, a Chinese marriage is a transaction between two households instead of two individuals. Marriage does not need to be passionate as it would divert one's energy, although producing heirs, especially boys, is a must. The basis of marriage and sex is not sexual desire or love but the obligation to continue the family line. Whether one has sexual desire for one's spouse is quite irrelevant. Heterosexually inclined people may not even know their spouses before the wedding banquet, and it is often coincidental if the couple happen to be sexually attracted to each other. Yet it causes little problem if they are not. Traditional Chinese focus their sexual concerns on marital procreation rather than different-sex pleasure. Therefore, the evaluation of sexual normality is not based on one's erotic object choice but on whether one acts according to the roles prescribed by the social hierarchy.[7] Indeed, PEPS often vent and gratify their homoerotic needs through intimate same-sex friendships, without even being aware of having a different sexual desire called *tongxinglian.* Marriage and same-sex relationships can coexist without much contradiction—the former is a social obligation; the latter is an expression of intimate emotions though not necessarily sexual ones.

Chinese society has an educational and social structure in which men and women are often separated. As early as the sixth century B.C., Confucianists had stressed the necessity of strict sex segregation between men and women according to the proper behavioral codes of *li* (propriety). Indeed, Confucius's students lived in his home. Homosociality and same-sex intimate friendship are socially institutionalized and legitimized as a crucial source of emotional support, with no need for homosexual connotations. Instead of provoking anxiety and guilt, same-sex intimacy is more often a source of comfort. Even in contemporary China, two men or women holding hands or leaning against one another may not cause public suspicion, sometimes not even when they stay overnight in the same bed in a hotel room or in a private home. It would be a problem only if a person was to go into a hotel with a member of the opposite sex. Given the social space for intimate homosociality, same-sex eroticism among friends could be positively perceived. For example, in the famous story in Wei Chin and Southern and Northern Dynasty (256-581 A.D.) concerning the seven famous male scholars, the Seven Sages of the Bamboo Breves, all of them had intimate relationships with one another. In one case, the wife of Shan Tao (205-283 A.D.), one of the scholars, found her husband having sex with two other scholars, Yuan Ji (210-263 A.D.) and Kang Ji (223-252 A.D.). Yet the wife shows no anger, jealousy, or hostility. Instead, her relaxed and positive comments about their sexual relationship indicate the rather relaxed attitude of the time, though in the patriarchal society a woman has to accept her husband having sex with other men, which, after all, does not threaten her status as a wife (Ruan, 1991).

Although traditional Chinese society laid great emphasis on the procreative purpose of marriage, sex within the same gender, sex with prostitutes, or a man having several wives and concubines were usually tolerated because the male-dominated family system was not challenged. Yet a man marrying a woman of the same surname would be strictly forbidden, as it would confuse patriarchal property inheritance. Similarly, a self-proclaimed gay man who refuses marriage may be disowned by his parents and the entire culture. The hostility is not targeted at same-sex sexuality itself, but at the idea of having a lifestyle that denies the cultural imperative to get married. Ironically, a heterosexually inclined person would be seriously condemned if she or he refused to get married, whereas a homosexually inclined person would be tolerated so long as he or she married and had children. In other words, one's sexual normality is defined not by the gender of one's erotic object choice, but by one's willingness and ability to fulfill filial piety, particularly the duty to reproduce.

The cultural tolerance of same-sex eroticism does not imply an affirmation of human rights or sexual rights. It is basically the male elite within the patriarchal marital system that enjoy immense sexual privileges, alongside their power within heterosexual marriages. That is why the term *wai-jiao* (external sex/relationship) is used to describe same-sex relationships, while *nei-jiao* (internal sex/relationship) describes marital relationships (Samshasha, 1997:164-165). In other words, same-sex relationships co-exist and parallel opposite-sex (marital) ones.

However, the rise of Neo-Confucianism and *li-xue* in the thirteenth century generated a rather antisex conservatism that went against earlier Confucian teaching about the naturalness of human sexuality. Control over eroticism became stricter in the Manchu-dominated Qing dynasty (1644-1911). Being the minority in terms of numbers and race, the Manchu rulers felt the need to implement strong ideological and social control, including the unprecedented legal code in 1740 on consensual sodomy between adults. As Vivien Ng (1991:88) said:

> Perhaps if the Qing rulers had believed that homosexuality was limited only to a very small percentage of the population, they might not have taken any action against it. But they were convinced otherwise. The boom in homoerotic literature in the seventeenth century, along with the frequent references to homosexual behavior in scholarly jotting, heightened their awareness of the extent of homosexuality, transforming it, in their minds, into a "problem."

Chinese culture has not supported or accepted homosexuality. The family-kinship system and the pressure to get married pose a limiting boundary to and pressure on same-sex erotic practices. People may gossip but rarely take action against it. Homosexuality is not treated as intrinsically evil and sinful. Gay-bashing as seen in America and Britain does not exist in traditional Chinese societies. The phenomenon of a group of young gang members beating up "gay-looking" people is unheard-of.

It is therefore no accident that homosexuality per se was not the concern of the law. Even in the Qing legal code of 1740, which was the first and only law in Chinese history punishing consensual homosexuality, with a penalty of 100 heavy bamboo blows and one month of imprisonment, the target of punishment is not homosexuality but all extramarital sex. In the Qing code, homosexual and heterosexual extramarital intercourse were not treated as different forms of desire and sexuality. The Qing code draws the line between procreative and nonprocreative sex. No categorical distinction was made between homosexuals and heterosexuals. Whereas the Qing code includes harsh punishment for homosexual rape, the penalty depended not on the gender of the person being raped but on her or his age and the extent of violence (Hinsch, 1992:144-145). Given the openness and frequency of homosexuality, especially in the wealthy classes and the theatrical world, it is doubtful whether this law was seriously enforced. For example, a writer in Kang Xi's reign said that "it is considered bad taste not to keep elegant male servants on one's household staff, and undesirable not to have singing boys around when inviting guests for dinner" (Mackerras, 1972:45). The popularity of male prostitution was even more remarkable. In 1860, a Western writer estimated there were thirty-five male brothels and 800 boys trained for pederastic prostitution in Tianjin alone (Ng, 1987:68). Western visitors as late as 1899 have observed Chinese tolerance of homosexuality: "Public opinion remains completely indifferent to this type of distraction, paying no attention to it at all, except to say that, since it seems to please the dominant partner and the other is willing, no harm is done" (Matignon, 1899:47).

The notion of homophobia is thus inappropriate to describe traditional Chinese attitudes toward same-sex eroticism, since the condemnation was not a categorical rejection of same-sex conduct per se, but the betrayal of family and social roles. "Homophobia," if the term is used in a non-discriminatory manner, is either explaining too much—as if Chinese culture rejects homosexuality as sinful or perverse, or too little—as if the Chinese understand homosexuality as a generic or essentialized category. Both fail to capture the unique specificity of the Chinese cultural attitude, which understands the sexual by the social.

CHINESE TOLERANCE OF SAME-SEX EROTICISM IN THE PATRIARCHAL-CLASSIST HIERARCHY

Contrary to modern Western culture, which divides human beings in a homo-hetero duality, the Chinese sexual world is constructed predominantly according to the hierarchy of class. The one with power—stereotypically, the upper-class adult male—could sexually dominate social inferiors such as his wife, second wife, or concubines. It is the upper-class male who has enormous sexual and social latitude to enjoy a wide range of sexual pleasures. He can also dominate and penetrate younger male servants who are socially inferior to him, without carrying a severe social stigma of being identified as a homo- or bisexual. Chinese obscenities would insult a person by referring to him as the dominated partner in a same-sex sexual act. That this same act must implicate the dominator never seems to worry the one who curses. The idea that the (male) inserter and the subordinate insertee may share the same social-sexual category— *homosexual* or *gay*—simply did not exist in the traditional Chinese mind. The social hierarchy of power differentiation is more important than the fact that both are biologically male or female. From the viewpoint of an emperor or a wealthy lord, there is rather little difference between his desire for a female or for a young male—the sexual activities of both would equally confirm and demonstrate his social power.

It is therefore dangerous to romanticize Chinese traditions of same-sex eroticism. The cultural tolerance of same-sex eroticism is neither unconditional nor wholehearted, but with a vital qualifier—it occurs only when the social hierarchy is not challenged. It is such hierarchical social inequality and its concomitant same-sex relationships that creates the majority of cases in the historical records of Chinese same-sex eroticism. The most distinctive features of homosexuality in Chinese history are ironically neither homophobia nor homoeroticism but classism, sexism, and ageism, which permeate and construct both homosexual relationships and mainstream culture.

Before the twentieth century, same-sex eroticism had always been a part of the sexual life of the elite social class. It was common for powerful (male) ministers to keep young boys as catamites (*luan tong*) and various rulers to keep favorites (*pi, chong*), both female and male. As early as the Warring States (475-221 B.C.), many (male) aristocrats reared and owned handsome boys, many of whom served as catamites. Heavy makeup and ornate outfits would be put on them to display their elegance and beauty. There were no categorical differences between female and male *pi* or *chong;* both had to serve their ruler, socially and sexually. Chinese historians, including major scholars such as Ban Gu and Sima Qian, put female and male favorites under the same category, without any sense of them as two types of persons or activities—heterosexual and homosexual.

Long yang, duan xiu (cut sleeve), and *fen tao* (split peaches)—the three major poetic and popular euphemisms for male homosexuality in the Chinese language—refers to the three young favorites of their emperors in the Han (206 B.C.-220 A.D.) and pre-Han dynasties.

Lord Long Yang shared the same pillow with his male lover, the King of Wei. One day they went fishing and had been very successful. But Long Yang suddenly felt very sad and wept. The king was very distressed and puzzled. Long Yang explained that he felt himself like a fish, who is able to catch the king's attention only so long as bigger fishes have not been

caught. The king was so touched that he ordered all officials not to talk of any other pretty male before him, or the offending official would be killed. The incident expresses not only the king's intense love for his male lover but also the general acceptance for such a relationship, at least for the socially privileged.

In the famous case of *duan xiu,* the Han dynasty emperor Ai-di (reigned 6 B.C.-1 A.D.) cut off the sleeve of his gown so that he might get up, rather than waking up his male lover, Dong Xian, who was lying asleep on it. Dong Xian became the chief minister by the age of twenty-two because of Emperor Ai's infatuation with him, to the extent that Emperor Ai decided to hand over the empire to him, by invoking the ancient precedent of the mythical emperor Yao's abdicating in favor of Shun instead of his own son. Although Ai-di had given the imperial seal to Dong, the opposition from major officials was so severe that soon after the death of the emperor, Dong lost all his privileges, and was pushed finally to commit suicide.

But were they homosexuals? We can only be certain of the homoerotic interest of the socially dominated ones who initiated sexual encounters. Ban Gu, author of *Han Shu* (Records of the Han), said, "by nature Emperor Ai did not care for women" (Ban, 1955:38-39). Yet the privileges of an emperor were so great that a same-sex erotic object choice would confirm rather than undermine his power. Neither the emperors nor their contemporaries ever comprehended these behaviors as *tongxinglian* because eroticism toward women or men was not dichotomized. For the socially inferior ones such as Dong Xian, the temptation of a huge reward in the form of social status and material benefits, together with his limited personal choices, made it difficult to tell his genuine erotic preference, which was almost irrelevant to his sexual choice. Dong Xian was married with children, which was again a familial event decided by parents and prescribed by culture rather than by himself.

The sadness of such hierarchical social power in same-sex eroticism is vividly expressed in the story of *fen tao:*

> In ancient times Mizi Xia won favor with the ruler of Wei (534-493 B.C.). According to the laws of the state of Wei, anyone who secretly made use of the ruler's carriage was punished by having his feet amputated. When Mizi Xia's mother fell ill, someone slipped into the palace at night to report this to Mizi Xia. Mizi Xia forged an order from the ruler, got into the ruler's carriage, and went off to see her, but when the ruler heard of it, he praised him, "How filial! For the sake of his mother he forgot all about the danger of having his feet cut off!" Another day Mizi Xia was strolling with the ruler in an orchard and, biting into a peach and finding it sweet, he stopped

eating and gave the remaining half to the ruler to enjoy. "How sincere is your love for me!" exclaimed the ruler. "You forgot your own appetite and think only of giving me good things to eat!" Later, however, when Mizi Xia's looks had faded and the ruler's passion for him had cooled, he was accused of committing crime against his lord. "After all," said the ruler, "he once stole my carriage, and another time he gave me a half-eaten peach to eat!" (Watson, 1964: 78-79)

The author of this passage, Han Fei, neither saw the relationship as homosexual nor classified the emperor and the favored Mizi Xia into the same category as "homosexual." Instead it is the social relationship of class and power that governs both the sexual relationship and Han Fei's attention. In particular, Han Fei worried that his Legalist ideal of objective and impersonal rule would be hampered by institutionalized favoritism, which is a political issue unrelated to the gender of the favorite (Hinsch, 1992:21).

That is why *chong* or *pi* (the favorite) rather than "homosexual" or any other sexual terms are used in this passage. *Chong* implies a hierarchical social relationship between the master and the servant, who could be female or male. *Chong* is a social term, not a sexual one, though sexual services for the master are often implied. "This tendency to describe homosexual acts in terms of social relationships rather than erotic essence continued in China down to the twentieth century, when terminology derived from Western science gained predominance" (Hinsch, 1992:21).

The prevalence of male favorites occupying high positions in the imperial courts was so serious that two political writings, *Ban Fa* and *Zhong Ling* in the *Guanzi* anthology, put favoritism first on the list of major threats to proper ruling and government (Rickett, 1985). Sima Qian, the great Chinese historian, wrote in the second century B.C. about male favorites for the emperors in the Han dynasty:

> It is not women alone who can use their looks to attract the eyes of the rulers, courtiers and eunuchs can play this game too . . . neither Chi (favorite of emperor Kao-tsu) nor Hung (favorite of emperor Hui-ti) had any particular talent or ability; both won prominence simply by their looks and graces. (Watson, 1961:462)

The great philosopher Mozi also warns of the political danger of favoritism:

> Rulers employ their relatives, or men who happen to be rich and eminent or pleasure-featured and attractive. But just because a man

happens to be rich and eminent or pleasure-featured and attractive, he will not necessarily turn out to be wise and alert when placed in office. If men such as these are given the task of ordering the state, then this is simply to entrust to men who are neither wise nor intelligent, and anyone knows that this will lead to ruin. (Hinsch, 1992: 30-31)

As same-sex relationships did not seem to be a social issue in traditional Chinese societies, they were rarely mentioned except as incidents within the wider narratives of the lives of the emperor and the male elite. The limited references to same-sex relations in pre-Han China is not the result of homophobia, but indicates that scholars and historians simply felt there was little need to record same-sex relationships. The historical description of the ten emperors in the West Han Dynasty who had sex with both genders was written in rather plain language, without much sense of contempt or hostility. Similarly, the wider range of post-Han same-sex historical records should not be seen as showing the increasing popularity of homosexuality, but rather that historians no longer confined themselves to recording the lives of emperors and major officials. Also, sexuality between women was systematically omitted, as a result of sexism rather than homophobia—Chinese history was mostly about those in sociopolitical power, i.e., men.

As sexual behavior, homo or hetero, must conform to hierarchical social relations, same-sex conduct that denies such social relations will be severely denounced, not because of homophobia, but because the social hierarchy between superiors and inferiors is threatened. The experience of Duke Jing is a classic case:

> Duke Jing of the state of Qi was so exceptionally attractive that a minor official presumed to stare at his extravagant beauty. The duke said to his courtiers, "Ask him why he stares at me, overstepping his rightful place." The official replied, "If I speak I will die, but if I do not speak I will also die—I was staring at a glance at the beautiful duke." The duke declared, "He lusts after me. Kill him!" Yanzi entered out of turn and said, "I hear that you are angry with an official." The duke said, "Correct. He lusts after me, so I will kill him." Yanzi replied, "I have heard that to resist desire is not in accordance with the Way (Tao), and to hate love is inauspicious. Although he was caused to lust after you, according to the Way it is not fitting that he should be killed." (Hinsch, 1992:22)

Duke Jing not only accepted the advice of Minister Yanzi, he initiated a sexual proposal to bathe with this minor official. What annoyed Duke Jing in the beginning was obviously not homosexuality, which he himself final-ly initiated, but this minor official's violation of the social hierarchy. What is also crucial is the advice given by Minister Yanzi, which follows the naturalist attitude that "eating and sex are human nature," thus arguing that it is indeed unnatural to resist a natural desire (for homoeroticism). For Yanzi, one should flow with nature; for Duke Jing, one should flow with social relationships. They expressed no intention to divide emotions or human beings in a homo-hetero duality. Duke Jing's sense of normality and manhood was not threatened by the sexual encounter with a man; for him it is merely a natural expression of *qing.*

The notion of *qing* is central in understanding Chinese conceptions of sexuality. For example, the late Ming novel *Bian er chai* (Caps and Hair-pins) powerfully articulates the discourse of *qing* in the context of same-sex eroticism (McMahon, 1988:76-77). *Bian er chai* is composed of four long stories, each named for a different kind of *qing:* "Qing Fidelity," "Qing Chivalry," "Qing Sacrifice," and "Qing Marvel." All four stories have similar narrations of a male intellectual who encounters another kind-hearted male, and they share an intimate and genuine *qing.* The couple would then experience certain social misfortunes but could still climb up the social ladder. All of the stories have a happy ending. In the beginning of the first story, "Qing Fidelity," the male protagonist says, "We are the people who really appreciate *qing.* Although our [same-sex] relationship has deviated from the norm [*li*], it flows with *qing* . . . a discourse that confines itself to the life and death of female-male relation-ships is not really *qing*" (Samshasha, 1997:390). Indeed, this story is about the love of a fifteen-year-old student, Chao, who is pretty, elegant, and smart, and the young scholar Lin, who is spontaneously attracted to Chao. Chao is finally touched by Lin's sincerity, and they live together. Because of Lin's academic enlightenment and guidance, Chao passes the examina-tion to become a scholar and officer. Yet Lin is later in danger of execution because of his insistence on justice, which irritates a powerful, rich person. The powerless Chao takes the risk to rescue Lin, and they finally depart officialdom to live a very peaceful life. Chao and Lin's family also become very close for many generations.

The unknown author of *Bian er chai* takes a nonconfrontational strate-gy of using the most profound mainstream categories of *qing* to develop a same-sex relationship that is congruent with the social morality of *qing* and *yi* (righteousness). Instead of oppressing PEPS, mainstream social values such as fidelity, loyalty, intellectual scholarship, and social justice are now mobilized to become key elements in a same-sex relationship.

In the third story, "Qing Sacrifice," the male protagonist, Wen, is imprisoned because he is set up by a rich man who refuses to let his daughter marry Wen. A prison guard is disturbed by the injustice and so lets Wen escape. Wen is then homeless and jobless, soon becomes an actor in the theater, and is then admired by a scholar, Han. Han and Wen gradually become intimate friends. Unfortunately, a wealthy villain wants to possess Wen and so kidnaps him. Out of *qing* for Han, Wen sells himself to this wealthy villain for a considerable sum of money, which helps Han with a scholar's examination. Because of his fidelity to Han, Wen commits suicide rather than submit to the sexual demands of this wealthy villain. Wen's action is so touching that even the godly spirit decides to intervene, and lets Wen reincarnate from the afterlife to continue his love with Han. Han passes his scholar's examination and gets revenge on the wealthy villain. Finally, Wen returns to the spirit world to become a god who guards the sea.

In this story, Wen and Han are portrayed as brave, righteous, and noble, not only in their genuine love but also in fighting against social oppression. Wen's fidelity, loyalty, and *qing* are so profound that he is rescued twice—first by the prison guard and later by the spirit that reincarnates him. Instead of casting a same-sex relationship as confronting the mainstream culture, social categories such as loyalty, love, self-sacrifice, and fidelity are manipulated as constitutive of the same-sex relationship in *Bian er chai*. More important, these stories do not replicate mainstream culture but are highly subversive of the heterosexist presuppositions of the notions of love, sacrifice, and long-term relationship. The most endearing *qing* actualizes itself in a same-sex relationship. It is a strategy of resistance in which same-sex relationships are legitimated not by denying the mainstream but by "queering the mainstream," a strategy that will be elaborated in later chapters.

Traditional Chinese same-sex eroticism should not be romanticized even as in this subversive narration of *Bian er chai*. Socially and economically underprivileged males must submit their bodies to the dominant elite, thus indicating a serious issue of classism that permeates same-sex and opposite-sex relationships.

In Chinese homoerotic literature, the erotic appeal of young men and women was interchangeable for the pleasure of their master. The descriptions of male favorites are structurally similar to those of female concubines. As early as the Jin dynasty (265-420 A.D.), the poet Zhang Han-bian wrote a poem to glorify the beauty and elegance of a fifteen-year-old boy, Zhou Xiao-shi, who was a private prostitute for him. The poet was deeply impressed by Zhou's delicate features, skin texture, and elegant costume. Yet it is crucial to note that Zhou was described as pretty rather than womanly. The poet did not seem to be governed or disturbed by a rigid gender duality:

> The actor Zhou elegantly wanders, the youthful boy is young and delicate, fifteen years old. Like the eastern sun, fragrant skin, vermilion cosmetics, simple disposition mixes with notoriety. Your head turns—I kiss you, lotus and hibiscus. Your appearance is already pure, your clothing is new. The chariot follows the wind, flying after fog and currents of mist. Inclined toward extravagance and festiveness, gazing around at the leisurely and beautiful. (Hinsch, 1992: 71-72)

In *Hong Lou Meng* (Dream of the Red Chamber), supposedly the most famous novel in Chinese history, Jia Lin pursues both young servant boys and girls when unable to have sexual relations with his wife, without feeling the need to differentiate between boys and girls. In *Jin Ping Mei* (The Golden Lotus), the male protagonist, Xi Men-qing, not only has sex with his wife and concubines, but also with his male favorite in a rather relaxed way, without feeling the need to take up a different identity for having same-sex activities. In *Rou Pu Tuan* (Prayer Mat of the Flesh), the protagonist, Wei Yang-cheng, is ashamed of his short penis, and decides to have a graft to gratify women. Before the operation, Wei tries to relieve his pent-up desire, and has sex with his sixteen-year-old servant boy when women are not available (Li, 1967:106-107). The homosexual sex scenes in these works of literature are described in a rather casual manner and are not the main part of the story. Indeed, they may not have caught the attention of the readers of that time as a dichotomous kind of eroticism needing a unique label and discourse.

The portrayal of young males of soft and elegant beauty has a long historical tradition in Chinese literature. For example, in the popular novel *Niehai Hua* (Flower in a Sinful Sea), which sold more than 50,000 copies and was reprinted fifteen times within the first two years of its publication, the author, Zeng Pu (1872-1935), portrayed the loving relationship between the fifteen-year-old courtesan Zhu Xia-fen and the protagonist, scholar Cao Yi-bao. Cao even bought Zhu's freedom from his master. Cao was said to be very much in envy of Zhu's youth and beauty, which was described in very positive terms—white and cute of face, smooth skinned, delicate and of a slim body shape, pretty eyes, small mouth, and elegant and soft gestures (Liu, 1984).

The best example to illustrate the Chinese "soft male protagonist tradition" is perhaps Jia Baoyu in *Hong Lou Meng*. Baoyu shows a persistent preference for the feminine over the masculine. On his first birthday,

Baoyu is given a wide range of objects, but he chooses only the so-called feminine ones including a comb, bracelets, and pots of rouge and powder. Baoyu is soft, delicate, considerate, beautiful, and has a deep love of poetry. He once says, "The ethereal beauty made from Heaven and Earth only belongs to females. Males are nothing more than remains and salivary excretion." He also says, "Females are flesh and bones composed of water; males are flesh and bones composed of soil. When I meet a girl, it is all so pure and serene, whereas when I see a boy, there is an irritable sense of defilement." In chapter forty-three, Baoyu's closest page, Tea Leaf, prays that "Master Baoyu is reborn in his next life as a girl . . . and do not let him be reborn as one of those horrible whiskered males" (Cao, 1973, SS 2.43.359). You San-jie, in chapter sixty-six, makes a strong comment on Baoyu: "I suppose you could call him effeminate. Whether he is eating or talking or moving about, there is certainly something rather girlish about his manner. That comes from spending nearly all his time in the women's quarters with no other males around" (SS 3.66.294). And in chapter seventy-eight, Grandmother Jia says, "Perhaps he was a maid himself in some past life. Perhaps he ought to have been a girl" (SS 3.78.556). In two instances, Baoyu's room is mistakenly thought to belong to a young lady. The decor was so feminine that both Granny Liu and the medical doctor called to examine Skybright think that they have entered a lady's bedroom.

Baoyu's erotic experiences are as subversive as his gender performance. He achieves sexual intimacy with females and males. However, it is inappropriate to classify him as bisexual, as he simply does not take gender as a base for erotic object choice. Baoyu, like most traditional Chinese, simply cannot be classified within the "homo-bi-hetero" spectrum. It is *qing* that touches Baoyu. He goes beyond class boundaries by exchanging presents with the female impersonator Jiang Yu-han as a token of mutual admiration, which finally leads to Baoyu being beaten by his father Jia Zheng. But even while Baoyu was beaten, he was still thinking of Jiang. It is crucial to note that Baoyu is beaten not because of homosexuality per se but because he breaks class boundaries between a wealthy male and the inferior female impersonator, who has already been "occupied" by a rich man.

Notions and practices of masculinity are culture-bound. Masculinity, or the notion of "being a man," is neither natural nor unmediated but is constructed in specific sociohistorical conjunctures. As compared to the well-muscled, rational model of the hegemonic male in the modern white-Western world, Chinese tradition emphasizes more the ascetic and spiritual aspects (*nei,* inner) rather than the external body (*wai,* outer). The

Chinese construction of *nanzi qi* (masculinity) focuses on the value of responsibility and fulfilling social and familial obligations. No wonder we find the male protagonists in mainstream Chinese literature to be pale-faced scholars stressing *wen* (scholarly intellect) rather than *wu* (martial arts). For a male to be soft, gentle, filial, and subtle is not a deprivation of his manhood but its fulfillment and completion.

Since the Han dynasty, there have been clear records of the ideal male using white face powder. He Yan, the son-in-law of Cao Cao (155-220 A.D.) and a famous scholar, for example, was praised as "by nature highly self-conscious, and whether active or at rest was never without a powder puff in his hand. When he walked anywhere he looked back at his own shadow."[8] The ideal male was portrayed as having "oiled hair, a powdered face, and small gleaming buttocks" (Hou, 1986:91). Pei Kai (237-291 A.D.), a scholar-official, was also praised for being feminine: "Pei Kai possessed outstanding beauty and manners; even after removing his official cap, with coarse clothing and undressed hair, he was always attractive. Contemporaries felt him to be a man of jade" (Ibid.:312). In the historical story of Dong Xian and Emperor Ai, Dong and other favorites all dress up as elegant, flamboyant dandies by ornamenting themselves as seductive beauties in light misty silk, gaudy feathers, and heavy cosmetics in order to seduce the emperor. But unlike modern times when such extravagant cosmetics and flamboyance signify effeminacy in a derogatory sense, male elegance in the Han dynasty is expressed as noble dandyism (Hinsch, 1992:47).

In most Chinese erotic painting, especially in the Ming and Qing dynasties, the male and female protagonists are often portrayed as having great similarities in appearance, features, and sensibility, making it difficult to identify gender except through the bound feet of the women. In Li Yu's *Heying Lou* (Reflections in the Water), young male and female cousins fall in love with each other as they first mistake the images of the reflection in a pond as their own, which shows how similar their appearances are (Ma, 1970).

The glamorization of the feminine male is also prevalent in the institutionalized same-sex eroticism in the theater world of the Qing dynasty (Dolby, 1976; Mackerras, 1972). Shen De-fu said that many government officials had turned from women prostitutes to boys as early as 1429 when the Xuande emperor had forbidden the officials to visit female courtesans or prostitutes (Ng, 1991). The Qing court even replaced female performing artists in the courts with male eunuchs and built male brothels for the officials.

In the theater, since women were forbidden to appear on stage, males would play female (*dan*) as well as male roles (*sheng*), and same-sex intimacy among these actors was commonly known. The recruitment of *dan* actors resembled that of male prostitutes. Young boys, mostly from the south, were purchased at the age of seven or eight, then sent to big cities such as Beijing or Tianjin for a demanding training program that lasted for several years, included singing, dancing, acting, and practicing anal intercourse with a series of progressively larger dilators. The age factor is crucial, as youth symbolizes femininity, innocence, and powerlessness. Colin Mackerras (1972) studied 150 *dans* in the late Qing dynasty and found that their average age was seventeen, and that most of them gave up their careers at around age twenty as they would be considered too old.

Pin-hua bao-jian is a classic novel describing the prevalence of same-sex relationships in the Qing theater. The author speaks through the character Tian Chun-hang, asking, "Why should we bother to distinguish between male and female, as long as the object affords erotic pleasure?" Another protagonist praises male-male (prostitute) sex: "A male prostitute shows a woman's face but does not possess a women's body. He is pleasing to look at without inciting adultery!" (Ruan, 1991:119). Though same-sex eroticism was rather prevalent in the theater during the Qing dynasty, it is doubtful whether these young boys who were sold by their parents into the theater went by their own consent.

Egalitarian same-sex erotic relationships, though rare, did exist in traditional China. During the Warring States period (722-221 B.C.) there was a romantic story about two young male students:

> When Pan Zhang was young he was extremely pretty, many people adored him. Wang Zhong-xian of the state of Chu heard about his fame and became classmates with Pan. They loved each other intensely and shared the same coverlet and pillow with unbound intimacy. They died together and everyone mourned them. When they were buried together at Lofu Mountain, on its peak a tree with long branches and leafy twigs suddenly grew. All of these embraced one another. At that time people considered this a miracle and called the tree Shared Pillow Tree. (Samshasha, 1997:48)

This story is not only the earliest analogy of same-sex love approximating the romantic fidelity ideal of a heterosexual marriage, but also the first historical record of same-sex love between two equal parties, rather rare in Chinese society where sexual behavior, homo or hetero, must follow hierarchical social relationships.

The most famous egalitarian institution of male same-sex relationships was the male *qi xiong-di*, a form of ritualized intimacy very close to the modern concept of marriage. In the province of Fujian in the nineteenth century, seafarers were known to pay a bride-price to "marry" young boys, who became their protégés. The older male was referred to as *qixiong* (adoptive older brother) and the younger as *qidi* (adoptive younger brother). *Qi* refers to a contract or agreement. According to this custom, two males must sacrifice a carp, a rooster, and a duck, then they exchange their dates of birth, smear each other's mouths with the blood of the animal victims, and finally swear eternal loyalty to each other. The younger *qidi* would move to the *qixiong's* household and be treated as the son-in-law by his husband's parents. The marriage would last for years, until the *qidi* had to fulfill the family responsibility of getting married to a woman, while the *qixiong* had to pay the bride-price for the *qidi's* wife. Shen De-fu, a seventeenth-century scholar, described such a same-sex kinship arrangement:

> Fujianese deeply treasure male homoerotic desire [*nanse*]. Whether rich or poor, beautiful or ugly, they find a companion of their own kind. The elder one is the sworn older brother, the younger the sworn younger brother. When the elder enters the younger's home, the younger one's parents welcome him as a son-in-law. The younger one's plans for the future, including the expenses for taking a wife, are all managed by the elder brother. Some among them are so devoted to each other that even past the age of marriage they still sleep on the same bed like husband and wife. (Wu-xia, 1912:9-15B)

It was a cultural strategy for PEPS to use familial and kin categories such as "adopted brother" to construct same-sex eroticism and integrate into the mainstream familial-kinship system, without segregating themselves from heterosexually inclined people.

Perhaps the best story concerning Fujian practices of male homosexual marriage comes from the famous late Ming poet Li Yu (1611-1680) in *Nan mengmu jiaohe sanqian* (A male mencius's mother raises her son properly by moving house). It is a love story about two men who fulfill their filial obligation not by denying their homoeroticism but ironically by marrying each other. The young scholar Xu Ji-fang, after his wife's death, decides that since he has fulfilled the social obligation of marriage, he will not marry again, but instead finds a catamite to be his second wife. He then falls in love with a beautiful boy, You Rui-lang. Xu sells his land to pay the five hundred teals bride-price to You's father. He even pays for the burial of You's mother and also invites You's father to live with them. Xu fulfills the role of a perfect husband and successfully gains the heart of You's father. You also becomes a perfect wife and mother, first by castrating himself to preserve his boyish beauty and to show his chastity to Xu, then by earning the encomium "Male Mencius Mother" because he twice flees dangerous situations to preserve his chastity.

In Chinese history, the customs of filial piety, virginity, chastity, bride-price, and motherhood are all key categories contributing to the heterosexual marital system. Yet Li Yu erects an alternative strategy that turns these categories upside down to produce and justify a filial same-sex relationship. It is a classic case of constructing and expanding the definition of the same-sex relationship not by denying, destroying, or dethroning the familial-kinship cultural imperative, but actually by appropriating and contextualizing it. The story is also subversive in terms of gender discourse, as feminine beauty, chastity, and motherly love are perfectly expressed by You, not as a mimicry of women or heterosexuality, but, as Li Yu repeatedly stresses, by You's natural feminine beauty, whereas women's beauty is only an artifice. Li Yu has thus denaturalized the one-to-one correspondence between "female" and "femininity," and "shows that the cardinal feminine virtues, chastity and motherhood, are not restricted to the female sex—indeed, that feminine gender is not restricted to the female sex" (Volpp, 1994:127).

Ironically, the best illustration of egalitarian homoerotic relationship is in woman-woman sexuality which, because of social denial and negligence, is relatively free from the rigid social hierarchy governing the male social order. It is women's peripherality in the patriarchal system that offers them "domestic space" for sexuality, especially in the system of polygamy, in which wealthy males could have many wives and concubines living together. As woman-woman sexuality does not directly challenge or threaten the male social order, it is tolerated and has never been a matter of serious concern. There is not even a word *nü feng* (female style/wind) to parallel *nan feng* (male style/wind, a euphemism for male homosexuality).

The major issue when writing Chinese *nü* (female) *tongzhi* history is the historical denial of women as sexual subjects. It is primarily a gender issue, not only an issue of sexual orientation. Traditional Chinese society denied and controlled the public expression of female sexuality. Because of women's inadequate public space and the male control of literacy, together with a patriarchal family-kinship structure in which women have little space for economic and social independence, there have been few historical records of woman-woman sexuality. We can only look through the margins, gaps, discrepancies, ruptures, and breaks, and be sensitive to secrecy, masquerades, and the silence of women's voices. As the female and male worlds were very separate, it was commonplace for women to establish intimate relationships with other women. In the Sung Dynasty, there were double dildos made from ribbed wood or ivory attached with silken cords. Van Gulik (1961) published detailed descriptions of the different types of dildos used by Chinese women for masturbation and mutual pleasure.

Li Yu wrote a popular play called *Lian Xiang Pan* (The Loving Fragrant Companion), concerning the relationship between two women. A young wife (Yun-chien), while visiting a Buddhist convent, falls in love with a beautiful and bright fifteen-year-old girl (Yun-hua) who reciprocates her feelings. Yun-chien prays to be reborn as a man so that they can be married. After many hardships, they decide to live together by making the girl the concubine of the wife's husband, thus gratifying all parties. Neither woman expresses any sense of guilt or shame, nor do the people around them resent such a relationship (Li, 1970).

A very similar narrative appears in *Fusheng Liuji* (Six Chapters of a Floating Life), the supposed autobiography of Shen Fe (1736-?). Shen depicts his wife's infatuation with a female singer. He wants to take her as his concubine so that his wife could be with her every day. But the plan is rejected by his upper-class parents, who despise the class background of the singing girl. The girl is finally forced by her own parents to marry another man. Shen's wife is very frustrated and depressed, falls ill, and dies (Ropp, 1981:146-147).

One of the most positive representations of woman-woman eroticism is found in the famous novel *Hong Lou Meng* (The Dream of the Red Chamber), in which there is a love story of two actresses—Wei-guan, who specializes in male roles, and Qian-guan, who specializes in female roles. They love each other both in real life and on the stage. When Qian-guan is excluded by her master, Wei-guan is so hurt that she writes the character "Qian" many times on the ground. When Qian passes away, Wei chooses to become a nun. Wei loves Qian so intensely that she burns incense for Qian. She tells her close friend, "I won't forget Qian. It's like a man loses his wife and remarries, but he is still faithful to his wife, so long as he keeps her memory green" (Cao, 1973:132-133). The main male character, Jia Baoyu, is deeply impressed by her sentiment, and comforts Wei sincerely.

The novel *Ge-lian hua-ying* (Flower shadows on a window blind) portrays an explicit sex scene between two young women who interchange sex roles:

> Two 16-year-old girls, Dangui and Xiangyu, slept together on one bed. At first, they felt shamed whenever they touched each other's bodies. After several nights, they began to kiss each other as a man kisses a woman, passionately and shamelessly. One night, they secretly watched their mothers having sex with an old man. Seeing this three-way sexual attraction left them highly excited. As a result, they

took off all their clothes and pretended to be a couple making love. First, Dangui, the elder girl, took the part of the "man." She told Xiangyu, "we may not have a penis as a man does, but we can use our fingers just like a penis." Dangui raised Xiangyu's legs, kissed and sucked her nipples, and touched her vulva. She tried to insert her finger into Xiangyu's vagina, but not even her little finger could get in. She wet her finger with her saliva, and finally succeeded in inserting it into Xiangyu's vagina. At first, the thrusting of Dangui's finger was painful to Xiangyu, but after many thrusts, Xiangyu felt excitement and pleasure. She applauded Dangui, calling her "my darling brother." At the same time, Xiangyu began caressing Dangui's vulva, and was startled to find it very wet. She asked Dangui, "Why did you urinate?" Dangui replied, "This is women's sexual secretion, and tomorrow when I play with you, you will get as wet as I am." After this, the girls made love every night; each one taking the man's role in turn. Later they made a false penis out of a white silk belt stuffed with cotton. They used it every night for their sexual pleasure. (Ruan, 1991:139)

Pu Song-ling's novel *Liaozhai Zhiyi* (Strange Stories from a Gossip Parlor), from the Qing dynasty, includes a love story between Fan and Third Sister Feng. Fan meets Third Sister Feng and they fall in love. Once, as they part, Fan misses Feng so much that she falls ill. Her parents know what is in her heart and try to find Feng. When Feng learns about Fan's condition, her tears "flowed like rain." After that, they "spent their time together, sharing the same bed and were very happy." However, Fan's parents are forced to marry Fan to a wealthy businessman. Fan kills herself on the wedding night. Feng rushes back and uses a special drug to revive Fan. Feng then tells Fan the truth, that she is actually a fox's spirit with a special attraction for beautiful women (Pu, 1969).

The most famous institutionalized illustration of woman-woman sexuality in Chinese history is perhaps the *zi-shu nü* (women who dress their own hair). From the early nineteenth to the early twentieth century, marriage-resistant sisterhoods developed in the Pearl River delta area of Guangdong, where the existence of sericulture and the booming silk industry made it possible for young women to become economically independent and celibate by choice. It is still unclear why these young women chose to be celibate, but scholars such as Topley (1967) found that the economic boom of the silk industry was a crucial socioeconomic factor enabling the prevalence of such sisterhoods. At the height of the movement it is estimated that 100,000 such women participated (Sankar, 1986). They either refused to marry or, if married, refused to live with their husbands. A woman could make the vow in front of a deity and eyewitnesses, and then comb her hair into a *shu-ji* (topknot) as a sign of her unavailability for marriage. The ceremony resembled the traditional marriage, and the *zi-shu nü* moved out of her parents' home, like a bride, and built a spinster house to live in with other *zi-shu nü*. If two *zi-shu nü* developed intense intimacy, they could perform the rites of marriage, vow to be lifelong spinsters, and then live as husband and wife. They would be supported by their natal family and treated as respected permanent members of the natal household. The couple could also adopt female children who would inherit their property.

Sexual behavior among these women was reported in the studies on *zi-shu nü*, and was seen by these *zi-shu nü* themselves as a natural expression of *qing* (Topley, 1964; Sankar, 1986:69-82; Siu, 1990:32-62). As early as 1928, Chen Tang-yuan documented the sexual practices among women in the silk industry in Shunde, Panyu, and Xiqiao (Chen, 1928). Sankar (1986) detected frequent but unstable "lesbian relationships" among her interviewees; Topley (1967:76) recorded that "informants called lesbian practices 'grinding bean curd' (*mo doufu*); they also referred to the use of a dildo made of fine silk threads and filled with bean curd."

Another type of woman in the Canton area, the *bu luo jia* (women who do not stay at home) refused to join the husband's family by returning to her parents' home after the wedding night, only visiting her husband at important festivals. Some would return to their husbands to bear children; some tried to stay at their natal homes until they passed childbearing age. These women would often live together in relationships that included sexual intimacy. Helen Siu says, "Elderly women I interviewed in 1986 recalled how they and their 'sisters' tightly wrapped their bodies with cloth in order to frustrate sexual advances during wedding nights, and how they escaped back to their natal homes before dawn after periodic visits to their husband's home" (Siu, 1990:53). With the decline of the silk industry in the area, many of these women migrated to Hong Kong to be domestic servants or join *chai tang* (Taoist or Buddhist vegetarian halls).

To conclude, same-sex erotic practices of both sexes are well-documented in Chinese historical records. For the following reasons, PEPS in premodern China should not be categorized as homo- or bisexual:

1. Same-sex eroticism was seen and constructed in traditional China as a specific social role rather than the essential condition of a certain personality. Traditional Chinese same-sex eroticism happened without the presence of "homosexuals." The basis of identity was not gender of the erotic object choice but instead class, kinship, and wider social relations.

2. Same-sex erotic acts in the traditional Chinese world occurred mostly in a social hierarchy of unequal power relationships, often with
little room for consent for the socially inferior party, who has little
choice but to follow the master's desire, socially and sexually.
Whether they have genuine erotic interests in their masters or people
of the same sex is simply unclear.
3. *Tongxingai* (homosexuality) includes not only *xing* (sex) but also *ai*
(love). But many "homosexual" encounters in Chinese historical
records are merely sexual acts that are brief, recreational, or frivo-
lous, which are not the same as a homosexual identity.
4. Rarely are traditional Chinese exclusively "homosexual." Most display a bisexual pattern; but the term "bisexual" is also inappropriate,
as it is a categorization based on the gender of erotic object choice, a
concept that did not exist in the minds of traditional Chinese. Until
recently, there was no Chinese word to describe a person who is
erotically attracted to both sexes. The term *shuangxinglian zhe,*
which is translated from "bisexual," appeared only in the last decade
and is incomprehensible to the majority of mainland Chinese.

MODERNITY AND THE DEATH
OF CULTURAL TOLERANCE
OF SAME-SEX EROTICISM

Given the cultural tolerance and rich historical records of same-sex
eroticism in Chinese history, it is lamentable to find not only contemporary China's conservatism and negativity toward homo/bisexuality, but
also the ignorance of Chinese intellectuals about the continuous prevalence of homoerotic practices in traditional China. The most ironic fact is
that contemporary Chinese, unfamiliar with the history of Chinese same-
sex eroticism, find such evidence unbelievable, continue to view homo/
bisexuality as a Western import, and conclude that traditional Chinese
culture is homophobic and antisexual.

Many scholars have attributed the death of Chinese tolerance of same-
sex eroticism to the colonial importation of modern Western sexology,
Christian homophobia, and the medicalization of homosexuality. Stephen
Likosky plainly states, "China, through much of its long history, has had a
rich and varied tradition of same-sex love. It was only with the arrival of
British colonialism in recent times that the stigmatization of homosexuality
appeared and prudery began to reign" (Likosky, 1994:24). Hinsch also says,
"in importing Western sexual morality, however, the Chinese also imported
Western intolerance of homosexuality" (Hinsch, 1992:167). H. J. Leth-

bridge contrasts the tolerance of Chinese culture with the homophobic hostility of Western Judeo-Christian culture:

> It would appear that in China, where the family unit was of supreme importance and where there was no mythological or metaphysical support for treating homosexual acts as especially abominable, homosexuality was not regarded as any more disruptive of the familial or social fabric than opium smoking, gambling or consorting with prostitutes, all of which were condemned by the virtuous citizen. (Lethbridge, 1976:315)

I contend that it is through the encounter with the West in the mid-nineteenth century, which sparked a series of indigenous efforts to modernize China, that same-sex eroticism was gradually defined as pathological. It was Chinese intellectuals' selective incorporation of Western scientific discourse on sexuality that generated the new attitude of negativity about same-sex eroticism. Dikotter (1995) writes:

> Instead of attributing social prejudice and official hostility towards homosexuals in twentieth-century China to an "importation of Western intolerance"—a simplistic and naive interpretation put forward by Bret Hinsch—the strong conceptual link between sex and reproduction was precisely what impeded the recognition that "homosexuality" was more than a non-procreative act. (p. 145)

In this section, I will examine the relationship between Chinese modernity and the fading of tolerance toward same-sex eroticism. Up until the late nineteenth century, Chinese authorities viewed China as the Middle Kingdom, a universal empire (*tian xia*). It is a Sino-centrism in which all foreign countries must participate in the tributary system, a suzerain-vassal relationship whereby trade was granted to foreigners as a gracious concession, not as a natural right for equal parties. The early Western arrivals, including the diplomatic missions of Lord Macartney (1793), Amherst (1816), and Napier (1834), did not disturb or threaten such Sino-centrism.

The first Opium War (1839-1842) was a turning point in modern Chinese history, as the Chinese sense of superiority about being the Middle Kingdom was seriously undermined. Chinese intellectuals were forced to see China only as a nation-state—*guojia*. However, the first stage of reform was merely to import Western technology and to subordinate Western scientific rationality to Chinese civilization: Chinese learning as the base, Western learning as the usage (*zhongxue weiti, xixue weiyong*). The

Sino-Japanese War (1894) shocked China, as even such a small country as Japan, modernized by Western learning, was able to humiliate the Middle Kingdom decisively. For the first time in Chinese history, Chinese intellectuals felt the need for a complete transformation of traditional Chinese civilization. A deep sense of cultural and political humiliation drove the Chinese to take more radical steps toward modernization. The lack of Western science and religion were perceived as proof of the inferiority and backwardness of Chinese culture. The Copernican universe of Western science was seen as more objective and scientific than the traditional Chinese worldview of yin-yang cosmic forces; Christianity's ethical universalism was seen as more attractive than the ethical particularism of the Chinese order; Western discourses on sexology were seen as superior and scientific.

Chen Duxiu criticized Confucianism for advocating superficial ceremonies, moral complacency, feudalism, the caste system, the denial of individuality, the oppression of women, and the cultivation of a weak and passive personality (Chow, 1960:295). Hu Shi, in *Bai shi bu ru ren* (Everything worse than others), says, "There is only one way out, to recognize that we are inferior in all aspects, not only in the material and technological aspects, not only in the political institutions, but also inferior in morality, in knowledge, in literature, in music, in art and in body" (Ibid.:289). Lu Xun even said, "rather than worship Confucius and Kuan Kung one should worship Darwin and Ibsen" (Ibid.:309).

It is crucial to note that the primary aim of Westernization was not admiration for Western culture but a strong anti-imperialist nationalism for building up a strong China. Many intellectuals did not really believe in complete Westernization, and their understanding of the West was very superficial and mostly ideological. But they were desperate to grasp Western science and democracy as the most powerful ideological tools for achieving modernity. The Republican period was an age of intense nationalism in which the goal of the May Fourth Movement was not individual happiness but nation building. All personal issues, sexuality included, appeared trivial and irrelevant. It was in such a context that Chinese intellectuals began to see the relationship between a modernized sexuality and a modernized nation.

Major scholars and reformers such as Liang Qichao, Yan Fu, and Kang Youwei attributed national weakness and backwardness to the physical inadequacies of the population, which included weak bodies and a poor knowledge of sex. The attitude commonly shared by reformers at that time was: "To strengthen the country, one should first strengthen the race, to strengthen the race, one should first improve sex education" (Wang,

1939:1). A famous sociologist, Yi Jia-yue, said, "To predict the rise or fall of the nation, one should look at the physique of the race; to assess the future of the state, it is enough to examine the bedclothes of our youth" (Yi, 1923:22149-22170).

Sexuality as an independent discourse on sexual conduct and desire was created, and suddenly became a vocal point of an acute nationalistic concern: "If sexual desire is not curbed, the sexual organs will weaken through wear and tear. This in turn will affect the physical strength of our sons and grandsons, eventually leading to the disappearance of our race" (Chen, 1979:338). In the several new intellectual journals focusing on issues of modernity and the new China, we find long discussions on sex, especially concerning masturbation and venereal diseases, both of which were thought to weaken the bodies of the nation. By the same token, there was immense concern about women, not because of a genuine feminist conviction, but because weak women would bear weak children, finally creating a weak nation. The new term *nüxing* (women) first appeared not referring to the notion of independent women, but as a patriotic call for the national building of modern China. Liang Qichao, for example, argued for the emancipation of women because it would "strengthen the race"—without healthy women, there would be no healthy child/nation (Dikotter, 1995:2).

It was in this time of immense faith that Western science would rescue China from backwardness that the concept of sexuality was first invented in China. Biological determinism and Western science replaced Confucian cosmological yin-yang discourse and dominated the discourse on sex. Instead of being tied up with the universe, human bodies were then seen as purely biological mechanisms through which hierarchical gender differences are naturalized and biologized (Dikotter, 1995). Zhou Jian-ren, a famous sex educator and the brother of Lu Xun, stressed that gender differences were rooted in an immutable biological fact of human bodies: "In conclusion, the male is relatively lively, whereas the female is relatively obtuse; these characteristics are comparable to the differences which exist between sperm and ovum" (Zhou, 1931:48). Western sexology's theory of women as little men with inverted sexual organs was popularly adopted by Republican reformers. "The most striking difference between the reproductive organs of both sexes is that the male sex is for the greatest part exterior (wai) whereas the female sex is for the greatest part interior (nei) . . . The female sex is exactly the opposite of the male sex" (Wang, 1939:103, 106).

Modern Western science, and biological determinism in particular, were seen as scientific proof of a gender hierarchy. The discourse of "nature" and the "scientific" was manipulated to justify such a gender hierarchy—passive women were seen as the natural complement of active men. As Frank Dikotter (1995) argues:

> The social roles of women and men were thus thought to be firmly grounded in biology: gender hierarchy was now represented as "natural" and "progressive." Instead of invoking the social duties of mothers, sisters, widows or orphans, writers debated the anatomical function of the womb in "women," the physiological effects of menstruation in "females," the nature of sexual desire in the "opposite sex." . . . Biological distinctions between male and female, which rarely assumed a primary function in imperial China, became essential. (pp. 9, 20)

In an unprecedented endeavor to "liberate" women from the tyranny of Confucianism and patrilineal oppression, women's bodies entered the public domain as the cultural symbol of China's modernity. As a commissioner of the Department of Civil Affairs in one province proclaimed:

> Women in this province have always been ashamed of their natural breasts which are thus bound and hidden. While having been practiced for thousands of years, this custom must be renounced, otherwise the physical condition of our people can never improve. Women are the mothers of all Chinese citizens. Their *natural obligation* is to breast-feed [our people]. Therefore, women's breasts are really the foundation of national development. If bound, they will gradually wither and then they will produce less milk. As a result, our people's health cannot progress. Therefore, breast-binding shall be prohibited from now on. Special attention will be paid to the mothers with sucking children. *Magistrates in all the countries should regularly report to me.* (Emphasis mine; Ching, 1931:2, quoted in Chao, 1996)

For the sake of a strong nation, women's breasts became the object of public and political surveillance. However, there was strong resistance in favor of breast-binding, based not on women's interest or benefits, but an outcry for the defense of "Chinese morality" in the face of the threat of Western colonizers:

> The act of breast-binding embodies our cultural virtues. Right now should be exactly the time to promote this practice. Therefore, his prohibition against breast-binding will lead to destruction of our

ethics and defilement of our way of humility. China is a country of ethics, as opposed to the West which is a society of barbarianism—not only do their women expose their breasts (in public), they even decorate their nipples with jewels without any sense of humility and shame! (Ching, 1931:2-3, quoted in Chao, 1996)

This debate also generated a highly heterosexist discourse on the biological differences between female and male, which justifies the male gaze and women's submission as "natural."

The reason why female breasts are larger (than male ones) and located right in front of the chest is that they are *naturally devised to attract the male gaze*. All animals are endowed with certain sex-specific spots for the purpose of arousing the interest of the opposite sex. As such, women naturally have two large breasts. Just imagining *looking* at the flat chest of a breast-bound woman: there is no fun at all! (Emphasis mine; Ching, 1931:6-8, quoted in Chao, 1996)

Although the rhetoric of Chinese modernity has also packaged itself in terms of women's liberation and gender equality, the female body has actually been reinvented and heterosexualized as the object of the male gaze in the public sphere. Though female breasts have long been eroticized in Chinese history, "their eroticism had not been collectivized until the legitimization and institutionalization of a public, and implicitly masculine, spectatorship in the early twentieth century" (Chao, 1996:148). The male-centered heterosexual desire to gaze at female bodies becomes the new grounds to justify opposite-sex desire. Heterosexuality, as a form of erotic desire independent of the will to procreate, is now constructed and naturalized in public discourse.

Republican China thus witnessed an unprecedented alliance between Confucian marital institutions and the scientific discourse of gender duality. It is perhaps crucial to note that the Confucian marital system is not homophobic per se. What it concerns and privileges is the reproductive-marital system—so long as one gets married and has children, whether one is homo or hetero is rather irrelevant. However, the Confucian emphasis on familial-marital institutions and reproduction is so overwhelming that it has been a crucial ground for a heterosexist and homophobic construction of sexuality. Western sexology provides the scientific discourses of biological determinism that heterosexualize the Confucian marital-reproductive institution. This close connection between Chinese modernity and heterosexualization allowed same-sex love to be medicalized and pathologized, now being perceived as a mental disorder and psychosexual essence that requires specific medical-psychological treatment.

The massive translations of modern Western male-authored sexology texts were crucial in this process of medicalizing same-sex love. The relationship between sexuality and marriage was now idealized and heterosexualized in the standard sequence as opposite-sex courtship, then romantic love, marriage, and, finally, passionate sex. Accompanying the import of Western science and sexology was the notion of romantic love, which began to prevail in Republican China. Passionate love was now romanticized as the sweetest sentiment of life, without which life was said to be incomplete. The emphasis on romantic love in modern China is perhaps best exemplified in the writings of Xu Zhi-mo. He writes, "I have no other methods but love; no other talents but love; no other potentialities but love; no other energies but love" (Lee, 1973:264). Lee Ou-fan called the China of the 1920s and 1930s "The Romantic Generation":

> Love had become an over-all symbol of new morality, an easy substitute for the traditional ethos of propriety which was now equated with external restraint. In the general temper of emancipation, love was identified with freedom, in the sense that by loving and by releasing one's passion and energies the individual could become truly a full and free man. (Lee, 1973:265-266)

What is yearned for is love, which always presupposes heterosexuality. As Yu Da-fu has said, "What I want is love! If there is a beautiful woman who can understand my suffering and who wants me to die, I am willing to die. If there is a woman—whether she is beautiful or ugly, who can love me wholeheartedly, I am willing to die for her. What I want is the love of the opposite sex" (Yu, 1947:17).

Chinese intellectuals were also disturbed by the new trend of Westernization. Writers such as Ding Ling criticized the obsession with romantic love as being self-indulgent, egocentric, and a decadence of the petit bourgeois young people. The poet Zhu Zhi-qing also wrote, "romantic used to be a good term, but now its meaning is reduced to slander and a curse. Romanticism was to release to the utmost one's animated emotions, thereby expanding oneself. But now what is needed is work and the animated emotions, undisciplined, cannot produce practical effects. Now is the time of urgency and such unimportant matters are not necessary" (Chu, 1928:372). Individual interests should be subsumed under national goals.

In other words, the process of Westernization is by no means a simple transplantation or cultural colonization but an active process of appropriation and recontextualization. Unlike Western sexology, which strongly advocates the pleasure principle of sexuality over procreation, Chinese sex reformers witnessed a primal concern for procreation—trying to find the most efficient way of producing a healthy and strong body/nation.

The Chinese appropriation of Western ideas was highly selective: homo-hetero duality and Christian homophobic hostility had never been popular; and their notion of sexual orientation continued to be absent from the Chinese sexual-social scene. It is only through the importation of biological determinism that the medicalization of homosexuality was tacitly accepted as a byproduct. Cheng Hao, in *The Sexual Life of Mankind* (1934), adopted the Western sexologist notion of "homosexuality as gender perversity," seeing homosexuals as having the gender traits of the opposite sex. He also criticized homosexuality as a bad habit that is abnormal, dirty, and inhuman. The notion that one person is both yin and yang was overwhelmed by a biologized gender polarity, thus making homosexuality appear to be unnatural and antibiological. Cheng even portrayed in his book the female and male biological reversal that was said to be the nature of homosexuality (pp. 133-134).

Chinese scholars, "enlightened" by Western scientific discourse, began to see homosexuality as a temporary aberration and a mental disease. In another rare case of direct discourse on homosexuality, Wang Cheng-pin (1934) wrote that if the sexual desire of a woman does not find a healthy outlet, "she will easily stray to the path of sexual inversion. If this kind of unnatural homosexuality is developed into an addiction, then even as she enters the age of marriage, she may not be able to have normal arousal but turn to the direction of abnormal perversity" (p. 114).

Chinese intellectuals began to address *tongxinglian* as a *bingtai* (diseased state) or *biantai* (metamorphosis), implying that such an abnormal state is generated by a normal person; the possibility of an exclusively homosexual desire is never envisaged, indeed not even in the 1990s in mainland China. Gui Zhi-liang, a famous gynecologist in the 1930s and 1940s, argued, "Homosexuality is a kind of intermediate or preparatory stage to heterosexuality; it is necessary for people to go through it." Gui thought that most people could pass (*guodu*) through homosexuality, but a minority would get blocked (*zu ai*) or bogged down (*tingzhi*) in the stage of abnormal homosexuality (*bu putong de tongxing lianai*) (Gui, 1936: 63-66). *Tongxinglian* is not seen as unchangeable, inborn, or an exclusive desire.

It was the sexologist's pathologization of homosexuality rather than the Christian homophobic attitude that was selectively and strategically adopted by Chinese intellectuals who had their own sociopolitical agenda in mind. Among the hundreds of treatises on sex education in the Republican period, only a handful mention homosexuality, mostly just as an aside.

Compared to the early Western sexologists' obsession with perversity, there was little discussion among Chinese intellectuals of homo, hetero, bi, or the entire notion of sexual orientation. While homosexuality had begun to be seen as unnatural and pathological, it was considered primarily as a bad habit and an abnormal form of behavior rather than an essentialized personality. Sodomy was seen not as an indication of a different sexual orientation but merely as a form of nonprocreative sex. The focus was not on homosexuality as a different form of erotic desire but as a bad habit that wastes semen because of illicit ejaculation. Thus homosexuality has a status similar to masturbation and spermatorrhea (*yijing*), which were the most obsessive concern of Chinese medical literature in the 1920s and 1930s (Dikotter, 1995:137-145).

In other words, Westernization was only a half-hearted project. Accounts by foreigners living in China illustrate the continued existence of homosexual activities amid the social disintegration and chaos of twentieth-century China. In 1898, Sir Edmund Backhouse (1873-1944), perhaps the first openly gay foreigner living in China, left England for China and began working for the British embassy there, where he lived until his death. From the time he arrived in China, he documented various aspects of daily life there, including his visits to male brothels and his many homosexual experiences with Chinese. In another case, a French diplomat, J. J. Matignon, who worked in Beijing during the late Qing period, vividly described from firsthand experience some of the male brothels operating in major cities such as Beijing and Tianjin (Samshasha, 1997). Indeed, for many Western Christians the sexual openness of Chinese society was proof of Chinese immorality, decadence, and inferiority. For example, Jesuit Matteo Ricci criticized the "homosexuality" of Beijing:

> There are public streets full of boys got up like prostitutes. And there are people who buy these boys and teach them to play music, sing and dance. And then, gallantly dressed and made up with rouge like women these miserable men are initiated into this terrible vice. (Spence, 1984:220)

As early as the nineteenth century, Sir John Barrow (1764-1848), in his book *Travel in China*, said that he should not write on this "disgusting topic" he found so common in China, but as he wanted his readers to understand China, he had to tell the truth (Barrow, 1806).

Anne-Marie Brady (1995), after detailed research, said that in the Republican period,

> Shanghai was a city with an active homosexual scene. Male prostitutes were available in the bars and brothels, and in bathhouses

where erotic massage was an optional extra. However it would be a mistake to view this as something separate from the heterosexual sex scene; homosexual activity was simply another option for the sex consumer. In the dance halls and night-clubs where partners could be hired to dance, both female and transsexual dancers were available. (p. 104)

In *Men and Women—The World Journey of a Sexologist* (1935), Magnus Hirschfeld recorded his observations of female and male homosexuality in China in 1931. He also gave a lecture at a meeting of the Chinese National Medicine Association held in Hong Kong on June 16, 1931, titled "Whether Homosexuality Is Inborn or Learned" (cited in Samshasha, 1997:277). It is perhaps significant that a typical Western sexologist's concern of the time—a scientific investigation of the cause of homosexuality (nature versus nurture)—was "imported" to China. For the first time in Chinese history, same-sex eroticism was treated as the essential and defining feature of a stigmatized minority called homosexuals for whom an investigation of the causes and prevention of homosexuality would be required.

The social anthropologist Pan Kwong-tan, who conducted extensive research on Republican Chinese sexuality, concluded that "cases of homosexuality among male students were not scanty. . . . Even in the co-educational schools of today, there are still many examples of lesbian relationships among the female students. Some of them even take vows to remain single" (Pan, 1947). Pan's translation of Havelock Ellis's *Psychology of Sex* (1947) and his own introduction, "Homosexual Examples in Chinese Literature," are particularly crucial because he represents the first generation of Chinese scholars who studied the issue of *tongxinglian* from the perspective of Western sexology. Pan adopts Ellis's approach of medicalizing and pathologizing homosexuality. When Pan's book was reprinted in 1993, the mainland Chinese deliberately changed the original title of Pan's article from "Homosexual Examples in Chinese Literature" to "*Xing Biantai* (Sex Perversity) in Chinese literature," indicating the pervasiveness of the medical paradigm of understanding homosexuality in contemporary China (Samshasha, 1997:16).

The prevalence of homosexual tendencies and behavior among modern Taiwanese men, especially of the younger generation, was forcefully illustrated in a survey conducted by Dr. J. K. Wen, a psychiatrist at the prestigious National Taiwan University. Among the 147 male and 96 female students interviewed, 26 percent of the male and 21 percent of the female students responded that they had "feelings of sexual admiration for a person of the same sex," and 14 percent of the male and 1 percent of the female students "had bodily contact with a person of the same sex and derived sexual pleasure from it" (Wen, 1978:106).

Homoeroticism can still be found in some of the literature of Republican China, though the concept of guiltless relaxation is fading, gradually replaced by a sense of perversity and abnormality, which has increasingly become the dominant discourse of *tongxinglian* in China. In a famous novel, *Obscure Night,* written by Yu Da-fu in 1922, the male protagonist, Zhifu, comes to know a nineteen-year-old tubercular man called Wu Chi-sheng. Wu's delicate features exert an "irresistible attraction" on Zhifu. The latter had more than once grasped Wu's hand and embraced him passionately, "feeling a kind of mysterious feeling passing through his mind like electric current" (Chen, 1992). Zhifu also compares their relationship to the love between the two French poets Verlaine (1844-1896) and Rimbaud (1854-1891), addressing it as the "pure love between the two." Subsequently, when Zhifu has to leave Shanghai, Wu goes to the pier to see him off. There they show great reluctance to separate from each other and exchange words of intense affection when Zhifu asks Chi-sheng to snuggle up to his coat if he feels cold:

> Upon hearing this, Chi-sheng, under the pale street lighting, took a look at Zhifu and surrendered his delicate body to Zhifu's embrace. Zhifu felt a kind of indescribable pleasant sensation passing from Chi-sheng's flesh to his own body. It was already twelve o'clock when they got out of the bathhouse. . . . Zhifu said, "Don't go. Come with us to the editor's office to sleep tonight." (Chen, 1992:15-16)

Xiao Qian, a Chinese writer, recently recalled his homosexual experiences in the 1920s and 1930s. He condemned such experiences as abnormal and pathological. But it is unclear whether he felt the same rejection at the time when these homosexual encounters occurred:

> The first time I came across homosexuality was in 1926. At that time, I was an apprentice in the Bei Xin Bookstore. There were two youngsters working there as well. In my memoir I called them Black Apprentice and White Apprentice. The three of us slept in the office, each of us had one table to sleep on. One night, White Apprentice did something stunning. It was a summer night. At midnight, he first climbed up my table, and then he went to Black Apprentice's. He didn't just lie down, he wanted us to sodomize him. Even today, I can still remember the pathetic look on his face when he almost fell on his knees to implore us. Black Apprentice and I both felt disgusted at and afraid of White Apprentice's perverted behavior. How-

ever, White Apprentice kept on imploring endlessly. I was only
worried about the next day's heavy duties. I really could not afford to
lose sleep and fuss with him any longer. Then I came up with an
idea. I took out an ultra-thick red and blue pencil. Black Apprentice
and I took turns to force the pencil into his anus. At the same time
while he was enduring penetration, he turned hysterically ecstatic
and gave thanks to us. (Xiao, 1996:13)

In this article written in 1992, Xiao repeatedly labeled the several
homosexual encounters he recalled as pathological. Yet the fact that White
Apprentice could initiate and request sodomy from his male friends in so
open a manner seems to suggest a rather guiltless and relaxed attitude
toward same-sex activity. Although Xiao Qian condemned such behavior
as perverted, the fact that he initiated a penetration into White Apprentice
and successfully made him "hysterically ecstatic" does not suggest a homophobic hostility, at least in 1926 when Xiao performed the penetration.
Psychoanalytically, one can even suspect a certain level of homoerotic
displacement when Xiao penetrated the so-called pervert—a scene Xiao
could recall so vividly even sixty-six years later!

Finally, in the autobiography of the famous Republican writer and
politician Guo Mo-ruo, love between people of the same sex was experienced openly as sweet and daring, yet it was becoming a target of social
taboo and gossip. Once the relationship was made public, the reaction
would fall between reprimand and partial acceptance. Guo recalled the
time when he was young:

At the time there were eight playful students in our school. They
were nicknamed "The Eight Planets" and I was one of them. . . .
There was a member whose name was Wang. He had such a beautiful face that people called him "The Flower of the Juan Juan Club."
The whole class tried to flatter and to seduce him like a swarm of
ants. Despite their efforts, he became particularly close to me. We
almost could not let a day pass without seeing each other. Every day
he waited for me at the steps of my store (owned by Guo's family).
Once I got out of class, I would call in sick and went out with him.
That was the time when I had the genuine feeling of "first love."
However, it was a first love toward a male. He had an affectionate
lover before, but he had left him when he turned to me. Our relationship had developed to a level that we could not be parted for one
moment. . . . Most of the time we met at night or in the evening. We
usually avoided the bustling city streets and chose to stroll along or
outside the city wards. The main reason he tried to avoid people was

his fear of gossip and rumors. . . . Once I fell asleep, I could feel
someone kissing me. There was a sweet juicy liquid flowing into my
mouth. I opened my eyes and realized it was Wang. I was over-
joyed.[9]

After 1949, the Communist government was eager to instill social and
moral order. Sexual puritanism was strictly imposed and enforced. Western capitalist influences were seen as corrupting Chinese culture; sexual
wildness in Shanghai and other big cities was seen as proof of such
"Western contamination." Centuries of tolerance toward same-sex eroticism had almost come to an end, with brothels and bathhouses for both
same-sex and opposite-sex pleasure closed down, and the privileges of the
foreigners withered away. Homosexuality was then seen as Western corruption and a legacy of the feudal past, now a crime of *liumang* (hooliganism). After 1949, PEPS could be arrested and sent to labor reform camp,
prison, or a clinic for electric therapy, or even shot dead in extreme cases.
Mainland China in the 1950s, 1960s, and 1970s underwent a very closed
and anti-Western stage, literally stopping most contact with the West,
which further hampered China in understanding and learning from the
Western lesbigay civil rights movement. The American gay movement in
the 1960s and 1970s added to the "historical amnesia" among Chinese,
who began to treat *tongxinglian* as a Western import that did not exist in
the Chinese past. Even when the Western lesbigay movement was occasionally reported on, the media would only publish the picture of a Caucasian drag queen to "prove" the promiscuity and perversity of homosexuality. Only in the 1980s did the Chinese population, especially in the coastal
cities, start to have extensive contact with the West, thus marking a different stage in terms of discourses on (homo)sexuality. A detailed discussion
will be conducted in Section II concerning the uniqueness and differences,
specificity and diversities of contemporary Hong Kong, Taiwan, and
mainland China in terms of same-sex relationships.

To conclude, it is only since the Republican period that China's long
history of cultural tolerance of same-sex eroticism began to fade. In the
process of Westernization, what Chinese intellectuals have accepted is not
homophobia per se but a scientific discourse of biological determinism
that marginalizes and pathologizes all nonreproductive sexuality. In an
ironic reversal, the contemporary Western world since the 1950s and
1960s has gradually departed from the mental illness model toward greater
respect for differences and individuality, yet China has abandoned traditional tolerance for the outdated Western mental illness model of sexuality,
developed at the turn of the century. In other words, it is only in recent
decades that *tongxinglian* has come to be seen as an immoral offense in

Chinese societies, especially in Hong Kong, a British colony for 150 years, where the general public has normalized Western homo-hetero duality and homophobic hostility toward same-sex eroticism. Yet, because of their own sociopolitical agenda, mainland Chinese intellectuals have not entertained the main thrust of modern Western sexuality, which divides human beings in a homo-hetero duality and treats homosexuality as a type of personality needing an inquiry into its cause (nature versus nurture). In a fascinating case, Dr. Li Zhi-sui, the private doctor of Chairman Mao Tse-tung for twenty-two years, wrote in *The Private Life of Chairman Mao* about Mao's insatiable appetite for both young women and the male services of "groin massage" (Li, 1994:358). It is crucial that Dr. Li perceives Mao's behavior only as a symptom of an overactive sexual appetite but definitely not as anything related to homo/bisexuality. Dr. Li's perception is not only a result of fear and respect for Chairman Mao, but the continuation of a historical attitude of treating same-sex eroticism as a behavior anyone can be involved in rather than a "personality" type. Despite the extensive influx of Western ideologies, the modern Chinese history of sexuality cannot be captured by any simple "Western colonizer versus Chinese colonized" or "foreign corruption versus native purity" dichotomy. Instead, this so-called Western hegemonic discourse has been appropriated, negotiated, resisted, subverted, and indigenized for a unique local agenda of its own.

SECTION II:
DIVERSITIES AND DIFFERENCES AMONG CONTEMPORARY CHINESE SOCIETIES

Chapter 2

Colonialism and the Birth
of Sexual Identity Politics
in Hong Kong

The Hong Kong *tongzhi* movement is a process of searching for an identity. It is an active process through which local *tongzhi*, trapped by two colonizers—British colonialism and Chinese culture—negotiate and appropriate resources from both colonizers to articulate their own indigenous identity and personal space.[1]

Sexual identity is not directly derived from sexual desire or behavior but is the product of a complex socioeconomic development that provides the necessary social conditions and personal space for adopting certain sexual-social categories to understand and organize oneself. Sex, apparently the core of lesbigay identity, is actually constituted by a complicated web of social relations of class, race, culture, and gender through which the meaning of sex is produced, sustained, and stabilized (Petula Ho, 1997). In the 1970s, when the colonial term *gay* was first imported into Hong Kong, it was not only a signifier of sexual orientation, but also a category of (middle) class, (white) race, (young) age, (well) educated, (English) language, and (male) gender (Chou and Chiu, 1995).

In this chapter, I will explore the social formation of the public discourses of homosexuality and the new social-sexual subject of *tongzhi*: When did Hong Kong Chinese start to adopt the apparently Western mode of constructing identity through sexuality? Why only in the 1970s did local PEPS begin to categorize same-sex eroticism as "being homosexual" or "being *gay*"? Why have these Western categories, when translated into Chinese, failed to take root in Hong Kong? Why do PEPS today prefer the identity *tongzhi* rather than "lesbian" or "homosexual"?

Identity, following the contemporary insights of poststructuralism and deconstruction, is an unstable and endless process of "becoming" rather than a fixed "being."[2] Instead of already "being gay," I would argue that thousands of Hong Kong PEPS "became gay" in the 1970s, many of them became queer, bisexual, or lesbian in the 1980s, and most of them have become *tongzhi* in the past decade. Such articulation by no means implies a linear account of historical development, but sensitizes us to different self-categorizations when PEPS use different cultural schemes to comprehend their same-sex experiences.

This raises an intricate issue: how to address our subject of research? Hong Kong *tongzhi*, especially in the 1960s and 1970s, had no uniform way to categorize and identify their own same-sex experiences. They have even less consensus on the issue of identity. Before the 1970s, there was no generic term for homosexual. More traditional Chinese terms such as *long yang, duan xiu,* and *fen tao* were used, but these are social roles describing same-sex practices, not generic terms for a specific kind of person. In the 1980s, the media started to use *"tongxinglian zhe,"* whereas more middle-class new-generation PEPS, women or men, tend to use the term *gay.* The importation and appropriation of Western sexual identity such as "gay" and "homosexual" is gendered, as women's sexuality and subjectivity is usually ignored or marginalized. Even through the 1990s, the mainstream media in Hong Kong often presuppose that "gay = homosexual - women + men" and "*tongzhi* = homosexual + male." There is no specific term for "lesbian," except that sometimes *gei mui, gei po,* or *doufu po* (bean-curd women) are used, which means "gay women" in a rather derogatory way. The terms "queer," "lesbian," and "bisexual woman" are occasionally used by more educated and Westernized women.

In this chapter, I apply "PEPS" to local Chinese who may not identify themselves with any discrete sexual identity. Lesbian, gay, TB (tomboy), *tongzhi,* or queer will be used when referring specifically to the self-identity used by a specific person. The terms "homosexual act" and "homosexual" appear in this chapter because the Hong Kong law books and debates used the same terms. I will start with an overview of the legal discourse on (male) homosexual acts before decriminalization in 1991. Then I will analyze the social controversy in the 1980s concerning the social and legal status of homosexuality in the context of the MacLennan Incident in Hong Kong. The third part will account for the rise of the new sexual-social subject. The last part will account for the classed, raced, aged, and gendered nature of this sexual-social subject, from gay, to *tongxinglian zhe,* to *tongzhi.*

THE LEGAL DISCOURSE OF HOMOSEXUALITY UNDER BRITISH COLONIALISM

It is through discourses that *tongzhi* identity emerges. The legal discourse on homosexuality in colonial Hong Kong has facilitated the production and reproduction of specific racial, sexual, gender, and class boundaries, and hierarchy.

In the early history of the colony, there was a rigid hierarchical distinction between the colonizer and the colonized, with all the high-ranking positions in the government occupied by white males, thus making white masculinity the norm for superior leadership. The colonizers thought that they had a "civilizing mission" to spread Western knowledge through "the project of instituting orderly, lawful and rational procedural governance" (Chatterjee, 1993). In such a colonial context, Caucasians are made to feel more masculine, strong, assertive, rational, decisive, and independent, and Chinese are labeled and made to feel powerless, passive, obedient, and incompetent. White heterosexual masculinity is further reinforced by the notion of citizenship in liberal capitalism, which is predicated on the notions of (bureaucratic) rationality, (objective) calculation, (impartial) legality, and (masculine) control. Contemporary feminists such as Seyla Benhabib (1992) and Iris Young (1990) have argued that the liberal construction of citizenship is formulated around rationalized hegemonic masculinity. In the context of British colonialism, the British aristocratic class, presented as the ideal Englishmen, became the major source of colonial officers. They were typically educated in English public schools, through which they acquired the so-called aristocratic culture, expressed through loyalty to rules and traditions, paternalism toward dependents, and, finally, class and cultural arrogance that justifies their mission to colonize "uncivilized" nations. Sinha's (1995) *Colonial Masculinity* has demonstrated in the context of India that colonial British officers were masculinized as the norm of "human being" whereas the Indian males were effeminized as inferior natives. The ideological construction and consolidation of white heterosexual masculinity as normative and the corresponding legal discourse on same-sex behavior is a crucial institutional device to discipline the sexual-social behavior of the colonized and to maintain the supremacy of colonial rule.

Of Hong Kong's 6.4 million residents, 98 percent are ethnic Chinese. As a former British colony, the law of Hong Kong is basically modeled upon British law. In the area of homosexual acts, the Hong Kong government in 1865 adopted the English Offenses Against Persons Act of 1861, which prohibited anal sex and bestiality. Before the Amendment Bill was passed to decriminalize homosexuality in 1991, it was an offense punishable by life imprisonment to commit anal sex even as a consenting adult in a private place. The main offenses covering homosexual conduct are contained in the Offense Against Persons Ordinance (Cap. 21.2) of 1901 in a chapter titled "Abominable Offense": "Any person who is convicted of the abominable crime of buggery, committed with mankind or with any animal, shall be guilty of a felony, and shall be liable to imprisonment for life" (Section 49). "Any male person who, in public or private, commits or is party to the commission of, or procures or attempts to procure the commission by any male person of any act of gross indecency with another male person shall be guilty of a misdemeanor triable summarily and shall be liable to imprisonment for 2 years" (Section 51). Attempted anal sex or indecent assault is classified as a misdemeanor and subjected to a maximum sentence of ten years (Section 50(a)).

This homosexual law is not a reflection of Chinese law or culture but the imposition of colonial law without any consultation with the colonized people. Both criminalization and decriminalization were initiated and instigated by the Hong Kong government. In Taiwan and the People's Republic of China's Criminal Law Code, there is no mention of homo/bisexual offenses at all.

Despite the harsh punishment for homosexual acts, the colonial government did not intervene in people's lives and culture unless necessary (Lau, 1982). This nonintervention policy was well exemplified in the case of homosexuality, as before the 1970s the government did not actively enforce the law. Since 1842, there were no cases of a convicted sodomite being sentenced to life imprisonment. Rarely were cases of sodomy brought to a court's attention, though in 1880 a young soldier named Peter Hardy was "convicted of an attempt to commit an unmentionable offense and sentenced first to three years imprisonment, which was afterwards increased by Sir John Smale, the presiding Judge, to five years" (Norton-Kyshe, 1898:26). In the following years, there was an increase in such cases, but it never exceeded three to four cases a year. The slight increase may be explained by the arrival of two full battalions of the Hong Kong Regiment from India in 1892. Away from their homes and families, these Muslim soldiers had no wives or women of their race with them, and were quartered in barrack dormitories of eight to ten males. Some soldiers, homosexual or not, may have sought sexual relief with their fellows or occasionally with Chinese males. In July 1887, for example, Keysir Singh was charged with attempted intercourse with a Chinese boy and sentenced to five years' imprisonment with hard labor. In December, one Abdoola was charged with the same offense with a Chinese boy, and was sentenced to the maximum penalty of ten years' imprisonment with hard labor (Lethbridge, 1976).

When a series of homosexual offenses occurred in the last years of the nineteenth century, although it was never more than three to four per year, it provoked deep anxiety in the British hegemonic institution. The ruling elite was threatened, and fearing not only that homosexuality would "spread" to the public but also that the imagined purity of the bureaucratic administration would be seduced and corrupted, it was quick to impose a harsh penalty for homosexual acts. In 1901, the colonial government passed the bill incorporating the Offenses Against Persons Ordinance, which prescribed penalties up to life imprisonment for anal sex, and up to two years' imprisonment for any act of gross indecency, irrespective of whether it was with or without consent, in private or in public. Until 1991, there was no such thing as an age of homosexual consent in Hong Kong, as all types of male homosexual acts, even between consenting adults in private places, were crimes.

Homosexual offenses remained few, and were not perceived by society as a social problem of any sort. Before the 1970s, there were extremely few prosecutions for homosexual offenses, and the police made no attempt to enforce the law against private consensual homosexual acts. Between 1914 and 1941 no cases of anal sex were brought to the Supreme Court, apart from one case of attempted anal sex in 1923 and several cases of gross indecency in the Magistracies. Statistics compiled by the court showed that after 1945 such cases were rarely brought to the court except in 1955-1956, when twenty-two people were accused, of whom thirteen were imprisoned.[3] The numbers may reflect not the real situation but the sensitivity of the police to such offenses. If more plainclothes police officers were assigned to watch public places where PEPS lingered, it is likely that the number of males charged in the courts with soliciting would have shown a substantial increase. As compared to twenty-two cases of anal sex or gross indecency in 1955-1956, there were none in the year before or the year after. The low overall figure for homosexual offenses does not imply that same-sex sexual behavior was rare in Hong Kong. Instead, it reflects a racial discontinuity: Chinese cases of same-sex intimacy, unless they involved explicit sexual behavior, were not usually recognized and categorized as *tongxinglian* by the Chinese community; and when non-Chinese homosexual cases occur, they might have been perceived by the Chinese community as merely matters of the *gweilos* or *lao wai* ("outsiders," especially Caucasians) and therefore to be ignored by "we Chinese." Thus, it was mixed-race relationships between Chinese and non-Chinese that received the most attention and constituted around half of the court cases of homosexuality before 1990.

Having gone through all the newspaper clippings from the late 1960s to the present concerning homosexual offenses, I have found that about half of the offenses in the 1970s and 1980s were between Caucasians and Chinese men, including the MacLennan Incident. In a culture where same-sex intimate friendship and physical closeness are highly valued and easily blended into the mainstream marital system, people do not have the entire homo-hetero framework to identify others or themselves as homo or hetero, thus making the general public rather insensitive to homosexuality. Even when people feel sexual tension, they may be too embarrassed to publicize it, and would rarely think of the possibility of reporting it to the police. For cases of female intimacy, it would be simply outside legal and social concerns, and would be trivialized as natural but negligible girlish behavior that, after all, would never threaten the hegemonic male order anyway. The stereotypical Chinese response would be trivialization: she would be "all right" when she grows older and marries a man.

On the contrary, whenever there was a male Chinese-Caucasian encounter, it seemed to have crossed the "insider (Chinese)-outsider (*gweilos*)" racial boundary, thus causing immense cultural anxiety among Chinese people, especially concerning the so-called "Chinese purity" and "Western contamination." Given the traditional Chinese stereotype of Caucasians as wild and promiscuous, sexual connotations are easily implied in the social perception of a Chinese-Caucasian intimate encounter. Because of an intense concern and scrutiny of Chinese-Caucasian relationships, such relationships become highly loaded, visible, and vulnerable to social gossip and suspicion, sometimes with the Caucasian party being blamed for corrupting the Chinese.

It was typically these mixed-race homophilic relationships that were most likely to be read as homosexual, especially in cases concerning an adult or middle-aged Caucasian male and an adolescent Chinese boy, which made up around one-third of all homosexual offenses in the 1970s and 1980s. Another one-third were attempted assaults upon Chinese adolescents by adult Chinese men. Rarely were there homosexual offenses concerning adults of the same race, unless violence, libel, or prostitution were involved.

Newspaper coverage in the 1970s reveals a cultural defense of blaming the West for corrupting the Chinese by bringing homosexuality to Hong Kong. Headlines include the following:

- *Tongxinglian* Is Banned by Hong Kong Law. But in a Westernized City Like Hong Kong, Buggery Cases Have Been Frequent. (*Sing-Tao Daily,* October 7, 1976)
- The Expatriate Lawyer Brought the Practice of Sexual Perversity from His Homeland. It Shocks the Hong Kong Government. (*Express Press,* August 16, 1978)

- Decent Youngster Completely Disregards Chinese Culture and, Corrupted by Western Immorality, Initiates Sex with American Naval Person. (*Sing Pao,* February 20, 1972)

It is crucial to note how the West was imagined and constructed by the Hong Kong Chinese as spreading homosexuality that "corrupts" the local culture, which is then imagined to have no such thing as homosexuality. There were two interesting cases in the 1970s in which Chinese, mistaking the stereotype of "Caucasian male = gay" for reality, cruised Caucasians publicly (during morning jogging and in a bus, respectively), and were caught immediately and finally prosecuted for gross indecency (Chen, 1973; Zhou-wai, 1983). The two Chinese "offenders" would have been highly unlikely to cruise other Chinese on the street. Even if they had, the Chinese being cruised might not read it as a blatantly homosexual act, and would be more unlikely to resort to the legal discourse of reporting it to the police.

Also in the 1970s, a series of homosexual offenses in the civil service pushed the government to reexamine its own homophobic laws. In May 1976, Assistant Financial Secretary Brian Jenny was found to have been cohabiting with a Chinese adult male for two years. It turned out to be the first homosexual prosecution of a senior government official in Hong Kong. However, because of technical legal mistakes, the charges against him were void. In October of the same year, two male Chinese government officers in the ICAC (Independent Commission Against Corruption) were prosecuted for having a sexual relationship and were eventually charged with suspended sentences of three and four months, respectively. As the offenses were all committed by government officials, the credibility of the government bureaucracy as civilized, moral, objective, and trustworthy seemed to be undermined.

Alarmed by these homosexual offenses in the civil service, the government hoped to reclaim the esteemed image and normality (read heterosexual masculinity) of the civil service, and decided to establish the Special Investigation Unit (SIU), which was formed with the principal task of discovering and prosecuting homosexual civil servants who could be potential blackmail victims. The creation of the SIU was the result of a series of blackmail and prosecution cases including that of John Richard Duffy, a thirty-four-year-old solicitor, who was jailed for three years after pleading guilty to sodomy and gross indecency charges in October 1978. Duffy then drafted a petition for clemency which alleged discrimination, and claimed that he was in a position to name many highly placed homosexual men. Fearing a witch hunt, 424 individuals including academics, lawyers, and social workers, with mostly Caucasian leaders, petitioned the government, criticizing the SIU and demanding the decriminalization of sexual conduct between consenting male adults. The fear was not ungrounded. As stated by the Law Reform Commission Report in 1983, government policy was that "known practicing homosexuals of either sex, should not be offered appointment in the civil service. . . . It was later acknowledged to be a circular issued by the office of the Secretary for the Civil Service" (1983:30).

The series of homosexual offenses in the 1970s, especially among civil servants and the Caucasian community, embarrassed the colonial government. But what was most alarming and shocking to the government and society at large was the MacLennan Incident, which proved to be monumental in the development of the *tongzhi* movement in Hong Kong.

FROM THE MACLENNAN INCIDENT (1980)
TO DECRIMINALIZATION (1991)

The social production of *tongxinglian zhe, gay,* and later the *tongzhi* identity in Hong Kong is inseparable from one of the longest and costliest legal inquiries in Hong Kong history—the MacLennan Incident.[4]

John MacLennan, a twenty-nine-year-old Scottish police inspector, was found dead on January 15, 1980, with five bullet wounds in his chest—the morning he was to have been arrested by the SIU for eight charges of gross indecency involving male prostitutes. The allegations flew: MacLennan had been set up on homosexual charges because he knew too much about alleged high-ranking homosexuals including Commissioner of Police Roy Henry, who was in a file of prominent homosexuals. An urban councilor, Ms. Elliot, claimed that the SIU had coerced Police Inspector Fulton to frame MacLennan on homosexual charges (Daryanani, 1980). Eventually, Fulton admitted that he was asked by the SIU to "set up" MacLennan by introducing him to male homosexuals so as to provide evidence to prosecute him (Yang).

There was intense public speculation and suspicion concerning this scandalous incident. The government responded to enormous public pressure by appointing Justice Yang Ti-liang, who later became chief justice, to chair the commission of inquiry to examine the case. After 134 days of public hearing, at a cost of $18 million, the commission published a 411-page report and concluded that MacLennan was bisexual and took his own life rather than face the charges. It was claimed that "an ordinary man," to use Justice Yang's words, was driven to suicide in an attempt to spare himself and his family the embarrassment the revelation of his homosexuality would have brought (Hadfield, 1981).

Questions remained. What made the MacLennan case so disturbing to Hong Kong's people and the government? Why had all previous homosexual offenses passed almost unnoticed by the public, while this case was so alarming? What really disturbed the public? What was the MacLennan case about—(homo)sexuality, (inter)racial tension, (colonial) bureaucratic scandal, (racial) pederasty, (male) gender nonconformity, or (political) secrecy in government?[5]

It is perhaps crucial to know how the whole case was exposed and detected in the first place: one night in July 1978, MacLennan tried to cruise a new friend, David Lau, an eighteen-year-old Chinese who had lived in Scotland since 1968. Lau rejected him but was not really annoyed. The incident would have passed unnoticed, like most hetero and homo cruising, but the father of Lau's friend, a retired police sergeant, after confirming the whole story, insisted on reporting it to the police. This man said that he would not want "someone even worse than a beast" to stay in the police force (HK Clipping, 7(7):1-3). Had this retired sergeant not reacted so bitterly to his son's friend's experience, the entire MacLennan Incident might not have happened at all. Why was such cruising so annoying to him? Did he feel the need to defend the integrity of the (heterosexist) civil service of which he was a member; did he want to protect young Chinese from the seduction of older expatriates, or simply to safeguard Chinese culture from Western corruption?

The MacLennan Incident exposed the "embarrassing" fact that a very substantial number of consensual sexual acts between male adults happen but are unlikely to be detected and prosecuted. Applying Dr. Kinsey's calculation that 10 percent of any given male population is homosexual, the Law Reform Commission (LRC) estimated a population of 250,000 male homosexuals in Hong Kong, representing approximately 10 percent of the total male population at the time (Law Reform Commission of Hong Kong, 1983).

The MacLennan case quickly turned from a personal and private case of suicide to a sociopolitical scenario that generated a debate over the territory's homosexuality laws. A subcommittee under the chairmanship of Justice Yang was appointed by the LRC five months later to deal with the question posed by the attorney general and the chief justice: "Should the present law on homosexual conduct be changed and, if so, in what way?" (Rayner, 1981). After three years of research, the subcommittee published, on June 9, 1984, a 400-page Law Reform Commission Report recommending decriminalization. The report stated that the crux of the issue was not whether the public approved or disapproved of homosexuality, but whether they expected the law to intervene in adults' private sexual behavior. Even the governor made a public statement in favor of legal changes—Sir Murray MacLehose argued that decriminalization would benefit society and that the discrepancy between Hong Kong and British law should be scrapped (Cheng, 1980).

The recommendation for decriminalization immediately stirred up an unprecedented debate in the Chinese communities concerning homosexuality. Owing to the controversial nature of the issue, the government held back from making hasty decisions on its own. In 1988, the Government Security Branch issued an official document, "Homosexual Offenses: Should the Law Be Changed?—A Consultation Paper" for public information, discussing three options: first, maintain the present legislation; second, reduce the sentence to a two-year maximum; third, decriminalize homosexual acts between consenting males in private.

The Crime Amendment Bill was historic in bringing together different institutions, including the church, academia, politicians, social services, legal, medical, and education professionals, and the general public, to engage extensively and intensively in a discursive struggle on the knowledge and meaning of (homo)sexuality. It is interesting to note that among those most militant against decriminalization were the Christian groups and those with a strong Christian background. Although the traditional Chinese cultural tolerance of same-sex eroticism had gradually been replaced by Western sexology, it was now the Chinese Christians who were unaware of this history of cultural imperialism and were keen to defend an imagined Chinese tradition that was said to have been hostile to homosexuality. The Hong Kong Chinese social and moral leaders, instead of clarifying such historical facts and reflecting upon the historical role of political, cultural, and erotic colonialism, actually accepted this fantasy about Chinese culture, now labeling homosexuality a Western decadence, and claiming that "there was no homosexuality in China."

The Christian Church

The anti-decriminalization platform was most strongly represented by the Joint Committee on Homosexual Law, established in 1983, comprised of thirty-one pressure groups, later increasing to 267 groups, mostly with Christian backgrounds. The Joint Committee claimed to speak on behalf of 450 school principals, 600 social workers, 200 teaching staff and administrators in the tertiary education establishment, 650 professionals, and 30 cultural and publication groups. The spokesperson for the committee, Dr. Choi Yunwan, a former medical doctor and present pastoral counselor and director of Breakthrough, said that decriminalization was "morally unacceptable," and was a threat to family life and the morals of the young. (England, 1983).

Breakthrough is a large, influential Christian para-church organization serving tens of thousands of Hong Kong youths through their publications, audiovisual productions, radio programs, and counseling services. Dr. Choi argued that homosexuals are usually emotionally disturbed and morally handicapped, and should seek psychological treatment. He announced a 70 percent success rate of *converting* "homosexual patients" into heterosexuals. Breakthrough also did a survey of 690 people, with 95.5 percent of interviewees rejecting decriminalization, and 89 percent said that a Chinese community would not accept homosexual behavior (Lee, 1983).

Despite his Christian background, Dr. Choi rejected homosexuality not because it was denounced by Christianity but because it was "unacceptable according to Chinese culture." Ironically, it was the Christian church that spoke most fiercely and defensively for the imagined Chinese tradition. What is equally interesting is the binary opposition these Christians erected: homosexuality was Western, immoral, unnatural, individualistic, and should be criminalized because it would disrupt the Chinese, moral, natural, family-based social order.

Individual Christian bodies also launched fierce opposition against decriminalization. The Hong Kong Chinese Christian Churches Union, which comprises more than 120,000 Christians from over 200 churches in Hong Kong, sent a letter to the governor saying that "homosexuality not only violates traditional Chinese moral concepts, it is also an abnormal form of physical behavior. It is a social illness and should be rectified and banned. We just do not want homosexuality" (Chan, R., 1983:9). An advertisement placed in the evening papers by the Chinese Protestant Alliance on June 14, 1983, petitioned the government not to change the law, and listed more than 200 churches and religious groups supporting it (Lam, 1983).

Yet the churches were by no means monolithic in their opposition. Their positions were obviously divided by race, class, education, and other sociopolitical factors. The racial division was particularly visible: most Caucasians that expressed their views supported decriminalization, whereas the strongest defendant for making homosexual acts an offense were all Hong Kong Chinese Christians who unanimously claimed the incompatibility of homosexuality and Chinese culture.

Since the 1970s, individual Catholic priests have been a strong voice for decriminalization. The Catholic Church was the first church to support decriminalization publicly. "Father Louis Ha of the Catholic Social Communication Office said homosexuality was undeniably bad morally but acts in private between consenting adults should not be punished by law" (Campbell, 1987b:16). Father Chris Phillips of St. John's Cathedral in Hong Kong took a big step forward in saying that biblical teachings were not against homosexuality. "The church always backs the oppressed. We should not condemn homosexuals because most of them are born that way" (Hamlett, 1987:9). As early as 1977, the Dean of St. John's Cathedral, Reverend Stephen Sidebothan, said that "until the law was changed homosexuals would continue to be at the mercy of blackmailers and other criminal elements" (Malcolm, 1977:23). Later, the Anglican Church of Hong Kong and Macau no longer opposed decriminalization. Rev Lam, the church's spokesperson, said that "when both persons, whether they are men or women, consent in the homosexual act in private, we should not regard them as criminals" (Hamlett, 1988:18).

The Education and Social Services Professions

It is crucial to note the involvement of Christian and missionary institutions in Hong Kong education and social welfare services where a majority of such services are initiated, organized, and financially supported by overseas missionary organizations (Kwok, 1997). It is thus not surprising to find a strong fundamentalist homophobic attitude in the education and social service professions.

One of the most virulent opponents of decriminalization was Hui Yin-fat, the legislative councilor and director of the Hong Kong Council of Social Services. His position is a vivid testimony to the popular naiveté concerning Chinese homosexuality. He argues that "homosexual activities are the product of capitalist societies and Western cultures" and that "homosexuality threatens the institution of marriage and is objectionable by reason of conscience. The abandonment of criminal penalties is likely to subject young people to exploitation and illegal activities" (Harte, 1988:18). Hui refers to homosexuals as "sick perverts" and believes that homosexuals can and should change their sexual orientation: "I would like to see young homosexuals come forward for treatment to learn about the opposite sex and become heterosexual. I condemn their depraved, unnatural and immoral practices that exert a destabilizing effect on society" (Hui, 1990).

The principal of the China Holiness College, Li Pak-hung, said that the recommendations made by the Law Reform Commission took no consideration of the welfare of the young who would be corrupted by homosexuality. "It will be a serious blow to educationalists and moralists who have been working hard to morally educate our growing generation" (Hawksley, 1983:23). The chairperson of the Teachers Association, Chow Kwong-chi, said, "gay conduct violates natural law and the Chinese tradition." He believes that giving legal protection to homosexuals will lead to more vice crimes (Chan, T., 1983:21). Another legislative councilor, Cheung Chi-kong, who is a secondary school principal, said that "it is a deviant behavior

. . . the act itself is not natural and should not be acceptable (Cheng, D., 1990:18).

On the other side, Peggy Lam, the executive director of the Family Planning Association, called for decriminalization to encourage people to come forward for HIV-antibody tests. She said, "as long as no harm is done to a third party, then it seems to me that it is a private matter" (Cheng, 1987:7). Dr. Ho Yau-fai, a senior lecturer in the Psychology Department at Hong Kong University (HKU), said

> there is no law either in China or Taiwan concerning homosexuality. Sexual orientation is a complex psychological behavior which can not be changed because of an amendment in legislation. There is no reason to believe that decriminalization of homosexual activities will lead to a downgrading of society's moral standards or that it will have a bad effect on young people. (Li, 1983:8)

He criticized the pro-criminalization camp as making "moral judgments" under the guise of scientific studies on homosexuality (Dobson, 1983). Dr. Nihal Jayawickrama, a law lecturer at HKU specializing in human rights law, stated that the existing law is a blatant violation of the human right to privacy (Hamlett, 1989). Indeed, as early as 1977, Henry Lethbridge criticized that anal sex between consenting adults, a crime without victims, ranks with murder as the most serious of all criminal offenses, with the maximum penalty being lifelong imprisonment (Ho, 1977).

The Political and Business Arenas

The Hong Kong business community has been rather conservative on gender and sexuality issues, worrying that their own sexist and homophobic practices, such as sexist employment ads and heterosexist staff welfare policy, might be criticized if a decriminalization bill were passed. Their conservative position becomes a vicious circle that makes *tongzhi* in the business community more reluctant to come out and speak for their rights. The situation in the political arena was no better in the 1980s, as there were no direct elections to the Legislative Council, making councilors highly insensitive to the public's needs, as they need not be accountable to the public.

Legislative councilor and influential industrialist Ngai Siu-kit said, "Decriminalizing homosexuality will destroy this family structure which means destroying society as a whole. Homosexuality is also against Chinese virtue and ethics. Homosexual acts should be punished because they go against traditional Chinese ethics and will result in the spread of AIDS" (Choi,

1987:19). Another Legislative Council member and a famous social leader, Szeto Wah, who is the president of the largest union and teachers' group, the Professional Teachers' Union, strongly opposed decriminalization as "it will encourage more people to take up such abnormal behavior" (Campbell, 1987a:10).

The Chinese Manufacturers Association, which represented more than 2,500 Hong Kong companies, rejected decriminalization for fear of the negative affect it would have on the environment for industry and trade. The spokesperson said, "homosexuality is at variance with the traditional moral standards of the Chinese people who form the great majority of the local population. Homosexuality has no place among traditional Chinese Confucian ethical teaching" (Lee, 1982:23). The vice chairperson of the Hong Kong Belongers Association, Sze Chu-sian, said that "to reform the gay law is to deform the moral fabric of the Hong Kong Chinese, to reform is degrading, retrogressive, indecent, alien, of no urgency and a downright encouragement for sexual aberration" (Course, 1983:14). Tsuen Wan District board member Chan Po-fong said that "99 percent of our citizens are Chinese, who emphasize and abide by a high value of morality. Homosexual acts are not tolerated in the community" (Wong, 1982:11).

Urban councilor Denny Huang said homosexual acts are abnormal behavior. Ho Sai-chu, a representative of the Chinese Chamber of Commerce and the only Hong Kong legislator who belongs to the Chinese People's Political Consultative Congress, said, "homosexuality is not acceptable to Chinese society. We must be careful" (Innis, 1990:15). James Tien, another legislative councilor, believes that "homosexual rights represent a scale of values which is out of harmony with Asian cultures" (Cheng, F., 1990:18). When one considers the level of homophobia displayed by legislative councilors it is not hard to understand the kind of pressure local *tongzhi* are facing. This is perhaps why most of them eschewed the development of an institutionalized homosexual lifestyle in the 1970s and 1980s.

Political alliances and battlefields are not fixed, but fluid and constructed. Szeto Wah once strongly opposed decriminalization, but changed his view when his Democratic Party, the most militant defendant of human rights, decided to support decriminalization in 1991. Another legislative member, Rosanna Tam, said firmly in 1987 that "decriminalization will indirectly promote homosexuality" (Hamlett, 1983:17). Yet she changed her position to vote for legal changes "to respect the heightened awareness of society in general of human rights values" (Lui, 1991:28). Whether genuine changes of view or simply sensitivity to the new socio-political climate, some hard-line opponents of decriminalization did soften their positions or even decide to support legal changes. Ten years of heated debate educated many people, challenged others, and reoriented everyone to mobilize themselves in this discursive construction of (homo)sexuality.

The Medical and Psychology Professions

In Hong Kong, medical and psychology academics in the 1980s had mostly received their education in the United States and the United Kingdom in the 1950s, 1960s, and 1970s, a time when the mainstream Western academic world was still struggling with the "mental illness" status of homosexuality. Thus, the decriminalization debate made no mention of heterosexism or *tongzhi* politics, but was obsessed with the mainstream medical and psychological agenda: the cause and cure of homosexuality.

Dr. Wong Chung-kwong, a lecturer in the Department of Psychiatry at Chinese University, said that homosexuality was learned and curable: "The inborn theory of homosexual behavior was not accepted in the academic field. Homosexuality is mentally unhealthy." Dr. Lam Man-ping, a counseling psychologist, working closely with Breakthrough and other Christian organizations, echoed this by saying that "this abnormal behavior is certainly not hereditary, but learned" (Man, 1983:20).

Yet there were voices from the medical profession that supported decriminalization. The most vocal was Dr. Ng Man-lun, a psychiatrist at the Queen Mary Hospital. He said that "we can call homosexuality a deviance but it is not a disease. It was dropped from the medical list of diseases long ago because we had no evidence to prove that it is a disease" (Lau, 1987:19). Dr. Ng also founded the Hong Kong Sex Education Association in 1985, which includes members who are teachers, social workers, and medical and health personnel. He said, "The minds and views of man [sic] have broadened in recent decades, and rapid advances made in sexual knowledge have also pointed out the irrationalities of many of our fears about homosexuality. To maintain the existing law would mean dampening the development of sex education, health services, and the general intellectual education in Hong Kong" (Liu, Ti, 1988:16).

The view of the Hong Kong Psychological Society was more in line with the Law Reform Commission: "Homosexuality is not a mental disorder. Criminalization runs against human rights and mental health" (Wood, 1984b:31).

Hong Kong University Psychology Department lecturer Norman Murphy said that his 100-page critique, "Homosexuality, Hong Kong, and Hubris: A Study in Deceit," arose out of his interest as a professional who was "upset by Dr. Choi Yun-wan's report which was based on religious beliefs about the sinfulness of homosexuality." Dr. Murphy criticized

Choi's analysis as weak and naive. "The present law governing homosexuality was not an inherent part of the Chinese tradition of law, but originated from fundamentalist Christianity. While the British themselves found these laws to be inappropriate and changed such laws for their own citizens in 1967, no such steps were taken for the colonized" (Chen, 1984:15). Murphy claimed to have conducted "the first scientifically sampled survey of the Chinese population" on decriminalization, which showed 251 versus 202 interviewees in favor of decriminalization (Wood, 1984a).

The Tongzhi Groups

The homophobic discourses, instead of suppressing and denying homosexuality, became a stunning force pushing PEPS to organize themselves to speak for their rights. For the first time in Hong Kong and, indeed, in Chinese history, PEPS acquired the unified and Westernized name homosexual or *gay,* as if they shared a certain common personality, motives, family background, lifestyle, and taste. Previously they were simply "doers" of certain sexual acts; they were now suddenly transformed from *doing* to *being*—they became a different kind of person called homosexual (*tongxinglian zhe*). It was the first time they entered into the public arena to define and construct their own subjectivity and identity. Groups were formed, and new identities, languages, and alliances were generated. A homosexual support group, the Association for the Welfare of Gays and Lesbians, was established in 1989, chaired by Reverend Fung Chi-wood, who was active among Hong Kong liberals calling for more democracy in the territory. The Ten Percent Club, the largest *tongzhi* group in Hong Kong, was formed in 1986 with the specific aim of fighting the homophobic law. It was through this unprecedented raising of self-identified PEPS' voices in the public arena that the Hong Kong *tongzhi* movement is said to have begun in the 1980s.

The *tongzhi* platform was not a "visible" camp because the spokesperson would have faced severe social stigma and even legal prosecution if found to be a *tongzhi* with sexual experience. As early as 1983, "a group of Hong Kong homosexuals . . . decided to take action against harassment and lack of human rights for gay people here. As a first step, they wrote to the British Prime Minister, Margaret Thatcher, urging her to ensure that the law in Hong Kong is brought into line with British law on homosexuality. The group followed up by enlisting the support of hundreds of gay activist groups in Europe, North America and Australia" (Martin, 1983:19). "In an open letter entitled *Everybody's Duty To Strive For Justice*, a group of homosexuals has launched a campaign to press for complete decriminalization of homosexual acts between consenting adults in private" (Holland,

1988:13). In the *Hong Kong Homosexual Political Manifesto* (Hong Kong Homosexual Representatives, 1988), a group of Hong Kong *tongzhi* asked society to combat homophobia and heterosexism. In a thirteen-point statement, the manifesto argued that the basic human rights of freedom of speech, of association, publishing, privacy, and marriage should be given to and respected by everyone irrespective of sexual preferences.

Throughout the debate, lesbian and bisexual issues were completely ignored. As Hong Kong University lecturer Ellis Cashmore said, "It will be an outrageous double sexist outrage. Men will be protected while females are ignored again. Many people treated lesbians as invisible. Women are under-represented in a number of institutions" (Wong, 1987:20). The law of Hong Kong is male centered. The legal definition of sex is phallocentric and behavioral, focusing on the penis: sex is defined as penetration by a penis into a vagina; orgasm is defined as ejaculation. Sex among women is not even recognized as such in the legal system. The entire debate on decriminalization is basically about the penis: whether anal penetration into a male body is a crime or not. In other words, lesbians are completely ignored.

Another interesting thing about the debate was that most involved parties employed the language of "scientific knowledge" and "objective truth claims" to justify their arguments, some even conducting their own "scientific" surveys to prove their point. The government presents itself as open and liberal, listening to public opinion and its objective knowledge. In 1984 when the LRC published a report on legal reform, it had tried very hard to go through a truth-seeking process concerning psychological, sociological, and legal knowledge about homosexuality. The LRC became a crucial agent in generating a social scenario in which scientific discourses became the most legitimate and then the most popular way to express opinions. What is important is not whose arguments are more scientific, or whether these people really believed in their "scientific research," but the fact that they all felt the need to speak in the scientific language of objectivity and rationality (Petula Ho, 1997).

The Government—The Bill of Rights and Decriminalization

The emergence of representative government, the public anxiety over the political future of Hong Kong after 1997, and the public debates on democratization were a crucial political context that finally led to the decriminalization of homosexuality in 1991. The direct election of the Urban Council in 1981 hallmarked a new era of representative politics and the exploration of civil society in Hong Kong. Various social platforms, pressure groups, and later political parties were formed, together with the rise of a new postwar middle class with an egalitarian and liberal democratic political orientation. Only in the last days of colonial rule had the colonial govern-ment taken unprecedented initiatives in pushing democratic reforms.

Since the Joint Declaration in 1984 by China and the British government, there has been great concern about the credibility of the Chinese govern-ment in safeguarding the human rights of Hong Kong citizens. The June Fourth Incident in Tiananmen Square in 1989 shocked the world. Not surprisingly, Hong Kong's people reacted strongly, worrying "Today Beij-ing, Tomorrow Hong Kong." One and one-half million people, i.e., one-fourth of the entire population, marched on two consecutive Sunday after-noons to protest against the massacre in Tiananmen Square. Public opinion in Hong Kong had pressured the government to quicken democratic reforms to safeguard human rights. In an attempt to rebuild confidence, the Hong Kong government passed the Bill of Rights in January 1991, which includes absolute protection for human rights and overrides all other laws.

Though the Bill of Rights does not explicitly prohibit laws criminalizing homosexual acts, such laws may conflict with Article 14, which protects individuals against arbitrary and unlawful interference with their privacy. As a strong case of reference, the European Court of Human Rights in 1982 found, by a majority of fifteen to four, that Northern Ireland's legislation on homosexuality, which is identical to Hong Kong's, was in violation of Article 8 of the European Convention on Human Rights—which is very similar to Article 14 of the Hong Kong Bill of Rights (Petersen, 1997). As the Bill of Rights contained a reference to freedom of sexual preference that was incompatible with existing legislation, the colonial government was eager to pass legislation for decriminalization. It is generally believed that homosexuality was decriminalized in 1991 in order to make the law com-patible with the Bill of Rights. Decriminalization became an honorable gesture of democracy to pave the way for the retreat of Great Britain.

Eventually, in July 1990, the Legislative Council voted thirty-one to thirteen in favor of decriminalizing homosexual acts between consenting adults, following almost ten years of public debate. The bill was finally passed in July 1991, but it remained a criminal offense for a man to have sexual intercourse with a male under twenty-one, despite a legal age of consent for heterosexual intercourse of sixteen. In spite of all its limita-tions, the 1991 decriminalization released local *nan tongzhi* from the basic fear of being prosecuted simply for having sex with a same-sex partner.

While some *tongzhi* viewed decriminalization as a complete victory, the government actually regained its control over the legal discourses of (homo)sexuality by creating the new discourses of (ab)normal sexual be-havior, reconfirming hegemonic heterosexual morality through regulation of privacy and the age of consent. Decriminalization was an act of tolerance and compromise rather than acceptance and liberation. As Ng Man-lung said, "there is a tendency in this report of the Law Reform Commission to recommend greater liberalization of the law with its right hand while encouraging greater social censure with its left" (Chan, B., 1983:19).

With the 1991 Crime Amendment Bills, the age of sexual consent for men became twenty-one, while for women it is sixteen. In other words, it is completely normal and legal for an adult male to have sex with his twenty-year-old girlfriend, yet he would be liable to lifelong imprisonment if his partner were a male of twenty. Why is there such discrimination after the decriminalization? Does it mean that males are less capable of deciding for themselves than women of the same age? Does it mean that homosexual sex is inherently evil? If a man has sex with a girl under sixteen, he is liable only to five years' imprisonment. Intercourse with a woman who is mentally incompetent is also punishable by five years' imprisonment. But a man who has anal sex with an incompetent person shall be liable to imprisonment for ten years. Why is it that anal sex is a more serious crime than vaginal sex? Why is anal sex considered abnormal in a way that oral, vaginal, and other forms of sex are not? The Chinese translation of "anal sex" is *jijian,* literally "chicken-rape," thus implying a bestial nature, and even if anal sex happens between two loving, consenting adults, it is still treated as (chicken) rape, thus turning "consensual sex" into a rape case. Further, why is there such discrimination against sex between males while sex between females is not even acknowledged? As the Hong Kong *nan tongzhi* win their battle of liberation from decriminalization, the fundamental issues of sexism and lesbian voices are left untouched.

The legal discourses have established a clear distinction between vaginal sex, which is said to be normal, natural, and legal, and anal sex, which is defined as perverse and pathological. In actual practice, it is only anal sex between males that is the target of legal and social censure. There have never been any reported court cases of heterosexual anal sex in Hong Kong history. In other words, gay men have been constructed as the potential criminals. The new definition of "private" is also created to target gay male sex. "Public" is now legally defined as a venue (a) when more than two persons take part or are present; or (b) in a lavatory or bathhouse to which the public have or are permitted to have access, whether on payment or otherwise. If two consenting male adults have sex in a hotel room, or in a private room with a friend present, or when three consenting male adults have sex in a private room, all these contexts will be defined as "public," and these people can be jailed for having consensual sex. Even after decriminalization, the police have continued to raid the cruising areas, especially toilets, to prosecute men who cruise men.

The colonial government has actively prioritized and privileged the notion of a "normal civil sexuality" (read conjugal heterosexuality) at the expense of all nonprocreative sex, especially sex between males. Even the supposedly objective Law Reform Commission Report said, "We believe that the law relating to marriage and divorce needs no amendment in respect of homosexual conduct by either sex. Specifically we have concluded and recommended that the law, should not be amended to permit persons of the same sex to enter marriage" (Law Reform Commission of Hong Kong, 1988:121).

Although the government proposed law reform, it was also the colonial government that first made anal sex a crime and that made little effort to follow British law when homosexual acts were decriminalized in 1967. In the debate on the Equal Opportunity Bill in 1993-1995, the government actually opposed protecting *tongzhi* rights in employment and other social services. Worse still, the government has never changed its policy that any civil servant found to be a homosexual will be fired. In a speech that summarized the debate on decriminalization in the Legislative Council, Chief Secretary David Ford stated blatantly that "a vote in favor [of decriminalization] does not signify personal acceptance of the rightness or wrongness of such an act, but only suggests whether such acts committed between consenting adults and in private merit the mobilization of the full machinery of law enforcement" (Chen, 1991:13).

Finally, while the government has taken an active role of political intervention, its space and boundaries of maneuver were indeed overdetermined by various sociopolitical and economic forces to adopt an apparently libertarian approach for decriminalization. A state-centered conception of power is therefore inadequate to comprehend the role of the Hong Kong government in the discursive formation of decriminalization. The fear of challenge by the Bill of Rights, the concern for a "glorious" retreat in 1997, the emergence of *tongzhi* and pro-*tongzhi* voices, and the maintenance of a respectable civil service and colonial bureaucracy all added to construct limiting boundaries and conditions for the government. The colonial government is only one of the actors in a complex field of discursive articulation (Petula Ho, 1997).

THE CREATION OF A NEW SOCIAL-SEXUAL SUBJECT: THE HONG KONG CHINESE GAY/TONGZHI

In Hong Kong, the very concept of sexuality came into popular usage only during the late 1970s. By then, the fluid conceptions of Chinese sexuality, which assume that every individual is capable of enjoying different sexual acts and practices, were replaced by the homo-hetero duality that defines people by the gender of their erotic object choice. Hong Kong people now speak of *tongxinglian zhe* (homosexual), *yixinglian zhe* (heterosexual), or *shuangxinglian zhe* (bisexual), often accompanied by the medical and psychoanalytic agenda of "normality," "pathology," and most fundamentally, "the cause of homo/bisexuality."

Through a review of clippings from the major newspapers in Hong Kong over the past thirty years (1967 to 1997), it is evident that the Chinese words for "homosexuality" appeared only in the late 1970s and then became popular during the ten years of debate on decriminalization. Many of my interviewees said that they first learned the words *gay* and *tongxinglian zhe* during the MacLennan Incident, when there was prolific media discourse upon the issue. According to the Law Reform Commission Report (1983), "Public discussion of homosexuality was virtually non-existent until the 1970s."

Tongxinglian or *tongxingai* is a translation of the Western medical term "homosexuality," which defines a minority group of individuals according to their same-sex sexual preference or orientation, as if everyone has a certain fixed and innate sexual essence. Many Chinese *tongzhi* find it uncomfortable to speak the word "homosexual" in Chinese, *tongxinglian zhe*. When they use it as an adjective describing a person, they will resort to English and say the English word "gay" in a Chinese sentence, sometimes turning the adjective "gay" into a noun by saying *wo shi yige gay* (I am a gay). The uneasiness of many Chinese *tongzhi* about using the Chinese language to address homosexuality as a generic identity is not because Chinese are passive, shy, or closeted. The main reason is that, in Chinese history, the notion of a sexual orientation, be it homo, hetero, or bi, never existed and was culturally alienating. Sexual identity politics have little market in Hong Kong. S/M, drag, transvestitism, and other marginalized sexual practices are not rare in Hong Kong, but no one has taken the label actively in public and made a political claim on behalf of that identity.

It is interesting to note how *tongzhi* and the mainstream media translate the term *gay*. The local (male) *tongzhi* use the Chinese word *gei*, which means foundation or ground but is pronounced exactly like "gay," thus desexualizing gayness by offering a rather positive reading. The mainstream media, however, turn *gei* into *gei-lo*, which is a derogatory label for gay men since *lo* carries the connotation of a male who comes from the lower classes. It is also a sexist term because it totally ignores and rejects lesbians and bisexual women. It is also classist in attaching "gayness" to the lower-class male. Linguistic translation becomes a process of bitter political struggle when "gay" is translated into *gei-lo,* which vulgarizes, masculinizes, and sexualizes homosexuality.

The other commonly used English term in *tongzhi* circles is "member," which is pronounced in Cantonese as *mem-bah,* implying a strong sense of inclusion but without specifying what kind of membership or club it is (Petula Ho, 1997). People tend to say ambiguously, "Is he a *mem-bah?*" or just, "Is he or is she not?" The ambiguity is not the result of self-denial or internalized homophobia, because even the activists would say *mem-bah.* It may indeed be a local strategy to avoid speaking the word *tongxinglian* directly in a homophobic world. More important, it reveals the indigenous approach of blending the "sexual" into everyday life and rejecting a rigid and discrete sexual identity.

It was the Commission of Inquiry and the LRC that helped to popularize the terminology of homosexuality and the entire homo-hetero duality. Although the Commission of Inquiry reported that MacLennan was a bisexual, it is the medical term "homosexuality" that is used in all the government reports. Three things should be noted here. First, the government rarely uses the politically positive category "gay" (happy) but insists on the medical term "homosexual." Even in the 1990s, all consultation papers, publications, and official statements by the government adopted "homosexual" rather than lesbigay or *tongzhi.* Second, bisexuality has not been seriously addressed. "Homosexual" is the only term to describe people displaying same-sex sexual behavior, although an individual may be a bisexual or may not like to identify with any of these sexual identities. Third, sexual behavior does not equate with sexual identity. MacLennan had sex with both genders, but we do not know how he understood his sexual identity. There are straight-identifying people who have sex with the same sex, there are lesbian- or gay-identifying people who have sex with the opposite sex, and there are bisexuals who have no sexual experiences at all. The LRC failed to comprehend bisexuality as an independent identity and the crucial distinction between sexual behavior and sexual identity, and produced a homo-hetero duality in which sexual identity is narrowly defined by one's sexual behavior.

The government's endeavor to discipline the sexual conduct of civil society, instead of repressing homosexuality, has the ironic consequence of generating a homo-hetero duality and the notion of sexual identity, thus leading to the formation of a distinctive *gay* consciousness, identity, and community. Hegemonic politics has generated its own counterpolitics.

It is only after 1991 that we see the rapid emergence of various *tongzhi* groups with a strong sense of self-identity. Before 1991, the Ten Percent Club was the only *tongzhi* group, with some other short-lived underground groups of very small size. Even then, the Ten Percent Club was not officially registered as a social organization because it would require an interview by the police in the police station, thus making *tongzhi* highly vulnerable to prosecution if anyone admitted to having sexual experiences with a same-sex partner. The Ten Percent Club was formed in 1986 by Alan Li, who returned to Hong Kong from Canada and saw the need to form a mutual support group for PEPS in the territory. The idea of "ten percent," based on the Kinsey report's claim that 10 percent of the population is homosexual, indicates the local *tongzhi* strategy to manipulate Western scientific research and the lesbigay movement to justify the legitimacy of their existence, a minority which is by no means a small community. The Blessed Minority Christian Fellowship, a subgroup of the Ten Percent Club, was set up in 1992 with regular monthly meetings of over 100 Chinese *tongzhi* Christians. It organizes Sunday services, theology courses, and various subgroups. The publication of the Chinese book *Tongzhi Christian Theology* has been vital in providing a theological and biblical ground for integrating the *tongzhi* and Christian identities (Chou, 1994).

Horizons was founded in 1991 by four gay Chinese men and Barry Brandon, a gay British man who had worked on the London Gay Switchboard. Horizons is a hotline service group providing information, education, and counseling for local *tongzhi*. Horizons' Chinese name, Hong Kong *Tongzhi* Counseling Hotline, is rarely used. This indicates their acquaintance with a more educated English-speaking crowd. Horizons has also organized a monthly tea dance in Club 1997 for the last five years, which manages to attract an average crowd of 150 gay men of different races. In recent years, Horizons has undergone the process of localization in terms of its membership, programs, and strategies. After Brandon left Horizons in 1993, it was run predominantly by local Chinese. The core members found that unlike the U.K. or U.S. experiences, where hotline services can best serve the more individuated lesbigay people, Hong Kong *tongzhi* prefer and need more interpersonal support and networking. Therefore, social groups, coming-out groups, peer counseling, and other subgroups have been formed to cater to the specific needs of local *tongzhi*.

Two *tongzhi* groups use Sanskrit words as their names: *Isvara (Ji Joi Se)*, established in 1994, was the first Buddhist *tongzhi* group in Chinese history. In both Sanskrit and Chinese, *ji joi* means to be relaxed and comfortable with oneself. *Isvara* aims to integrate Buddhism and the *tongzhi* identity, promoting harmonious communication between Buddhists and the *tongzhi* community. The other group is *Satsanga (Tong Jian)*, which was established in 1993 to focus on counseling and community service. The Sanskrit word *Satsanga* means communal practices of goodness and perfection. *Satsanga* provides counseling services, and organizes courses to enhance members' psychological health. It emphasizes the integration of *tongzhi* and non-*tongzhi* into the larger society. Indeed, some key activists in *Satsanga* are not *tongzhi* themselves but straight professionals devoted to the political cause of antidiscrimination. This demonstrates the indigenous cultural attitude of going beyond the sexual duality that classifies people as homo and hetero. Freemen *(Xiao Yiao Pai)*, founded in 1996, is a social group of exclusively *nan tongzhi*. It is an apolitical and nonintellectual group for recreation, fun, and socializing. The term *xiao yiao* means the joyful pleasure of freedom.

Zhan Chu Cai Hong (Over the Rainbow, the Hong Kong version of PFLAG) was established in 1997. The founders recognized that the most difficult issue for most Chinese *tongzhi* is their family relationships. Anthony Man and Roddy Shaw, the coordinators, stressed that the group is searching for a suitable mode in which their members can come out in Chinese society, instead of conforming to the strategies employed by the lesbigay movement in Western cities.

The Joint Universities Queer Union (JUQU) was started by a university student, Tommy-zai, in January 1997. Within four months, it had gathered more than 200 *tongzhi* students from various universities in Hong Kong. JUQU provides a warm and supportive space for fellow *tongzhi* to get to know and communicate with one another. Since then, *tongzhi* film showings, group discussions, and *tongzhi* orientation camps for new students have been organized on campus.

XX Party appeared in 1994. While XX represents the two X chromosomes of women, the meaning of XX is open to a number of readings and interpretations, another example of the Chinese preference for an ambiguous (sexual) identity. It is not really a group but a meeting space or platform for women who are concerned about sexuality and *tongzhi* issues. It has monthly open meetings at Club 64, a *tongzhi*-friendly bar, welcoming all women, *tongzhi* or not, to participate.

Queer Sisters (QS), established in 1996, was originally named *Fei Kung Kung Tongzhi Jie mei*. *Jie mei* means sisters; *fei kung kung* means "going beyond the boundaries" or "without the boundaries." The word "queer" is used most often by this group, to express the desire to go beyond homo-hetero boundaries and be more inclusive of all kinds of sexual minorities. Queer Sisters emphasizes that they are not lesbians and prefer not to be labeled. They later changed the Chinese name to *Tongzhi Jie mei,* and focused on issues concerning women's sexuality, but not necessarily *tongzhi* issues. QS is not only a *nü tongzhi* group, it is also a feminist group. QS is very vocal in advocating female sexual rights, defined as the right to explore, expose, and choose their own sexualities and sexual lifestyle. It is interesting that the most common way of referring to the group is either as QS in English or *Jie mei Tongzhi* in Chinese. The word "queer" is too Western, having a specific U.S.-U.K. historical context, thus having little chance of being popularized in Hong Kong, especially after the politically similar but indigenous term *tongzhi* was coined.

Lui Tung Yuen, established in September 1996 by five *nü tongzhi* all in their early twenties, is a *tongzhi* group with a membership of more than one hundred women. It organizes workshops, discussion groups, and social gatherings where *nü tongzhi* can socialize in a relaxing, safe, and nonmale context.

The recent rapid development of all-female *tongzhi* groups indicates the extent of sexism in the mainstream *tongzhi* scene in Hong Kong. All along, few women's voices have been heard. Regretfully, *nan tongzhi,* themselves victims of oppression for their sexual orientation, may not be sensitive to male privilege, and sometimes share mainstream sexist and misogynistic attitudes toward women, especially in terms of ignoring the specific needs of *nü tongzhi* in facing multiple forms of oppression. In most *tongzhi* groups that claim to include both sexes, women usually constitute less than 20 percent of the membership. Most *tongzhi* groups have very few female members, and the content of many *tongzhi* gatherings focuses on male issues such as decriminalization, cruising, and sauna culture.

The development of a discourse on homosexuality in Hong Kong is also contingent upon *tongzhi* writers who provide the necessary language, perspective, and impetus for Chinese *tongzhi* to speak up using indigenous language, perspectives, and sensibilities. Edward Lam, Michael Lam, and Samshasha are the most outspoken freelance writers in Hong Kong who discuss *tongzhi* issues in popular magazines such as *City Magazine, City Entertainment Magazine,* and *Crossover Magazine.* The first *gay* column in the media appeared in 1980—"Minority Rights" by Samshasha in *City Magazine.* In 1981, the Pink Triangle Press published Samshasha's *25 Questions About Homosexuality,* a simple Chinese question-and-answer book concerning the basics of homosexuality. In 1984, Samshasha published *Zhong Guo Tongxingai Shilu* (The History of Homosexuality in China), which is historic in recollecting incidents of same-sex eroticism in Chinese history.[6]

The return of students from overseas, who have started various *tongzhi* groups, has also been crucial to the development of the movement in Hong Kong. Samshasha, Julian Chan, Michael Lam, Jack Lo, Alan Li, Michael Lai, and Edward Lam, all young gay men who were key players in building up the *tongzhi* movement, had all lived in Western countries. They were crucial agents in bringing the Western *gay* discourse to Hong Kong. For example, the first four chairpersons of the Ten Percent Club—Alan Li, Julian Chan, Jack Lo, and Michael Lai—from 1986 to 1994, all came back from Canada, the United States, or the United Kingdom. All of them use English names instead of Chinese ones. Their Westernized background and economic independence, which distinguished them from the majority of local *tongzhi,* enabled them to come out to spark off the movement.

The establishment of the 1997 Tongzhi Forum has helped to popularize the term *tongzhi.* The publication of eight Chinese books with the term *tongzhi* in the title since 1994, all written by this author, was also vital in making *tongzhi* a popular and positive social term for self-identified PEPS. *Tongzhi* groups (*Satsanga,* Horizons, Queer Sisters, *Lui Tung Yuen,* Ten Percent, and *Isvara*) also have their own newsletters and journals, which are crucial in terms of building an information network, a site for *tongzhi* voices, and a space for developing a healthy community. All these groups have put the Chinese term *tong (zhi)* in the official name or the journal of the organization, thus further enhancing the popularity of the category *tongzhi.*

The process of identity politics from the 1970s to the 1990s is not linear. The change from *long yang* to *tongxinglian zhe,* to *gay* to *lesbigay* to *tongzhi* is by no means discrete. Different labels and identities are used interchangeably by different persons in different contexts for very different reasons. Some people use *tongzhi* as it is more Chinese, some like its desexualizing element, some dislike it for this same reason, some enjoy its transcendence over the homo-hetero duality, and some would like to de-homosexualize *tongzhi.* The English term "gay" is still commonly used, alongside the Chinese category *tongzhi.* These different articulations and interpretations are not exclusive or incompatible; they overlap, interact, compete, supersede, and sometimes collapse into each other.

The *tongzhi* community has become more diversified, with different groups putting energy into different issues such as gender politics (Queer Sisters), Christianity (Blessed Minority Christian Fellowship), Buddhism (*Isvara*), men's leisure (Freemen), women's socializing (*Lui Tung Yuen,* XX Party), hotline counseling (Horizons), sexual politics in college (JUQU), and social services (*Satsanga*). Instead of splitting and weakening the *tongzhi* movement, it is such sensitivity to differences among and outside *tongzhi* that reminds the *tongzhi* movement of the danger of becoming another hegemonic platform of otherizing and marginalizing those who fail to fit the mainstream—usually those from the working class, women, the elderly, and *tongzhi* who cannot speak English.

CLASSISM AND THE CULTURAL
CONSTRUCTION OF TONGZHI

As Hong Kong, and, indeed, the entire Chinese tradition, does not have a discrete lesbigay culture of its own, it becomes highly vulnerable to the influence of the modern Western model of identity politics and *gay* discourse. For a PEPS to become *gay* in 1970s Hong Kong often meant becoming Westernized. In the 1970s, when *gay* identity was first adopted by the Chinese community, it was a class privilege of those who spoke English. "Middle class" is here defined not only by income or property, but also the cultural capital in Boudieu's sense, in terms of class aspirations (Boudieu, 1984). The prerequisites for passing as *gay* were that one had to possess a minimum command of English and knowledge of Western gay culture. Those who were elderly or working class did not seem to qualify as *gay*. They were at most "homosexuals," conforming to the mainstream media representation of having "dirty" sex in public toilets as a form of obscenity or even perversity. In other words, the *gay* discourse had a tendency to absolutize homo-hetero sexual differences at the expense of all other social-sexual differences.

The formation of gay identity is possible with the rise of the Hong Kong identity, a new generation of postwar Hong Kong Chinese who prioritize homoerotic desire at the expense of family obligation in an unprecedented way. "Hongkongese" (*Xianggang ren*) was only invented in the 1970s. Before that, residents in Hong Kong would either identify themselves as *Zhong Guo ren* (Chinese) or by the specific lineage kinship or province one belonged to, e.g., *Shanghai ren, Guangdong ren*, etc. Most residents of Hong Kong came from China in the 1940s and 1950s, boosting Hong Kong's population from .6 million in 1940 to 3 million in 1960. These mainland refugees treated Hong Kong merely as a temporary residence, expecting to return home when China became less turbulent. Yet the rapid economic and social development of Hong Kong has generated a new sense of belonging for these refugees. In the 1970s, the newborn postwar generation, with no direct experience of China, began to identify Hong Kong as their home. This new generation identified themselves as *Hong Kong ren* (people), and are highly conscious of their differences from their parents and the mainland Chinese, who represent all the negative connotations of backwardness. This new social class, itself the product of an expanding market economy, is eager to establish a Westernized middle-class lifestyle and cultural capital, both to confirm to and celebrate their achievement and identity, and to distinguish themselves from the mainland Chinese.

What is unique about the Hong Kong Chinese born after 1945 is their background of being Westernized, middle class, well educated, English speaking, and economically and socially independent. They are generally influenced by liberal and carefree Western cultural symbols, represented by rock and roll and the Woodstock culture. The 1970s was a time when traditional family control over young people was challenged by the new wave of socioeconomic changes that began to prioritize individuality and privacy. The younger generation started to enjoy a space of privacy unavailable to their parents and predecessors. They are the product of an urban culture, having a considerable level of anonymity and personal freedom in issues of love and sexuality. Sex, instead of a familial-kinship obligation only possible after marriage, now gradually becomes a site of individual pleasure and the basis on which different kinds of preferences and identities are built.

Rapid urbanization since the 1960s, together with the wage labor system, have created new social conditions for the birth of a homosexual identity: those young people began to organize their personal lives around their erotic and emotional preferences. In a social structure based on close family relationships, there was simply no social space to *be gay;* it was even more difficult to *be lesbian,* since this would require an economic system where individuals become independent socioeconomic units, and where identities are not bound by a familial-kinship network. Sexuality was now released from the cultural imperative of procreation, and became the ground for individual pleasure and identity (D'Emilio, 1993). With nine years of compulsory and free education since 1971, the expansion of tertiary education, the trend toward delayed marriages, the government's massive program to build housing, a rapidly developing urban economy, and the bombardment of the Western discourse on sexuality, young people have had much greater space to develop their emotional and sexual lives independent of the family-marital system. It is in such a sociocultural context that homo and hetero identities have been created.

Central to the idea of *gay* is not only a positive, self-claimed identity stressing the right to one's body and homoeroticism, but the modern Western discourse of romantic love and individualism. The narratives of passionate love and sexuality are now individualized and said to be the core of selfhood, treated as an independent arena separate from the sociocultural domain. This individualized notion of sexual love laid a crucial ground for the introduction of the Hong Kong Matrimonial Ordinance in 1972, which bans concubinage and makes heterosexual monogamy the only legal form of marriage.

The 1970s also witnessed the unprecedented opening of several *gay* venues, namely Disco Disco (DD), Dateline, and Waltzing Matilda. In the 1990s, there were around thirteen *tongzhi* bars and discos in town, the best known being Propaganda, Why Not, CE Top, H_2O, Smart S, Garage, Secret Party, Wally Matt, Zip, Petticoat Lane, G Spot, Flex, and Circus. There are also about ten licensed *tongzhi* steam baths: Rome Club, Bobson Fitness Club, AA, AE, BA, Blue Blood, CE Top, Game Boy, KK, and JJ Park. Presently, nearly all of these discos, saunas, bars, and karaoke clubs have only English names, without Chinese names. The songs and videos displayed are predominantly Western ones. This is obviously not an attempt to attract Western tourists, as most customers are local Hong Kong Chinese. Rather, because of 150 years of colonialism, Western names and images stand for high-class culture, taste, modernity, sexual liberality, and trendiness. What is consumed in these *tongzhi* venues is not just a space for same-sex pleasure, but appeals to a very specific racial, class, and cultural imagery—to be white, Westernized, modern, classy, stylish, and young is what the Hong Kong *gay* image is about.

The Lesbian and Gay Film Festival is another crucial agent for building up the local *tongzhi* movement in a colonial context. In the last seven film festivals (1989-1998), more than 95 percent of the films and videos shown were in English without Chinese subtitles. This meant that *tongzhi* who do not have a high English proficiency are excluded from the festival, and would feel inferior for being unable to understand the seemingly glamorous Western world. For the well-educated middle-class *tongzhi* who constitute the core of the local activists, the experience of frequently exposing themselves to English-language lesbigay films becomes a vital colonial experience in which Western lesbigay discourses, experiences, and images are normalized, naturalized, and universalized as the prototype of what homo/bisexuality should be. In other words, the festival has produced and reproduced the cultural stereotype that Western lesbigay experience is the ideal prototype that "underdeveloped" Hong Kong Chinese *tongzhi* should model themselves upon, as if the best way to be *gay* is to be anglicized.

Indeed, most local *tongzhi* groups tend to use their English names, with the Chinese translations merely as an official token. Activists may not even know the Chinese name of Horizons, Queer Sisters, or XX Party. By the same token, very few local Chinese male *tongzhi* use their Chinese names in *tongzhi* circles. English first names are expected even for working-class people who do not speak English at all.[7]

In the 1970s, the discourse of *tongzhi* eroticism was highly racialized—the primary choice for gay men in the scene was between Chinese or Western partners. Julian Chan, the founder of *Isvara*, said that in the

1970s the first question asked of another PEPS was, "Do you fancy *ren* (human, meaning Chinese) or *gwei* (devil, meaning Caucasian)?" The most extreme though not uncommon case for such racialization of eroticism is expressed by Julian Chan himself: "At that time, I found sex with Chinese felt like incest. I simply couldn't accept that Chinese could love another Chinese" (Chan, 1997:52).

Homoerotic desire is not sufficient to constitute *gay* or *tongzhi* identity. The most common "type" of *tongzhi* would be a young, middle-class male who speaks fluent English and is fashionable and stylish. However, if we meet a sixty-five-year-old man in shabby traditional Chinese clothing, speaking in a rural dialect and knowing neither Cantonese, Mandarin, or English, even if he has sexual interest in men, we may not call him *tongzhi* or *gay*. Instead we would say he is a *tongxinglian*. Women, especially working-class ones, are less likely to take up a *tongzhi* identity than men, even those who have an erotic desire for other women. For a working-class middle-aged woman, her major concern may be the everyday struggle to put food on the table. How can she prioritize and privilege sexuality as a basis for her identity when it is so threatening to her identity as a working-class, full-time housewife?

A-Chun (forty-seven) said that he cannot be *gay* even though he loves men:

> I was married in 1975 when I was twenty-five. I had sex with other men only two years after marriage. I was cruised by a man in a bathhouse. Then I learned about DD and Dateline. It was fun and exciting but I rarely went there, as these places are not for me but for young middle-class gay men who speak English. I felt excluded there. They have their own circle, manner, style, language, and subculture. I cannot be *gay* though I love men. I am married and have two daughters. *Gay* is not a lifestyle for me. I go to toilets occasionally and meet my friends there.

Doing is not the same as being. Being *gay* in the 1970s in Hong Kong implied a specific class, age, education, and language location. A-Chun is a good example whereby the construction of gayness has stopped him from equating doing with being. He does not seem to be homophobic and has little problem in accepting his same-sex eroticism. He has his PEPS friends and activities, except that he does not take up a *gay* identity and lifestyle. Class is a big issue here.

Perhaps the best locale to illustrate the cultural hybridity of colonialism in constructing Hong Kong *tongzhi* space is in Lan Kwai Fong (LKF), a small L-shaped lane in downtown Central with around fifty drinking and eating establishments. LKF exists only at night; in the daytime it is just another ordinary backstreet. Since the opening of Disco Disco in 1978, LKF has gradually become a totemic brand name, signifying European avant-garde, elegant cuisine, expensive suits, wild drunkenness, casual flirtations, trendy youngsters, arrogant *gweilos* (Westerners in Hong Kong), and chup-pies (Chinese yuppies). It has also become symbolic of queers in Hong Kong. It is "queer" rather than *tongzhi,* as LKF is a highly Westernized locale in which indigenous working-class *tongzhi* may not feel comfortable. In short, LKF is an enclave for "The Other," a certain sexual and racial minority in Hong Kong (Cheng, 1997).

Disco Disco, the first *gay* venue at LKF, was the euphemism for "gay" in the 1970s. It was opened in 1978 by Gordon Huthart, a famous gay man in Hong Kong who had been jailed for homosexual acts with Chinese adolescents. It was his experience of repeated prosecution that gave him the inspiration for starting up Disco Disco, a place for the trendy, the outrageous, and the hip, including a crowd of expatriate and middle-class lesbigay people. Disco Disco signifies the birth of the most visible "*gay* circle" as the urban, young, Westernized, English speaking, trendy, and stylishly dressed.

LKF is the "home" for certain social/cultural minorities who cannot fit into the mainstream. In the 1970s, Hong Kong Chinese PEPS had real difficulty facing the two colonizers. They were pressured by the Western, colonized *gay* discourse to come out as *gay* but also by Chinese parents and culture to get married and be filial. Worse still, the meaning of mar-riage has changed from a familial-kinship affair to a matter of individual romantic intimacy. In a situation where the majority of people cannot afford to rent apartments of their own, and at a time when no one is expected to move away from his or her parents before marriage, it is almost impossible to become *gay*—to take up homosexuality as a lifestyle and one's primary identity. LKF, as a glamorous Westernized "ghetto," ironically becomes a "big closet" helping thousands of local PEPS to get in touch with Western *gay* experiences and build up their self-image, confidence, and pride. A trip to LKF represented an escape to a "free world of *gay* paradise." When PEPS use English names and speak English to Westerners in a Westernized place, they have already engaged them-selves in the Western imagery of the free world. LKF becomes an imagi-nary space of otherness, a safe home for the sexual minority who may not be able to become *gay* without such a space. Without LKF, some local PEPS may not have the knowledge, social network, role models, or confi-dence to live a healthy social life.

Yet it regrettably enhances the stereotype of homo/bisexuality of being a "Western import corrupting innocent Chinese youth." It further reinforces the marginalization of the working class and elderly *tongzhi* who are rarely represented in the media or on the *tongzhi* scene. The discourse of colonialism is oppressive because it prevents the colonized from speaking unless they speak on the colonizer's terms, in this case, the specific modern American discourse of middle-class gay identity politics.

Gay identity is neither imposed from the West nor a simple product of British colonialism, but is a complex and hybridized process of cultural translation whereby Hong Kong Chinese actively reinterpret, reread, and recontextualize Western identity categories. The simple linguistic translation of "anal sex" into *jijian,* "homosexual" into *tongxinglian zhe,* "gay" into *gei-lo,* "member" into *mem-bah* have already inserted an indigenous cultural reading into the so-called "original" text. *Gay* and other sexual identities were manipulated by Hong Kong Chinese in the 1970s for their own empowerment and identity building. Despite a colonial discourse in which the English-speaking world is standardized as the prototype, "Western identity" has been a powerful tool of resistance and empowerment for thousands of local *tongzhi* who at the time were trapped by the traditional Chinese pressure to get married. *Gay* became a powerful symbol providing a new language to understand oneself: "I am gay, so what!" "I am gay, I don't want to get married to the opposite sex." Once a *gay* identity is established, it gives *tongzhi* a different scenario of meaning-structure to organize their lives, prioritizing sexuality and individual happiness over parental expectations and family relations.

Some of the interviewees recalled the significance of LKF, especially Dateline and DD, in building up their *tongzhi* identity. John (thirty-nine) shared his experiences of becoming *gay* through LKF. He first went to LKF in 1979:

> I became gay in LKF. It is a place for gay people. I remembered one day I was cruised by a Caucasian at the pier in Central. He then introduced me to Dateline and DD. I started to cruise people there and met my first lover at Dateline. I knew almost everyone, including the staff, DJ, customers, and managers. It became my second home. The idea of LKF still makes me feel warm; I miss the experiences very much. . . . If I didn't meet this *gweilo* and go to LKF, I might not know the gay world. I would have gotten married and never have confirmed that I am gay.

Class is the big issue. At that time, John lived with his seven family members in a 200-square-foot flat in Wong Tie Sin. He said:

How could I date? If my boyfriend calls me every night, everyone knows that it is the same guy. What can I do? When I chat on the phone, my mum and dad are sitting next to me! My house is so small, packed with seven people, no rooms. How could I say any pillow talk in a soft voice? I never bought any *tongzhi* books, dared not even keep any *tongzhi* leaflets or notices. It is a very split life. Only in LKF could I be gay. Otherwise, I can only be the filial son of my parents. So I am Chinese during the daytime at work and at home. And I am gay during the nighttime in LKF.

Language is a crucial factor, most vividly articulated by Giana (thirty-two), who first went to LKF in 1982:

In LKF I can drop my mother tongue—no one speaks Chinese to you. I feel that I am away from my family, friends, and the entire culture. Listening to English is great. Speaking a foreign language in a place full of foreigners and "weird" people makes me feel so different, I become more wild, relaxed, and gay. You feel as though you're farther from home, as if you are in a Western city, a nobody's land where you can be gay freely, do whatever you like, without any worry. I went there not for sex, but a place full of "devils" *[gweilo]* who make me feel very warm because we are all "devils" in that world. I can just relax, be myself. I feel safe and secure. This is the only district in Hong Kong where I can hold hands with my partner, without fear.

English in Hong Kong has become a crucial cultural and class marker that divides people into those who know the language (middle class) and those who do not (working class). When local *tongzhi* insert English words in an otherwise Chinese sentence, they are not only describing new experiences, because these Western terms have no equivalent in Chinese, but also implying their English-educated and classy cultural identity. In a colonial society where English is associated with social distance and power, speaking English draws a boundary between Hong Kong identity and traditional Chinese culture. It is also a boundary within Hong Kong— between those who are familiar with Western, thus modern, values and culture, and the majority of Chinese, who are not.

Before the "birth" of LKF, the social life of most male PEPS was limited to toilets, saunas, and some cruising areas in the Hilton Hotel and the Ambassador Hotel. All these places were exclusively male. With the prolific development of *tongzhi* venues in Wanchai, Causeway Bay, Tsim Sha Tsui, and other places in Hong Kong, LKF has gradually lost its monumental meaning for the new generation of *tongzhi*. Still, LKF remains a status symbol for a specific class and race group of *tongzhi*. Daniel, an engineer of twenty-six, enjoys the ambiance:

> I like Zip and Club 97—they are good socializing places. You have people of similar social background, class, profession, and status. You consume the specific ambiance, well, which is constituted by the specific lighting, music, drinks, language, people of certain ethnicity, staff, service, style, food, decor, literally everything there, giving you a fantasy as if you were in London, L.A., or New York gay world. You can be gay and relax. No shame.

There is a strong "we versus they" dichotomy in LKF: to be in, you must wear the right clothes, have the right look, acquire cosmopolitan knowledge, speak a certain level of English, and have a minimal sensitivity to cultural and sexual diversity. The racial differentiation in LKF is clear. Some bars, such as D'Aguilar 26 and Green Parrots Bar, are mostly for Chinese with customers playing Chinese guessing/yelling games and dice. Other bars—Oscar's or La Dolce Vita—are mostly for the expatriate crowd.

LKF is a highly stratified place with clear boundaries in terms of race, class, gender, and culture. *Tongzhi* venues in LKF are mostly for men, except Petticoat Lane, which attracts many expatriate women. Propaganda is a male cruising place. Zip, Flex, and Club 97 are very Westernized male social places that are not comfortable for working-class non-English-speaking *tongzhi*. Tod, a Chinese *tongzhi*, was denied entry to Zip on the grounds that it was "members only." He then saw different expatriates, and Chinese accompanying expatriates, entering without showing any sign of membership. Tod confronted the bouncer, but no further explanations were given. The incident was bought up on the Internet on the Hong Kong Queer e-mail list with few responses from the expatriate circle (Cheng, 1997).

LKF has undergone a process of localization within the larger society. As expressed by a headline in 1990: "LKF Also Needs Open Reforms: Hook Up with Chinese Society Culture" (*Ming Pao*, July 11, 1990). The LKF Mid-Autumn Festival in 1989 began the process of localization both in terms of targeting the local crowd and by serving more indigenous and cheaper cuisine. Another crucial hallmark was the opening of Club 64 in 1990 by twelve Chinese partners from the intellectual and cultural scene. Club 64 is a *tongzhi*-friendly bar, with frequent meetings of local *tongzhi* groups. Since then LKF has been enhanced by a Hong Kong Chinese intellectual flavor (Cheng, 1997).

Not all *tongzhi* are comfortable with LKF. Because of its strong stigma as a *tongzhi* place, LKF has alienated some *tongzhi*. Daniel (thirty) admitted that many local *tongzhi* may hesitate before going to LKF. "After all, it is the place to see and to be seen. For the really closeted, LKF is a place to be avoided."

Stephanie (thirty-six) described LKF from a woman's viewpoint.

> I first went to Dateline in 1987. I realized that it was only for gay men. There were no women, not even one. A gay man friend brought me there, so it's OK. Half a year later, I met my first girlfriend. One night we went to Dateline again just for a look, to see whether there were lesbians or not. No! People stared at you. A Caucasian gay man came to us and said, "Do you know what kind of bar this is? It's a men's bar, not for women!" I was really annoyed. We left and never went there again. Lesbians are rejected in a *tongzhi* bar—can you believe it? I assumed that there is a bond among homosexuals; I was wrong. Sexism is so pervasive in our society that many people, especially male, simply don't feel it is a problem. Gay power only means gay male power.

Katherine (twenty-three), another local *tongzhi*, echoes these feelings:

> These *tongzhi* venues are all targeted toward a small segment who are usually middle-class, male, well-educated, young, and have a good job. If you are old, handicapped, economically poor, unemployed, or a woman, then you may find many of these *tongzhi* venues quite irrelevant to you.

During one interview, Sammy (thirty-four), a local *gay* activist, told me proudly that he can never remember women's names. I was stunned and asked him if he could remember his mother's name. The list of these examples of sexism is endless. Local *nan tongzhi* need to tackle their own sexism in a daily context before a genuine integration of female and male *tongzhi* is possible. Many *nü tongzhi* find it absurd simply to prioritize sexuality and ignore their gender experiences. They would insist on a *tongzhi* community sensitive to sexism and misogyny, together with classism, racism, ageism, and other forms of oppression. As Katherine said:

> Local gay male activists always ask us to ally and work together, but they tend to underscore the implications of gender differences for a woman. We are either excluded, ignored, or just a token when *nan tongzhi* need us.

In other words, *gay* is not just a sexual identity but rather a (middle) classist, (Westernized) racist, (young) ageist, (male) sexist, (capitalist) consumerist, (urban) city-centric, (English-speaking) Anglocentric category, all of these actually constituting Hong Kong society as such. Working-class and elderly *tongzhi*, especially women, are much less visible in Hong Kong. Unlike the Taiwan *tongzhi* scene, which at least has several *tongzhi* bars for middle-aged people, the Hong Kong *tongzhi* scene seems to exhibit a strong fetishism for youth and beauty. Apart from Satsanga, which organized one meeting discussing age issues for *tongzhi* in 1995, no *tongzhi* group has ever organized any activity specifically for older *tongzhi*. Being highly insensitive to ageism, it is not surprising to find that elderly *tongzhi* rarely attend *tongzhi* meetings, as they would likely be ignored.

The popularity of the term *tongzhi* does not imply that the classism, ageism, racism, and sexism inherent in the gay identity of the 1970s automatically faded away. *Tongzhi* identity has to be worked on, constructed, and negotiated. The search for a self-label is an endless process of redefining and reinventing the self by integrating the fragmentary and contradictory self. *Tongzhi* identity is fluid, multiple, and political, always in the making. Without continual effort to explore the hierarchical power relations within *tongzhi* communities, *tongzhi* could become another oppressive and hegemonic category that reproduces the sexist, classist, ageist, and colonialist elements of the wider society—issues that I will deal with in later chapters.

Chapter 3

Tongzhi Discourses
in Contemporary China

THE ABSENCE OF HOMOSEXUALS,
BISEXUALS, OR HETEROSEXUALS

In 1995, I stayed in Beijing for three months to conduct research on same-sex eroticism. I was first referred to two *tongzhi* activists in Beijing, who then introduced different friends to me. I also went to the parks, bars, and discos where *tongzhi* meet one another. Formal interviews were impossible. I chatted with around 200 people, for an average of one hour each (Chou, 1996a). Most of the people I spoke to were in their twenties or thirties, not because they are more representative, but because they felt freer to express themselves and come to the cruising areas in the first place.

Not a single informant used the label *tongxinglian zhe* (homosexual). They used the Chinese term *tongxinglian* (homosexuality) not as a noun for a different kind of person (i.e., *tongxinglian zhe*), but to refer to a practice. They would call themselves *wo men zhe zhong ren* (we this kind of people), *na zhong ren* (that kind of people), or say *ta shi gao tongxinglian* (she or he is playing around with homosexuality). In the book *Wo Men Huo Zhe* (We Are Alive), in which twenty-two mainland Chinese wrote their own *tongzhi* stories, the term *tongxinglian* was used more than thirty times, but never as a noun *tongxinglian zhe* for a type of person (Wu and Chou, 1996). Similarly, in the movie *East Palace, West Palace*, supposedly the first *tongzhi* movie in China, when the main male character first discloses his sexual identity, instead of saying *wo shi tongxinglian zhe* (I am homosexual), he says *wo shi tongxinglian* (I am homosexuality). This continues the traditional Chinese discourse where there is simply no linguistic and cultural equivalent to the concepts "homosexual," "lesbian," "gay," or "bisexual." The only exception is that some young males will use the English word "gay" in their otherwise completely Chinese speech, using mix-coded language to say: *wo shi gay, ta shi gay, zamen doushi gay* (I am gay, s/he is gay, we are all *gay*). When this new generation adopts the Western notion of sexual identity, they find no cultural equivalent in Chinese language or thought, and resort to using the English term "gay" in a Chinese sentence. They are actually integrating two very different cultural traditions by inserting the concept of homo-hetero duality into Chinese language and culture. Bilingual language becomes necessary to find words for new experiences when no native term exists for a Western concept. The term *tongzhi* is commonly used by young PEPS in major cities, especially in Guangdong province because of the pervasive influence of Hong Kong media.

The resistance to taking up a "homosexual identity" among PEPS should not be seen as a product of homophobia. Many Chinese *tongzhi* stress that sexuality is only one of the integral parts of life, and does not mark them as categorically different persons. Traditional Chinese culture treats homosexuality behaviorally—as an option that most people could experience—rather than psychologically, restricting *tongzhi* to a sexual minority having fixed inherent traits. In a culture that never segregates sexuality from the wider social life, and where same-sex eroticism is well contained within everyday life, separatist identity politics may generate a homo-hetero duality that both irritates the majority and stigmatizes the PEPS.

As traditional Chinese did not have the concept of a sexually oriented person called homo or hetero, when a daughter or son says that he or she loves the same sex, the classic parental response is: "When are you going to get married then?" or "Your bad habit will be changed when you get married." The implication is: "Are you still my daughter or son who will fulfill your cultural role and responsibility as a Chinese?" In other words, if the Chinese *tongzhi* fulfills the cultural expectation of getting married, her or his private life can be relatively free. The primary concern of modern parents is not so much the child's intimate relationship with people of the same sex, but that she or he becomes "lesbian" or "gay," a sexed category that privileges sexuality at the expense of his or her position in the family-kinship system, thus making the child a nonbeing in Chinese culture.

Given the cultural reservations about a separatist sexual identity, it is impossible to know the exact numbers of homo- and bisexuals in mainland China. Chinese experts have estimated that 1 to 5 percent of the total population of 1.2 billion are *tongxinglian,* much lower than the Kinsey scale, but which still amounts to as many as 60 million people (Laris, 1996). A recent random-sample survey of university students in Beijing, however, found that among male students, 29.2 percent reported having some homoerotic feelings or experiences, 16.6 percent reported having had a physical sexual experience with another male, and 8.4 percent felt themselves to be predominantly homosexual (Aggleton, 1996). A 1990 study by Liu Da-lin found that 7.5 percent of male and 8.6 percent of female college students either had a *tongxinglian* experience or were attracted to people of the same sex (Liu Da-lin, 1994-1995).

The search for the numbers of *tongxinglian zhe* is culturally problematic. The problem is not only the severe stigmatization of such a label, but that even those PEPS who accept their same-sex eroticism may not identify with the labels "homosexual," "lesbian," or "gay" because they may not feel the need to segregate themselves from those who love the opposite sex. Awareness of homo/bisexuality is low even among PEPS, both because it may not be a big issue to them and because the definition of these sexual categories may be beyond their comprehension. Therefore, the Chinese government was not completely "wrong" to claim the absence of *tongxinglian* in China, as this label is associated not with genuine love of the same sex but with promiscuity, Western corruption, gender perversity, and AIDS. Among all the PEPS in China, it is only those who exhibit Westernized attire and lifestyles, cruise in toilets or discos, or unmarried individuals without proper jobs who are most likely to be perceived as *tongxinglian zhe*. For those who are married, grew up in healthy families with normal childhood experiences, have proper jobs, and exhibit gender-conforming behavior, their same-sex intimacy may be seen by the public and even themselves as merely having occasional sexual indulgence (e.g., reading porn), naughty excitement (e.g., heterosexual prostitution), or a bad habit (e.g., masturbation) which can be changed. That is why many Chinese can accept their children having intimate same-sex lovers, but they cannot accept their children being "gay," "homosexual," or *tongxinglian*.

During my Beijing research, I seized every chance to chat with people on the street concerning their views on *tongxinglian*. Among the eighty persons I chatted with, I encountered no homophobic hostility. Instead, their responses ranged from frank admittance of ignorance ("Are there such kinds of people in Beijing?") to curiosity over the causes of *tongxinglian* ("How come some people are *tongxinglian*?") to treating it as a kind of disease ("Can it be cured?") to viewing it as a form of gender nonconformity ("These men are sissy boys who sway while walking, wear lipstick, earrings, and exhibit effeminacy") to a rather relaxed attitude of tolerance ("Oh, yes, it is now very popular to *gao* [play around with] *tongxinglian*"). The response shows curiosity more than resentment or hatred. Only about one-fourth of the persons replied by stressing that *tongxinglian* is abnormal and pathological. Moreover, they considered it a disease rather than a sin or perversity. While *tongxinglian* has been medicalized and pathologized by the mainstream psychological and medical authorities in China, the typical Christian homophobic hostility commonly found among the Hong Kong population has never been popular in mainland China.

Until the 1990s, the majority of mainland Chinese were basically unaware and unconcerned about the issue of homo/bisexuality and sexual orientation in general. Rarely would a mainland Chinese identify herself or himself as heterosexual, homosexual, bisexual, fetishist, transvestite, or S/Mer even if such practices were not uncommon. The landmark study on sexuality by Liu Da-lin (1992) found that one out of three peasants had not even heard of *tongxinglian*. Heterosexual-identified people were as rare as, or even less numerous than, homosexual-identified ones. Again, it is not because of heterophobia, but simply because rarely would they take up heterosexuality as a sexual identity. Even when one is married, one becomes a wife, husband, mother, or father, i.e., a role in the kinship network, not a "heterosexual." If a Chinese asks his or her mother or father whether she or he is a heterosexual, the parent may find it weird and say *"Shen jing bing!"* (you are crazy).

Sexuality, whether it refers to *xing yishi* (sexual consciousness), *xing quxiang* (sexual orientation), or *xing lunshu* (sexual discourse), until the 1980s had rarely received important consideration among the Chinese population or in scholarly discourse. Even now, the English term "sexuality" does not have a proper Chinese translation, as Chinese have never treated sex as a discrete domain abstracted from social and family life. The turn of the century, when the Western notion of sexuality began to be imported to China, was a time of intense patriotism for nation building. Thus, the entire discourse on sexuality was catalogued under the political goal of building a strong China. "Sexuality" had not yet gained independence. After 1949, the discourse of class took precedence over everything, and a concern for sexuality would be denounced as bourgeois individualism and Western corruption. It was through the language of class struggle that the entire population was constructed as one undifferentiated whole in which only the class matrix dominated and determined the life and death of every resident. Same-sex eroticism was ignored rather than discriminated against. During the Cultural Revolution, all social relationships, marital ones included, were viewed as political relationships. What was important was not one's sexuality, but one's political position. To treat gender or sex as a category distinct from class would be seen as reactionary. Zhang Bei-chuan, one of the most famous mainland scholars of *tong-xinglian,* said:

> In the 1950s, 1960s, and 1970s, *tongxinglian* was rarely mentioned in society, and when it was, it was treated as an immoral is-sue—whenever the government talked about the ugly phenomena of society, it referred to three things: prostitution, drug addiction, and *tongxinglian.* But the 1980s witnessed the influx of Western sexology. The publication of the Chinese translation of Masters and Johnson's *Xing Yi Xue* [Medical Science of Sex] was monumental in [de]medicalizing *tongxinglian.* But for the general public, con-sciousness of *tongxinglian* is still very low. (Interview, February 11, 1998, Hong Kong)

In a culture that is not hostile to same-sex intimacy, and which does not divide people into homo and hetero, people can be gratified within same-sex relationships while being heterosexually married, without being con-scious of having a different sexual desire. This largely explains the late age of self-identification of PEPS. Among the 200 informants I chatted with, about 30 percent confirmed their same-sex eroticism only after turning twenty-five years old. That number may be high because most of my informants are active and well acquainted with the "scene," and hence were aware of *tongxinglian* much earlier than most other PEPS in China. One male PEPS (thirty-four) for example, said:

> When I was young, I felt comfortable with men, but I didn't feel anything wrong or sexual. That was the age of sexual innocence. Even straight people may not be sensitive to their erotic desire before marriage. I was married at twenty-five. My same-sex needs were channeled through relationships with other *ge ermen* [male friends]. We are very close. Men are very close here. When I was thirty-one I was cruised by a man in a toilet. Then I knew that I was turned on by men. It was great fun. My relation with my wife is very good. To me, sex is not very important, *qing* is more important. I don't want be gay, I am a husband.

When this informant said, "I don't want be gay, I am a husband," he was conscious of a choice whether to take up the *gay* identity, and his choice not to take up this identity has nothing to do with self-denial. He also said, "Then I knew that I was turned on by men. It was great fun." Sexual identity should not be confused with sexual liberation. Instead, he emphasizes his role of husband rather than his same-sex eroticism. He accepts "doing *tongxinglian*," not "being *gay*," which is threatening to his kin-marital status as a husband.

Such historical absence of homo-hetero duality and Western sexual identity labels for same-sex eroticism have significant implications.

1. The phenomenon common among British and American men, who seem to be obsessed with picking up women but may react violently when approached by a friendly gay man, is uncommon in mainland China. Several Hong Kong *nan tongzhi* informants who went to China in the 1970s had similar experiences of having sex with young mainland Chinese men. These young mainlanders had neither heard the term *tongxinglian* nor felt guilty about their same-sex behavior. If these mainlanders had been exposed to Western culture, they might have denied their own homo-eroticism, and refused to have sex with men. Through Hollywood and Hong Kong movies and outdated psychoanalytic theories of sexual deviance, many mainland Chinese are rapidly changing their attitudes toward sexuality, and have begun to adopt the homo-hetero duality and homophobia in reading human intimacy. The best example is Hong Kong, a very traditional Chinese city, which, after 150 years of colonial rule and modernization, now exhibits a typical Christian homophobic hostility toward same-sex eroticism.

2. Many works on Chinese homosexuality rely uncritically on Western categories of sexual identity, thus failing to capture the indigenous Chinese constructs of same-sex eroticism, even accusing PEPS of being "closeted" and "dishonest" for refusing Western sexual constructs. Western lesbigay people, who have experienced a long historical period of homophobic violence, have only gained their social space in recent decades. As *gay* scholar Robert Aldrich describes, "Western society has for centuries been uncongenial to homosexuality, law considered homosexuality a crime, medicine labeled it a disease, religion called it a sin, psychology analyzed it as a perversion or personality disorder and general social mores castigated it as a disgusting deviance" (Aldrich, 1993:7). Decriminalizing sex between consenting male adults is a recent development in most Western jurisdictions. So when Western lesbigay people look at the contemporary Chinese world, a notoriously totalitarian country especially from the Western perspective, some of them expect Chinese same-sex lovers to identify themselves as "gay" and "come out of the closet." Most reports on Chinese *tongxinglian* stress that they are just coming out of the dark ages: "Chinese Closet Door Now Ajar" (*SCMP*, September 5, 1997); "Gays in Beijing Stretching the Limits of Tolerance—Gay Chinese Come Out" (*Eastern Express*, September 17, 1994); "Out of the Shadow" (*Newsweek*, April 15, 1996).

3. Whereas the Hong Kong *tongzhi* circle has been highly Westernized in terms of "bi-phobia," mainland Chinese *tongzhi* are rather relaxed. There is neither a bimovement nor biidentity in China, unlike the Western world, where bi-phobia in both the straight and lesbigay worlds suppresses and denies the voice of bisexuality. Homosexuality is seen as opposite to and incompatible with heterosexuality. Such a notion of "monosexuality" is the crucial conceptual ground accounting for the serious bi-phobia in the Western world and Westernized places such as Hong Kong. On the contrary, most people in China rarely feel the need to categorize people as bi, since bisexuality is rather ambiguously integrated into the normal social fiber. Homo and hetero tendencies are not mutually exclusive or even discretely differentiated. In mainland China, marriage is still primarily a social obligation everyone must fulfill, thus a PEPS getting married would not be seen by herself or himself or her or his *tongzhi* friends as betraying the "circle." Instead, bisexuality is seen more positively, both for relieving the pain of having sex with one's spouse, and also for the capacity to go beyond gender. One *tongzhi* said, "I adore bisexual people. Life would be much more complete if I could be intimate with both sexes. You need to have a very broad heart in order to go beyond the mundane boundaries of gender."

4. Many Chinese PEPS have close friendships with straight people. When asked to list their three best friends, 90 percent of Hong Kong *tongzhi* listed other *tongzhi*. But in China, when asked the same question, only around 40 percent of PEPS listed all three friends as PEPS, and around 10 percent said their spouses were one of their best friends. One *tongzhi* shares his experience of having a close friendship with a straight man he loved:

We are each other's best friend for the last ten years. We were so close that we saw each other every day during college and for several years afterward. Once when we were sleeping on the same bed, I just could not help but touch him. His body was so sexy and seductive, very masculine. Can you guess his response? He let me touch him, and the day after he told me that he did it only because of me, and he really fancied women. I was disappointed, but at least the whole thing was smooth. So he knows that I am this kind of person. Last year when I experienced the darkest period of my life—being sacked, my father's death, financial difficulties, and awful experiences in the cruising areas, it was his support and care that kept me alive. He is the only person who gives me the greatest and warmest feeling. Now that my parents gone, I only have him. I care for him, his wife, and his daughter.

5.   The mainland Chinese reluctance to take on discrete sexual identities has led to a different scenario of sexual behavior and safe sex practices. It is found that those who take up the *tongzhi* or *gay* identity are more willing to confront the issue of safe sex. Many interviewees who refused sexual identity said that they "are not this kind of people." They quote very different reasons, ranging from being married, having decent jobs, receiving advanced education, or coming to cruising areas only occasionally, to justify their resistance to taking up a *gay* identity, which has significant implications for safe sex practices. As one said:

> I am not this kind of person [read *tongxinglian*]—then why should I use condoms? I only come here occasionally. I am married, have a decent job, my cultural quality [read education] is high, so I know how to avoid AIDS.

Another PEPS admitted that he has frequent sexual encounters with other men in public restrooms. He refused to use condoms on the grounds that these sexual encounters are really "playful":

> I only played with them, just hand-drop. I would only be penetrated by the one I love, and I know how to choose the one to love and won't hang around with the *liumang* [hooligan]. I am very selective and careful, so I don't need condoms. And how would a decent person carry a condom? If the police caught me in the park or toilet and found my condom, I would be in trouble. I am single and not married yet, so why should I carry condoms?

In a recent survey, Zhang Bei-chuan interviewed 422 male PEPS. Among those who had had anal sex experiences, 59 percent had never used a condom, and for every twenty experiences of anal penetration, the interviewees had used a condom only once, regardless of whether they were the one to penetrate or the one being penetrated. Although 87 percent of the respondents said that "using condoms correctly is an effective way to avoid AIDS," they also shared the difficulties of getting condoms: too expensive (12 percent), nowhere to keep the condoms (50 percent), and inadequate places to buy condoms (38 percent) (Zhang, 1998b).

The vulnerability of PEPS to HIV/AIDS is accelerated by the absence of public discussions on this topic. Although drug addiction is still the predominant cause of transmitting HIV in China, the paucity of public information and discussions on same-sex eroticism and the transmission of HIV/AIDS have created a dangerous situation where the rate of HIV/AIDS could explode. The unwillingness of the Chinese government to acknowledge the widespread presence of PEPS, together with the resistance of some PEPS to the gay identity, only make the gathering of information about sexual practices and HIV extremely difficult.

6.   The exploration of Chinese discourse on same-sex eroticism has exposed key issues not only for Chinese but for everyone worldwide: does the enhancement of social acceptance and respect for same-sex eroticism need to be conducted through a homo-hetero duality? How meaningful is it to understand human intimacy by defining identity by the gender of erotic object choice? Is the concept of sexual orientation a culturally specific one? Why should we divide people into homo and hetero in the first place? If we are liberated only as *gay* people, do we inscribe ourselves into the divisive and exclusionary structure of the homo-hetero duality that we claimed to go beyond in the beginning?

WHY ARE CONTEMPORARY MAINLAND CHINESE SUFFERING THE MOST?

As I stressed in Chapter 1, the so-called tolerance of same-sex eroticism is predicated upon a hierarchical power structure of classism and sexism in which it is the male elite who mostly enjoy the social and gender status to penetrate the socially inferior male. There is a wide gap between tolerance and acceptance. Same-sex eroticism is tolerated only when one is married and does not form a homosexual identity or publicize one's same-sex relationship. This is the source of oppression, especially for women, whose space for social and sexual autonomy is already very limited.

Compared to PEPS throughout Chinese history, contemporary Chinese *tongzhi* are having the most difficulty. The major reason is, ironically, the popularization of courtship culture and the romanticization of marital relations. In traditional China, marriage has nothing to do with romantic love or sexual orientation. One is married not only to one's husband or wife, but also to the parents-in-law and the entire kinship household. Same-sex eroticism can coexist with marriage without conflict. As marriage is not required to be passionate and intimate, the marital bond is more like a "working partnership" managing the household and the kin network. Courtship is thus called "making a friend" and is not categorically opposite to friendship.

However, with the advocacy and popularization of romantic love in the twentieth century, marriage becomes a personal pursuit of (sexual) happiness. Instead of pleasing one's parents and parents-in-law, one has to please one's partner, emotionally and sexually. Post-Mao Chinese are supposed to date before they get married, and to choose their own partners instead of allowing parents to make the choice. During courtship, one has to be intimate, passionate, seductive, flirtatious, sexual, willing to caress, and even be jealous. The invention of courtship culture has therefore inflicted much pain upon PEPS, who now have to pretend to be turned on by a person of the opposite sex. The marital bond is now an important social relationship in which husband and wife must be very intimate. Therefore, marriage has become an oppressive and torturous institution for PEPS in a way it never was before. PEPS who live in cities, because of the pervasive exposure to Hollywood movies, Hong Kong culture, and Western ideas of romantic love and individualism, might ironically be worse off. They are enlightened and inspired by Western images of individual freedom, yet their parents and society still expect them to get married—which means to date and have passionate sex with the opposite sex.

Most mainland Chinese *tongzhi* I chatted with are either married or are planning to marry.[1] Many *tongzhi* said that the only reason to get married is to get a divorce. They would pretend to be very hurt by it, and could then pursue their own happiness.

There is a crucial gender factor here. I have come across many male but not one single female *tongzhi* who has used the strategy of "single-married-divorced-single" to attain personal freedom. Such a strategy of "fake marriage, then genuine divorce" is gendered, as a wife occupies a very different position within the family and marital relationship than a husband. Men have much greater sexual space within the marital relationship and social power for divorce. To say the least, a husband, irrespective of sexual orientation, is quite unlikely to be raped by his wife, whereas a woman who loves women may worry about her sexual space and autonomy within marriage. The tension is not just sexual, but has to do with the entire scenario of personal space for a woman after she is married. As a *nü tongzhi*, Xiaosheng, said,

> After the gay man makes his wife pregnant, the obligation is basically finished and he is free. But for a woman, to get married automatically means to be a housewife, a wife and mother, and that means an exploited laborer, a lifelong sacrificer for children, and a domesticated caretaker respectively. For a gay man to get married, he is neither a housewife nor sexually exploited by his wife.

Before the twentieth century, Chinese women could not initiate divorce, while their husbands could divorce them based on one of the "Seven

Outs": barrenness, wanton conduct, neglect of parents-in-law, garrulousness, theft, jealousy, and incurable disease. According to the Marriage Law of 1950, a woman can divorce her husband if he agrees, and vice versa. But in reality, they need the permission of the work unit (in an urban area) or the production team (in a rural area), as well as parents, relatives, the head of the work unit, and neighbors, who would strongly persuade the couple to stay together, thus making divorce a highly difficult and often painful process.

Many *tongzhi* have made use of the new Marriage Law of 1980, which makes "the absence of love" legitimate grounds for divorce. The new law states, "If love and affection [*ganqing*] have been destroyed, and if mediation is ineffective, a divorce should be granted" (Honig and Hershatter, 1988:207). Such emphasis on love as the basis of marriage is partly a reaction to the overwhelmingly political marriages during the Cultural Revolution and partly a result of rapid socioeconomic development since the late 1970s. The divorce rate has increased rapidly from 4.7 percent in 1979 to 9.97 percent in 1993 (Hung, 1995). It is this new trend of pursuing personal happiness that enables many *tongzhi* to divorce her or his spouse.

In contemporary China, marriage is not simply an interpersonal or household issue; it is an economic, moral, and political institution that serves as a social control agent, disciplining the livelihood of every residence. Most housing used to be assigned by the state through the *danwei* (working unit). The principle of allocating houses is that people live with their parents or in communal dormitories in the workplace until they get married. Single people are not entitled to independent housing but have to share housing with several colleagues in a small dormitory. Many people get married in order to receive a housing allocation; others refuse to divorce for the same reason. Many divorced couples still live together, as there are not enough houses to go around. Such a pattern of residence, in which most people live with their parents, brothers, and sisters before marriage, and with partner and children after marriage, minimizes pre- and extramarital relationships (homosexual or not). Steady, stable, and public lesbian and gay relationships become dangerous, making anonymous sex through newspaper notice boards, in public toilets, public bathhouses, and parks almost the only choice for many men. It is in such unsanitary conditions that contagious diseases, AIDS included, could easily be contracted and spread if safe sex practices are not rigorously observed. The situation is more worrisome as AIDS is commonly associated with foreigners (read Caucasians). Thus, mainland Chinese are rather unaware of their chances of contracting AIDS through unsafe sexual contact.

What is even worse for *tongzhi* is that all the neighbors in the residential building are also the colleagues in the work unit. It is a compact system of social control where everybody knows everybody, where neighbors and colleagues are often the same, thus making any form of social deviance highly difficult to sustain. Jobs have always been assigned by the work unit and the Party, and cannot be chosen and changed freely by the individual. Only in the last several years has there been more room for individual choice of jobs. There is also a powerful street neighbor committee at the entrance of each residential building, making extramarital relationships easily detected. It is a social arrangement that prioritizes heterosexual monogamy, making it difficult for all nonmonogamous relationships to survive. The absence of relaxed places for PEPS to meet and know one another has made the derogatory public images of PEPS a self-fulfilling prophecy.

A cause of yet more unhappiness for *tongzhi* is their romanticization of the Western lesbigay world, which is perceived as nonhomophobic, carefree, and liberating. Most Chinese residents cannot get a visa to the West so the only images and knowledge they have about the Western lesbigay world are the media images of lesbigay marriages and parades where thousands of lesbigay people march openly and proudly. They tend to romanticize the Western world as a lesbigay haven, and are shocked to be informed of the prevalence of gay-bashing and the extent of homophobia in the United States and the United Kingdom. Some simply find it unbelievable. They might, ironically, have felt more envious—though also empowered—had they traveled to Hong Kong, Thailand, or other places where they could see the wild commercial discos, saunas, karaoke, and bars where hundreds of lesbigay people gather and meet one another. They would refuse to marry, but would find the parental and social pressure insurmountable. They are desperate for a healthy *tongzhi* circle but find mainland Chinese cruising areas (toilets and parks) full of blackmail, libel, prostitution, deceit, and frustrating stories. It is almost meaningless for them to know that traditional Chinese culture was tolerant toward same-sex eroticism as it was a world they never experienced. What they and their parents can recall are wars, chaos, migration, pain, poverty, starvation, political oppression, and fanatic movements such as the Cultural Revolution. Their impressions about traditional Chinese culture are generally negative.

With the opening of China in 1978, economic development has become entangled with a kind of cultural imperialism by which Western ideas and commodities, from romantic love and possessive individualism to Hollywood films and McDonald's, have become the fashionable icon of the new generation. A *nan tongzhi* in Beijing told me:

For me, "West" is something more modern, liberal, individualistic, and progressive; "Chinese" represents something old, traditional, static, and resistant to change.

He has been to Hong Kong and has no problem dichotomizing the West with the East, and locates Hong Kong as a Westernized city. He tends to lump together the notion of the capitalist West with very different categories including modernity, modernization, industrialization, progress, urbanization, democracy, liberation, freedom, and openness. Such political and ideological confusion is perhaps best exemplified when he remarked:

> Hong Kong is a highly successful sample of capitalism, a mixture of Western and Eastern culture. For the past thirty years, Hong Kong has undergone a drastic process of industrialization and urbanization, emerging from a small fishing village to become a major modern financial center, a liberal and prosperous modern city.

It is perhaps crucial that he shifted from "capitalism" to "mixture of Western and Eastern," then "industrialization and urbanization," and finally equated all these with "a liberal and prosperous modern city." When asked about their understanding and associations of "West," "East," "Chinese," and "Hong Kong," my informants demonstrated a rather ethnocentric stereotypical polarization which has hierarchized the West as the superior Other over the inferior East and "Chineseness." It is the kind of situation where globalization actually means Westernization. This echoes Frantz Fanon's notion of a "dependency complex," in which the colonized cherishes a desire to "imitate, appropriate the culture, lifestyle of the colonizer," at the expense of local, indigenous culture and values (Fanon, 1967:30). Since the late nineteenth century, China has been in a semicolonial position in which Western power exerted a considerable amount of ideological and cultural control over a nominally independent country. This is akin to the "hegemonic phase" Abdul Mohammad talks about in which "the natives accept a version of the colonizers' entire system of values, attitudes, morality, institutions. . . . This stage of imperialism does depend on the active and direct 'consent' of the dominated" (Mohammed, 1986:81).

LEGAL DISCOURSE AND MEDICALIZATION

What is new in postwar China is the intervention of state apparatus, especially the police, court, and legal system, to prosecute (male) PEPS for their sexual activities. This state intervention, together with the medicalization and pathologization of same-sex eroticism, were another crucial reason for the difficulties of contemporary PEPS in China, and also Taiwan and Hong Kong, especially in the 1970s and 1980s.

Same-sex eroticism and sexual conduct have never been illegal in Chinese history, except for a loosely enforced law passed in 1740, the only other exception being a Hong Kong law criminalizing same-sex sexual conduct, which was the product of British colonialism. In post-1949 China there was not one word in the legal statutes concerning *tongxinglian.* However, it is typical of Chinese legal practice that the actual status of the "offense" depends very much on the interpretations and the social consequences decided upon by individual police and courts rather than the objective qualities of the conduct itself. PEPS had been subject to public criticism, police harassment, detention, imprisonment, or even execution during the Cultural Revolution. Yet the treatment was not the result of homophobia per se, as all kinds of extramarital sex, together with reading, spreading, and smuggling heterosexual pornographic materials could also be subject to prosecution. As Professor Qiu Ren-zong argues:

> The law in China does not treat *tongxinglian* as illegal . . . and for those *tongxinglian* who are caught by police because of prostitution, harassing heterosexuals or having sex in the public venue, the problem is not *tongxinglian* per se because heterosexuals will also be caught for having the same behavior. (Qiu, 1997:337)

Since 1949, the dominant legal stance toward *tongxinglian* has been the hooliganism model and the mental disease model. The former is a Chinese Communist label for all kinds of social deviance, the latter a product of Western cultural colonialism regarding modern sexology, neither perspective having prevailed in traditional China.

In past years, all legal prosecution of PEPS was based on the highly ambiguous Criminal Law 160, under the section "Offense of Obstructing Public Order," which states: "All *liumang* [hooliganism] behaviors should be subjected to arrest and sentence." But what constitutes *liumang* behavior is subject to the interpretation of individual police and courts, without many objective references. The official attitude can change spontaneously, and a gap always exists between the official platform and actual practice. In a 1984 decision, the Supreme People's Procuratorate holds that people who commit sodomy should be prosecuted "if the circumstances are odious and the consequences are serious" (Supreme People's Procuratorate, 1984). One of the most famous attorneys in China today, Dun Li, once said, "though homosexuality exists in different societies and cultures, with some minor exceptions it is considered abnormal and disdained. It affects social order, invades personal privacy and leads to criminal behavior. As a result, homosexuals are more likely to be penalized administratively and criminally" (Ruan, 1985:186). In 1987, the head of the Shanghai Municipal Committee on the Determination of the Administration of Psychiatric Justice, Zheng Zhan-pei, said, "because homosexuality violates public morality and therefore disturbs public order and affects the physical and mental health of young people, it clearly constitutes criminal behavior" (Zhang, 1994:633).

Because discretion and arbitration rights reside with individual court authorities, positive legal verdicts on same-sex eroticism exist. Indeed, there have been at least two reported cases of same-sex marriage in 1990 (in Fujian) and 1991 (Guangxi) respectively, in which a male couple and a female couple both applied for marriage and were permitted by the provincial government after approval from the central authority (Li, 1998:378). In 1991, the Chinese Public Security Bureau decided to drop the case against two women in Anhui charged by the father of one of the women for cohabitation and having a sexual relationship, on the grounds that "under the present circumstances in our country where the law has no explicit regulation on what homosexuality is and what criminal responsibility may pertain, the situation you have reported cannot, on principle, be accepted to be heard as a legal case, and it is not appropriate that this should be submitted for legal punishment as an instance of hooliganism" (Chou, 1996a:140).

This is the only case in which a legal authority has made an official statement on the legal status of *tongxinglian.* Yet such a statement of tolerance may only be the result of misogyny and sexism, whereby women are not perceived as sexual subjects, and sexuality between women is not seen as a threat to the (male-dominated) social order. After all, the police continue to abuse their power to prosecute and blackmail men who have sex with other men. Sometimes, a gang of hooligans will pretend to be police, exploiting the paranoia and anxiety of PEPS to extort money from them. Even real police officers may not bring PEPS to the police station, but just fine them on the spot and send them off. It is possible that such money will be kept by the officers themselves. Even when they are blackmailed by criminals, abused by individual police, fired from their jobs, or sent to mental institutions, many PEPS dare not voice their grievances for fear of the subsequent humiliation and trouble.

In recent years, police usually carry out raids only when crimes are reported, such as theft or robbery; during the "strike-hard" periods when the government imposes especially stringent punishments; or when big events occur, such as the Asian Olympics in 1990 or the World Women's Congress in 1995. There has been a procession of changes in police and other authorities' attitudes toward PEPS in recent years: from a status of immorality, to mental illness, to hooliganism, to more tolerance and understanding; and from long-term imprisonment, to one to two weeks, to three to five days of detention, to a fine, to verbal warning without informing the work unit or family. Significant legal changes occurred in 1997. Since January 1, 1997, the Criminal Procedure Act of the PRC has included the legal principle of "presumed innocence" in clause 12, which says: "without any judgment reached by the People's Court, everyone is presumed to be innocent." Also, the crime of *liumang* has been completely deleted from the law books. Though abuses continue, the police and the courts can no longer use hooliganism to prosecute PEPS. Since then, *tongzhi* activists in China have confirmed very few cases of legal prosecution of sexual behavior between consenting males. After all, the most commonly applied legal ground has been abolished. The new Criminal Law in 1997 also added clause 301, which criminalizes "collective gathering for obscene activities." Yet this law does not seem to target *tongxinglian* at all, as it does not specify the gender of the participants, and "collective gathering" is clearly defined as at least three people. Therefore, no matter how such a law will be interpreted by individual judges, it cannot be used to prosecute two consenting adults for same-sex behavior in private.

If the legal statute regarding hooliganism was directly targeted at men who cruise other men, the discourse on mental illness has had the far more pervasive impact of medicalizing and pathologizing same-sex eroticism. It is a historical tragedy that Chinese modernization in the Republican period happened at a time when the first paradigm of homosexuality in the Western world treated homosexuality as an illness. While the West in the 1960s and 1970s was marked by significant breakthroughs both in the political lesbigay movement and the theoretical discourse on sexuality, this was unfortunately a closed-door period in China, which shunned Western influence. Post-1949 medical and psychological scholars, influenced by early Western sexology and the psychoanalytical paradigm of medicalizing and pathologizing homosexuality, were almost unanimous in using electric shock treatment and behavioral therapy to "cure" homosexuals. Electric shock, aversion techniques, and behavioral treatment have been widely used to "cure" PEPS. According to one report,

> homosexuals are . . . sometimes given painful electric shocks to discourage erotic thoughts. An alternative approach is to offer herbal medicines that induce vomiting. Both . . . are hailed by doctors in

China as remarkably successful in "curing" homosexuality. (Kristof, 1990:7)

Although *tongxinglian* is not a criminal act in mainland China, it is still classified as a mental disorder according to the latest Chinese Classification of Mental Disorders (CCMD-2-R), passed in 1994 by the Chinese Psychiatric Association (CPA), despite its removal from international manuals such as the ICD-10 and DSM-IV. In 1996, when a famous scholar and psychologist from China visited Hong Kong, I met him and introduced my Chinese books on *tongzhi* issues. To my surprise, this famous scholar, who claimed to have cured more than 100 PEPS in the last ten years, asked me sincerely and innocently: "What kind of disease is *tongxinglian?*" The 1990 Encyclopedia of Criminal Sciences, for example, listed it as a type of "sexual deviation" and "illegal behavior" (Yang et al., 1990).

Zhang Bei-chuan, in his book *Tongxingai* (1994:17), made this overall comment: "almost all mainland scholars stressed that *tongxingai* is a psychological illness . . . an abnormal behavior that should be disciplined and penalized." Any review of contemporary mainland Chinese scholarly literature on *tongxingai*, sadly, would confirm Zhang's comment. Gao Cai-qin, in the book *Xing Yu Rensheng* (Sex and Human Life, 1989:20), said that "*tongxinglian* . . . is a mental disorder that cannot be self-controlled . . . it threatens social order, undermines youth health, and destroys family harmony." Psychologist Gan Lin hosted the radio program *Jinye Bu Shefang* (No Defense Tonight), which became the source of a book with the same title. Gan said, "the medical cause of *tongxinglian* is still under research . . . we must educate children in the correct gender role identity so as to prevent *tongxinglian*" (1993:106). In 1987, a leading forensic psychiatrist, Dr. Zheng Zhan-bei, stated that "*tongxinglian* is against social morality, interferes with social security, damages the physical and mental health of adolescents, and ought to be a crime" (Ruan, 1991:132). A 1993 article in the *Beijing Review* says: "In China, from the view of public morals, homosexuality is synonymous with filth, ugliness and metamorphosis" (Hao, 1993:45).

The most famous sexologist in contemporary China, Liu Da-lin, in his books *Xing Ziyou Pipan* (Critique of Sexual Freedom, 1988) and *Xing Shehuixue* (Sociology of Sex, 1989), criticized *tongxinglian* as "a deviation from normal human biological and psychological nature. Their lives are always nasty and low-brow, unable to keep mental health and work progress." Liu also argued that these people "should be subjected to punishment by society." Jin De-chu, in *Baisi Nanjie Tongxinglian* (Intrigue and Unresolved Homosexuality), said, "the behavior of *tongxinglian* is obviously contradictory to human sexual features ordained by nature, it is undoubtedly a sexual perversity" (quoted in Zhang, 1994:577). Yang

Feng-chi, in *Zhongguo Qingnian Keji* (Chinese Youth Technology), said that "*tongxinglian* is a distortion of sexual orientation . . . the genuine male *tongxinglian* plays the passive role, the genuine female *tongxinglian* plays the active role" (1994:42-43).

Almost all the authoritative textbooks on mental health and pathology, such as *Linchuang Jingshen Bingxue* (Clinical Psychopathology, 1984), published by Shanghai Medical University; *Jingshen Yixue Yu Xiangguan Wenti* (Psychopathology and Related Problems, 1990), published by Beijing Medical University; the first Chinese book on sexual deviance, *Xing Pianli Jiqi Fangzhi* (Sexual Deviancy and Its Cure, 1989), edited by Liu Yan-ming, define *tongxinglian* as a sexual and psychological perversity. Another authoritative textbook on psychopathology, *Jingshen Bingxue* (Psychopathology, 1994), a book with sales of more than 100,000 copies, was written by more than fifty medical experts. The book has only one small section of 2,000 words on *tongxinglian,* describing how *tongxinglian* can be cured through electric shock treatment (pp. 768-769). In another academic book, *Zhongguo Funü Falu Shiyong Chuanquan* (Chinese Women's Legal Practical Book, 1993), published by Fulian (the official Women's Association), *tongxinglian* is catalogued under the category Criminal Behavior: "*tongxinglian* . . . is a form of sexual perversity. Since childhood, these people play the opposite gender role . . . the causes of *tongxinglian* are now still undecided" (p. 303).

Since 1949, *tongxinglian* has been associated with Western capitalist corruption. The academic book *Xing Kexue* (The Science of Sex, 1983:33), edited by Xu Ji-min, emphasized the close link between *tongxinglian* and capitalism: "To avoid the popularization of *tongxinglian,* it is necessary to criticize capitalism and to insist on the Four Basic Principles of Socialism." *Tongxinglian* is also associated with criminal behavior: "*Tongxinglian* is a behavioral and psychological abnormality" which may lead to "theft, prostitution, and murder" (Beijing Renmin Jingcha, 1989:11-12).

Tongzhi activist Wan Yan-hai quoted psychologist Zhang Ming-yuan's 1981 article in the Shanghai magazine *Mass Medicine* as "the first contemporary public discussion of *tongxinglian* in China" (Chou, 1996a). The irony is that this article discusses *tongxinglian* behavior in the *Hong Lou Meng,* a book which in the Qing dynasty was not perceived as representing *tongxinglian* but simply ordinary intimate sentiments.

Because of the pervasiveness of the medicalization of *tongxinglian* since the early twentieth century, the primary contemporary agenda in the discussion of *tongxinglian* is still the "causes turning a normal child into *tongxinglian*." Even the two most respectable contemporary mainland Chinese books on *tongxinglian*, i.e., Zhang Bei-chuan's 675-page book *Tongxingai*, and Li Yin-he and Wang Xiao-bo's *Tamen De Shijie* (Their World), have major chapter titles such as "Causes of *Tongxinglian*" (Chapter 4, in Zhang) and "Reasons for the Formation of *Tongxinglian*" (Chapter 2, in Li). Many PEPS in China, especially those who have had little direct contact with the Western world, have certain sociological explanations for the causes of their same-sex desire and behavior. These fit closely with the (mis)conceptions of Chinese sexology and mostly fall into three categories, described in the following sections.

First Sexual Encounter

Many mainland Chinese PEPS attribute their same-sex eroticism to their first sexual experiences, as if they would not have "become" *tongxinglian* if they had not been "seduced" by *tongxinglian* in their youth. One *nan tongzhi* said:

> There are two kinds of *tongxinglian,* one is inborn, the other is seduced. Originally, I am not this kind of people. At age ten, I was cruised by an old man. He was old and ugly, has no market in this circle, so uses sweets and money to seduce little boys. I was too small to resist and even found it amusing. I got used to sexual pleasure with men and just fixated in that stage. Since then, I have never gotten rid of *tongxinglian.* I hate that old man very much, for turning me into a *tongxinglian.*

His personal narration fits very well with the ideas of Chinese scholars such as Li (1992), who list "seduction by other *tongxinglian*" as one of the causes of *tongxinglian.* It is difficult to tell whether it is such personal narratives that convince Chinese scholars that they have found the cause, or whether Chinese *tongzhi* are exposed to information such as Li's and thus construct and comprehend their own experiences from such a (hetero-sexist) perspective. Yet one thing is clear: both the popular and scholarly narratives are overdetermined by the pervasive medicalization of *tongxinglian* since the early twentieth century.

Gender Inversion

It is very popular for mainland Chinese scholars to perceive *tongxinglian* as gender inversion, and to categorize *tongxinglian* into four types: effeminate or masculine men, and masculine or feminine women: "*tong-*

xinglian is an inversion of nature because it is associated with confusing gender boundaries in a child's upbringing, between the strong masculine spirit (*yanggang zhi qi*) of the male and the soft feminine beauty of the female" (Wan, 1990:110).

Zhang Bei-chuan (1994) argued that a domineering mother is a crucial factor in causing a child's *tongxingai:*

> Many scholars realize that these domineering mothers, together with feeble and weak fathers, are the perfect soil for generating male *tongxingai*. In such families, boys lack an appropriate role model, cannot establish normal male identity and consciousness. (p. 264)

> To cure the effeminate boy . . . we must let his parents know that, this effeminate boy may develop into a *tongxingai,* "transvestite addiction," "transsexual addiction" . . . intervention is necessary to prevent the child from developing into "transvestite addiction" and "transsexual addiction." (p. 267)

Li and Wang (1992) in their book *Tamen De Shijie,* also share this obsession with "gender perversity":

> Being spoiled by parents is one of the causes of *tongxinglian,* because *tongxinglian* is practically a kind of narcissism. (p. 46)

> For those men who identify with the female, there are three reasons for their tongxinglian . . . (a) Overdependence on the mother, which makes the boy identify with women, lacking identification with men. They treat themselves as women, express female features and qualities, they walk waveringly, speak softly, and have a weak character . . . (b) The second reason is womanly socialization . . . from our questionnaire, many informants in their childhood had worn flowery clothes, did knitting, played female games, and had feminine nicknames. (c) The third reason for those identifying with the female to become *tongxinglian* is because they are born with weak physical bodies. Because of their weak bodies, they rarely join male games and physical activities, but hope to be protected by strong ones, developing a kind of addiction to strong partners. (pp. 49, 51)

Childhood Experiences

As *tongxinglian* is supposedly caused by certain sociopsychological factors, childhood experiences become the crucial site in revealing its "cause." Such a search for a cause is very popular among both scholars and PEPS themselves. A *nü tongzhi* informant (twenty-nine) said:

> Before I was born, my parents were very desperate for a son. They were very disappointed when I was born. They insisted on giving me the masculine name they planned for a son, and in many ways treated me like a boy, giving me male toys and letting me play with boys. They always praised me for having *nan qi zhi* [male qualities]. I think that is the reason why I became a *tongxinglian.* I got used to the male role. I think I have a male heart trapped in a female body.

A *nan tongzhi* (thirty) said:

> I was born in a very feminine environment, with four sisters and no brothers. So I always played with girls and got used to the female norms, fantasies, and qualities. That's why I became quite girlish. Worse still, my father has a rather weak character and was always dominated by my mother. I always looked for a strong male father figure but I found none. So when I met my teacher at age thirteen, I was charmed by him and could not help falling in love. That is how I became *tongxinglian.*

Indeed, in the extensive survey of 422 *nan tongxinglian* in China conducted by Zhang Bei-chuan in 1998, 12.5 percent of the interviewees think that "it is through social learning that they become *tongxinglian*"; only 30 percent think that they are born *tongxinglian.* There is a high rate (30 percent) of "seeking medical authorities to cure my *tongxinglian* inclination." This, together with 14 percent and 18 percent who think that homosexuality and bisexuality respectively are abnormal, partly explains the fact that 28 percent of the interviewees have a strong desire to commit suicide, and 10 percent did attempt suicide. In the area of gender identification, only 26 percent of the interviewees object to the belief that "male homo/bisexuals can be divided into two kinds—the effeminate and the masculine ones."

Given the overwhelming extent of prejudices, stereotypes, and misunderstandings, together with the dominance of outdated psychoanalytic and mental illness paradigms, most PEPS in contemporary China have experienced guilt, shame, confusion, self-hatred, and a low self-image. The heterosexist discourse of medicalizing homo/bisexuality has become implicated in the construction of the self, as clearly revealed in many of the narrations of PEPS themselves. Yet they are neither passive nor helpless, but actively manipulate resistant strategies to expand and enrich their personal and social space—an issue I explore next.

INDIVIDUAL STRATEGIES
OF TONGZHI EMPOWERMENT

In this section, I will discuss individual *tongzhi* spaces of empowerment in mainland China. Five specific stories will be discussed, not because they are typical or representative of mainland Chinese *tongzhi*, but because their stories elucidate certain unique features of the mainland Chinese *tongzhi* struggle. It is found that despite the oppressive environment, Chinese *tongzhi* manage to manipulate indigenous cultural resources to expand and reactivate their personal and social space.

Story 1

James (twenty-seven) has lived with his boyfriend Xiao-Liu (twenty-nine) in Beijing for three years. They live together with James' parents, brother, and his brother's wife.

When I first met James at a private *tongzhi* gathering, he was not at all interested in sharing his story with me. He was more eager to talk about money, money, and money, together with information about all sorts of fashion brand names and VCDs (video compact diskettes). Consumerism, economics, and class seem to be much more his concern than sexuality. Several times, when I talked about sexuality, he smoothly changed the topic. At first, I suspected that he might be hiding something. Then I realized that my suspicion was caused by my own obsession with sexuality. James said,

> Why always ask about my sexuality? I know you are doing research, and want to ask about my sexual experiences with men. I don't care. I enjoy my life. Sex is not that important to me. I don't want to stress that I am gay, not because I am scared, but there are more things in this world that I care for, like my parents, environmental issues, and the economy. I did not see my relationship with Xiao-Liu as homosexual, we are just lovers like everybody else. I don't want to hang around only with *gay* people in *gay* bars and *gay* cruising areas. I have more straight friends than *tongzhi* ones.

At a time when I was obsessively pursuing my research on mainland Chinese PEPS, James' statement was the best critique of imposing a homo-hetero duality onto PEPS. It was during our second encounter that James shared his story. James is the eldest son in his family. He experienced his first same-sex love with a schoolmate when they were both seventeen. After graduation, James went to a university, and his lover went to work in a factory. Their relationship started to turn sour and they finally split up. James was very hurt and thought that there was no prospect of having a steady and promising relationship with a man. Four months later, James received a letter from his former lover, saying that he now had a girlfriend and was planning to get married. Toward the end of the letter he said: "our previous relationship is *biantai* [pervert]. I am now converted to normality by the real love of my girlfriend. You should try to enjoy the love of women. Or maybe, you should see a doctor."

Obviously, the letter was devastating to James, especially at a time when he was still fantasizing about getting together again with this classmate. That night, James drank two bottles of dishwashing liquid together with fifty pills. He was unconscious for two days. James' best friend thought that James might die, and decided to tell James' parents the full story, after they pressed him desperately. James survived, but has serious stomachaches and kidney problems as a result.

Since then, James' parents have been very kind to him. They never mention *tongxinglian*. Even in recent years, rarely did they encourage James to get married, which by Chinese standards is incredible as most Chinese in their twenties would be pressured to get married. James said,

> My parents seriously worry and care for my health. They prefer our family members to stay together so that we can take care of each other. I think my previous suicide attempt really scared them, and they would do everything to avoid it happening again. So when they feel that I really love Xiao-Liu, who is such a nice guy, they are quite happy. From their point of view, Xiao-Liu is mature enough to take care of me, which is more preferable than I get married and have to take care of my wife and the household. Another thing is, Xiao-Liu works as a professional, is very mature, and he is rich. . . . At first I only introduced Xiao-Liu as a good friend of mine. Then he often came to visit me and have dinner together with my parents. He gets along very well with my parents. They would invite him to stay overnight if it is too late, I mean in the same bed with me. *He gradually attended all our family dinners and became part of my family.* Until two years ago when he changed to a new job where there was no housing allocation for him, my mother simply invited him to move in! Isn't that cool! *My parents treat him as their son, and never say a word about sex.* I think it is better to come out by

action than by words or arguments. I can't expect my parents to understand the concepts of *tongxinglian*. The terms *gay* and *tongxinglian* could be very scary for my parents as they would be associated with perversity and Western corruption. *But they understand intimate* ganqing *and* guanxi, *they accept Xiao-Liu fully, not as a gay man, but as my intimate friend.* (emphasis mine)

James has thus manipulated the sharing of food as a cultural marker to bring Xiao-Liu into his family. As James said, "He gradually attended all our family dinners and became part of my family." James further uses quasi-kin categories to construct his relationship with Xiao-Liu. ("My parents treat him as their son, and never say a word about sex.") James stresses the sexist nature of Chinese culture in this regard. "As Xiao-Liu and I are both rather masculine, our normal masculinity makes our homosexuality highly invisible. A sissy boy and a tomboy lesbian would have a difficult time especially in the family." In other words, the cultural tolerance of homosexuality is qualified—it is the male elite who play the so-called male role who are mostly tolerated.

James also shared a fascinating experience that best illustrates the public's insensitivity to *tongxinglian*. On the last day of one semester, James and his classmates had a wild party. They sang, danced, and drank. At midnight, James' roommate took his girlfriend into their room and had sex. When James came back to the room with his boyfriend at about 4 a.m., this opposite-sex couple was already there, asleep in the nude. About an hour later, several policemen suddenly came in and turned on the light. They arrested and took away this opposite-sex couple, saying that someone from the opposite building had reported seeing some "obscene behavior" between a nude man and woman. Most interestingly, James was also sleeping in the nude together with his boyfriend. But the police did not say a word about them. They simply did not "see" *tongxinglian;* they had no such concept. They thought James and his boyfriend were just close friends, whereas this opposite-sex couple was obscene. James finally remarked, "That was seven years ago. I am afraid if that happened now, we might be caught and charged with *liumang*."

Story 2

Song and Jenny are another *tongzhi* couple who live together. I interviewed Song (thirty-three) in early 1998 when she attended a business conference in Hong Kong. When Song was twenty-three, her parents arranged for her to marry the son of a Communist Party member. Song resisted, but her parents insisted that they desperately needed the help of this party member. The marriage proved to be a total failure. Although Song's parents at first rejected the possibility of divorce, they agreed to let Song go to Beijing to study. It was at Beijing University that she met her present lover, Jenny (twenty-nine), who was a student majoring in economics.

Both Song and Jenny were each others' first girlfriend, and both had little difficultiy accepting their relationship. Song said, "It is just beautiful!" They have been together for five years. All their best friends know about and accept their relationship. Song explained,

> Beijing is changing very fast, people are now very pragmatic and care less about the ideological debate. Our friends are all university graduates. They are only concerned about two things—whether our love is genuine, and whether we can manage the pragmatic arrangements like divorce, housing allocation, and retirement plans.

Song stressed several times that their relationship is one of *tongzhi*—they share the same (*tong*) goal/spirit (*zhi*) of life:

> *Tongzhi* is not just about sex, but the sharing of worldview and the goal of life. For our generation of mainland Chinese who have come through the Cultural Revolution, the appropriation of the identity *tongzhi* is a fantastic integration of a sexual minority with the revolutionary struggle. It is now the sexual minority who ironically take up the most sacred political label of the mainstream world. It's really great!

When she first came to Beijing to study, Song had been separated from her husband for seven years. She initiated the divorce, and now lives and works in Beijing in the government. Although she is allocated a house in the work unit, she prefers to live in Jenny's apartment, which was allocated by Jenny's American firm in Beijing. Song lied to her work mates, saying that Jenny is her cousin. She admitted that she gained much freedom and space by moving away from her work unit. Song also warned me,

> If you want to find *nü tongzhi*, don't just approach the "out" ones, as there are only a handful. Go chat with the married women. I have been working as a volunteer counselor for a women's hotline in Beijing for half a year. I came across several married women who have little interest in having sex with men. Their sex life was a mess and they felt like whores. One even flirted with me during the phone chat. I am not saying that they are *nü tongzhi*. That is not the point.

These categories may be meaningless for them. Chinese women simply have little choice for their lives, especially in terms of sexuality. Women's sexuality has been buried in marriage and domestic responsibility.

Song and I also had a serious chat on women's issues in China:

I never thought of being the "second sex." Since I was born, I got used to the idea that "women hold up half the sky." For us, equality of the sexes is natural, not something achieved through the feminist struggle. My mother worked on the farm. She did all the plowing, raking, seed mixing, and harvesting, with no sense of treating work as liberation, and my father cooks very well. Western feminists see women as individuals with inalienable rights. But in the Chinese world, the family rather than the individual is seen as the basic unit of society. I have been asked by Caucasian feminists and lesbians about my views on the one-child policy. Of course I support it. The policy stops the most populous country in this world from suffering the human disaster of having billions of people starve to death. A Caucasian criticized me for denying the child's right to survive and the woman's right to have as many children as she likes. As a person who has come through the Cultural Revolution and all kinds of human disasters, of course I understand human rights. But exactly because I understand these, I support the policy that creates a better social environment for the next generation. We simply have different priorities from women in the Caucasian world.

Story 3

The rapid development of *tongzhi* venues in big cities has drawn many female and male *tongzhi* from smaller cities and towns. A common problem facing young *tongzhi* who migrate to large cities is that, unable to find a job that can support the high cost of living, some of them may become prostitutes. Peter (twenty-five) is a good example. Peter grew up in a poor village in Hunan where he finished his primary school education. He went to Guangzhou at age fourteen with his uncle. In his five years in Guangzhou, he worked as a waiter, hawker, gardener, cleaner, and, most of the time, prostitute. At age nineteen, a Hong Kong businessman brought Peter to Shanghai. Peter worked in his factory for three months, until they split up. For nine months Peter then lived with an American gay man who was forty years older. Peter then changed jobs several times and since last year has worked as a waiter in a bar where there are many Caucasian customers. Although Peter did not really love this American gay man, he is very grateful to him. He said,

> When I moved into his place, I was really fascinated by his collection of *gay* videos and magazines. It was very empowering to know about the Western *gay* world. I grew up in a society where "gay" is "pervert" and should be cured by electric shock. When I watched all these videos, or when he translated the articles in *OUT* or *The Advocate* for me, I felt that I was born again. I decided to be a happy gay.

When I first met Peter in Shanghai, he was wearing a tight mini T-shirt, stylish blue jeans, and a baseball cap. When a friend introduced me as a university lecturer from Hong Kong, Peter immediately changed from Mandarin to English, though his English was not at all fluent. It is still unclear whether Peter just grabbed every chance to practice English, or he thought speaking English was superior, or English represents a Western fantasy and space that he desperately needed. During the chat, he asked me seriously about the possibility of emigrating to Hong Kong. He is desperate to leave China. "I will do whatever I can to leave this country, either by marrying a Caucasian man or buying a fake visa, whatever. There is little hope for *gay* men in China. I must go." Peter told me that some male prostitutes are not gay but use sexuality as a tool for social mobility and economic advancement.

Peter is very positive about his prostitution: "I am young and good-looking. What's wrong with that? Everyone sells something about themselves; I sell my body. And you need a lot of talent and skill to cruise your patrons, otherwise no one picks you up. I work only part-time. I choose my working hours and clients." Peter has earned a lot of money. He has even stolen money:

> Once I stole 7,000 yuan from a Taiwanese businessman. Well, don't condemn me; it is only a few pennies for him. I spent 4,000 to buy a fake residence and work permit, and I gave the rest to my parents. That is my tactic to please them and to delay my marriage. Money is the best tool in the world. My brother and sister in Hunan earn only 300 dollars a month. But every New Year when I went home, I gave my parents several thousand! That's why my parents are not that eager to pressure me for marriage. I only meet them once a year, and it's easy to entertain them. I won't get married. I am gay and I want my freedom.

Peter is very critical of Chinese culture. He prefers Caucasians as he thinks they are more creative and romantic. It is a racial and cultural fantasy of "Western modernity" that enchants the new generation. Public morality and attitudes among young people are rapidly changing. Individuality and mutual happiness have become primary values cherished by the young urban generation. Peter admitted that China is now much more open than before:

> As long as you do it in private, police will not disturb you. But if I cannot tell my parents about my sexuality, how open is it? In recent years, there are more *gay* people who are willing to come out of the closet and dress up distinctively. The driving force behind the growing openness in Socialist China is ironically capitalistic economic growth and the concomitant convenience of telecommunication. People are now busy earning money and would not bother with your private life. So I think we should talk about pink dollars. It's stupid to hit on *gay* rights. I think we should follow the market economy and open up *gay* consumption and lifestyle. Money is the best package for *gay* rights.

Once when I was chatting with two of Peter's friends concerning Chinese and English names, both of them said that they did not know Peter's Chinese name at all, though they have known him for two years. Until recent years, it has been rare for Chinese to introduce themselves only by an English name. Again, it is Peter's strategy to involve himself in Westernized discourse and depart further from his natal home in Hunan, which for him only represents poverty, suffering, and oppression. A Western given name also symbolizes egalitarian relations and culture which are rarely found in the Chinese hierarchy of human relationships and titles.[2]

Peter is also actively using the Western discourse of romantic love to bargain with his parents. He would emphasize the factor of "genuine love" for a happy marriage, and use the notion of romantic love to delay marriage, saying that *yuan fan* (a sort of romantic coincidence) has not come yet. While his parents still pressure him for marriage, Peter's Western lifestyle and handsome income have ironically given his parents good reasons for accepting his resistance.

Peter provides an example of a *tongzhi* who manipulates the space of economic development, urban migration, and Western *gay* discourse to develop a new form of sexual-social identity and subjectivity. For PEPS in contemporary China, Western *gay* discourse provides a ready-made array of weapons serving to counteract indigenous traditions, values, and customs they find oppressive. In Peter's words, "the Western world has its own problems, but I don't care. It provides me with the best tool for self-liberation."

Story 4

Although Song attained her *tongzhi* space partly through divorce, some women choose to stay in marriage while enjoying same-sex relationships. Ning (thirty-six) has been married for ten years and has no intention of divorcing. Instead of coming out and being a visible *tongzhi*, she argues that such visibility would only destroy the space she is presently enjoying with the married woman who lives next to her. She told me,

> There are no lesbians here! How can one be a lesbian in this country? In my case, I was married ten years ago when I was twenty-six. Now I have a child of nine. What can I do? If I "come out" to my husband and parents, I become a devil in people's minds, not so much because of my *tongxinglian,* but for failing in my obligation and responsibility as a wife, daughter, and mother. I accept my homoerotic desire, but why should I make a big fuss and destroy the harmonious family order I have in my life? Why should I become a different person just because I have sex with a person of the same sex? . . . When two men or two women sleep together, it is acceptable when you are friends, relatives, or classmates. Of course, if you have sex, it cannot be publicized. But what constitutes sex? If sex must be penetrative, then I do not want sex. If sex is the most intimate expression of our love, our relationship is very sexual. I prefer to emotionalize sexuality rather than sexualizing all emotions like some Americans do.

I took her words seriously. She is comfortable with her sexuality, having no feelings of guilt or shame for her sexual desire and behavior. So why should her sexual desire, rather than her class, ethnicity, family, or any other social categories, decide her personal identity? In other words, why should her sexual desire be her primary identity? And why is gender of erotic object choice singled out to determine her sexual identity? What kinds of social hierarchy are we establishing in prioritizing the gender of erotic object choice at the expense of all other social and sexual categories?

Her story does not end here. She had a marvelous relationship with a partner before she came to Beijing. She missed the relationship deeply:

> We loved each other very much. We slept together, we shared everything, chatted every day. We were a couple. But at that time, I simply did not have the language of love of the same sex to construct or even to comprehend our relationship in that way. You know, my perception of *tongxinglian* was very derogatory, associating it with

broken families, casual sex, and AIDS. We loved each other, of course. If I stayed in my previous village and did not move to Beijing, our relationship would have continued even if I married a man. I can love my girlfriend while maintaining a harmonious relationship with my husband, without serious conflict. It is easier to camouflage a relationship between women than a heterosexual one. *Tongxinglian* is more invisible and less threatening than extramarital heterosexuality. I brought my previous girlfriend back home—she stayed and slept with me. No one would suspect anything. Basically, if you don't have sex in front of them, no one would associate female intimacy with *tongxinglian.* It would cause me more trouble if I came out as a "lesbian," a Westernized category that challenges the basic family-kinship structure and my cultural identity as a Chinese. What benefits could coming out to the public bring me?

Tongzhi, lesbian, gay, or queer is a subject position that has to be constructed and self-identified. Same-sex eroticism does not necessarily contradict one's marital status. It is only when one takes up the lesbigay identity and constructs his or her experiences and lifestyle around this sexual identity that sexuality comes into conflict with marital status. The tension is most acute when one wants to proclaim the sexual identity as a public statement about one's body. Ning treasures her social role as a wife, daughter, and mother so much that she finds the lesbian identity threatening rather than empowering. As she said, "I accept my homoerotic desire, but why should I make a big fuss and destroy the harmonious family order I have in my life? . . . It would cause me more trouble if I came out as a "lesbian," a Westernized category that challenges the basic family-kinship structure and my cultural identity as a Chinese. What benefits could coming out to the public bring me?"

To classify Ning as a lesbian is to impose an imagined binary difference based on the gender of the erotic object choice, and to fix and inscribe such differences onto her body, claiming such an identity to be her natural and core self. Yet Ning's experiences clearly expose the limitation of universalizing the homo-hetero duality to all cultural practices of same-sex eroticism.

Story 5

This story is about Wing (forty-seven), who is now an editor at a magazine. He is married with three children. He had his first sexual experience with a male during the Cultural Revolution. He said that the Cultural Revolution was the happiest period of his life, even though he was separated from his family for ten years. He was sixteen when the Cultural Revolution broke out in 1966. Because his father had a close relative in Hong Kong, he was labeled "Black Gang." His father had to kneel on broken glass, live for five years in a pig house, and had to parade publicly wearing derogatory placards while being kicked and spat upon by hundreds of people. Wing's entire family broke up. His parents and siblings were sent to different cities for political reeducation. Wing was sent alone to a northern city where he spent ten years in a steel plant work unit. He was grouped in a small team with twelve other young men, working and living together in a dormitory. Wing said,

> Politically, my whole family suffered painfully. But sexually, that was the most beautiful period in my life. I had sex with all of my workmates—we even had an orgy. You see, all of us were young virile men staying together for years without wives or girlfriends around. We worked together and then returned to the dormitories to spend our leisure time together. We were all away from our parents, siblings, friends, and neighbors for years. We only had each other.

Wing then shared some of the experiences they had during those years:

> We had sex games like using our dicks to pick up shoes, ejaculation, and biggest size competitions. It's great fun. There was simply no concept of sexual orientation or sexual identity, it was just a natural expression of male sexuality. It would be pointless to ask who is *gay* and who is not. The relationship was human-sexual rather than homo or hetero. If we had known about all these concepts of sexual orientation, we might be too scared to touch each other, thinking that it was perverted. Well, all of us are married now, but marriage is only a social obligation and has nothing to do with sexual orientation. I sometimes wonder what is the point of dividing human beings into homo and hetero. Intimacy goes beyond social categorization and sexual identity.

Ten years later, Wing was sent by the Party back to his hometown. A marriage had already been arranged for him.[3] He had no choice but to marry a woman whom he did not know at all. Wing wished that the marriage could change his "bad habit," but he soon realized that his homoerotic feelings did not diminish but intensified instead. Although he did not enjoy sex with his wife, he is proud to have three children. Wing said, "This family is very important to me; it is a harmonious *jia* [home/family]. Although I rarely have sex with my wife, we really care for each other, and our children perform very well at school."

When Wing went back to his hometown in 1976, the only place he could have sex with men was a public toilet. He went there once or twice a month, and gradually made several friends. Most of them were married. Some deliberately married ugly, fat, or uneducated village women, which, in their minds, minimized the feelings of guilt for ruining a woman's life. Unfortunately, Wing was caught in the toilet by the police. Although there is no law against same-sex relationships, he was penalized and abused for "hooliganism." During the five days of detention, he was forced by several police officers to have sex with another man they had caught in the toilet. Wing was then brought by another police officer to a small room where he was stripped, spat upon, and raped. He was raped by the same police officer again the next night. Although the police did not notify his work unit and family, Wing was so devastated that he never went to the cruising area again. He attempted suicide twice afterward.

Wing appeared to be very calm when he shared his story, as if he was telling someone else's story. His calmness was most disturbing when he told me how he was spat upon and raped. He described the details in a very plain way. It seems that only by "otherizing" and alienating the self could he talk about such experiences, otherwise too painful to be remembered. Wing later remarked that many *nan tongzhi* in the scene have had the experience of being caught by police and later attempting suicide. The latter is sometimes caused by the former. Among the 200 *tongzhi* I chatted with, thirty-nine of them have attempted suicide, a high proportion of 20 percent, not to mention those who did not disclose their attempts to me.

Once, Wing was on a business trip to another city for ten days. He met a nineteen-year-old boy and they had sex on the first night. Wing was infatuated by the beauty of this youth. Only on the last day of the trip did Wing realize that this young man had lied to him—he was twenty-five, not nineteen; he had only a primary school education instead of secondary school; his mother was not seriously ill; and he was a money boy (prostitute). But Wing had already lent him 2,000 yuan, and also bought him lots of expensive presents. When Wing wanted the money back, they had a terrible fight. The young man scolded him: "Stupid old man, look at yourself! How would I fancy you?" Wing was only thirty-eight at the time, although he already looked fifty. In the *tongzhi* circle, middle-aged men are usually not popular and become vulnerable to all forms of abuse.

In the past two years, Wing made contacts with some *tongzhi* from Hong Kong, and he started to publish positive *tongzhi* stories in some magazines, trying to refute the mainstream medical viewpoint. Yet, as he said,

> Here in China, you must be highly careful. All minority works are highly sensitive in mainland China. My articles have been canceled

by the editor and I have been warned. You must know the overall political trend and your own assets. Otherwise, your entire career and life can be ruined in one night.

The previous five cases are neither ideal nor without pain. All of the subjects live in very difficult situations. They have attempted suicide, been married, divorced, arrested, raped and/or cheated. Yet, they each have manipulated their own unique circumstances to enhance their personal space.

James (Story 1) integrates his sexuality into family life, not by confronting his parents, but by integrating Xiao-Liu into his family. James has manipulated the cultural markers of food and kin categories in helping Xiao-Liu become a quasi-kin member of his family. He also retains and develops his parents' cultural innocence and tolerance toward same-sex eroticism. Instead of provoking a debate on the status of *tongxinglian,* Xiao-Liu established an intimate relationship with James' parents and literally lives with them. Song and Jenny (Story 2) manipulate their middle-class economic space and the divorce law to afford an independent life of their own. Peter (Story 3), despite his limitations of receiving only a primary school education and having a rural background while living in a large modern city, manages to identify positively with the Western *gay* discourse, which became a major source of empowerment and liberation for him. The Western discourses on romantic love, carefree lifestyle, and individualism are strategic tools for Peter to negotiate with his parents' expectations of marriage. Ning (Story 4) enjoys the traditional space for female intimacy and develops a positive space while rejecting the Western strategy of coming out. Wing (Story 5) enjoyed his teenage years of sexual innocence. Although he has been arrested and cheated, he still maintains close friendships with *tongzhi*. He also empowers himself and others by writing positive *tongzhi* representations under a pseudonym.

Tongzhi is not a monolithic discourse. Even within the major cities of mainland China, *tongzhi* of different gender, age, class, education, marital status, and economic power resort to different resources to enhance their *tongzhi* space. James lives with his boyfriend, redefining the meaning of marriage and male intimacy without openly challenging the marital institution; Song divorced her husband in order to stay with Jenny; Peter firmly resists marriage by expanding his economic assets and Western affiliation; Ning adopts a nonconfrontational model to enjoy the cultural space for female intimacy; Wing stayed in marriage to enjoy the warmth of a family, while his male friends deliberately married less desirable village women to minimize their guilt.

Although some *tongzhi*, such as Peter, have to exile themselves from the family to attain personal freedom through the appropriation of *gay* identity and lifestyle, for other *tongzhi*, such as James, Ning, and Wing, the mainstream categories of family relations, filial piety, and marriage actually help them attain personal happiness and protect them from social mistreatment more effectively than the categories of coming out and human rights. It is the complexity and diversity of their strategies that enrich the scenario of *tongzhi* resistance. What we need is not a single monolithic discourse on "The Chinese *Tongzhi* Strategy," which would be impossible and undesirable. Instead, the differences and diversities among *tongzhi* should be explored and celebrated, to empower and vitalize the uniqueness of each individual *tongzhi's* struggle.

COLLECTIVE STRATEGIES OF TONGZHI EMPOWERMENT

Chinese and Western scholars commonly agree that in the first thirty years of the PRC, sex and sexuality were absent from public discourse; "sex was a taboo during the period 1949-1980 with any material relating to sex strictly forbidden" (Evans, 1997:1). The Cultural Revolution represented the most acute expression of such sexual puritanism, in which the slightest suggestion of sexual interest was seen as bourgeois corruption and antirevolutionary. In a survey of 23,000 people across fifteen provinces by Professor Liu Da-lin in 1990, 40 percent of the informants said that they never took their clothes off during sex. Liu suggested that contemporary Chinese people are perhaps more ignorant about sex today than they were before the revolution (Liu, 1992).

Since the 1980s, China has undergone drastic changes. There has been an explosion of popular discourses on sexuality, including (female) nudes, (female) erotica, and the (female) seductive images that are displayed in magazines, posters, newspapers, videos, calendars, periodicals, and TV ads. Telephone hotlines and counseling services on sexuality are also commonly found in major cities. Chinese modernity is a highly sexualized and racialized discourse where Westernized erotic images become a marketing strategy for commodities and a symbol of avant-garde spirit. Such drastic socioeconomic changes open up new forms of desire, identities, discourse, and spaces of resistance for PEPS.

Commercial Absorption of the Political

The economic reforms stipulated by Deng Xiaoping since 1978 ignited rapid socioeconomic changes which have significant bearing on the rise of the public sphere, legal rights consciousness, and the flourishing of socio-economic activity with active participation, cooperation, and coordination of private individuals.[4] The crucial changes, including the right to choose and change jobs, the trend of delayed marriages, less rigid policies on housing allocation, the popularity of intercity migration, increasing opportunities to live away from one's family, greater tolerance toward sexual expression in the media, and the abolition of the crime of *liumang,* all have had significant impact on the survival space and identity building of *tongzhi* in China.

In recent years, a more visible "*tongzhi* scene" has emerged in major cities. Apart from public toilets, which have long been cruising areas for male PEPS, there are now discos, bars, and parks patronized by a large male PEPS clientele in major cities. The "scene" is now predominantly occupied by young middle-class men who, because of their social space, gender privileges, and economic power, have the time, aspiration, money, and social space to afford the visibility of these new public spaces. What exists in China is not a visible *tongzhi* organization, but many personalized social networks. In Beijing, for example, there is also an active *nü tongzhi* community in which, through dispersed interpersonal networking, gatherings of more than forty people occur regularly in different circles for relaxed socializing.

Bars are an interesting cultural space in modern cities where Chinese and Caucasian, East and West cease to be discrete or mutually exclusive geographical locations but act as social processes that condense and interact in this specific context. Bars and discos become a modern space where PEPS gather to generate a new form of identity and survival space.

Before 1996, there were no "*gay* bars" or "*gay* discos" in mainland China. PEPS like to "colonize" and "queer" a mainstream bar or disco. The strategy is first to find a bar that is PEPS-friendly and has many Caucasians and hip young customers. They then choose a certain weekday to ask others in the PEPS community to go, not as public forum or political gathering, but simply to find a friendly place where they can meet and be sociable without fear or having to wear a heterosexual mask. Although an exclusively PEPS venue could be very empowering for those who feel deeply oppressed, PEPS also enjoy the assimilative strategy of queering the mainstream venue. However, in 1998, there was an obvious trend of new bars started by *tongzhi* for *tongzhi.* In a Beijing bar, for example, the *tongzhi* couple who owns the bar organizes a casual chatting forum every weekend, with a steady crowd of thirty *tongzhi.* This casual gathering becomes a crucial venue that helps to build up a visible and healthy *tongzhi* community. In a big new *tongzhi/gay* bar in Shanghai, there are dozens of intrabar telephones for customers to "cruise" with anyone who happens to pick up another phone. There are several computers that customers can use to send and receive e-mail, play Internet games, download pornographic pictures, and connect to other users all over the world. These high-tech instruments are crucial devices to construct and fantasize a cyberspace of the "queer planet," which is said to be free and liberating. In this context, to be *gay* is not only to love the same sex, but is a cultural and class response to the yearning for a racialized discourse of modernity through which the Western metropolitan *gay* images and lifestyle are appropriated and fantasized.

In Beijing, for example, it is also important that these PEPS bars are mostly located in the Westernized and diplomatic districts where there are large crowds of Caucasian customers. On Bar Street in the diplomatic district there are more than fifty bars, if we can include the dozens of bars on the adjacent street. The location of the bars already segregates the customers from the general population, marking such places for the trendy, Westernized, English speaking, young, middle class, single, liberal, and avant garde. When a PEPS goes into a bar, he or she is literally entering a different space. It is a specific time (night), a specific language (English-Mandarin mixed code), a specific racial combination (a high ratio of Caucasian clientele), a specific class (middle-class and freelance workers and artists), specific music (Westernized, trendy music and MTV), specific drinks (Western drinks and beer), specific dress (casual wear and trendy Western attire), specific gender (predominantly male), and a specific topic (sexuality). Most of these bars in Beijing and Shanghai have no Chinese names, only English ones.[5] During Western festivals such as Halloween and Christmas, they will organize wild parties and beer competitions. In other words, these bars and discos become cultural and class markers that differentiate themselves not only from the general population, but also a certain class of PEPS—urban, middle class, English speaking, trendy, young—from the majority of PEPS. These venues serve as a "qualifier" for being *gay* and *tongzhi*. A traditional elderly woman dressed in shabby old-fashioned clothes does not seem to "qualify" as lesbian or *tongzhi*. These venues are thus both empowering to certain PEPS and exclusionary or even oppressive to the majority. What is emerging is a hierarchy of PEPS culture in which the highest level consists of the urban, English-speaking, middle-class, young male PEPS who take the lead in developing the directions of *tongzhi* culture.

These bars and discos are places where PEPS move away from their families and work units—they are neither filial sons and daughters as at home, nor diligent workers under a complex web of state and social control. They can grasp this rare chance in everyday life to openly confirm sexuality in a way they want—as *tongzhi, gay,* or lesbian.

The emergence of these venues also helps redefine private-public boundaries, as sexuality is no longer a private realm always associated with and confined to the domestic and marital institutions. The emergence of same-sex erotic culture and identities within the newly developed main-stream consumption venues questions the rigid private-public distinction by relocating (private) sexuality into the public domain of the market economy. Although the state apparatus directly intervenes in the work-unit, family, and cruising areas, these new consumption venues are governed more by the capitalist market mechanism. It also challenges a strict homo-hetero duality, as same-sex eroticism circulates and flirts with everyone in these mainstream bars, discos, and parks.

Although the liberal discourse of individualism and romantic love have motivated many PEPS to seek out a *"gay* lifestyle," the emergence of *gay* culture in the large cities of Beijing, Shanghai, and Guangdong has not been without social cost. Many mainland Chinese see *tongxinglian* as a product of modern capitalism in which a new generation of young people has been corrupted by Western decadence—dressing up in outrageous attire with Westernized sexuality and a confrontational lifestyle. "Gay" becomes a symbol of Western bourgeois urban sexual adventure, which, in the Chinese context, is seen as a threat to the social order, public morality, family values, and Chinese culture. The development of a discrete *gay* culture is double-edged—it is empowering to *gay*-identified people, but simultaneously it may provoke a homo-hetero duality and homophobic consciousness that has never prevailed in China.

The Academic Struggle for Demedicalization of Tongxinglian

In a society where PEPS have little social space to come out, most people would think that they have never come across any PEPS, and their conception of *tongxinglian* would not come directly from PEPS themselves but from the media and academic world. Apart from the rare appearance of *tongxinglian* in the tabloid papers, usually associated with rape, murder, cheating, and all forms of perversity, the images portrayed by the academic world become the only medium through which the general public understands *tongxinglian*. It further explains the significance of negotiating with the academic and medical world concerning same-sex love.

With the Open Door Policy, beginning in the the late 1970s, some positive discussions of *tongxinglian* started. In 1985, the sexologist Ruan Fang-fu published an essay titled *"Tongxinglian: An Unsolved Puzzle"* in the widely circulated *Good Health Magazine*, under the pseudonym Hua Jin-ma. Ruan argued that *tongxinglian* should not be subjected to persecution or medical treatment as they are no different from heterosexuals in terms of intelligence, physical strength, creativity, and desire for stable relationships.

In the 1990s, it is less taboo to discuss *tongxinglian* as a scholarly issue. There have been three unprecedented books on *tongxinglian*. In 1995, Fang Gang published a journalistic book, *Tongxinglian Zai Zhongguo* (Homosexuality in China), which has been criticized as being heterosexist and sensational. Li Yin-he and Wang Xiao-bo, a married couple who are both sociologists, published *Tamen De Shijie* (Their World) in 1992, the first specialist study of male *tongxinglian* in Beijing, arguing that *tongxinglian* should not be seen as sick, immoral behavior or perversity. However, as the title of the book implies, Li and Wang portrayed *tongxinglian* as distant from the mainstream culture, therefore presupposing a we-they dichotomy between *tongxinglian* and the mainstream world. The third book was Zhang Bei-chuan's *Tongxingai*, published in 1994. Zhang did not use the more standard word for homosexuality, *tongxinglian*. He replaced *lian*, denoting an obsessive kind of love, with the loftier *ai*, in order to show that same-sex love is neither an illness nor immoral.

Philosophy professor Qiu Ren-zong is another scholar crucial to *tongzhi* cultural development. On December 6-8, 1994, Qiu organized, on behalf of the China Academy of Social Science, the first public symposium on *tongxinglian* in China, with fifty scholars, professionals, and *tongxinglian* in attendance. By the end of the symposium, they announced a twelve-point manifesto, "The Consensus and Suggestions on AIDS and *Tongxinglian*," stressing the normality of same-sex love and the social harm caused by discriminating against *tongzhi*. Qiu also said,

> China is now faced with immense population control [problems]. Same-sex love is an effective and natural way of population control. It is inhuman to force PEPS to marry. It will only end in human disaster, even suicide. Letting PEPS remain single would be the most natural solution to help PEPS and the country. The one-child policy has abrogated the Confucian ideal of having as many sons as possible to ensure family male lineage, [so] why tie sex to procreation at all?" (Personal interview, July 11, 1995)

Despite such positive developments, *tongzhi* representation in the media is still discouraged and even prohibited by the government. In 1996, the Ministry of Propaganda and other offices more than once decreed that books focusing on *tongxinglian* should not be published, for fear that these books would "promote" *tongxinglian.* Yet, in 1998, Li Yin-he successfully broke through this "censorship" by publishing *Tongxinglian Ya Wenhua* (Homosexual Subculture) a book that rewrites her own *Tamen De Shijie* published in 1992. Although the new book still retains the chapter "Cause of Homosexuality," it is a step forward, especially in terms of discussing Foucault and queer politics in the last chapter.

In March 1998, Zhang Bei-chuan, together with other academics, published *Friend Exchanging* newsletter, the first *tongzhi*-positive newsletter published by a mainstream academic institution (The People's University in Beijing). It prints 3,000 copies of each issue, sending them to *tongzhi* and certain mainstream institutions free of charge. Zhang has regular contact with hundreds of *tongzhi*, which has helped him become a passionate advocate for *tongzhi*. Zhang's work is well supported by *tongzhi* because it is crucial to build a bridge between the government and the *tongzhi* community to help the government and the establishment understand *tongzhi*. Otherwise, it is difficult to go beyond the mainstream stereotype of *tongzhi* as *liumang*, promiscuous and pathological. Zhang writes in the first issue of *Friend Exchanging*:

> Homosexuals, like their heterosexual counterparts, also look forward to living with their loved ones. But because of sociocultural backwardness, many homosexuals live under severe discrimination, unable to establish stable and healthy monogamous relationships. . . . "Discrimination" has now been commonly acknowledged by the international health community as the key factor for spreading AIDS. In the age of AIDS, changing the social environment that discriminates against the homosexual community is a pressing obligation and task for academia. (1998:4-5)

Apart from *Friend Exchanging*, there was significant progress in the media in 1998 on *tongzhi* issues. In June 1998, the mainstream magazine *Hope,* which sells a half million copies, launched a twenty-one-page feature on *tongxinglian,* with many articles, mostly by *tongzhi*-positive scholars. On May 30, 1998, the *People's Daily,* the official Party newspaper, included a short article on page three titled "German State Passed Law to Cancel All Unjust Laws in Nazi Court." The article states, "After Hitler came to power in 1933, in order to consolidate the Nazi Fascist regime, he launched cruel measures to oppress all anti-Hitler elements and other people, including homosexuals. On May 28, 1998, the German state passed a law to cancel Hitler's unjust laws, to reclaim for the victims." It was an unprecedented move of the Chinese Communist Party to "endorse" a positive statement on homosexuality.

Technological Enhancement of Tongzhi Space

In a society where the heterosexual marital institution, housing policy, and work system together form a tight web of social control that minimizes any form of social deviance, it is very difficult for PEPS to know one another and maintain steady relationships in a safe and comfortable context. The technological innovations in recent years, especially the pager and the Internet, have immensely enhanced the survival space of PEPS. Pagers, which have rapidly become popular in recent years, are commonly used by PEPS as the most easily accessible and safest way to make personal contacts, with no need to expose one's real name, work unit, family background, or ethnic origin. *Tongzhi* no longer have to go to the cruising areas to make contacts, thus relieving the fear of blackmail, arrest by police, or identification by the straight world. In the survey by Zhang Bei-chuan (1998b), 26 percent of the interviewees had been blackmailed in the previous twelve months, and 40 percent had been sexually harassed by other PEPS, thus indicating a pressing need for a context where PEPS can meet other PEPS safely. As one *nan tongzhi* (twenty-seven) said,

> I don't want to go to the fishing pond—there is lots of robbery, cheating, and stealing. And you have to worry about police raids. You show your real face and there is no way to hide or deny when anything happens. That's why I use a pager. I prefer to meet friends who are introduced by my friends. We contact by pager and meet not by the fishing pond, but in McDonald's or Kentucky Fried Chicken. I could be completely relaxed there, as it is not a *tongzhi* ghetto but just an ordinary place.

Though the Internet is not yet widely accessible in China, it is a highly effective way to break through the oppressive boundaries created by the tight family-kin structure and the social control system of work units and residential arrangements. Given the enormous possibilities to maneuver in cyberspace, the gradual popularization of the Internet in China has helped to generate a small but a rapidly growing *tongzhi* community which will prove to be a pioneering force in building up indigenous *tongzhi* discourses in China. Pagers, mobile phones, fax, e-mail, Internet, and other high-tech devices have been appropriated by *tongzhi* to build up an unprecedented space of virtual communities.

Since mid-1997, several Chinese and expatriate *tongzhi* have operated a pager hotline for information about HIV, other sexually transmitted diseases, and relevant counseling services. Several Internet homepages such as *Gay* China have been established for Chinese *tongzhi* to make contact in a safe and warm environment. The Internet has also been widely used, especially by overseas Chinese *tongzhi*, to disseminate positive information about *tongzhi* and to have regular exchanges of information with mainlanders. In the spring of 1997, a few Chinese *gay*-identified students and scholars in North America tried to establish a group for lesbigay studies. After much preparation, the Chinese Society for the Study of Sexual Minorities (CSSSM) was established on September 1 and held its first annual meeting in Los Angeles. The main goal of CSSSM is to reduce prejudice and discrimination against sexual minorities in the Chinese culture, with a focus on the situation in mainland China. CSSSM has resorted to the cost-effective Internet for information dissemination through the biweekly Internet journal *Taohong Man Tianxia*.

Apart from CSSSM, Lavender Phoenix and ICCO were both set up in 1997 in the United States. Lavender Phoenix, a support group for lesbian and bisexual women in and from mainland China, was started in August 1997 by five mainland Chinese lesbian and bisexual women in the United States. It had an e-mail list of twenty-five women from the start and tries to focus on lesbian issues related to its members.

These *tongzhi* groups in the United States are faced with immense difficulties. Apart from the Orientalism, tokenism, and racism faced by Chinese *tongzhi*, they also have to tackle the homophobia and political conservatism of the Chinese community. More important, the American background and resources are anxiety provoking for the Chinese government. It is difficult to directly influence Chinese people and policy once any mainland activist leaves China. For example, on November 11, 1997, Gary Wu, executive director of the International Chinese Comrades Organization (ICCO), sent an open letter to President Jiang Zemin in a press conference, asking the Chinese government to respect the human rights of lesbian and *gay* people in China:

> As early as the late 19th century, there were nearly one thousand publications centering around the issue of homosexuality in the west, whereas in China there were nearly none. . . . In China there are no laws banning homosexuality. However, up till now many gays and lesbians have been arrested or fined by other charges. . . . This discrimination and even persecution has endangered the human rights of homosexuals. . . . Therefore, we urge that (1) The Chinese government should positively treat the issue of homosexuality and protect the rights of gays and lesbians. . . . (4) The Chinese government should allow local gay and lesbian organizations.

Although this letter is addressed to Jiang Zemin, it is unlikely that Jiang will ever read it, and neither will the vast population in China. Instead, the main target seems to be the Chinese-speaking and English-speaking media in the United States. The letter starts by comparing Western "progressiveness" to Chinese "backwardness" in terms of the far greater number of Western publications on homosexuality, and asks for the Chinese government to respect the human rights of lesbians and gays in China.

From the Chinese government's viewpoint, when Gary Wu left in 1997, he immediately criticized China on the issue of human rights. Gary Wu soon started the ICCO under the International Gay and Lesbian Human Rights Commission. In an interview with the *San Francisco Chronicle* (the largest paper in San Francisco), the reporter took a rather Orientalist perspective in describing Gary as "an aggressively outspoken proponent of the rights of Chinese gays and lesbians—a pioneer for sexual freedom in the world's most populous totalitarian empire" (Burdman and Tuller, 1997:7).

It is indeed inaccurate to say that the Chinese government oppresses lesbian and gay people. Though PEPS have been oppressed and abused by individual police officers for having sex, heterosexuals are also oppressed for having extramarital relations. It would be fair to say that both traditional and contemporary Chinese ruling authorities simply do not have the concept of lesbian and gay issues. The Chinese government's concern is obviously not *tongxinglian* itself but social order and stability. It hits a governmental nerve when the most well-known *tongzhi* in mainland China seeks the help of the American Human Rights Commission to set up a *tongzhi* human rights group, and to attack the Chinese government on the highly sensitive issue of human rights.

Ironically, the sensitive act of sending an open letter to Jiang Zemin may irritate and pressure the Beijing government to take a hostile attitude on lesbian and gay issues, not because of homophobia per se, but because political mobilization, human rights, mass organization, and affiliation with an American human rights organization are the most sensitive political issues.

Depoliticization of Mainland Chinese Tongzhi Culture

In China, the government's strict control of free expression and free association means that mass demonstrations and registration of PEPS organizations are not only impermissible, they might have disastrous results for millions of PEPS in China. In contemporary China, collective movements, political action, and human rights are most sensitive issues that can cause disaster to anyone who advocates them publicly. The politicization of same-sex eroticism, and indeed any kind of politicization or political movement, would quickly be perceived as a threat to the legitimacy of the Communist Party.

It does not imply, however, that the Chinese state is omnipotent. Although the central government can act in a rather authoritarian manner, China is simply too big and populous to implement omnipresent state control, especially with giant but inefficient bureaucratic government machinery. Therefore, while the government takes a hard line on political issues, especially related to the Western world, individuals do have room to maneuver in nonpolitical arenas. This, together with government's and the culture's insensitivity to *tongxinglian* and the homo-hetero duality, explains the strategy of depoliticization of *tongzhi* work in China.

On November 22, 1992, *tongzhi* activist Wan Yan-hai organized China's first open forum for male *tongxinglian*, Men's World, with thirty-five participants, including scholars, writers, government officials, and reporters. It was a "cultural salon" that lasted for six months. While the first meeting was held at the Sea Horse, a famous restaurant in Beijing, other meetings were held at the offices of the National Health Education Institute. Yet the Public Health Ministry soon ordered the salon to shut down. According to Wan, who lost his job for organizing the event, it resulted not from homophobia but from factional infighting among health officials. The liberal head of the Health Education Institute, Chen Bing-zhong, was forced to resign. The manager of the Sea Horse was fired, and the Sea Horse, now defunct, never repeated the event.

Mainland China has no organizations to fight for *tongzhi* rights. Indeed, the entire notion of "*tongzhi* rights" and "*tongzhi* movement" has been criticized by many activists who reject confrontational politics. They recast *tongzhi* culture as an apolitical and government-friendly culture. Most activists also opt for an apolitical strategy of *tongzhi* culture to negotiate with the government and academic world. *Taohong Man Tianxia* is a vocal supporter of such depoliticization; the second issue in 1997 included a crucial article written by the editor-in-chief "exploring the politicization and de-politicization of *tongxinglian* in mainland China." The article urged gaining government support and cooperation:

> There are fundamental differences between *tongxinglian* rights and civil democratic rights . . . democratic rights extend to the whole society . . . what *tongxinglian* demand are the freedom to be true to oneself, and do not seek to confront existing political institutions nor threaten the existing government. . . . The fundamental issue of *tongxinglian* is not fighting for political rights but the welfare and happiness in the everyday life of *tongxinglian*. To radicalize the conflict with the government, and to politicize the issue of *tongxing-*

lian neither helps nor reflects the collective wish of *tongxinglian* to seek for such social space. . . . The ambiguity of the general public towards *tongxinglian* has both good and bad sides. Bad as it lacks information concerning the scientific and objective facts. Good as there is a vacuum without too many deep-rooted misunderstandings. *Tongzhi* activists should gain the support and cooperation of other social circles, and use scientific and objective facts to fill that vacuum. . . . I suggest locating the issue of *tongxinglian* not as a human rights issue, as proposed by Western world, but to relate it to divorce, aging, marriage, and other social issues. (Web page, *Taohong Man Tianxia*)

The modern Anglo-American lesbigay discourse, generated in the civil rights movement in the 1960s, is itself the historical product of modernity, individualism, and human rights discourses. Identity politics and legal discourses of rights have been the major strategy of resistance. However, China lacks the tradition of homophobic hostility to sustain confrontational politics, nor has the homo-hetero duality generated separatist and discrete sexual identity politics. The primacy of family-kin social constructs has produced a different scenario of same-sex eroticism: instead of prioritizing human rights and *gay* rights as a universal principle, *tongzhi* discourses in China tend to focus on integrating sexuality into social relations both at the individual level and in the collective building of healthy *tongzhi* communities, partly through the social struggle toward demedicalization of homosexuality. Even the minority middle-class, young urban male who takes up the *gay* identity does not have the cultural "privilege" to segregate sexuality from the family-kin relationship. As I will elaborate in Chapter 7, "coming home" can be proposed as an indigenous strategy of empowerment for *tongzhi* in China.

To conclude, rapid socioeconomic development since the early 1980s has generated new forms of social, economic, and sexual desire, identities, and new relations of power and resistance. Same-sex eroticism has taken a new shape. The rapidly opening market economy, the continual potent reaction against the total politicization during the Cultural Revolution, massive usage of pagers, mobile phones, and the Internet, the influx of Western individualist and libertarian discourse, and the trend of delayed marriage, together with the proliferation of commercial discourses on sexuality, have been vital in generating new spaces for *tongzhi*. Interestingly, most *tongzhi* activists in China do not take a segregational approach but have a strong sense of "*tongzhi* work" being part and parcel of the wider socioeconomic development and the ultimate social project of human liberation. In the workshop "Directions and Strategies and *Tongzhi* in

China" in the 1998 *Tongzhi* Conference held in Hong Kong, with 200 attendees from seventeen countries, there seemed to be a consensus concerning the strategy of depoliticization and nonconfrontational approach. Indeed, the attendees suggested replacing the category *tongzhi* "movement" with *tongzhi* "work" or "culture" because the term "movement" in the last forty years has been derogatory and disastrous in mainland China.

It is through this close link between same-sex eroticism and wider social relations, itself a historical continuation of understanding and constituting the sexual by the social, that the discourse of *tongzhi* liberation is tied up with the wider social development of economic reforms, housing policy, technological innovations, marriage and divorce laws, and greater respect and emphasis on personal choice and happiness. Chinese modernity is not only a socioeconomic project, it also generates discourses of bio-power and body politics of eroticism in which new spaces of discipline and control, empowerment and resistance, desire and identities are invented, negotiated, and constructed.

At a time when China is moving toward greater diversities and away from any fixed notion of so-called "Chineseness," it is high time to critically examine different indigenous perspectives and strategies of *tongzhi* empowerment that really cater to the needs of different segments of PEPS in China, and to explore the struggle of PEPS in their own unique context. Mainland Chinese PEPS do not seem to pass through the same historical development of lesbigay movements as in other societies. Neither can the specific historical experiences of Chinese PEPS be subsumed under any monolithic notion of "China versus America" or "East versus West." Instead, it is the specific political situation of dictatorial Communist rule, rapidly changing housing and work policy, severe pressure for marriage, close kin networking, vibrant economic development, and migration trends, together with the self-identified process of PEPS identity formation, that push Chinese PEPS to pursue their own strategies of resistance. As China has not yet adopted fully the homo-hetero duality and the concomitant homophobic consciousness, it is an urgent task to explore and vitalize multiple perspectives, strategies, and spaces of *tongzhi* empowerment.

Chapter 4

Going Beyond "Cultural Carnival versus Political Confrontation": Pluralities of Contemporary Taiwanese *Tongzhi* Discourses

Whereas *tongzhi* discourses in mainland China and Hong Kong have generally been suspicious of confrontational politics, Taiwan *tongzhi* discourses actively appropriate and indigenize the confrontational strategies.[1] Among all the contemporary Chinese societies, the discursive practices of Taiwan *tongzhi* activism have the most substantial spectrum ranging from active intellectual theorization to aggressive political activism, strategic media manipulation, strong women's voices, prolific university activism, and a substantial variety of socializing venues and commercial commodities. Throughout the 1990s, Taiwan has had more than thirty university *tongzhi* organizations, fifteen *tongzhi* radio programs, and twenty *tongzhi* social organizations together with more than 100 Chinese *tongzhi* books, not to mention the dozens of saunas, bars, and discos in the commercial scene. The flourishing of *tongzhi* activism has been marked by an explosion and diversification of strategies of resistance, which can broadly be divided into the cultural strategy of carnival eroticism that opts for the unique approach of *jiti xianshen* (collective coming out), and the confrontational politics that fight for the legal rights discourse. These two approaches are neither oppositional nor discrete but mutually implicated. Indeed, it is the diversity of Taiwan *tongzhi* discourse that makes it a good test case of indigenizing identity politics and confrontational strategy in a cultural tradition that did not divide people into homo or hetero.

In this chapter, I will focus on the 1990s, in which the Taiwanese *tongzhi* movement began and grew at an incredible rate. I will start with an overview of Taiwan's political situation, which has significant bearing on the emergence and directions of Taiwanese *tongzhi* discourses.

141

Imperial China first sent a military expedition to Taiwan in the sixth century. Before the Ming dynasty (1368-1644), Taiwan remained an exotic and "underdeveloped" region in the Imperial Chinese texts. Taiwanese aboriginals (*yuan zhu min*) not only differ in their skin color from the mainland Han people, their language and cultural practices are notably distinct from the Han culture. In 1662, the famous Ming General Zheng Chenggong expelled the Dutch army from Taiwan. As a matter of fact, the newly formed Qing government dispatched official troops to maintain social order in 1684. In the seventeenth century, Taiwan had been ruled by Spain and Holland for sixteen and thirty-eight years, respectively. In 1895, Taiwan was ceded by China to become a colony of Japan for fifty years due to mainland China's defeat in the Sino-Japanese war. After World War II, when Japan "returned" Taiwan to China, Chiang Kai-shek's Guomindang (Nationalist) government, which proclaimed itself the real Chinese government, fled to Taiwan, ruled Taiwan, and named itself as the existing Zhonghua Minguo (Republic of China). The serious conflict between Taiwanese and the mainlanders as represented by the Guomindang government resulted in the riot of the 2-28 Incident on February 28, 1947, in which the local protest was brutally suppressed by the Nationalist government.

After that, Taiwan was under the autocratic rule of the Guomindang. The intense threat from Communist China (PRC) had provided Taiwan's government with a good excuse to exercise martial law controlling the speech, activities, and assembly of the general public, to the extent that even children speaking the local Minan language at school would be penalized. Anticommunism was so overwhelming that all activities perceived by the government as antisocial could be labeled Communist and therefore violently suppressed. The general population was very discontented with the autocratic rule, especially with political oppression, including the Formosa Incident in 1979, when several key opposition political leaders were mysterious murdered, along with tens of thousands of oppositional activists being arrested and jailed since the late 1940s. It has been estimated that 3,000 to 5,000 people were killed during the White Terror (Cheng Ai-ling, 1997). On the other hand, rocketing urbanization and industrialization in the 1970s and 1980s gave birth to a new generation of urban, well-educated young people who are blatant in their demand for democracy and political diversity. In 1986, the DPP (Democratic Progressive Party) was founded and became the leading oppositional party. The DPP was soon recognized by President Jiang Jingguo (Chiang Chin-kuo), who made a historical statement by proclaiming, "I am a Taiwanese too" and started to recruit nonmainlanders to the government, including the current President Lee Teng-hui. In 1987, martial law was waived, and a general presidential election was held in 1996, an unprecedented event in Chinese history.

The lifting of martial law has released the deep-rooted anger, discontent, and tension concerning Taiwanese identity and cultural heritage (Murray and Hong, 1991). Although the mainlanders (Chinese moving from the mainland after 1945) constitute about 12 percent of the population, they dominate the political scene, whereas the local Minan people, who speak the Minan language (*Tai-yu*) rather than Mandarin, constitute about 70 percent of the population. Presently, many Taiwanese identify themselves as Taiwanese more than Chinese (*zhong guo ren*). The English term "Chinese" fails to differentiate two very different categories—*hua ren* (ethnic/cultural Chinese) and *zhong guo ren*, which literally means China's people. After martial law, the previously sanctioned voices of "Taiwanese independence" (*Tai-du*) gained much social support, including implicit recognition by the current government, although there are also voices for unification with the PRC, as advocated by political parties such as Xin Dang, founded in 1994.

The ignition and skyrocketing development of Taiwan's *tongzhi* movement can be located in the demise of the autocracy in which oppositional and marginalized voices were eager to be heard. Taiwan suddenly became a highly political society with a multiplicity of sociopolitical forces fighting for visibility and power. The emergence of Taiwan's *tongzhi* movement was effected and sheltered by the social outcry for human rights and social justice, hallmarked by the political movement of aboriginals, Taiwan independence activists, labor unions, environmentalists, the Hakka, political pluralists, and, most important, the women's movement. Before we focus on the Taiwanese *tongzhi* movement in the 1990s, we must first examine the emergence of *tongxinglian/tongzhi* identity in postwar Taiwan.

FORMATION OF TONGXINGLIAN CONSCIOUSNESS AND COMMUNITY BEFORE 1990

Before the 1970s, public discourse in Taiwan had barely any reference to homosexuality and had never referred to homosexuality as a generic identity. According to the stringent security measures adopted by the Qing Dynasty, immigration was strictly controlled. As a result, the female-male ratio in Taiwan became unbalanced, reaching 100:120 in 1896 (Wu, 1998:25). At that time, the term *Lohanjiao* referred to men without wives who idled around taking part in illegal activities. There were many reported cases of anal sex among *Lohanjiao* and other males. In the most famous case, the Wangjiao incident (1768), multiple same-sex relation-ships were involved (Ke, 1991:114-115). According to the record of the Qing Gaochung Shilu, the Qing government had already acknowledged the existence of *Lohanjiao* and thought that the *Lohanjiao* in Taiwan were no different from the *Guoluzi* (indigenous terms for males involved in same-sex intimacy) (Wu, 1998:23). Although the reported cases were exclusively male, in one of the Four Strange Criminal Cases in Taiwan during the Qing Dynasty, a nun seduced a female Buddhist disciple in southern Taiwan (Ke, 1991:117).

It is only since the 1970s that same-sex eroticism became a social issue in public discourse. The rapid socioeconomic development of industrial-ization and urbanization have generated new forms of social space that reorganize the discursive practices of marginalized groups. For example, areas around the Taipei railway station that people frequented daily were conducive to the affiliation and assembly of male PEPS, who have few healthy channels for social contact. The concentration of strangers in-creases anonymity and relaxes the social constraints of family-kin moral networks on the individuals. During the night, Taipei Park (New Park, now known as the 228 Peace Memorial Park) and nearby Changde Street in the area of the Taipei railway station became the major cruising area for men. This was not without danger because public surveillance under mar-tial law was very prevalent. One may commit an offense of unlawful assembly simply by being with two other persons.

Autocratic rule, added to the cultural insensitivity to the homo-hetero division, has silenced the issue of homosexuality in public discourse. The population was mostly concerned with economic livelihood, and had little concern for sexual orientation. For example, Kong Er Ling-Wei (1919-1994), the niece of Sung Mei-ling (the wife of President Chiang Kai-shek), wore a man's military uniform during her entire public life. There was gossip saying that she had crushes on women, yet people inside or outside the government did not label her on the basis of sexual preference.

Although there were no generic categories based on sexual orientation, sexual relationships between persons of the same sex were regarded as abnormal. The derogatory term *ren-yao* (nonmale and nonfemale) appears most frequently among the words relating to same-sex eroticism. In 1948, *He Ping Daily Post* carried the headline "Police Caught *Ren-yao*" and reported a male transvestite who married a railway cop. In 1951, the *Independent Night Post* carried the caption *"Ren-yao Tsang Case"* in which a transvestite married a railway worker. It is worth noting that the displaced gender roles of the two males were emphasized but their sexual-ity was barely mentioned. The fact that these two men (railway staff) had sex with men did not seem to cause any social stigma. Sexual orientation is thus reduced to gender categories—only (male) gender nonconformists will be seen as *ren-yao*, while the gender conformist in a same-sex relationship will "pass" as they display normal gender behavior. After reviewing these two cases of *ren-yao* media reportage, Wu Jui-yuan (1998) comments:

> These reports indicate that the Western conception of homosexuality has not been popularized. At that time, it was only a joke when two people with the same sexual organs married each other and it was a wonder when a man dressed in woman's garments. . . . "Homosexuality" refers not to the essence of certain person, but a kind of perverted behavior. (p. 39)

The import of Western discourse on sexuality has contributed to the emergence of sexual identity and the community of *tongxinglian*. Since the Korean War, Taiwan's government has maintained a close alliance with the United States, which provided Taiwan with financial assistance (1951-1965) and military "protection" (1950-1979). The American presence had inculcated a strong sense of cultural superiority, with English constituted as a superior language, white as a superior color, and American culture symbolizing progress and freedom. At the same time, Americans in Taiwan were highly privileged, as the strict social sanctions on Taiwanese did not apply to them. When the government set up strict guidelines to govern the length of hair and ban local dancing parties, no measures were taken to limit gatherings of foreigners. The American culture, venues, and gatherings represented the liberated and exotic world and were very attractive for young Taiwanese who were eager to break free from Taiwanese cultural and political bondage. To be Westernized, ranging from having an English name to a Western partner, good English proficiency, Western attire, and acquiring lesbigay terminologies was a survival strategy of local PEPS to construct a sexual identity and lifestyle unavailable in Taiwanese culture.

It is in such a context that the terms gay, Tomboy, homosexual, and the entire homo-hetero duality have been gradually transplanted into Taiwan. For example, Guang Tai's novel *Taobi Hunyin De Ren* (A Person Who Shuns Marriage, 1976) adopts many English terms such as gay, homosexual, queen, and straight. Because all the newly adopted generic terms for PEPS are English, homosexuality was presented as a Western import or, even worse, a sign of Taiwanese moral degradation. When the novel was first published, 4,000 copies sold immediately. By 1988, it had sold 100,000 copies (Wu, 1998:70). A popular singer in the late 1960s, Wang

Xiao-ning, who sang mostly Western songs, was labeled a TB (tomboy).
She always had short hair, wore trousers and suits, went to American bars
and clubs, and never denied her lesbian identity. The term tomboy also
appeared in the novel *Yuan Yi Wai* (Beyond the Circle, 1967) by Xuan
Xiao-fo. In the book *Nuer Quan*, Zheng Mei-li (1997) interviewed a TB
who shared the impact of Wang Xiao-ning upon the *nü tongzhi* circle:

> When Wang first appeared in the circle, I was in secondary school. . . .
> From 1966-1976 Wang was the star celebrity, always in a three-piece
> suit, white shirt, tie and very short hair, very hippie [hip] look. When
> we went outdoors, we formed a motorcycle group. The police called us
> bad guys, bad girls. Every TB is like that (p. 128).

Indeed, as "homosexual" was only associated with sexual indulgence
and gender confusion, many people differentiated homosexuality from
same-sex love. Even as late as July 1994, when the media extensively
reported the double suicide of two schoolgirls, the school was so disturbed
by the rumors of homosexuality that it issued a pamphlet saying that
"same-sex love is not homosexual" (*tongxingai bushi tongxinglian*), thus
ironically defending the (traditional) space of same-sex love by shunning
and otherizing the Western discourse of homosexuality (Sang, 1996:20).

In the 1960s and 1970s, Taiwanese PEPS managed to construct a visible public space, most notably the New Park and bars scene. Bai Xian-
yong (Kenneth Pai)'s historic novel *Nei Zi* (*Crystal Boys,* 1983) further
brought media exposure to New Park. As a convenient transport point,
New Park became the center attracting (male) PEPS of all walks of life,
and thus earned its title, Head Office. New Park was the most visible,
famous, and for many (male) PEPS the only public space where they could
suspend their "heterosexual masks" and make contact with other PEPS.
Zhong-Shan Park in Tai Chung, and Ai-Ho Park in Kao Hsiung, together
with newly established bars, pubs, discos, and theaters gradually became
well-known cruising areas for PEPS. New Park, the nearby Sin Nan-yang
Theater, and the Madrid Restaurant have been called by author Lin You-
Xian the cradle for PEPS in the 1970s (Wu, 1998:48).

The 1970s also witnessed the formation of consumerist space for male
PEPS. Ta-K is the owner of the first Taiwanese PEPS bar, Champaign,
which opened in 1970. By 1987, Ta-K had opened sixteen bars. These are
male bars—the first T(Tomboy)-bar opened as late as 1987. Yet they are
not gay bars in the Western sense, because they are not exclusively for
PEPS, and even the PEPS customers may not identify with any particular
sexual identity. The PEPS coined the term *bo-li zhai/quan* (glass boy/
circle) for themselves. The term *bo-li* is used to symbolize the fragility of

the male anus, paraphrasing the English term "gay bowl" in which the anus is described as "the opening of a bottle." The term was first used in the 1960s by triad gangsters referring to the bottom or the anus. It was then used to refer to *tongxinglian*. The symbol of *bo-li* as anal sex is also a sexist representation that defines homosexuality merely as male homosexuality.

The local venues Ye Ren (Wild Person) Coffee Shop and Ming Xing (Celebrity) Coffee Shop have also been crucial for PEPS to make contact under the cover of celebrities and Western customers. It is a relatively safe place for PEPS to establish a social network crucial for a healthy self-identity. Literature has also been important in constructing *tongxinglian* consciousness and community. Bai Xian-yong wrote short novels including *Lonely Seventeen* (1961) and *Shining Stars* (1969), both depicting the male clientele of the New Park, although neither these characters nor Bai address same-sex eroticism as a generic sexual identity. And when *Crystal Boys* was published in 1983, several major literature critics insisted that it was not a homosexual novel (Cai Yuan-huang) but about juvenile delinquents (Long Ying-tai). Cai Yuan-huang even said that it was embarrassing to read the novel, and he used Freudian theories of strong mothers and weak fathers to explain the cause of homosexuality (Wu, 1998:89).

With the popularization of the categories gay, homosexual, lesbian, tomboy, and the visibility of this social group, the media began to ask the public to be concerned about "these popular phenomena" on the grounds that innocent youth will be corrupted by it. Newspaper headlines said, "members of the *quan* (circle) in the New Park draw outsiders into the *quan*." The fact that the media began to use the category *quan* demonstrates the visibility of PEPS subculture activities. Yet the media exposure of PEPS was marked by vulgarization, criminalization, and medicalization. During this time Taiwanese academics and professionals absorbed the Western discourse of sexuality through newly available translations of Havelock Ellis's and Freud's work. Taiwanese medical doctors and psychologists began to study the cause and prevention of *tongxinglian*. This also explains why when the Chinese term *tongxinglian* was used in the 1960s and 1970s, it usually followed the word *huan shang* (infected) or *gao/nao* (play/fuss around with), implying that *tongxinglian* is a medical and immoral category.

As homosexuality was seen as a mental disorder, it was usually doctors who commented on it. In 1975, the Department Head of Urology at Taiwan University, Ging Wan-xuan, stated: "Homosexuality is an abnormal phenomena that is rarely found in Taiwan. It will not increase in the future as Chinese people cannot accept it" (Wu, 1998:41). In 1980, Wen Jung-kwang and Chen Chu-cheng published an authoritative medical report on *tongxinglian*. The report explained in detail a case in which a "homosexual patient" had 104 encounters with his doctors and finally was "cured" and "converted" to heterosexuality. Gender role confusion was highlighted as the key factor "causing" homosexuality, thus implying the need for rigid gender role education in schooling and parental guidance. The report was then published by Taiwan's Central News Agency and was extensively reported in newspapers with headlines such as "Taiwan University Found the Cause of Homosexuality," and "Abnormal Family Causes Homosexual Child." Wen was the most influential scholar in the 1970s and 1980s, with his successful cure of a homosexual popularly quoted. In 1982, a social work lecturer, Peng Huai-zhen, described homosexuals as having "smaller hands, less hairy, thicker lips, big eyes, artistic hair style, habitual body swinging and more substantial facial expression" (Wu, 1998:43). In 1983, Peng published the first scholarly book on *tongxinglian,* called *Tongxing-lian, Zisha, Jingshenbing* (Homosexuality, Suicide, Mental Illness). In the preface, Peng stressed the therapeutic value of social science and medical objectivity: "It is only with the help of social science and medical knowledge that we can prevent and cure homosexuality." While Peng's book quoted Wen as proof that homosexuals could be cured, both Peng and Wen relied on the analysis of Havelock Ellis for the cause and cure of homosexuality.

Because of the pervasive medicalization of homosexuality, many PEPS themselves have few alternative constructs of self-understanding but have adopted and even internalized heterosexist frameworks to construct their own same-sex experiences. In the famous novel *A Person Who Shuns Marriage*, Guang Tai (1995) writes in the postscript that *tongxinglian* is caused by abnormal family relationships, especially a domineering mother. Guang Tai, the first openly gay person in Taiwan, who came out in 1975, cites the Freudian Oedipus complex and the notion of a fierce mother as the real cause of homosexuality:

> Why is there such a "wrong sexual orientation" as homosexuality? . . . I realized that it is completely family factors that contribute to this abnormal development of personality, especially when the mother plays the wrong role. (pp. 266-267)

In the novel, the male protagonist, Andi, also perceives homosexuals as people who are "confuse[d] about their gender roles" (p. 199), and thus he insists that he is only attracted to straight men who for him are the real men—"I still think that a man who does not like women is very strange, so I will not fall in love with them, I would rather fall in love with straights"

(Tan, 1989:43). He sees a "real" gay man, including himself, as a woman trapped in a man's body who psychologically and sexually desires heterosexual men. In his second novel, *Meng Huan Kuai Che* (Dreamland Express), Guang Tai even said that a heterosexual man is not heterosexual enough unless he has sex with a woman. The male protagonist was turned off to the straight man he fancied when he found out that the straight man had no sexual experience with women. This is a highly behaviorist and heterosexist definition of what constitutes a man.

In media representations, the notion of *ren-yao* was commonly used with pseudoscientific discourses tracing explanations such as broken families and abnormal childhood as "causes" of *ren-yao*. A newspaper report on August 14, 1971, in *Da Zhong Bao* (Public Daily Post) said:

> Every evening around the Museum area, there are *ren-yao* wearing abnormal clothing for their gender . . . most *ren-yao* were teenagers who escaped from home, . . . were seduced by this kind of people [read *tongxinglian*] and gradually [*tongxinglian*] acquired their bad habits. (Zhong-fong, 1971:8)

After the first case in Taiwan, in 1985, AIDS became a label attached to homosexuality. In 1985, the Health Department discussed the possibility of sending government officers into the *tongxinglian* community to investigate the situation of AIDS and safe-sex practices. The proposal was turned down because "it may cause the [officer] obsessive indulgence and unable to free himself [from homosexuality]" (Li-fong, 1985:10).

With the rapid development of PEPS subculture, the media had great interest in sensational reportage of this "weird sexual circle." In 1983, Taiwan police broke into the Jin Kongque hotel and caught an organized syndicate of male prostitutes. Eight men who dressed up as women to serve male customers were caught, yet the fifty male customers were released. This event helped to popularize the term *Niu Lang* (cowboy), which originated from the Oscar-winning movie *Midnight Cowboy* (1969), which was banned in Taiwan until 1989. In the coverage of this event, the media repeatedly used the term *ren-yao*, showing a serious misunderstanding of homosexuality as gender perversity. Thus, the male customers were set free, whereas those who "betrayed" their "original gender roles" were caught.

The extensive vulgarization of *tongxinglian* ironically helped PEPS to identify themselves with the necessary categories to organize their identity and everyday life around the experiences of same-sex eroticism. It is a kind of "reverse discourse" talked about by Foucault (1978) in which heterosexist media coverage helped PEPS to discover their own identities and their anger toward institutionalized oppression.

Despite the oppressive social situation in the 1960s and 1970s, PEPS do explore different devices to negotiate the space for same-sex love. Tan Chong-kee, in his thesis on contemporary Taiwanese homosexual fiction, argues that Bai Xian-yong establishes an "alternative family" for the outcast boys in *Crystal Boys*. The novel begins by depicting the severe pressure on male PEPS such as Li Qing, who is expelled from school because of the exposure of a same-sex relationship with a chemistry student. This is a serious blow to his father, a military officer who always dreamed of Li Qing following the same path. Li Qing is then disowned by his father. Desperate and sorrowful, Li Qing enters the secret kingdom of New Park in Taipei. The loss and pursuit of the father figure is a crucial theme of the novel, indicating the crisis of the traditional patriarchal father-son relationship in postwar Taiwan. Although the novel does not use any generic term such as homosexual, *tongxinglian,* or *gay* to describe the actors of same-sex eroticism, and the only term used as a noun is *bo-li quan* (glass circle), the PEPS seem to have a clear sense of having a social network based on same-sex eroticism. *Tongxinglian* is seen not only as a behavior, but a basis on which social community and alternative family can be established. In an often-cited passage at the beginning of *Crystal Boys*, Bai (1983) writes,

> In our Kingdom, there is no day-time but only dark night. When the sky turns bright, our Kingdom has to hide because it is an illegitimate Nation: we have no government, not being recognized or valued, we are just a group of disorganized citizens. (p. 3)

It is crucial that Bai constructs the "imagined community" of the Kingdom/Nation. Bai also describes in detail the "alternative family," which is marked not only by erotic attachment, but hierarchical older-younger male relationships blended with different forms of prostitution. Despite the apparently unequal power relations, this hierarchy serves as the survival system for young boys who are rejected by their family-kin network and thus have little socioeconomic capacity for independence.

The alternative family of homosexuality attains its own identity not by denying but by appropriating the mainstream cultural values of filial piety, *qing, yi,* and brotherhood. For example, Coach, the "master" in the alternative family, is described in a loving relationship with another character called Ah Xiong. Coach is different from a pimp: his relationship with his boys are marked with mutual respect, responsibility, and care. Coach helps his boys to establish stable and promising livelihoods by finding conventional work or a caring "daddy." The boys call Coach master *(shi-fu)* and he calls them apprentices *(tu-di).*

The traditional Chinese martial art family practices are also cited to illustrate the cultural resonance of this alternative family. If an apprentice wants to join a martial arts family, he has to leave home, travel a long distance, and live with his master. He has to respect his master and also his seniors as older siblings. This martial arts family, like the same-sex alternative family, is a subset and a continuation, rather than denial, of the existing family-kin structure and values. Bai Xian-yong uses kin-family categories to construct an alternative family structure not based on kinship bloodlines, therefore expanding and subverting the (heterosexist) conception of a family.

On a Chinese New Year's Eve, which traditionally has been the most crucial day for family union, Li Qing and other boys come to visit Coach and send presents to him although they no longer live as prostitutes. In another case, Coach helps his boy, Wu Min, to move in with the patron Mr. Zhang. When Wu later attempts suicide after he is thrown out by Mr. Zhang, it is Coach who helps, paying the hospital bills and asking the siblings to donate blood. Wu's *qing* toward Mr. Zhang is so genuine and intense that when Mr. Zhang is seriously ill, Wu plays the role of a filial son and takes care of both his own father and Mr. Zhang. It is also interesting to note that Wu's father, being working class and dependent on him, has little problem with Wu's homosexuality (Tan, 1998:Ch. 2).

In another example of loyalty and alternative family structure, Tan Chong-kee quotes Chen Ruo-xi's *Zhi Hun* (Paper Marriage, 1986). In this story, the protagonist, Ping Ping, is caught working while using a student visa, and faces deportation from the United States. In order to stay, she marries a Caucasian gay friend (Shawn). They live together and support each other as close friends. Although Ping Ping rejects homosexuality as moral corruption and sexual promiscuity, she accepts Shawn as her close friend. When Shawn is diagnosed with HIV, Ping Ping does not reject him but rather cancels the divorce to take care of him. It is the cultural attribute of *yi* (loyalty and righteousness) and *qing* that help Ping Ping to go beyond her prejudice against homosexuality. She says, "When I was alone and helpless, he held out a helping hand. Now that he is sick, abandoned by his father, afraid to tell his mother, shun[ned] by his neighbors while his friends dwindle, I cannot leave him, or I will never forgive myself for the rest of my life" (Tan, 1998:218).

Ping Ping and Shawn once attend a Catholic service in which the priest gives a sermon condemning Sodom's homosexuality. Ping Ping does not agree with the Christian fundamentalism but compares it to the stubborn dogmatism of the Cultural Revolution. She resorts to the Eastern religion of Buddhism to forestall Christian homophobic violence. She writes in her diary, "The Buddha is all compassionate and does not keep count of the past, Buddha only asks you to put down your sword now and you become a Buddha on the spot. This spirit of forgiveness is closer to my ideal" (p. 277). Chen Ruo-xi suggests an indigenous strategy of overcoming mainstream prejudice—since there is rarely religious fundamentalism or homophobic violence in Taiwan, it seems counterproductive to resort to confrontational politics to combat bigotry. Instead, many Chinese tackle homosexuality by containing and dissolving it within the family-kin system. The cultural elements of compassion, *qing,* and *yi* can be mobilized to establish a harmonious social relationship that goes beyond sexual orientations (Tan, 1998:Ch. 2).

FEMINISM AND THE FORMATION
OF THE TONGZHI MOVEMENT

It was the lifting of martial law in 1987 that helped Taiwan step into a new historic era of political liberalization in which different marginalized and forbidden voices could speak out extensively and collectively in the public arena. The women's movement is particularly important in the emergence of Taiwan's *tongzhi* movement. Four decades of patriarchal and authoritarian rule of the Guomindang resulted not only in an all-male political scene, but included the arrest, imprisonment, and murder of thousands of political opponents, predominantly male, leaving wives and families in misery. Before the lifting of martial law, dozens of women had already become leading political activists, fighting not only for the release of their husbands but for the democratization of society. As the issue of gender inequality has been politicized and prioritized in the public discourse since the late 1980s, it has been an obvious way to bring up the issue of women's sexuality and compulsory heterosexuality. It is worth noting that shortly after 1987, most universities in Taiwan set up *Nü Yan-She* (Women's Studies Societies) in which students form discussion and action groups concerning sexuality and gender politics.

From the beginning, Taiwan's *tongzhi* movement has been closely tied to the women's movement. The *tongzhi* movement was begun by a *nü tongzhi* organization—*Women Zhijian* (Between Us, WZJ), formed on February 23, 1990. WZJ defines its own aspiration as to "light a lamp for closeted lesbians who think they are alone and without help. We will let them HEAR us (through answering their phone calls by volunteers working on shifts), let them SEE us (through our publications, our showing up on the media, and the writing of newspaper columns), and let them FIND us (through the conducting of consciousness-raising forums and friend-making activities)."[2] The positive media coverage of WZJ in *Xin Wen-hua* (New Culture) and *Awakening*[3] (a feminist journal) in 1990 had a striking social impact and immediately attracted hundreds of *nü tongzhi* who otherwise had no public channel to make contact with other *nü tongzhi*. From 1990 to 1998, 3,000 *nü tongzhi* joined WZJ. In 1994, WZJ published the first *nü tongzhi* biweekly journal, *Girlfriends,* with a circulation of 2,000 copies per issue, aiming at establishing social networks and a strong collective identity and culture.

In 1992 the *Taiwan TV World News Report* sent a woman reporter undercover to a T-bar and secretly filmed the activities of *nü tongzhi,* adding derogatory captions and subtitles when the program was broadcast. WZJ immediately criticized the voyeurism of the news agency. *Awakening* published an editorial, "Please Respect *Nü Tongzhi,*" and a famous cultural critic collected more than thirty signatures from celebrities condemning the news agency. It was the first time that the feminist movement and cultural professionals made public statements for the *tongzhi* community. The event was one of the first victories of the *tongzhi* movement, as even a senior government official in the News Department criticized the reporter's action as voyeuristic and unprofessional.

The alliance between *tongzhi* and feminism is not without tension. The women's movement, despite its impressive efforts and contributions, has rarely tackled the issue of *nü tongzhi* politics—the subject of the feminist movement is supposed to be heterosexual. Yuxuan Aji (1995b), a founding member of WZJ, laments that

> even the most radical feminist organization [read *Awakening*] does not challenge the existing family system, but merely pursues equality between the sexes within the heterosexual classification system. In the recent example of changing marriage law no. 1052, which lists "adultery and gross indecency with the same sex" as legitimate reasons for divorce, perhaps homosexuals should be happy that Taiwan law finally acknowledges the existence of homosexuals, but only as a penalty. . . . Progressive feminist organizations only stand for the position of heterosexual women, to embrace heterosexism and to dismiss the human rights of homosexuals. (pp. 16-17)

It was only in July 1995 that *Awakening* printed its first feature on the relationship between feminism and lesbianism, mostly as a response to *nü tongzhi* criticism. The feature sparked hot debates in the following five issues of *Awakening,* which are the most systematic and comprehensive dialogues in Taiwan's history concerning the relationship between feminism and *nü tongzhi* activism. Some heterosexual feminists think that (1) they should pretend to be *nü tongzhi* so as to share the oppressive experiences of *nü tongzhi*; (2) they should also come out to share their deviant sexual fantasies and experiences; (3) the distinction between homosexuality and heterosexuality is itself a patriarchal construct to stratify women; and (4) feminism needs lesbianism. On the other hand, some *nü tongzhi* argue that (1) *nü tongzhi* and heterosexual feminists are located in different power positions; (2) heterosexual feminists should be much more sensitive to their heterosexual privileges when they join the *tongzhi* movement; (3) feminists should try to eliminate the homophobia and heterosexism within the feminist camp; and (4) separatism is still needed to respect the subjectivity of *nü tongzhi*. In August 1995, a feminist who is intensely involved in the *tongzhi* movement wrote:

> So long as the closeted situation of *tongzhi* does not change, the issue of heterosexual "spokespersons" and "appropriation" cannot be resolved. It's like the "progressive male" in the women's movement: the question is not whether progressive men are qualified to be the core subject or spokesperson of the women's movement, but how can we actually change the power relations . . . the article (by a heterosexual feminist) seems to forget that lesbianism can be a kind of feminism, and feminism can be one kind of lesbianism. . . . Rather than seeing others . . . feminists should see and pursue the possibility of greater liberation of gender within their camp. (Gu, 1995:10-11)

Hu Shu-wen, also a feminist involved in the *tongzhi* movement, refers to an *Awakening* forum attended by several famous feminists:

> That forum almost became a gate for coming out. As these heterosexual feminists curiously ask: are there really a lot of *nü tongzhi* within the women's movement? Has *nü tongzhi* subjectivity been formed? But how can we answer these questions? When will these heterosexual feminists understand—do we need to come out ourselves and for others to say discretely that "I am," "she is," "they are" . . . For these heterosexual feminists, there may be an unbridgeable gap between homosexuality and heterosexuality. . . . When we actively ponder and get involved in the *tongzhi* movement, we have already come out. But you [heterosexual feminists] keep on worrying that it is merely a hollow movement without a subject. The subject has already faced you, yet you refuse to see it. (Hu, 1995:14)

While many *nü tongzhi* have been grateful for being "fed" and "hidden" by the women's movement, it has a qualifier—that these *nü tongzhi* remain invisible. In a touching article written by *nü tongzhi* and feminist Yuxuan Aji, she shares her pain for being unable to come out to her feminist sisters because of the overwhelming heterosexism and homophobia within the women's movement itself:

> With these sisters in *Awakening* I struggled and grew . . . only because I chose to be a lesbian, I have to quietly disappear, change my name and be reborn. Isn't it absurd? The notion of woman-loving woman, woman-identifying woman is celebrated (in the women's movement), but when I really love a woman, I have to disappear instead of becoming a heroine. When I turn from a progressive heterosexual woman into someone who identifies and practices homosexuality, complete vulgarization becomes my inescapable fate. Feminism and Western queer theories can only help me avoid drowning, but I must find my way out with other *tongzhi*. (Yuxuan, 1995a:16-18)

While feminist discourses have provided a powerful cover and cushion for *tongzhi* voices, it is also crucial not to deny the tension between these two camps. Gender and sexuality are not the same issue. Indeed, the entire controversy was also stirred up by the *tongzhi* critique of the feminist proposal of a new marriage law. For example, *Awakening* argues for a woman's right to divorce if her husband is a homosexual. But because same-sex marriage is not recognized at all, the feminist proposal would only kill the space for *tongzhi* resorting to heterosexual marriage to resolve social and parental pressure. Some women's groups responded quickly to incorporate same-sex marriage and other *tongzhi* rights into their agenda. On March 8, 1995, several women's and *tongzhi* groups launched a parade for the "Revisions of the Civil Ordinance on Marriage Law," advocating the right to marry the same sex. The right to adultery has also been discussed because the entire discourse of marriage and divorce has been predicated upon the monogamous marital institution, in which relationships must be one-to-one. In June 1995, several *tongzhi* groups formed the *Tongzhi* Human Rights Group to fight for same-sex marriage.

On March 8, 1996, *Tongzhi* Front for Space Rights, an alliance of twenty-five *tongzhi* organizations joined the women's parade Women 100 Action. Apart from the feminist agenda for women's rights, *Tongzhi* Front also proposed a ten-point political platform:

1. Welfare policy should not be based only on the heterosexual family—celibates, homosexuals, and nonheterosexual monogamous families should enjoy equal rights
2. The *Tongzhi* right to marry should be recognized

3. A *Tongzhi* couple's rights for insurance, inheritance of the partner's property, and other heterosexual privileges should be protected
4. A foreign same-sex partner should be allowed to stay in Taiwan
5. *Tongzhi* should have the right to adopt
6. The present sex education material, especially the homophobic and heterosexist elements, should be eliminated
7. The formal curriculum in primary and secondary school should change the heterosexist definition of family
8. A *tongzhi* resource center should be established
9. When the sexual identity of a *tongzhi* is exposed, the right to work should be protected
10. A nondiscriminatory health and medical policy should be instituted

In December 1996, a large parade was organized by women's groups and joined by *tongzhi* on the issue of the right to walk at night. The issue was raised because of the murder of Peng Ruan-ru, the supervisor of Women Division in the Democratic Progressive Party. At the parade, *tongzhi* were also fighting for the right to walk at night—free from police raids and harassment. An Internet Web site, "Women's Net," was immediately set up to arouse social concern for discrimination against women. Within three weeks, Women's Net collected 20,000 signatures, indicating an efficient and cost-saving way of social mobilization.

While WZJ symbolizes the birth of Taiwan's *tongzhi* movement, it is university activism that has brought the movement to an unprecedented strength. In a society that highly values intellectual scholarship, it is significant that the first campus *tongzhi* organization is at the most prestigious university in Taiwan—Gay Chat at the National Taiwan University. Gay Chat was founded in March 1993, as *Nan Tongxinglian Wenti Yanjiushe* (Study Group for the Problem of Male Homosexuality). Although the university authority was hesitant, it found no reason to cancel the group as it is only a "study group" that does not publicly confirm the sexual identity of its members. It is also crucial that the founding chair is a straight woman who is an activist in Taiwan's *tongzhi* movement. In 1995, Gay Chat published a magazine, *Tongyan Wuji* (*Tong* Words Without Taboo) and in 1994, the book *Tongxinglian Banglian* (Homosexual Federal-State), which soon become a bestseller.

Soon after the birth of Gay Chat, *tongzhi* students in other universities felt encouraged to organize groups of their own. While these campus groups are mostly for socializing and networking, some target a more political level of combating homophobia and heterosexism. For example, Sting (Study Team of Identity and Gender) at the Central University was established in December 1993. In November 1995, Sting organized the

Tongzhi Arts Festival, using the medium of cultural and artistic festivals to explore gender and sexuality issues, so that all people, *tongzhi* or otherwise, can participate. The format of a cultural carnival also helps tackle the difficulties of coming out in the family-oriented Taiwanese culture. In April 1994, Sting set up the "Members of the Same-Sex" Internet Web site, which sparked a crucial trend of *tongzhi* using electronic media, especially e-mail and Web sites, to form alliances, discuss sexuality and gender issues, and to create a safe environment where *tongzhi* get to know each other. By 1998, there were at least sixty Chinese Internet BBS (Bulletin Board System) in Taiwan. Cyberspace has become a crucial force and platform for socializing, networking, pornographic pleasure, political alliance, and intellectual dialogue. In a society in which personal exposure of *tongzhi* identity could be disastrous, the high level of anonymity on the Internet becomes a tactful strategy for *tongzhi* to manipulate high-tech devices to organize activism and promote critical discourse.

In November 1995, the *Kuer Wenhua Yanjiushe* (Queer Culture Study Society) at Central University was formed, trying to contextualize queer politics into the campus. The chairperson writes in the second issue of its newsletter, *Ren Tong* (Identification): "As the categories of homosexual, heterosexual and bisexual are inadequate to capture the complexities and diversities of human eroticism, *Kuer* provides a rational way to understand sexuality and to counteract heterosexism. *Kuer* respects the choice of heterosexuality, but also argues for the rights of all nonheterosexual erotic practices." The newsletter also discusses *jia-ren* love (usually labeled incest) and intergenerational love (usually called pederasty). In November 1995, Gay Chat and Lambda, together with around ten university *tongzhi* groups, organized the *Tongzhi* Arts Festival, again using the fun fair format of organizing book and movie shows, games, arts exhibitions, theater performances, drag shows, and seminars. It helped not only to break down the elitism of the *tongzhi* activism of National Taiwan University, but also to organize cross-province activism to strike for a national event to maximize the *tongzhi* alliance and its social impact.

The lesbian and bisexual women's group *Taida Lambda* (Society for Studying Female Homosexual Culture) was set up in November 1994 and officially registered in February 1995 at National Taiwan University. The birth of *Lambda* was a watershed in the relationship between *nü tongzhi* and feminist groups on campus, because before 1994 *nü tongzhi* students would usually "parasite" upon the *Nü yan-she* (a women's study group on campus), and it caused some anxiety among the heterosexual members and debates concerning the priority of *Nü yan-she*. *Lambda* symbolizes the difference in focus between *nü tongzhi* and feminist campus groups. In

August 1995, *Lambda* published *Women Shi Nü Tongxinglian* (We Are Lesbians), a collective work by a group of *nü tongzhi*. This first Chinese book on *nü tongzhi* became a classic reference, which has sold 6,000 copies.

The establishment of WZJ and *Lambda* indicate a crucial gender specificity in terms of *tongzhi* empowerment. As women's sexuality has always been marginalized and trivialized, and the public space is constructed as a male territory, the domesticity of women has made "women's public space" a contradictory term. Therefore, publications become an effective way to mobilize *nü tongzhi*. Gian Jia-xin, whose master's thesis is on Taiwanese *nü tongzhi* discourses, called it "publication networking," in which *nü tongzhi* come out and connect to others not through traditional public space but by the Internet, writing, publishing, or simply buying and circulating the magazine. "Publication networking" is a highly privatized public space in which *nü tongzhi* connect with one another in a safe and comfortable way. Gian Jia-xin (1996) argues that publication networking is an active form of "collective coming out" which fits the situation of Taiwanese *nü tongzhi*:

> Taiwan's *tongzhi* community handles the issue of coming out rather differently from the Western mode of coming out personally. Since the 1950s, the Western lesbigay movement has used coming out personally as the most crucial strategy. In the 1990s, what Taiwan's *tongzhi* movement relies on is not the sacrifices individual *tongzhi* make for the movement but a strategy that really protects the security of individual *tongzhi*. It is what publication networking has attained. . . . It also demonstrates a new ethics of movement, a new politics of anonymity: the concept of citizenship in contemporary democratic politics is based on the notion of an identity, a name that can be publicized, and anonymity is usually manipulated for nasty blackmail. Yet, the *nü tongzhi* publication networking and the politics of non-coming out reorientate the political implications of anonymity—it stops the individual from accumulating personal assets through the movement, and thus minimizes interpersonal and group conflicts, and returns personal assets to the movement itself. (pp. 49-50)

Taiwan's *tongzhi* movement has been marked by a vocal feminist discourse, intellectual theorization, and university activism in which feminism, gender theories, and queer politics are the constitutive elements. Although the bar scene, saunas, and the New Park have been flourishing, the popularity of Western feminist and queer discourses have also lured radical heterosexual academics to engage positively in *tongzhi* discourse.

On April 28, 1996, Professor Zhang Xiao-hong of National Taiwan University organized a conference called *Yuwang Xinditu* (Queer Desire: Gender and Sexuality), inviting dozens of academics and *tongzhi* activists to participate. By June 29-30, 1996, the much larger International Conference on Sexology Education, Sexology, Gender Studies, and Lesbigay Studies, with 300 academic and activist attendants, was organized by Josephine Ho, a dedicated feminist also keen on *tongzhi* issues (Ho, 1997a, b). The conference continued in 1997 and 1998 and has become the biggest academic event on issues of sexuality, with around twenty academic articles published in the annual proceedings of the conference.

Yet the rapid growth of *tongzhi* activism on campus is not entirely a rosy picture of victory over homophobia. Instead, homophobic backlash has been provoked by the extensive achievements of *tongzhi* activism. In December 1995, the Blackmail Incident occurred at National Taiwan University, in which two male students who ran for the Student Union exposed *tongzhi* candidates' names and identities. These two students declared themselves heterosexual, and then demanded that the *tongzhi* students come out. They printed 3,000 posters to publicize the names of the twelve *tongzhi* candidates with the English word lesbian or gay after each name. The event blatantly exposed the unequal power relations between *tongzhi* and the hypocritical heterosexual world.

Another incident of backlash against *tongzhi* happened in 1995 when a professor at National Taiwan University, who later became the head of the Health Bureau of Taipei, did a research questionnaire on behalf of the Health Department on the issue of AIDS. However, it was a homophobic and prejudicial questionnaire that labeled *tongzhi* a high-risk group and treated *tongzhi* as sex addicts. Although there was only a 2.61 percent response rate, this professor is still preparing to publish the research. *Tongzhi Gongzuofang* (Workshop), a political activist group formed in November 1993, together with women's groups and five *tongzhi* groups, launched a demonstration with about eighty participants. It became the famous Guinea Pig Incident, as *tongzhi* feel that they become experimental guinea pigs exploited by academics for their own self-interest. It was the first time *tongzhi* took to the streets to protest against homophobia and discrimination.

RESISTANCE THROUGH CULTURAL CARNIVALS

Taiwan's *tongzhi* movement is also a movement of the media. In a highly literate and rather intellectual city where printed media have a high level of readership, Taipei *tongzhi* have been rather successful in manipulating the media to generate their own discourses. The first positive representation of homosexuality in the mainstream media was a 1984 feature in *Zhang Lao-shi Magazine,* a popular mainstream magazine, which stated that: "In our research, it is found that rarely are the homosexual couple playing the role of total masculine and feminine. Most of them advocate a more equal relations of sharing rights and responsibility" (quoted in Wu, 1998:72). In 1986, the first Taiwanese film focusing on homosexuality, *Nie Zi* (*Crystal Boys,* or *The Outsiders*), which was based on a novel with the same title, was shown on screen.

Four decades of martial law and political control have created a crying social demand among Taiwanese intellectuals for Western radical social thought. In the printed media in particular, serious publications concerning neo-Marxism, deconstructionism, postcolonialism, and feminist and queer theories became trendy commodities and sometimes even best sellers. It is trendiness and marketability, plus political correctness, that have repeatedly helped *tongzhi* win prestigious literature awards. For example, in October 1990, *A Songbird That Lost Its Voice* won first prize, one million Taiwan dollars, in the Independent Post Fiction Award; in September 1991, *Tongnu Zhi Wu* (Dance of the Child Girl) won the Union Post Literature Award, and in 1994 the China Times One Million Award was given to Zhu Tian-wen's *Huangren Shouji* (Journal of the Loner). In 1996, *Ni Nü* (Rebellion Girl) won the Crown Press Award. It is a favorable commercial environment in which *tongzhi* issues successfully capture the attention of mainstream academia, cultural critics, and journalists. Qiu Miao-jin's (1969-1995) autobiographical lesbian work *Eyu Shouji* (The Crocodile Journal) (1994) is particularly important as an unprecedented self-exploration of a woman's own same-sex eroticism without using a pseudonym. Qiu committed suicide, but six months later *The Crocodile Journal* won the Prize of Recommendation of the China Times Literacy Awards in December 1995.

Within the printed media, *tongzhi* discourses have been highly articulate in both intellectual and mainstream media. On the intellectual side, the journal *Isle Margin* has made a crucial breakthrough in terms of exploring and popularizing queer discourses. *Isle Margin* was founded in 1991, a highly intellectual and subversive journal that incorporates Western radical theories such as deconstructionism, neo-Marxism, feminism, and queer politics into the indigenous Taiwanese context. In March 1994, *Isle Margin* (No. 10) published a seventy-five-page feature on queer politics. This first feature in the Taiwanese media was organized by three queer-identified young writers, with lots of nude, erotic, and subversive photos. Western queer politics became a strategic weapon for *tongzhi* to expand their own agenda and to critically engage with mainstream conservatism. The feature has a strong Western reference, as the first two long articles were translated novels from the original text of *Kiss of the Spider Woman* and Jean Genet's *Journal Du Voleur* (The Thief's Journal). As queer discourse is a language the mainstream culture is highly unfamiliar with, to counteract the *tongzhi* voice would require a serious reading of queer discourse, something conservatives are both unwilling and unable to engage. The feature also includes an article, "A Little Ku-er Encyclopedia" elucidating forty-eight mostly Western lesbigay terms such as fetishism, camp, queer, lesbian, dyke, feminist, straight, queer, sadomasochism, out, sex versus gender, butch, and femme. By spending much effort to explain these Western categories, the article tends to privilege and glamorize Western categories and culture as superior, avant-garde, and progressive.

It is also crucial that in the *Isle Margin* feature, queer is translated as *kuer*. It is a cultural reconstruction and indigenization rather than a copy or reiteration of the "original." As stated by Chi Ta-wei in *Kuer Qishilu* (Queer Archipelago, 1997) "*Kuer* does not equate with queer although it is translated from it. I am afraid that no Chinese term can accurately translate "queer" because queer derives from the specific U.S.-U.K. history of erotic practices" (p. 10). While *kuer* appropriates the insights of queer politics, especially in terms of the fluidities of identities and eroticism, it differs from "queer." Queer was a bigoted term appropriated by lesbigays in the cultural context of the AIDS epidemic and Reagan/Bush homophobic conservatism. On the contrary, in Taiwan *tongzhi* is a newborn baby facing primarily the issue of integrating sexual identity in the cultural context of a family-kin system that contains and discusses, rather than bashes, PEPS. Instead of choosing the derogatory term, Taiwanese *tongzhi* translated "queer" into a positive term, *kuer,* which literally means avant-garde, subversive, and cool, and is an identity mostly used by the small circle of young *tongzhi* academics in the universities. The outrageous and confrontational politics of queer simply do not have the equivalent cultural anger in Taiwan, Hong Kong, or mainland China to sustain in-your-face confrontation.

In October 1993, *Isle Margin* allied with the newly founded *Ai-Bao* (Love Paper, a *nü tongzhi* magazine) to edit and publish a feature, *Nüren guo/jia rentong* (Women's Nation, State/Family Identification), that interrogates the issue of women's sexuality, lesbianism, and nation/state discourses. *Ai-Bao,* which was established by a group of university *nü tongzhi* in 1993, seriously examines feminist and queer issues. It is also the first *tongzhi* magazine to be sold publicly. Given the social popularity and intellectual respectability of *Isle Margin,* these two queer features are crucial in positioning *tongzhi* issues as an intellectual, serious, and subversive force.

Eslite is an intellectual journal that was founded in December 1991. In August 1994, the *Eslite Book Review Journal* ran a fifty-four-page feature on homosexuality, consisting of fifteen serious articles, mostly on Western lesbigay issues. In the first article, "Running Out of the Closet," the author uses a lot of Western English terms such as dyke, fag, gay games, Stonewall riot, closet, gay power, and gay rights in otherwise Chinese text, thus tending to establish the superiority of Western lesbigay categories and experiences (Eastern Flower, 1994:18). The second article introduces the Stonewall Incident and ends by questioning the "backwardness" of Taiwanese law: Is homosexual marriage legal in Taiwan? Could homosexuals adopt children? Does insurance for government officials include homosexuals? Could homosexuals kiss in public? (Tan, 1994:21).

Eslite is also the most intellectual chain bookstore in Taiwan, with large collections of *tongzhi* books. It plays a crucial role in promoting sexuality and *tongzhi* issues as a very serious forum of study. In 1994, Eslite bookstores organized the "Woman-Woman Man-Man Cultural Festival," which included theater, films, book exhibitions, seminars, and public forums. In April 1996, Eslite organized a public drag performance on the street outside one of its bookshop, which attracted thousands of citizens.

Fem Bookstore, opened in 1994, is a feminist bookstore that contains rich *tongzhi* references and sells many low-budget *tongzhi* publications. It is a crucial site providing Western and local queer and feminist books, and also a venue for *tongzhi* gatherings and seminars. Fem Bookstore also publishes *tongzhi* books. Indeed, more than 100 *tongzhi* books have been published in Taiwan in the 1990s, many of them soft pornography. The first nonfiction Taiwanese book on *tongxinglian* was *Zhongguoren De Tongxinglian* (Chinese Homosexuality), published in 1990 (Zhuang, 1990). Although this book is still heterosexist in terms of discussing the causes of homosexuality, it contains substantial *tongzhi*-positive voices.

Among more mainstream publications, *G/L* is the first upmarket glossy Chinese *tongzhi* bimonthly magazine, which sells for NT$200 (US$8). It is very successful in terms of marketing strategy and sales. The first issue, in June 1996, sold 20,000 copies within three weeks, and the magazine began to earn money from its third issue. Since 1997, it has also published a male pornographic magazine, *G/L Passionate Love,* which is highly profitable. *G/L* is a name that is deliberately undefined, as it can stand for glory and liberty, gentlemen and ladies, gay and lesbian. While *G/L* has been criticized as too commercial, middle-class, male, and Americanized, the editor-in-chief, James Ang, stressed that pink dollars, together with political votes, are the best forms of coming out. James Ang argues that to commercialize *tongzhi* discourse is a big movement in itself. In the opening statement of the first issue, he professes, "the time is ripe for a lesbian and gay magazine that provide[s] tips on living, leisure and consumption" (Ang, 1996:8). The main feature in that issue is "The Culture of Gay and Lesbian Consumption," which begins with the statement: "Our age is hallmarked by the motto: business is guiltless, consumption is right" (p. 19).

It is obviously crucial in a capitalist society such as Taiwan that the *tongzhi* movement is sensitive to the issues of classism and consumerism. Yet classism and consumerism are exactly the issues that are rarely prioritized in Taiwanese *tongzhi* discourses, as if sexuality is always more primordial than class (for middle-class intellectuals?). Taiwan *tongzhi* activism is a rather intellectual and middle-class movement that rarely tackles the class privileges and social distinctions between rich and poor, urban and rural, and college intellectuals and working-class grassroots.

Despite its commercial orientation, *G/L* serves a multiplicity of purposes, for leisure, information, political rallying, identity formation, and, most important, the popularization and normalization of *tongzhi* representations in the mainstream culture. For example, in October 1997, *G/L* did a major feature on the police raid on Changde Street titled "Martial Law in Taipei After Ten Years of Lifting Martial Law." At midnight on July 30, 1997, around fifty men near New Park were arrested, interrogated, and brought to the police station. These *tongzhi* were simply out walking at night and committed no crime. Some were photographed by police and some families were notified by the police. *Tongzhi* groups reacted strongly by forming the *Tongzhi* Civil Action Alliance, which fights not only for *tongzhi* rights but the civil rights of every citizen to walk casually at night. Two weeks later, thirty-seven organizations signed an open letter to proclaim the right to walk at night. Nine radio programs reported this event, turning the police raid into a social and public discourse of citizenship. Given the popularity of the magazine, this feature in *G/L* played a crucial role by documenting the homophobic violence of police and also rallying social support for *tongzhi* rights.

Tongzhi columns in mainstream newspapers are another major channel through which *tongzhi* issues have been transformed from voyeurism of "sexual perversity" into a "decent" mainstream issue. Although the *tongzhi* columns in *Pots* biweekly and *Li Pao* have only limited circulation in Taiwan, the *Times Weekly Independent Morning Post* includes the first full-page *tongzhi* feature (*Tongzhi Park*) in a mainstream paper. More important, since June 1994 *China Times* has run a *tongzhi* column, *Kan-*

jian Tongxinglian (Seeing *Tongxinglian*), on the family page in which Lin Xian-xiu and others write about homosexuality in a very positive way.

These examples should not be taken naively as media's conversion to supporting the *tongzhi* movement. *China Times Daily,* which is one of the two biggest newspapers in Taiwan, has the *tongzhi* column *Kanjian Tongxinglian,* and its book-publishing division also produces *tongzhi* books such as *The Crocodile Journal.* However, the *China Times Weekly* always contains scandalous and voyeuristic stories and gossip on *tongzhi.* It is clear that the *China Times* conglomerate, like most other media enterprises, neither supports the *tongzhi* movement nor has any consistent ideological convictions on *tongzhi* issues. Instead, the primary concern is profit and public credibility. As far as *tongzhi* issues make money or serve as the newest academic chic and political correctness, *tongzhi* is a marketable commodity that can be glamorized or vulgarized at any time. Indeed, sensational tabloid magazines such as *Unique Reports (Dujia Baodao)* or *Times Weekly (Shidai Zhoukan)* have never changed their voyeuristic gaze on *tongzhi,* featuring particularly scandalous stories about crimes, suicide, or cruising spots.

The mainstreaming and normalizing effect of *tongzhi* discourse is also remarkable, with fifteen radio *tongzhi* programs throughout 1990s, including the *tongzhi* program *Taipei Tonghua* from the Taipei city radio station. In terms of film festivals, the first *tongzhi* film series was shown in the November 1992 Golden Horse Festival, when the term *tongzhi* was first imported by Hong Kong activist Edward Lam. More than twenty *tongzhi* films were shown in the 1992 festival.

Perhaps the best example to illustrate the strategy of cultural intervention in political *tongzhi* discourse is the New Park incident, in which *tongzhi* groups confronted the government not by political demonstrations or legal prosecution but with a cultural carnival. On December 25, 1995, the mayor of Taipei announced the Reconstruction Plan of Core District in Taipei City where the area including New Park will be rebuilt, which would imply the end of the cruising area in the New Park. Taiwanese *tongzhi* reacted strongly and twenty-five *tongzhi* groups immediately formed the Tongzhi Front for Space Rights (TF). TF argued for *tongzhi* rights to enjoy public space, and criticized the government's plan as disregarding the needs and interest of *tongzhi,* as if the public interest includes only heterosexuals. New Park has long been the major public survival space for many male PEPS. Yet, instead of using confrontational strategies, TF resorted to the cultural carnival of Rainbow Valentine Week in 1996.

Rainbow Valentine Week included two parts: first the Ten Dream Lovers Election, in which dozens of polling boxes were set up in *tongzhi* venues all over Taiwan for *tongzhi* to elect dreamy lovers. Since all the candidates were celebrities, the media found it marketable to interview and explore the views of the celebrities on homosexuality. With the help of the media, TF successfully turned this into a talk-of-the-town media event in which it was the celebrities rather than *tongzhi* who were confronted on their views and experiences of homoeroticism. What came out was not individual *tongzhi* but homoeroticism itself, as even the straight-identified celebrities can have positive *tongzhi* voices.

The second part of the event was the Rainbow Dressing, in which all Taiwanese *tongzhi* were invited to dress in rainbow colors from February 8 to 14: in red on the eighth, in orange on the ninth, in yellow on the tenth, in green on the eleventh, blue on the twelfth, purple on the thirteenth, and in rainbow colors on the fourteenth. Since thousands of citizens would accidentally wear red on the eighth, orange on the ninth, and so on, the event creates a social aura in which homoeroticism flows everywhere and flirts with everyone. Instead of a psychological essence monopolized by a stigmatized minority, homoeroticism is now constructed as a natural and seductive desire that everyone can explore. While this strategy of "queering the straight" will be further discussed in Chapter 8, Rainbow Valentine Week demonstrated different possibilities of resistance and empowerment:

1. From anger and political confrontation to a cultural carnival of exploring sexuality
2. From minoritizing politics of gay identity/rights to everybody's exploration of homophobia and homoeroticism
3. From antagonizing the mainstream to queering the mainstream
4. From stressing sexual difference to a balance between difference and sameness
5. From homo-hetero duality to inviting everyone to join a joyful gathering
6. From a rigid identity politics (Who is and who is not gay?) to a destabilization of homo-hetero duality (Why can't you be?)
7. From coming out as a sexual identity to coming out as homoeroticism itself
8. From homo and hetero as dichotomous to fluid eroticism in which homo and hetero intermingle in all aspects of social life

GLAD is another event that actively explores the nonconfrontational strategy of going beyond the homo-hetero duality. The annual GLAD (Gay and Lesbian Awakening Day) event first started on June 1, 1995, organized by Gay Chat, Lambda, and other university *tongzhi* groups. It is similar to a cultural carnival, including activities such as movies, a fun fair, seminars, an auction, a drag performance, and candlelight sharing. It manipulates popular rumors about the homoeroticism of the famous ancient scholar and politician Qu Yuan by selecting his memorial day, *Duanwu Jie* (Dragon Boat Festival), as the Chinese day celebrating same-sex love. Qu Yuan wrote several affectionate and tender poems to his emperor, comparing himself to beauties and fragrant plants. He finally drowned himself in the Miluo River more than 2,000 years ago. Although the mainstream textbooks have desexualized their relationship and insisted on a patriotic reading of Qu Yuan's act, his homoeroticism has been established by recent scholars (Wen, 1944:245-258). What is more important is the endeavor to indigenize Taiwanese *tongzhi* discourse by creating their own "cultural symbol" and pride day. June 1 is chosen because it is the Dragon Boat Festival and a public holiday to memorize Qu Yuan. While the celebration of the Stonewall Riots is also in June, Taiwanese *tongzhi* decided to select a Chinese person, also commemorated in June, to act as a local *tongzhi* pride day. Besides, the traditional food for this festival is a rice dumpling tied in a triangle shape, which can symbolize both S/M and the pink triangle. GLAD in 1995 was a big fun fair in which more than 1,000 people participated. In 1996, 1997, and 1998, GLAD continued to become a glamorous carnival on campus that is open to everyone.

GLAD is highly successful not only in terms of rallying *tongzhi* and social participation in the celebration of *tongzhi* visibility and power; more important, GLAD critically explores indigenous possibilities of *tongzhi* resistance. As was well stated by Chi Ta-wei, an organizer of the GLAD event and a key advocate of *kuer* politics in Taiwan, GLAD is a conscious negotiation and integration of two different approaches—human rights and cultural carnival eroticism:

> we have seriously pondered the Chinese and English name of this event. Should we add "human rights" or "festival" into the title? . . . we want both . . . we can strategically choose to come out as a community, rather than any single individual. (Chi, 1995:23, 27)

Chi also responds to the criticism that there is no subjectivity in GLAD, as people do not see individual homosexuals as such. Chi said, "it is a collective coming out. . . . It is homoeroticism that flows to everywhere to everyone, you can feel it and enjoy it if you are open enough" (p. 27).

GLAD and Rainbow Valentine Week have been seen by many *tongzhi* as the two most successful examples of media activism in the 1990s. Their success lies not only in rallying massive social support from both *tongzhi* and mainstream society, nor simply in the fact that after these two events the media have rarely produced bigoted representations to demonize *tongzhi*, but, more important, both events articulate an indigenous perspective of *tongzhi* resistance. As clearly stated by Gian Jia-xin (1997),

> Up till now (1996), the Taiwanese *tongzhi* movement does not opt for direct radical confrontation with heterosexism. Instead, it culminates positive representations of *tongzhi* culture, and fights for the rights of self-naming through the struggle against vulgarization and silencing. This mode of the movement is different from the Western lesbigay movements, which since the 1969 Stonewall Incident have been based on personal coming out, public demonstration, and political votes to fight for the rights of gay citizenship. (p. 4)

Interestingly, while the mainstream media have very positive representations of these two events, certain *tongzhi* opt for more confrontational strategies that criticize the events for being assimilative and compromising, without directly challenging the existing system. Ni Jia-zhen, for example, said:

> The subjectivity is blurred in these events, even heterosexuals can easily cross the border to participate in these performances, as if Taiwan society has demonstrated its cultural multiplicities and openness to let homosexuals to perform in fixed time and place. On another level, it is actually a denial of homosexuality. In terms of cumulation of power and consolidating identification, the ambiguity of subjectivity has blurred and weakened the focus of the battlefield. (Josephine Ho, 1997:145)

It is perhaps crucial that Ni Jia-zhen refuses to use the term *tongzhi* but insists on a more essentialist category, "homosexual." Ni seems to have reservations about heterosexuals joining the *tongzhi* movement to fight against heterosexism. The notion of a "border" creates a clear we-they dichotomy that "we homosexuals" cannot afford to lose. Ni also worries that in the cultural event of collective coming out, *tongzhi* subjectivity will be undermined by heterosexuals who become activists and even spokespersons in the movement. Yet it is exactly this kind of we-they dichotomy that GLAD and the Rainbow Valentine Week are eager to go beyond.

CONFRONTATIONAL POLITICS AND BEYOND

Taiwanese *tongzhi* discourses can be broadly divided into two different approaches—the cultural carnival and confrontational politics of rights.

While the former creates a relaxed environment in which everyone irrespective of sexual orientation can join the carnival to explore sexuality, the
latter is a more confrontational approach, using identity politics to fight for
tongzhi rights.

Taiwan in the 1990s witnessed the massive manipulation of confrontational politics both in parliamentary and street protests. Physical fighting
in the parliament is as frequent as the massive demonstrations on the
street. After forty years of autocratic martial law, human rights and freedom of speech have become the common consensus of all political parties,
including the government. Indeed, the government's endeavor to join the
United Nations has further pushed the government to exhibit concern for
human rights and democratic reforms. It is in the government's interest to
show a genuine concern for minority rights to differentiate itself from the
Beijing government, which is otherized as corrupt, backward, bigoted,
totalitarian, and authoritarian.

However, obvious cultural boundaries constrict the space of confrontational politics, which is predicated upon identity politics and coming-out
strategies. A *nü tongzhi* activist, Wang Xiao-shan, identifies the dilemma
clearly:

> The greatest problem for most Taiwanese *tongzhi* is neither state
> oppression, work discrimination, nor religious hostility, but parents.
> If we moved away from our home town and did not live with our
> parents, many of us could live a rather relaxed life, especially the
> younger ones, who have few problems accepting our own *tongzhi*
> identity. In other words, despite the apparent glamorous achievement
> of the Taiwanese *tongzhi* movement, most activists cannot be out in
> the national media. Before 1995, only Guang Tai, Qi Jia-wei, and
> Bai Xian-yong had come out in the national media. That is why
> people have developed the notion of collective coming out. (Person-
> al interview, June 25, 1998)

In this section, I will use the issue of same-sex marriage and a public
hearing on December 28, 1993, to illustrate the contributions and limitations of confrontational politics in the Taiwanese *tongzhi* context.

The issue of same-sex marriage was first raised by AIDS activist
Qi Jia-wei in 1986 when he applied for a same-sex marriage. Although his
effort stirred up social concern for "gay marriage," the absence of *tongzhi*
community support at that time minimized the social impact. The issue
was brought up again in 1995 when women's groups proposed changing
the marriage law. At that time, same-sex marriage was elevated from a
personal struggle to a *tongzhi* community struggle as symbolized by the

Tongzhi Human Rights Group. The issue of same-sex marriage was great-ly dramatized in 1996 by Xu You-sheng's marriage. Xu's fame, together with support of the *tongzhi* community, turned the marriage ceremony into a stunning social and international event covered by more than 120 report-ers and seven TV station crews, and broadcast on prime-time TV in Hong Kong and Taiwan.

Xu's marriage provoked intense controversy among the *tongzhi* and the mainstream community. While most *tongzhi* feel deeply empowered by the event, some also expressed their worry that it glamorized coming out by obscuring the fact that it is mostly middle-class, gay males under little parental pressure who could afford to come out. In Xu You-sheng's case, his parents had passed away, thus relieving the greatest problem oppress-ing most Chinese *tongzhi*. Indeed, the first AIDS patient to come out (Lin Jian-zhong, who is a *tongzhi*) is also a person whose parents had passed away (Lin, 1995), thus indicating the severe parental pressure Taiwanese *tongzhi* are facing. Further, Xu's partner is a Westerner, and they went to Taiwan only for the wedding, as they originally planned to return to New York. The fact that Xu works as a professional writer rather than as a nine-to-five office worker frees him from the homophobic discrimination most Taiwanese *tongzhi* would have to face if their identities were ex-posed.

In the video *Not Simply a Wedding Banquet—A Documentary About the First Gay Wedding in Taiwan* (1998), directors Mickey Chen and Mia Chen feature not only Xu You-sheng's marriage but also the opinions and experiences of many Taiwanese activists on the issue of coming out. The video critically exposes the cultural specificity of the strategy of coming out. Many *tongzhi* in the video blatantly express their reservations about coming out. At the end of the video, Mickey and Mia also quote a main-stream television survey stating that the percentage of those against gay marriage in the Taiwanese population increased by around 20 percent on the day after Xu's marriage in November 1996.

During the debate over same-sex marriage, many *tongzhi* activists re-sorted to the American experience of gay marriage as grounds for parallel legal changes in Taiwan. For example, an article concerning homosexual marriage in the book *We Are Lesbians* cites experiences in Denmark, Sweden, and the United States, and then concludes by saying that "as we [Taiwanese] want to be included as an advanced country, how can we omit the crucial historical moment [of same-sex marriage]?" (Jiang, 1995:195).

As argued by Taiwanese *tongzhi* writer Lin Xian-xiu (1997), who has been living in New York for many years:

Since the debate over same-sex marriage in the USA, Taiwanese *tongzhi* have wanted to bring a similar controversy to Taiwan. The recent marriage of Xu You-sheng became the focal point. However, both the supporters and opponents use the American experiences and arguments . . . and both parties fail to develop indigenous perspectives and therefore, are unable to really impress the Taiwanese audience . . . Taiwan is not the USA, having a different national and cultural situation. The American civil rights movement can only be a reference, and should not be seen as a standard formula to be copied. (pp. 66, 72)

Lin also talks about his first encounter with New York, which included the empowering experience of seeing gay people kissing on the street, yet he soon felt that Greenwich Village is only a "concentration camp of gay people," as the entire society outside the ghettoized gay area is very hostile to gay people. He said, "The homosexual district is merely Taiwan['s] New Park enlarged fiftyfold" (p. 39).

Indeed, in Xu You-sheng's autobiography *Dan Ai Wufang* (It's All Right to Love), he sets up a dichotomy between American gay life, which is portrayed as liberal and free, and his own pre-New York gay life in Taiwan, which he describes as miserable and oppressive. But his writing shows that his friends in secondary school, college, the army, at work, and his sister are actually quite supportive to him when his sexual identity is exposed (Tan, 1998). Xu also shares his experiences of visiting New York gay venues and regarding American gay icons as his own *tongzhi* ancestors, as if cultural differences, racial tensions, and linguistic barriers and class differences can all be suspended in front of "sexuality." Xu says, "this cosmopolitan city [New York] is called the heaven of immigrants, having varieties of people as many as stars . . . that's why it is called the capital of world homosexuals (Xu, 1997:96). Xu continues,

Every time I come here [to a Different Light Bookstore], I pause in front of the biography section to glance at my *tongzhi* ancestors. I really feel at home, as if grandpas, grandmas, uncles, and aunts are all there on the shelves. All these giants have been glorified by the textbooks, and behind them are something we have in common that is little known: homosexual orientations. . . . Every time I walk by, I feel I'm paying tantalizing homage to all my ancestors. (Xu, 1997:178)

In view of this quote, Tan Chong-kee (1998) comments:

> It matters little to Xu that the biographies consist almost entirely of white Western middle and upper class persons. This does not mean he is "colonized" although he is rather naive to think that they sufficiently represent his own ancestry, rather, it brings home the point that Western gay tradition and its contemporary manifestations in New York (gay residential enclave, gay bookstore, public display of affection, etc.) gave him more comfort and reassurance than anything else thus far. The only common point between these Westerners, and himself, is sexuality. It is little wonder that for him, sexuality eventually becomes the master category. (p. 34)

Tongzhi confrontational strategy has also been to be vocal in the political arena. In 1995, Zhuang Song-fu used his *tongzhi* identity as the platform to run for membership in the Parliament. Although he lost the election, it is the first time a *tongzhi* used the *tongzhi* banner, with a clear *tongzhi* platform such as the equal rights bill to rally support. In November 1995, before the election, seven organizations with eleven university groups formed the *Tongzhi* Observer, which watches over the election process and also advocates the motto "*Tongzhi* political voices exchange for *tongzhi* votes." It further proposes "Ten Rules for Good Legislators" to urge all legislative candidates to support the antidiscrimination policy. However, Zhuang's campaign and the *Tongzhi* Observer did not seem to arouse much social support. In particular, the major political parties refuse to put *tongzhi* issues on their political agendas.

On December 28, 1993, six *tongzhi* groups (WZJ, Speak Out, Asian Lesbian Network, Love Paper, *Tongzhi* Workshop, and Gay Chat) combined with a legislative counselor and an AIDS group to organize the Public Hearing Forum Enhancing Homosexual Human Rights. For the first time in Taiwan, the issue of homosexuality entered parliamentary institutions and the political arena in the language of human rights. They issued a public statement that:

> Antidiscriminatory law should be part and parcel of Taiwan's government effort to actualize the policy against all forms of social discrimination, to safeguard the rights of *tongzhi* and minority groups. We demand that the antidiscrimination law include the rights of homosexuals not to be harassed by police, the right to work and receive education. (Wang, 1993:16)

However, response from the government was very apathetic. In the public hearing forum, a supervisor of the Education Department said:

> I do not know the cause of homosexuality, but I think heterosexuality is normal. I want to remind you that if homosexuality is like taking drugs, is taking drugs a human right? I want to warn those who have indulged in these organizations—what kind of social cost are we going to pay? I don't want the development of your action to corrupt other people. (Josephine Ho, 1997a:130)

In this public hearing forum, both the format (public forum of consultation) and the content of the discussion (queer theories, the Kinsey report, human rights discourse, legal reform) have actively manipulated the American model of lesbigay liberation through the legal discourse of rights. As noted by Tan Chong-kee (1997:8), since Taiwan's government does not have a strong Christian homophobic background like the American conservatives, and sometimes even adopts the language of equality and human rights on the *tongzhi* issue, one needs to ponder whether direct confrontation and outrageous presentation are the best means to attain liberation.

Chu Wei-cheng (1997b) queries the entire identity politics of coming out, which may confine the *tongzhi* platform to the ghetto of the politics of we-they antagonism:

> Many people do not want to come out as *tongzhi* . . . as sexual orientation is only one facet of our whole being, its importance may not be more primal than her/his class, ethnicity, race, political and religious belief. And identity politics always implies a we-they dichotomy. . . . "When we come out, we should confirm and fight for everyone's right to love people of the same sex." This perspective broadens the *tongzhi* movement, from fighting merely for *tongzhi*'s minority rights to proclaiming everyone's erotic rights and freedom (to explore different erotic practices). Isn't this kind of social alliance capable for broader support and impact? (p. 11)

On the level of personal politics, Zhou Qian-yi (1997) said in the feminist magazine *Stir:*

> The present stage of Taiwan's *tongzhi* movement is based on the politics of identification. The subjectivity of the movement is legitimized by the fixity of one's sexual identity, which is defined by the gender of one's experiences of erotic object choice. Those who have same-sex partners would be seen as having a legitimate *tongzhi* identity and become the legitimate protagonists of the movement; but for those who had heterosexual partners, who now have a hetero-

sexual partner, will have heterosexual partners, and those who have no sexual experiences, their alliance with the *tongzhi* movement and identity will be challenged. (pp. 39-40)

She ends the article by articulating *tongzhi* as a "subject position" rather than the "essence of the subject": "eroticism is a complex process of endless negotiation, it is highly difficult to fix oneself to any notion of essence. What we possess is only a specific position to speak, for having a temporary and transitional erotic essence" (p. 42).

It brings us back to the issue of coming out. The same issue of *Stir* includes a panel discussion on coming out in which the first question is: "Is the Taiwanese *tongzhi* movement stuck on the issue of coming out?" Xiao-xing, a core member in the WZJ, replies by challenging the ethnocentrism of this question, arguing that Taiwanese *tongzhi* have developed different strategies of empowerment and exhibiting visibility. It is only by the standardization of the San Francisco model of coming out that the Taiwanese *tongzhi* movement can be judged as "getting stuck."

This implies not the denial of confrontational or coming-out politics but the need to contextualize *tongzhi* discourses. The success of Taiwanese *tongzhi* discourses in the 1990s lies in a rich blending of different perspectives and strategies of resistance. For example, the biggest and most successful mobilization of the equal rights movement in the 1990s was the New Park Incident. Although it appears to be the most confrontational event, as *tongzhi* had a clear enemy (government) and the aim was to reallocate social resources at the policy making level, *Tongzhi* Front actually adopted the most nonconfrontational strategy by organizing the Rainbow Valentine Week. It is a cultural subversion that neither bashes the government nor antagonizes the mainstream, but invites Taiwan's population to explore their own homoeroticism in the most relaxed and joyful way. This event demonstrates the possibility of using cultural carnivals to contextualize the discourses of equal rights. More importantly, homoeroticism is constructed not as a private property of stigmatized "gay" people, but rather as something everyone can explore, share, and enjoy in a specific context. What has come out in this event is not individual *tongzhi* but homoeroticism itself.

Taiwanese *tongzhi* have manipulated multiple platforms and strategies to exhibit visibility and power. For example, on September 5, 1997, there was an 8,000-person demonstration against the government's conservatism and budget cuts for education. The *tongzhi* community, especially teachers and university students, joined the demonstration and held banners such as "*Tongzhi* teachers are good teachers," and "Combat homophobia at school." Since hundreds of different banners were displayed during the march by thousands of people, it was impossible to identify who were *tongzhi* and who were not. In other words, *tongzhi* discourses and voices came out without exposing individual identities. While the demonstration is clearly a confrontational identity politics led by the constituents of education, *tongzhi* grasped this opportunity to contribute a *tongzhi* perspective on this apparently non-*tongzhi* mainstream issue. Instead of confining themselves to the issue of sexuality as merely a minority politics of "*gay* rights," *tongzhi* communities refuse to abstract sexuality from the wider social structure. By allying with progressive heterosexual groups on the mainstream issue of education, *tongzhi* challenge and subvert the homo-hetero duality, not by denying their own *tongzhi* specificity, but by actively exploring the intermingled connections between sexuality and class, culture, gender, and, in this context, education. It implies an integrative and connective conception of identity in which *tongzhi* is not merely a sexual category but also social and cultural.

Instead of a simple dichotomy between the politics of identity and the politics of difference, Taiwanese *tongzhi* discourses demonstrate the strength of indigenizing different strategies of resistance. As Taiwan proceeds toward liberalization and democratization, *tongzhi* grasp the new sociopolitical space to self-generate discursive practices that are always in the plural and in the process of contextualization. Taiwanese *tongzhi* vividly demonstrate the pluralities and diversities of coming out. Instead of coming out merely as individuals, to confront the straight world, which would leave them open to insurmountable social-family pressure and could reproduce the homo-hetero duality, Taiwanese *tongzhi* also come out as a community, in festivals, through academic discourses, through fun-fair gatherings, in mainstream demonstrations, and, finally, to turn the tables to invite everyone to come out and explore their own homophobia and homoeroticism.

SECTION III:
GENDER, RACE, AND TONGZHI
POLITICS IN HONG KONG

Chapter 5

When Potato Queens Meet Rice Queens: Racial-Sexual Dynamics in Colonial Hong Kong

Colonization is not just about force or coercion, but legitimization and naturalization of specific racialized relations, which are crucial for producing genuine consent and a desire of the colonized to be dominated. Modern colonialism operates as institutionalized hierarchies of specific knowledge and power relations between the colonizers and the colonized through the social construction of desire and subjectivity, which permeate everyday practices. Though Caucasians constitute less than 2 percent of Hong Kong's population, their colonial privileges are grounded and perpetuated by a long history of global unequal power relations. More often than not, the colonizer's categories become part of the colonized's common-sense framework that shapes the perception of their world and even becomes their own constitutive categories. In this chapter, I will examine the social formation and the multiple power dynamics of Chinese-Caucasian *tongzhi* relationships. Although Chinese *tongzhi* may masquerade to play very submissive roles, I found that Chinese-Caucasian relationships cannot be characterized by any simple dominant-dominated duality. There are multiple and contradictory structures of power relations which intersect to produce interracial dynamics.

I interviewed eighty Chinese (four females and seventy-six males) in 1996-1997. The result of that research has been published in *Houzhimin Tongzhi* (Postcolonial *Tongzhi*, Chou, 1997). All of the interviewees have interracial relationships and have lived in Hong Kong for more than three years. I conducted the interviews in a fairly unrestricted fashion, simply absorbing views, opinions, attitudes, and perspectives, not to capture an exhaustive picture, but to articulate crucial structures and themes in their constructions of social-sexual identity as Chinese *tongzhi* living in colonial Hong Kong. I chose to focus on the Chinese *tongzhi* rather than the Caucasians living in Hong Kong, though I did interview quite a few Caucasians (seven females and thirty-three males). An analytical report of Caucasian lesbigay people in Hong Kong would be another valuable book. Given such a focus, the interview process is biased by the class, language, and educational background of my interviewees. In general, the *tongzhi* in interracial relationships have more education, better English proficiency, and are mostly middle class and predominantly male.

SEXUAL-RACIAL POLITICS IN PERSONAL ADS

Interracial *tongzhi* relationships in Hong Kong are basically a male scene, divided into the so-called *potato queens* (Chinese male *tongzhi* who prefer Caucasian males) and *rice queens* (Caucasian gay men who prefer Chinese/Asian males). It is difficult to find women potato or rice queens. The fact that I have to add the noun "women" in front of rice queen and potato queen shows its male nature. I have spent much extra effort but can only find a few women, Chinese and Caucasians together, who have an exclusive interest in women of a different race. Women do have interracial relationships with women, but for different reasons, with different patterns and dynamics.

There is a remarkable gender difference here. Of the thirty-three male Caucasian interviewees, all have had sexual relationships with Chinese. More than half had at least thirty Chinese sexual partners, with four of them having had more than 500 sexual partners each, mostly through saunas and toilet sex. They admit that most of their Chinese partners cannot speak fluent English, and the relationship is largely sexual. Many Caucasian male interviewees have the experience of having Caucasians as close friends but Chinese as sexual partners. The language barrier, cultural differences, and class disparity, together with racial segregation, make intimate interracial friendships difficult.

Sharp differences exist between lesbian and gay Caucasians in terms of the attitudes toward and practices of interracial sex. Gender seems to be far more crucial than sexual orientation in this regard. Marie (thirty-one), a French lesbian, said,

> I don't think many women can accept having quick sex with a stranger. Whether she is lesbian or straight makes little difference here. That's why never in this world are lesbians into toilet [sex], no matter how liberated the lesbians are. Even when we cruise, it is flirtation rather than just for fucking. I cannot just pick up a pretty woman on the street and do it. I need to build up the relationship and

erotic attraction. Communication is the key word. If I don't know her and have feeling for her, how can we have sex?

Most women interviewees agreed with Marie and said that the emphasis on communication is the main reason for the absence of toilet cruising or bathhouses for lesbians. Indeed, we simply do not have a term for women having exclusive interest in women of a different race. Marie did mention "snow dyke" and "rice dyke," but she said the terms are rarely used by lesbians. In 1996, I directly asked twenty-eight local *nü tongzhi* whether they know any *nü tongzhi* who have interracial relationships. Most of them said "never." It turned out that I only interviewed four local women, with two others refusing to be interviewed. Indeed, one *nü tongzhi* who is a frequenter of local *tongzhi* bars such as H$_2$O, Circus, Smart S, and Secret Party, where most customers are women, said that she has never come across any Caucasian women in these bars.

The local *nan tongzhi* scene is very different. As Johnson (twenty-six), a self-identified potato queen, told me,

> Every Friday night, if you go to the tea dance organized by 1997 Bar, you would find around 100 Chinese and 100 Caucasians, all male, cruising one another. Or you don't have to wait until Friday. Every night you go to Wally Matt, PP, Zip, CE Top, or Flex, you would find so many interracial relationships in Hong Kong, all male. But be careful, most people would not like to be called rice queen and potato queen.

Jenny (thirty-one), a British lesbian, felt strongly that the "rice/potato queen" is a male phenomenon. She said, "If gay men insisted on communication before having sex, most of the quick sex simply could not occur. Just think, how many local Chinese can speak fluent English to share their inner feelings?" She is quite critical of gay male toilet/sauna sex: "Sex is personal business. But when so many gay men have quick sex with anonymous people, it really poses a very appalling and derogatory image of our people (lesbigay) to the straight world. This image of promiscuity is also unfair to lesbians."

The notion of cruising is gender specific. Women and men have very different patterns of cruising. That applies to *tongzhi* and straight, Chinese and Caucasians. Among the thirty-three male gay Caucasian interviewees, 100 percent have had sex with Chinese partners, and 50 percent have had more than thirty partners. Of the seven lesbian Caucasian interviewees, only two said that they have had sex with Chinese women, only one sexual relationship in both cases.

This does not mean that interracial relationships among women are free from racism and colonialism. Ada (twenty-nine) has lived in the United States for six years. She said that she has always been ignored in white lesbian circles:

> The stereotype of Chinese women is so ingrained that these Caucasians simply fail to see Chinese lesbians. I would only pass as a lesbian if I played the Caucasian game of dressing like a white lesbian—butch look, no makeup. The white lesbian and gay community has developed very established culture on lesbian and gay attire—the appropriate look to be gay. Yet most Chinese do not fit into that look.

One of the best sites to illustrate the gender-racial power dynamics in Hong Kong is the *tongzhi* personal ads. *Hong Kong Magazine* (*HKM*) and *Contacts Magazine* were selected as they are the two magazines having the most interracial *tongzhi* ads. They are magazines intended for an English-literate audience and all these ads are written in English, though a considerable number of writers and readers are Chinese.[1]

Women are generally less eager than men to write personal ads. In the case of *Hong Kong Magazine* and *Contacts Magazine*, which have columns for "women wanting women," there is on average one women's ad in every issue of *Contacts* and two women's ads in *Hong Kong Magazine,* around 10 percent of the number of "men wanting men" ads. Women do not seem to be comfortable with the sexual connotations of personal ads; they are also uneasy about seducing and flirting with a stranger through a cold medium. Even when women write personal ads, there are obvious differences. Here is a vivid example in the "women wanting women" section of *Hong Kong Magazine:*

> **American couple,** one Chinese and one Caucasian, seek other couples for several outings. Films, plays, tennis, dining and other nonsexual fun. (*HKM,* July 5-18, 1993)

Most ads from men seeking men would explicitly state the sexual implication. Yet this mixed-race female couple stated the purpose of meeting as merely a socializing and *nonsexual* encounter. This ad does not specify the age, appearance, nor any physical features of the authors and the couples they expect to meet. This has never happened in the gay male ads in these two magazines. The fact that they are already a couple now wanting to meet another couple has significantly desexualized the encounter they are expecting.

tions for the relationship. He markets himself in a financially privileged position to attract potential targets—slim and good-looking Asians under twenty-two, who this over-fifty Caucasian may otherwise stand little chance of having.

> **I am looking** for a slim, handsome Chinese boy under 23. Please reply to this improbable request if you would like to know a kind, mature Westerner, who would like to help you in other ways. (*HKM,* February, 1995)

The financial implications are clear here when this "mature Westerner" seeks a "slim, handsome Chinese boy under 23." It is interesting that a male of 22 would be regarded as an adult if he was Caucasian, but is treated as a "boy" because he is Chinese.

> **Generous European businessman.** Seeks young, slim, sexy lover-boy. Send photo with letter. (*HKM,* October 16, 1995)

> **Kind, sincere, Western, mature** guy, generous to the right person, looking for a handsome, slender and cute Chinese boy over 21 for ongoing relationship. Maybe I can help you through college. ALA, please send photo. (*Contacts,* February 1, 1995)

> **Mature Gweilo seeks young Chinese** boy as a adopted. Must be of pleasant personality as well as slim and gorgeous! I am a professional person—no ties, kindly, a bit fat, enjoy the good life and able to help the right boy. Please write with photo soon. (*HKM,* August 21, 1995)

Again, "slim and young" are characteristics required to qualify a Chinese partner for a middle-aged Caucasian. Asian bodies are fetishized, signifying a hierarchical power play between Asians and Caucasians. Financial implications are clearly stated in the above three ads with the term "generous" in the title or, more plainly, "I can help you through college."

Although the infatuation with youth and beauty has considerable cross-cultural relevance, especially in the gay world (Ebert, 1976; Rotello, 1995), it has an obvious colonial reference in Hong Kong in which only Caucasian older gay men are fantasized about by young Hong Kong Chinese men, while older local Chinese gay men are often marginalized and ignored. Indeed, the most striking feature of these personal ads is the invisibility of older Chinese, who seem to lack the "right color" to enter this erotic game. It indicates a crucial asymmetrical power structure: while the Caucasian ads are mostly written by middle-aged men seeking almost exclusively young, slim, and nubile Chinese, the Chinese do not seem to have the same option of being so selective.

In all the personal ads in these two magazines, never is there any Chinese over age fifty marketing himself as "mature, kind, generous," seeking a slim, young, gorgeous Caucasian boy under twenty-three who should speak Chinese to communicate with him. The crucial point here is why such an ad would appear bizarre or even unimaginable, whereas the "dominant Caucasian versus submissive Chinese" pattern is supposed to be "natural and normal." The boundaries and limits of erotic imagination in the colonial world seem to have clear rules of power differentiation codified by age, body shape, financial situation, social status, and, in a word, power.

It is unfair to criticize only these patronizing Caucasians. It takes two to tango. Many young male Chinese *tongzhi* are willing to play this "submissive" role, with various reasons ranging from enhancing their economic position, social status, career path, and language ability to gratifying their racial and sexual fantasies. Without Chinese playing the "submissive" roles, the Caucasian counterparts would have difficulty recognizing, sustaining, and enjoying their imagined "potent and powerful" self-image, and the apparent "naturalness" of the entire racial scenario would be destabilized. For example:

> **Chinese, 20 still young,** but not good-looking, not attractive, not sexy, not hairy, not fit, not tall, not experienced, not mature, not very intelligent but Thoughtful and Sincere, looking for friendship and love. (*HKM*, June 17, 1996)

"Youth" is a relative concept. A Chinese of twenty, already stresses that he is "still young" in the title, as if he may not be young enough for certain Caucasians, or maybe he finds his age his strongest selling point. Although he does not specify the race of his "target," in an English-speaking magazine *(HKM)* and a column used for interracial personal ads, it seems obvious that Caucasians are his major target. More interestingly, he resorts to the cultural strategy of self-depreciation, such as "not good-looking, not attractive, not sexy" and stresses that he is "Thoughtful and Sincere." In positioning himself as a desirable object to be consumed by an Orientalist Western subject, he simply perpetuates a racial stereotype that Caucasians may not actually want.[2]

Young, good-looking, small, passive type, Chinese. Seeks masculine, educated, athletic, strong type Westerner for developing monogamous relationship. (*HKM,* May 3, 1996)

Chinese cute 21+, slim (Your prisoner, sonny, toy) desires WM 30+ father, cowboy, coach, cop. (*Contacts,* March 1994)

Lonely Chinese, cute shy and submissive. Enjoys travel abroad, films, music and French. Seeks a gentle, sincere, caring and straight acting man for 121 fatherly relationship or more. Phones and photos appreciated. (*HKM,* December, 1993)

Westerner wanted. ME: student-look, smooth, feminine, 25, 1.65m, slight chubby, non-smoker, overseas educated. Enjoy being cared and fun. You: 25-45 mature-minded, experienced, passionate, hairy, for friendship, fun, or even more. (*HKM,* August 15, 1997)

Nice, Chinese, boy, pleasant-looking, 5′10″, decent, educated. Wants to share love and life with a caring professional Westerner, whom I can look up to. (*HKM,* March 1, 1996)

In the captions, these Chinese stress that they are slim, cute, young, small, good-looking, and/or boyish. They all look for "professional, masculine, athletic, caring, or/and fatherly Westerner" whom they "can look up to." These may be stereotypical, but are by no means exceptional.

I Supply Chinese tea. You'll bring your white cream. (*HKM,* February 6, 1995)

This Chinese seduces his intended Caucasian readers by visualizing the ejaculative power/potency of Caucasians. He also manipulates the Orientalist stereotype of Chinese tea, which symbolizes an artistic, tender, soft, and traditional Chinese seeking a Caucasian for wild sex.
    In cases where Chinese do not position themselves in submissive roles, Western cultural commodities are normalized and naturalized as the basic reference for seeing this world and their selfhood:

Chinese Forrest Gump seeks Caucasian Forrest Gump for stable, serious, long-term relationship. (*HKM,* February 20, 1995)

"I'm gonna rock your world!" If you're big-framed with a big heart, this chubby chaser is ready for you. And if loving you is wrong, I don't wanna be right. Write now, don't just think about it. (No serial killers or sick insects) please. (*Contacts*, December 11, 1995)

Although Hollywood films and songs are used in these ads, the following Chinese uses a cultural icon of the Western intellectual world—Freud—to engage with Caucasians. It is also interesting that a Chinese of thirty feels the need to stress that he is boyish in order to attract Caucasians.

> **Where they love,** they don't desire, and where they desire they don't love. Never mind about what Freud said. Here I am looking for desirable and lovable love. Me: 30, 5′6″, 125 lbs, boyish Chinese. You: 30-42, caring, intellectual, cuddly-bearish Westerner. Letter and photo and genuineness appreciated. (*HKM*, February 20, 1995)

Western culture is the basic reference for communication in these personal ads, with English as the only medium of communication. The ads become distinctive markers for class differentiation. Only those Chinese who have considerable mastery of English can play this game. Rodney Jones, in *Potato Seeking Rice—Language, Culture and Identity in Gay Personal Ads in Hong Kong*, states that "race" is the most crucial difference between local and Western gay personal ads. For example, in Coupland's study of British personal ads, ethnicity occupied only 7 percent among all variables to describe the author, and the target only 5 percent (Coupland, 1996). Even in gay ads in *Advocate Classifieds*, only 43 percent of the authors specify their race and 11 percent that of their ideal partners, compared to 93 percent and 41 percent respectively in the Hong Kong gay ads analyzed by Jones. These personal ads are contradictory: they provide arenas for *tongzhi* but also reproduce the mainstream racist, sexist, classist, ageist, and sometimes homophobic discourses (stressing straight acting). As Rodney Jones (1997) comments on these personal ads:

> While they provide an avenue for interaction in a society that limits opportunities for expression of homosexual identity, at the same time they support the very social order which imposes these limitations. Gay identity as it is expressed in personal ads often recreates the worst stereotypes of gay men found in heterosexist discourse: anonymous, furtive, materialistic and pre-occupied with sex. . . . Finally, the ads support an economic hegemony which marginalizes working class gay men and strengthens the association between gay culture and both capitalism and Western culture. (p. 15)

RICE AND POTATO QUEENS IN THE 1970s

After 1842, Hong Kong was racially segregated between British colonizers and the subordinate Chinese. "Hong Kong society was structured initially along racial lines, with the Chinese merchants and Chinese laborers coalescing into one community, in juxtaposition to the British merchants and the colonial government" (Leung, 1996:2). Until the 1970s, the Legislative and Executive Council, the top policymaking body in Hong Kong, was dominated by British merchants and government officials of British origin. In 1950, the Governor of Hong Kong appointed two of the wealthiest British merchants to the Legislative Council. The first Chinese was appointed to the Legislative Council as late as 1880. Even in 1941, only fourteen Chinese were appointed, and they were all successful merchants, had an English education, and belonged to elite Chinese groups such as the Tung Wah Hospital. Before the 1980s, almost all the top bureaucrats in Hong Kong's government were British. In 1950, among the forty-three Administrative Officers, only one was a local Chinese, and all the rest were overseas expatriates (Scott and Barnes, 1980). In the mid-1970s, for example, expatriates filled 82 percent of the highest grades of bureaucrat. "If one concentrates solely on the top five, the secretary rank and grade A officers, [who] often double as heads of departments, the proportion becomes 92.9 percent" (Lau, 1982:52). Even in the 1990s, residential, linguistic, economic, and social segregation between Caucasians and local Chinese was still remarkable, with the former enjoying considerable economic, occupational, linguistic, and racial power.

The rapid socioeconomic development of Hong Kong began after World War II and most has occurred since the 1970s, when there was a huge influx of Western culture in all facets of life, including Western *gay* discourses. Most young people in Hong Kong had little direct access to the West. Before the mid-1970s, most of the prime-time television programs in Hong Kong were Western movies and soap operas. Most interviewees said that the first naked or sensual bodies they saw were white blondes in Western movies, magazines, or advertisements. When asked about their favorite idols and television programs in the 1970s, all interviewees named imported Western programs such as *Superman, The Six Million Dollar Man,* and idols such as Sean Connery, Clint Eastwood, and Clark Gable. What Hong Kong people faced was not only British political colonialism but also Western cultural imperialism, especially from Hollywood films and other cultural products, which have permeated most aspects of their everyday lives. There were Chinese stars, of course, but they were too real, too mundane, and too "Chinese" to be fantasized about. It was the

Western icons that were equated with being adorable, sexual, and seductive.

The prominence of white Western images in media representation corresponds to their global prominence in the wider socioeconomic power structure. Most Caucasians came to Hong Kong as professionals, merchants, or civil servants who could enjoy much better benefits and privileges than their Chinese counterparts. Even for those who came empty-handed, racial privileges easily gained them good jobs, money, and romance. Westerners represented power and status, a superior class, superior taste, superior culture, superior race, because of a superior color—white.

The equation between color and power is most visible in the use of language. English was the only official language in Hong Kong before 1974. Only after the Joint Declaration in 1984 came the process of localization that allowed Chinese language and people to be promoted to higher status in the colonial administration. Yet one hundred years of colonial rule have inculcated a strong sense of English supremacy. English has become a status symbol, legitimizing and naturalizing the superiority of English-speaking culture.

Most Chinese *tongzhi* now between thirty and fifty years old went through a stage of eroticizing Caucasians. Caucasian languages, bodies, features, and complexion were preferred. The idealized homosexual subject is raced, predicated upon the images of a white body. As one local *nan tongzhi* (forty-three) said,

> The notion of the ideal male is modeled upon the white male body. But Chinese simply have different features. The desirable gay body conforms to mainstream standard of what is a desirable male body: slightly tanned skin, broad shoulders, big chest, big penis, and washboard stomach. Even when we go to the gym everyday, it only confirms the white game. White gay male is the norm, so we [Chinese *tongzhi*] are doubly belittled both in terms of sexuality and culture. There was a strong sense of inferiority that this generation of Chinese *tongzhi* may not understand.

To be *gay* in the 1970s in Hong Kong was not about sex with any man, but a set of sociocultural significations within specific coloniality that structures erotic desire toward bodies of a specific race, class, and age. Phenomenologically, in most Chinese-Caucasian relationships, the Chinese member was supposed to be younger, smaller, and more feminine than the Western member (Petula Ho, 1997). It echoes the "older men, younger women" power differentiation in heterosexual relationships. In heterosexual relationships, we still occasionally find an older, taller, or richer woman with a younger, shorter, poorer man (Burton, 1991). But in the local *tongzhi* world, it is almost inconceivable to have an obviously older, stronger Chinese picking up a young blond. Similar hierarchical interracial gay relationships can easily be found in other parts of the world, from the Long Yang Club in London, Asians and Friends in America, to the *gay* venues in Bangkok or Manila. The popularity and "naturalness" of this global interracial *gay* hierarchy seems to suggest a deep-rooted racial-economic construct that goes beyond personal taste and choice.

Michael (forty), who entered the scene in the late 1960s, told me about the 1970s scene in the two major *gay* bars, Dateline and Waltzing Matilda:

> All the Chinese there were *potato queens*. There were hardly any sticky rice [Chinese male *tongzhi* who prefer other Chinese *tongzhi*]. Male *tongzhi* treated one another not as brothers but sisters. We tended to effeminize ourselves. In the 1970s, the husband-wife model was very popular. A Chinese would refer to himself as "wife" and his Caucasian partner as "husband." It was a rule that the Chinese partner moved into the husband's place, doing housework, usually with financial benefits. It might not be the actual picture for all couples, but the pervasiveness of such racial representation was so overwhelming that deviations in actual reality can only be a scandalous secret. I know of no couple in the 1970s where the Chinese was older than the Western partner.

I think Michael's personal experiences are worth quoting at length as he represents rather common experiences shared by many *tongzhi* in the 1970s:

> When I was growing up, most of the male images I was exposed to were white, virile, masculine bodies. I identify myself as *gay* rather than Chinese. At that time, I thought being *gay* and Chinese was a contradiction. Being *gay* means wild, bold, sexual, and modern, being Chinese means tame, filial, asexual, and traditional. You see, all my stereotypes about the Caucasians were positive. I despised Chinese.

> I am the eldest son in the family. Since I was young, I forced my younger brothers and sisters to do housework. I was the leader, potent and strong. But when I met my British lover, Carl, I suddenly became his little woman. I moved into his house, did all the housework. I thought it was so natural. I quit my job in the factory and

literally was his wife. Once you give up work you tend to adopt a different attitude at home. It was ridiculous to do the housework when Carl came home at night, so I tended to finish all the housework during the day so as to free myself to have a nice chat with him at night. Our group of sisters would meet during afternoon, have tea in Hilton Hotel or Repulse Bay, then play mah-jongg at home, and gossip and gossip. Then, I go back home, prepare dinner with the domestic servant and serve him. That sounds weird now. But at that time, to have a Caucasian husband was our dream.

In the 1970s, if I dated women, I should prepare for marriage and child rearing. But I was not ready yet. I was only twenty-three when I met Carl. He took care of me entirely and did not pressure me. To be a Chinese man is very tiring, especially when your parents have a lot of expectations for you. There was only one thing in my parents' mind—I should get married and earn money. That was painful to me. How could I marry a woman?

After Michael split up with Carl, he still hung around with his Caucasian friends. His attitude changed when he was thirty-two:

Until one day, one Caucasian told me that I have little market in the Caucasian world because I was too old. I was really annoyed—too old! A Caucasian of forty, fifty, or even sixty is never too old. Indeed, this Caucasian who teased me was himself a sixty-year-old Caucasian living with two young Chinese boyfriends at midlevel. I was only thirty-two, full of ambitious plans for my future, and I was criticized as too old. I suddenly realized that what I really lack is a pair of blue eyes.

Gerald (thirty-six), a close friend of Michael, is very critical of these Caucasians of the 1970s.

They have the *M. Butterfly* complex of objectifying the so-called Oriental mystique: the gentle body texture and cute face. Many of these rice queens have been rejected in their homeland for being old and ugly. When they came to Hong Kong, they were fascinated by their colonial power. So many Chinese young boys rushed for them. How would they be serious and respectful toward Chinese? They will criticize your English—poor grammar, awful pronunciation, and vulgar manner. They will say they love you but then go out for sauna and toilet. We are just playthings, easy to get, cheap to keep, quick to dump. Many of them stayed in Hong Kong for short-term contracts and have little commitment. Only those who are impotent are most faithful to you. But why should I choose an impotent old man?

The golden age for this kind of patronizing Caucasian is past. Political correctness and the rapid growth of the economic and social status of Hong Kong Chinese have made patronizing Caucasians far less marketable than before. Gerald said, "Their days are numbered. The new trend is to learn Mandarin and have mainland Chinese connections. Having an old Caucasian partner would be seen as colonialist and stupid, even if it is genuine love." From what I have gathered, Caucasian gay men in the colonial age of the 1960s and 1970s can be broadly classified into three categories.

The first group are the Chinese culture fanciers. Most of them were young students and socialists moved by the passion of Chairman Mao and the Cultural Revolution. They took an antiracist and anticolonialist attitude when they came to Hong Kong. Most of them left Hong Kong or mainland China several years later because of disappointment with Communist China. Those who remained began to enjoy the colonial privileges they had never experienced before.

The second group are the "wounded" ones. They were casualties of a Western homophobic world where they might have gotten married with the wishful thinking of using marriage to pacify or even change their homoerotic desire. They failed to be "converted" to heterosexuality; some lived double lives, some divorced, some remarried, some were alcoholics, most were unhappy—all found themselves too old for a young boyfriend. Having no time to waste, some came to Hong Kong, and suddenly found themselves in a very privileged position. Many of them have settled in Hong Kong.

The third group are the patronizing ones who were mostly middle-aged gay men who had little market in their homeland. There was nowhere else in the world where they could easily pick up a pretty nineteen-year-old boy who could speak some English, was not a money boy, in a modern city where English-speaking people dominate. One British interviewee is typical of this category. He has been in Hong Kong for twenty-one years but cannot speak any Cantonese or Mandarin. During the interview, he made rather patronizing comments about Chinese. The only positive comments he had about young Chinese men is that "They are very cute, respect the elderly, and won't argue with you." In the phone chat when we fixed the appointment, this British gay man suddenly asked me, "Are you cute?" He had not seen me and knew nothing about me. Obviously he had gotten used to asking Chinese strangers the same question. Since I did not respond at all, he added, "You must be cute, right?" The fact that he could cruise me in such an abrupt manner, disregarding how I felt, is a vivid testimony to the unequal power relations between Caucasians and Chinese. During the interview, I caught his slip when he said "toy" instead of "boy." He denied having said, "My previous Chinese toys are cute and lovely." He later defended himself, saying, "Well, I am kidding, but Chinese boys are nice toys. It's a compliment!"

In colonial times, those Caucasians not identifying with colonialism would have a hard struggle. Joe (fifty-five) is an Irishman who had stayed in Hong Kong from 1962 to 1964, then came to Hong Kong again in the late 1980s. Joe was a devoted socialist in the 1960s and was very disappointed by Caucasians in Hong Kong:

> Those British on expat terms were the worst. Many of them did not survive well in Britain. They suddenly became princes here, without the slightest concern for the general public, who were living in poor conditions. I knew a gay man who was also a socialist when he arrived in Hong Kong. But after a couple of years, stuck in his big house with two domestic maids, he had a different Chinese teenage boy every weekend. He just indulged in his colonial privileges and fantasies, kept on telling me [about] all those fascinating sexual services provided by the Chinese boys. But he also criticized Chinese people most fiercely. Had I not decided to leave Hong Kong in 1964, I would have been one of these chauvinists.

The racial hierarchy is also constituted by the economic disparity. In the 1960s and 1970s, most young Chinese people had little earning capacity; they depended upon their Western partners. Danny (forty) said,

> It was Caucasians who introduced me to the world of French movies, coffee shops, red wine, sailing, and valentine romance. I have so many privileges, like the right not to pay the bill and to add my name on some of his properties. How can I not fancy Caucasians? I hung out with white people, I dressed like them, talked like them, thought like them, and believed that I was one of them. Gradually, I realized that I was physically turned on by Caucasians but emotionally closer to Chinese. It is a problem.

All of my Chinese interviewees said that they would not eroticize an older, wealthy Chinese man, while having no problems with having a Caucasian gay partner who was fifty years old. Danny put it most bluntly:

"A Caucasian of D grade is still very attractive, even old, fat, short, and chauvinist. But a Chinese man must be A grade in order to turn me on. For me, Westerners are superior, they are bigger, taller, stronger, and harder. In a word, they are better."

Tongzhi have many different reasons to fancy Caucasians. It is impossible to generalize and reduce the interest to any single dimension, such as race, money, cultural interest, class, status, or sexual attraction. For many PEPS in the 1970s, to have Caucasian partners was a crucial strategy to build up their own positive self-esteem and identity. At that time, most PEPS did not have much social space to establish steady same-sex relationships. Many PEPS dared not give one another real names and telephone numbers. Living arrangements were a big problem. Even in the 1990s, most young Hong Kong Chinese still live with their parents before marriage and cannot afford an apartment of their own. Astronomical property prices have forced many *tongzhi* to continue living with their parents and siblings. Unlike their Western lesbigay counterparts, who usually go home for sexual activity, Hong Kong *tongzhi* seldom utilize their homes for casual sex. While gay saunas are rapidly declining in the Western world because of the AIDS epidemic, they are mushrooming in Hong Kong. In an overcrowded and homophobic society, toilets, saunas, discos, and bars are the only places where many *tongzhi* can relax and do not have to fear identity exposure. They go to a *tongzhi* bar, buy a drink, just relax, and chat with anybody there, not necessarily looking for sex. Albert (thirty-five) even said:

> *When I was young, the only way to be gay was to live with a Caucasian.* They have big houses of their own, whereas Chinese live in very crowded conditions, which made an independent *gay* lifestyle impossible. As we are brought up in a culture stressing responsible, steady, and monogamous relationships, to be a potato queen is a way to fulfill the cultural expectation for a steady partner, yet retaining one's own *gay* identity. (emphasis mine)

Albert had a painful experience with a Chinese classmate in secondary school in the 1970s. They loved each other but did not know what to do:

> No role model, no prospect, no confidence. I thought *gay* was a dead-end road. The relationship lasted only for two years. He later wrote me a letter, saying that it was abnormal. I was very hurt, feeling helpless. I could tell nobody, shared with no one, and saw no way out. If I had not met my American boyfriend, I would definitely get married like everyone else.

Desire is not static. Albert's boyfriend brought him to the United States, where he stayed for five years. Albert split up with him and came back Hong Kong in 1985. He recalled an experience in the United States when he was driving with a Chinese friend. Another car came toward him and the driver yelled, "Go back to China!" His friend, who has never been to China, yelled back, "You Caucasians go back to Europe!" Albert admitted that his experiences in the United States really helped him to reorient his racial fantasy:

> I joined a men's consciousness raising group. But the men there were very heterosexist, presupposing heterosexuality as the only norm for love, romance, and sex. I then joined the gay male group. I felt that I was still not an integrated person, as my ethnic and cultural background are always ignored. I was always interrupted and when I shared my Chinese experiences, people would be silent, then say, "Oh, interesting," and change the subject. I was taken seriously only when there was a seminar or panel discussion on "racism." I was reduced to a racial token to confirm the political correctness of the white culture.

This is only one side of the story. Postwar Hong Kong was a place of drastic change. After World War II, Hong Kong began to industrialize and modernize into an international finance center. The postwar generation began to have an enormous sense of pride about being Hong Kong Chinese. From the mid-1970s onward, local television was "conquered" by local productions with local icons. They were neither Western nor Chinese but indigenous Hong Kong programs and celebrities. This marked the birth of a Hong Kong identity and culture. David (thirty-seven) shared his story of the localization of eroticism:

> Before 1974, I thought only blondes were pretty. Chinese males were dumpy and boring, having no sense of humor. I think I have internalized the Western representation of Chinese men—the idea that all Chinese males are eunuchs and have no sex appeal. That's why the production of the Cantonese soap *Jia-bian* [Family Crisis] in the late 1970s was so shocking, as there was the first Chinese gay character in Hong Kong media—Yam Tat-wah. I was shocked and entranced. Yam was so cute and charming. All of a sudden, I started to look at handsome Chinese men. That was really a new thing to me—the shock was like Bruce Lee kicking down Caucasian and black fighters in his worldwide film. Oh! Chinese men can be charming and attractive.

Kenneth (thirty-five) had a different experience of localizing erotic object choice. He said that his ability to eroticize Chinese is inseparable from his appreciation of Chinese culture. He has been going to Beijing on business since 1984 when he was twenty-two. He was shocked:

> In the 1960s and 1970s in Hong Kong, these Caucasians would touch you without asking your permission. I got used to such an inferior position and didn't see anything wrong with it. The Caucasians living in Beijing are very different. They speak Mandarin and have much more respect for Chinese. But in Hong Kong, the longer the Caucasians stay, the more colonial they become.

With the rapid increase of the economic power and cultural status of Hong Kong and the decrease of the economic power of the West in the last twenty years, there has been a corresponding change of erotic choice and aesthetic taste in the *tongzhi* community. Many ex-potato queens are now either "too old" according to mainstream Caucasian "gaydar," or they have accumulated adequate cultural confidence and social power to approach Chinese. Kenneth, who was very critical of his previous potato queen mentality, now has a Dutch boyfriend:

> When I came back to Hong Kong from Beijing, I was very hostile to rice queens. I tried to date Chinese but nothing really happened. Just when I was thinking of going to Beijing again for work, I met my Dutch boyfriend. He had just finished one year of study in Taiwan and was doing research in Hong Kong. He was twenty-five, very mature and bright. This relationship was really therapeutic to me. I realized that I had been swinging from one extreme to another, from worshipping Caucasians to hating them.

They have been together for seven years. Kenneth said,

> It is the best relationship I ever had. It is a love beyond color. It is naive to judge relationships just because of the skin color. The categories rice queen or potato queen are very dehumanizing and stereotyping.

All the *tongzhi* interviewees agreed that in recent years there have been crucial changes in power relations between Chinese and Caucasians. In some cases the Chinese *nan tongzhi* feels strongly that he is taking the lead. Kevin (twenty-two) just started a relationship with a British man, Ray, who is thirty-one years older than him:

He is in a very unfavorable position. He is rich and I am still a student. So when he takes me to an expensive restaurant, hotel room, or a short trip, he is bound to treat me. And he is now fifty-three—not many Chinese would like an "old devil." Chinese are no longer Susie Wong or Charlie Chan. Actually, it is me who believes in multiple relationships. Ray is very dependent on me, very insecure, always fearing that I may leave him for a young, virile man.

In another case, a twenty-nine-year-old Chinese engineer, Derek, said that the old colonizers would be replaced by the new colonial ruler—the Beijing government and the elite cadre in Hong Kong. Derek had lived in the United States and Canada for twelve years and said that he was closer to Caucasians than Chinese. He does not want to be labeled as Chinese:

> I am Chinese of course, but I am also Hongkongese, Chiuchowese, Thai, East Asian, Asian, Canadian, or American, and I am also male, engineer, *tongzhi*, vegetarian, Buddhist, feminist . . . I mean, I don't want to be defined by my skin color or ethnicity. I was born in Thailand, went to Hong Kong at eight, left Hong Kong at fourteen, went to Hong Kong three years ago. See, I won't even say "came back" to Hong Kong.

Derek says that neither Hong Kong, Thailand, nor China is his homeland. "Homeland is not a geographical place, it is something in the mind. It is the footsteps that I have experienced." Derek has never had a Chinese boyfriend. He finds most Chinese to be too parochial and ethnocentric. "They never care about issues outside Hong Kong, and have no interest or knowledge about Bosnia, Palestine, India, or even the Taiwanese aboriginals. In Hong Kong, I found myself closer to Caucasians than Chinese. At least, most Caucasians here have some migration experiences of living in different cultures, and they are more concerned about the global situation. That is something we share." Derek now has a thirty-six-year-old German partner. He dismisses the notion of colonialism in their relationship:

> Things are never so simple. Who is colonizing whom? Economically, I am far stronger than him. He is only an anonymous musician, earning just enough to pay his rent for his small room in Wanchai. I owned my handsome apartment, now costing five million dollars. I earned hundreds of thousands from the local stock market in the last three years. You can see, finance is far more vital than race in this relationship. He has proposed moving to my place, as I have an extra room. It's for me to decide. I am thinking of moving to Lamma

Island with him. He is very happy but has little say. You see, he has to depend on me. Race is not always important.

Choosing a place to live is a good indicator of power relations. It fits with resources power theory: the person with better resources, which includes income, social status, network, and other social power, is more likely than his or her partner to be the decision maker in situations such as dining out or choosing a place to live. At a time when the economy of Hong Kong is far better than in many Western countries, local Chinese have much stronger pride and self-esteem, and exhibit very different racial preferences and power dynamics in *tongzhi* erotic practices.

This research also found a crucial demarcation between Caucasians who have stayed in Hong Kong since the 1970s and newcomers who arrived in the last five years. Most newcomers were born in the 1960s and 1970s, growing up in an age of antiestablishment sentiment and political correctness. They are generally critical of sexism, racism, and cultural imperialism. When they came to Hong Kong, they no longer enjoyed the colonial, economic, and racial privileges of their predecessors. Most of them would insist on a nonpatronizing relationship with a local Chinese. They may live in Wanchai, Lamma Island, or other middlebrow areas. They are not rich; some may even have been unemployed in their homeland. Many did not have full-time domestic servants and are eager to learn Cantonese or Mandarin, for survival purposes or out of cultural admiration.

Jim and Steve are two cases that vividly illustrate the new forms of racial politics in Hong Kong. Jim was born in Texas and grew up in New York. He recalled his painful experiences of being bullied by other American kids because of his body shape and strong Texas accent:

> I came from a small village. My parents own a small farm. When I came to New York at nine, my accent was always mocked, the whole class would repeat my English. Do you know how painful it is for a nine-year-old kid? There was lots of name calling like Bony, Shortie-Tex, Monkey Jim. Look at me, I was short and skinny, five feet four and 115 pounds. American male culture is obsessed with masculinity, which is defined by the size of muscles. As a gay man, I am not marketable in the United States.

Jim knew a Taiwanese classmate at college, who introduced him to Chinese culture. Jim actually changed his major from Economics to Asian Studies.

I have great interest in Chinese culture. With Americans I feel intimidated because I have to act in an ultramacho way. With Chinese I am very relaxed and no one makes fun of my body shape or Texas accent.

Jim came to Hong Kong in 1992. "I feel comfortable here. I think I am lucky to have Andrew, my Chinese boyfriend. If Andrew were Caucasian, I don't think I would pursue him. He is so bright and attractive, how would he choose me? It is my racial privilege, I must admit it."

Steve (twenty-seven) also has a very high opinion of his present Chinese partner. Steve's father is an Anglican priest in London. "I came to Hong Kong to become gay. My father would kill me if I came out to him. No way. My choice was to get married or leave the country. I decided to go as far as I could. Hong Kong was a good choice."

Steve had rather painful experiences when he first arrived in Hong Kong. His first lover was a thirty-one-year-old Chinese who said he was twenty-seven and thought Steve was around thirty. They met at a friend's party and immediately started a very smooth and gratifying relationship. Five weeks later, when Steve accidentally said that he was twenty-three, the Chinese *tongzhi* was shocked:

> There was a dead silence. He was just speechless, and kept on asking if I was serious. He then said, "I want a man, not a boy." I was very disappointed. He was actually planning to live with me. But just because I am younger than him, he got annoyed. I think he has this colonial mentality of expecting a Caucasian older and stronger than him. People cannot tell from our appearance that he is eight years older than me. Even he himself got it wrong! Why does age matter if both of us treasure the time we share, so deep and so genuine?

Steve's second relationship was not much better. It lasted only seven weeks.

> He had tons of problems with coming out. I felt that I had to take care of his family problems. You know what—he did not give his telephone number to me, just asked me to page him—even after seven weeks of relationship. He said that his parents and siblings would speculate. And he would cancel our candlelight dinner appointment at the last minute, just because his mother mistakenly prepared a nice soup for him. It was the dinner to celebrate my job promotion, and he canceled it only fifty minutes before the appointment. How frustrating!

When Steve was struggling to decide whether he should leave Hong Kong, he met his present partner:

> It is very deep and tender, like Chinese tea, you need to feel it slowly. He is independent, relaxed, and cheerful. Our marriage, oh yes, our marriage is improving all the time. We are having two independent but very intimate lives.

It is difficult and indeed dangerous to portray any singular dominant-dominated or top-bottom relationship in Chinese-Caucasian *tongzhi* dynamics. Unequal power dynamics remain, but individual variations, together with the wider socioeconomic changes, often go beyond the single factors of race or colonialism, and make the categories rice queen and potato queen highly contestable.

LANGUAGE, FOOD, AND SEX

In this section, I will look at interracial *tongzhi* relationships through the micropolitics of naming, language, food, sex, and migration plans.

In contrast to Western democratic countries such as the United States, heterosexual interracial marriage was never illegal in Hong Kong or China. The reason is not that Chinese are not racist, but that family-kin sanctions and stigma were strong enough to constrain interracial marriages. There is little social integration between Chinese and other racial groups in Hong Kong. This creates a kind of societal bilingualism in which two largely monolingual communities coexist without interacting with each other (Lin, 1996). It is like a "salad bowl" where different colors occur together but never mix or integrate. Patrikeeff (1989) argued that the visible gulf between Chinese and foreigner is camouflaged by the lack of strong antiforeigner sentiment on the part of the Chinese. Most interviewees agreed that when they go out as a couple, people are not shocked, nor is the couple despised; people are just curious.

This research found that most mixed-race couples do not have joint leisure activities. Given the social distance of the two ethnic groups, each finds it difficult to integrate into the other's racial circle. In the rare case of racial integration, it is always the Chinese *tongzhi* who adjust themselves to integrate into the Caucasian circle. In other words, considerable understanding of Western culture and fluent English, defined not by themselves but their Caucasian partners, are the basic requirements.

If language signifies a kind of worldview and value system, then who speaks whose language becomes a good entry point to understand the power dynamics of interracial relationships. Among the Chinese *nan tongzhi* interviewees, only Sing (thirty-four) uses his Chinese name. Sing was brought up by patriotic parents who have a strong sense of cultural dignity as Chinese. He recalled an unpleasant experience with his first American boyfriend in Hong Kong:

> I was very disadvantaged in the relationship as I had to drop my mother tongue and speak his language. I could not express myself fully and always failed to find the right word for my feeling. Once I argued with him about his racial and language privileges in our relationship. Then I realized that even when I questioned his linguistic privileges, I had to speak English. But he never understood it, he kept on saying how great my English is. In my social circle, I mean Chinese, I am superior because of my English proficiency, but in his social circle, I mean Caucasians, I feel so inferior because I always fail to get the joke, the punchline, and the key words. I look so stupid and dumb. It is my first experience of the entire relationship depending so much on language.

All the other Chinese interviewees used English names. When speaking Chinese, their sentences are interspersed with English words. Rocky (twenty-six), a locally born working-class Chinese, used a considerable amount of English when he spoke to me. Obviously, his Chinese, which is his mother tongue, is far better. His friend told me later that Rocky rarely speaks so much English. Why did he decide to use English when talking to a university lecturer doing research on interracial relationships? Is it his way of balancing the unequal power relations by stressing his "cultural capital" of English proficiency? Did he feel superior by demonstrating his ability to speak good English with idiosyncratic terminology? Or does the Western language and culture help him to be gay? The answer may be mixed, but to speak English seems to signify a different horizon of imagination for him. He feels himself to be different.

Most Caucasians take it for granted that Hong Kong Chinese should speak English to them. English is the only medium of communication with their partners. Only a few interviewees occasionally spoke Mandarin or Cantonese, but it was never more than 5 percent of their total communication. The burden obviously falls upon the Chinese to acquire enough fluency of English to successfully negotiate and improve mutual understanding.

Very few Caucasians have made a consistent effort to learn Cantonese. About 70 percent of the Caucasian interviewees said they had attended Cantonese classes. But none persevered, with most following a start-stop-start-stop process. Among the forty Caucasian interviewees, only one can speak Cantonese, while five speak Mandarin. Among the interviewees who have tried to learn Cantonese, no one mentioned the motive of enhancing their understanding of their Chinese partners. All mentioned more practical reasons such as doing business or career requirements. Many Caucasians are frustrated by their Chinese partners' lack of enthusiasm about teaching them Chinese. On a societal level, Hong Kong Chinese always respond to Caucasians' Cantonese by using English, which is very discouraging for Caucasians. As one Caucasian puts it,

> Whenever I speak Cantonese to Hong Kong Chinese, they reply in English. How frustrating! A Hong Kong Chinese friend even told me that he simply cannot think and speak in Cantonese when he is with Caucasians, as if he feels inferior about Cantonese, or he treats Cantonese as a private language that should exclude outsiders. And many people just laugh at my Cantonese. . . . There are very few social contexts which are conducive to Caucasians learning Cantonese beyond the basics. I have been here twenty years and can only say simple things like "thank you" and "how are you" in Cantonese. How stupid!

Chinese *tongzhi* have some unique reasons for excluding their Caucasian partners from learning Cantonese. One said, "It is nice that he does not speak Chinese. Otherwise my parents would be more keen on him. My family and sexuality are strictly segregated. I prevented him from learning Chinese." Another *tongzhi* said, "I can control whether to translate the Chinese to him or not. I control what he can listen to and how the message will be conveyed to him. It is the little space where I control the relationship and he becomes so vulnerable. But when he joins my Chinese circle, I have the dilemma of whether to converse in English, thus entertaining my partner, or conversing in Chinese for my Chinese friends."

The picture is changing, especially for Caucasians who have arrived in the last five years. One young British gay interviewee, Crook (twenty-six), said that language is the main reason why most of his relationships with Chinese have failed. Crook said that it is difficult in a different culture to decide when he should ask for explanations and when he should just take bizarre behavior as a cultural difference. It is more difficult to tell the difference and decide when to do what. He shared his experiences about his previous Chinese partner, Tommy:

> His mother always calls him. Once, after the chat, I asked him what did his mother want. Tommy was so cross—dead silence for five minutes. Then he said that I ask the same question every time his

mother calls. Even now, I don't know why he was so angry. And I will never know—we have split up. I think it is stupid not to speak Chinese. It's to my benefit to know what is on people's minds.

Crook can now speak fluent Mandarin but little Cantonese. While he feels there is a high level of social acceptance of Caucasians speaking fluent Mandarin, he sometimes feels excluded because his Mandarin is too fluent:

> It is too threatening to Chinese, who always feel the cultural need to draw a distinction between Chinese and *gweilo,* insider and outsider. Language is a cultural marker of differentiation and exclusion. Chinese seem to be threatened by my superb Mandarin, as if their sense of insider-outsider distinction cannot be sustained. I think even if I were born here and dreamed in Chinese, I would still be regarded as a *gweilo* by Chinese.

This research also found certain patterns of division of housework along racial lines. The pattern of "masculinizing the Caucasian and feminizing the Chinese male" is still valid if cooking can be categorized as a traditional women's activity. For *tongzhi* living with Caucasian partners, many *tongzhi* take a predominant role in terms of housework, especially cooking. Peter, a Chinese *tongzhi,* did have some complaints about his Australian boyfriend, who is nineteen years older than he is:

> He never cooks a nice meal, or cleans the kitchen . . . he justifies his laziness by accusing me of being too clean. The problem is that I am always the one who notices the dust and dirt. Indeed, he is funny about washing; he will wash the pans before the glasses. I am not pleased, but what can I do? That is a typical Chinese problem—we accept it even when we are not satisfied.

Power relations work at a more subtle level, especially in an age when everyone talks about equality and liberty. Herman (twenty-eight) was very energetic in talking about how he shares housework equally with his Belgian partner: "Billy is different. He does a lot of housework now. Men have to be taught especially in terms of housework. . . . Now I cook, he washes, I clean the house, he drives me to the supermarket."

But when I ask Herman why cooking is his task whereas washing is Billy's, why cleaning the house is his whereas driving him for shopping is Billy's, Herman attributes this to personal choice and ability. The clear racial division of labor with the tedious and repetitive work left to the

Chinese *tongzhi* does not seem to disturb Herman. More interestingly, Herman seems to have detached himself from "male identity," as when he refers to Billy's masculinity by saying, "men have to be taught especially in terms of housework." It sounds as if Herman does not consider himself a man.

Patrick (twenty-five) claims proudly that Rico, his Italian lover, helps him with domestic duties. "Rico does share the housework with me. He irons his own clothes, he makes sandwiches for work, he sometimes cooks for me, and he always vacuums and dusts."

This concept of "sharing" and "help" are very crucial in understanding domestic politics: When his Caucasian partner does the housework, it is defined as "helping" Patrick—the Chinese is really supposed to do the housework. When Rico does his own part, he is praised for "sharing" the housework! When they go out and do things together, Patrick always does the things his partner enjoys. Patrick said: "My boyfriend likes watching movies and having Italian food and we tend to go out a lot." Patrick talked of "we" as himself and substitutes his partner's interest as "his" by losing himself in the "we." Indeed, going out for a meal was cited by many *tongzhi* as their favorite treat. Here lies another common tension in the Chinese-Caucasian relationship.

Food and taste are a system of communication and expression of social relations. For Boudieu (1984), "taste" is the collection of dispositions of an individual's social position. Taste is mobilized as a boundary marker and a basis for social distinction and exclusions that serve to naturalize domination and subordination. Caucasian interviewees seem to have fewer complaints than Chinese concerning food. Maybe they appreciate Chinese food, and they have adequate choices of Western-style food and restaurants in Hong Kong. Talking about his American boyfriend, Lewis (thirty-five) said,

> He has no concern for the freshness of the food, and can have supermarket canned food and McDonald's for the entire week. But, you know, freshness is a central tenet of Cantonese cuisine. It is difficult to compromise. He thinks the rich long-boiled soup or *yum cha* in a Chinese restaurant is a waste of time. When I boiled the nice soup, he just tried a little bit. He prefers beer to long-boiled soup. I become the only one to eat it. And that kind of soup can't be boiled just for one person. Besides, I always take the skinniest pieces of chicken while saving the juicy parts for him. But I don't think he noticed it. He just ate.

In terms of sex, most Chinese interviewees said that Caucasians were more romantic and creative, yet are disturbed by their nonmonogamous practices. Many *tongzhi* claim to prioritize relationships over sex, and said that had the relationship been strong enough they would not mind a rather mediocre sex life. As Richard (forty-three) said, "Sex is only twenty or thirty minutes, sometimes several seconds, but the relationship is everything, it can last forever. Moreover, sex is not just penetration or ejaculation. We kiss, caress, touch and hug, the whole body is sexual."

Concerning nonmonogamous relationships, most local *tongzhi* said that they are looking for a stable loving relationship, including those who go to cruising areas for one-night stands. Contrary to the popular stereotype, only about 20 percent of *nan tongzhi* interviewees said that they enjoy anal sex. Around 20 percent said that they dislike anal sex for being painful, dirty, and unsafe. The majority (60 percent) said that it depends on the context and partner. They will have it if their lovers demand it. Most *tongzhi* prefer oral sex, mutual masturbation, body massage, hugging, touching, and kissing.

Approximately 70 percent of Chinese interviewees having mixed-race relationships are in an open relationship where both partners are free to engage in sexual encounters with other people. The remaining 30 percent are in monogamous relationships where sexual exclusivity is expected of both partners. Open relationships do not imply promiscuity or having sex whenever possible. Interviewees all stressed that there are tacit rules. The two main rules followed by all are safe sex and no emotional commitment in casual sex. Some interviewees add other rules such as: cannot bring partner back home, cannot stay overnight with the casual sex partner, cannot show off these sexual relationships with other *tongzhi*. Simon (thirty-five) has been with Tim, his Australian partner, for fifteen years in an open relationship:

> We love each other deeply and also enjoy casual sex with others, which is conducive to our stable and loving relationship. Both of us prefer the penetrative role. So we are not the best couple in terms of sex. If we don't allow ourselves casual sex, our relationship might have serious problems.

Simon has a three-stage theory on gay male relationships:

> Sex is the most important in the first stage of the relationship, usually the first three to six months. If the sex life is not gratifying, the relationship will be in crisis. But the importance of sex will decrease as the relationship becomes more stable and promising. In the second stage, sex is less important than the overall relationship, and it is the social and economic practical considerations that are crucial in

sustaining the relationship. In the third stage, both parties identify the other as the lifelong partner, and casual sex with strangers is usually compatible with the loving relationship. But you may have no interest in casual sex any more, you look for something more enduring and solid.

Peter (twenty-nine) has another three-stage theory:

Most gay relations in Hong Kong fit into this model: sex, love, then friends. We usually start with sex, hot and spicy, then it may turn into passionate love, and when the passion fades, you become friends. Well, we don't have marriage to support or control us, otherwise, the third stage may be marriage instead.

Both Simon and Peter agree that most local *nan tongzhi* in relationships end up as friends rather than partners. Peter admitted that he has very few "couple" friends, though he knows more than 200 *nan tongzhi* in Hong Kong. Indeed, rarely would local *tongzhi* groups organize anything for couples—almost all activities are for singles. Peter explains:

Hong Kong *nan tongzhi* have to work twice as hard as our Western gay counterparts for a steady relationship. We are the first generation in Chinese history who has a clear sense of gay identity. The previous generations have left us no positive role models but only heterosexual ones. We are still pressured by our parents to get married. Living in such a small place as Hong Kong, there is little space for steady relationships. Once I had a partner, but it was so hard to keep. Both of us lived with our own parents—we had literally no place for dating. Whenever we went out, we acted like friends, colleagues, or classmates. We were highly cautious not to be seen as camp or gay. So we couldn't be spontaneous and could not even hold hands. The relationship ended in four months, already the longest relationship I ever had in my life!

Many local *tongzhi* maintain a strict segregation between (public) work and (private) sexuality. They avoid exposing their identity to their colleagues at work. Many *tongzhi* have devised tactics to tackle the anxiety of identity exposure. Having two different names is one way; changing names when chatting on the phone is another—male names would be changed to female names: Eric to Erica, Chris to Christine, Louis to Louisa, Tony to Tonia, Andy to Mandy.

The fear of identity exposure is a crucial reason many *nan tongzhi* in Hong Kong are obsessed with acting straight and often discriminate against the so-called effeminate male. Indeed, the terms "straight-acting" and "straight-looking" often appear in the Chinese-Chinese *tongzhi* personal ads. As William said,

> I am always teased as being camp and feminine. My bodily gesture of moving my fingers while talking, touching my face and stomach, and the high pitch were all targets of attack by *nan tongzhi*. One even called me a lesbian. We, the campy ones, have been criticized for giving the *tongzhi* community a bad name. Some *nan tongzhi* simply refuse to go out with us. It's a pity, but the local *tongzhi* community is full of discriminaion—those who are old, short, fat, poor, ugly are all discriminated against.

As 1997 approached, there was surprisingly little discussion of immigration plans among *tongzhi* with their Caucasian partners. All Caucasian interviewees held foreign passports, and could leave Hong Kong if they wanted to. The Chinese were rather disadvantaged in terms of mobility. Benson (thirty-one) dared not bring up the subject of migration with his British boyfriend, Rod, fearing that it would jeopardize their relationship. Rod was very annoyed by the Tiananmen Massacre, and decided to go back to Britain. At that time, Benson's family also decided to leave Hong Kong for Toronto. Benson was a social worker, a profession that has enormous scope in Toronto. Britain was too depressing a place for his career, especially as a foreigner. Benson was quite disturbed:

> Rod kept on asking me to go to Britain with him, saying how gentle and warm British people are. He even accused me of listening too much to my family's choice of migration. But he never thought of the possibility of going to Toronto with me. When I went to Sheffield with him, I realized that I had made the wrong choice. I might end up working in a Chinese takeout for the rest of my life. But I was only twenty-four, had just finished my master's degree in social work in Hong Kong. So I left.

Interviewees were asked also whether they have become more "Chinese" or "Western." All the Caucasian interviewees said that they have not lost their basic beliefs in Western values nor their lifestyle. Some can cite only superficial lifestyle changes such as eating more rice and more Chinese dishes. Compared with their Western partners, many Chinese *tongzhi* admit fundamental changes in their value system and personality after having a Caucasian partner. Their responses include:

- "I am becoming more assertive, independent, verbal, and open, especially in sex."
- "I now feel that I have a Caucasian soul trapped in a Chinese body."
- "I work hard and play hard, with sailing, tennis, and lots of wild parties. Very Westernized, right? Chinese just work and work."
- "I read the English newspaper and never the Chinese one."
- "I feel like a tourist in Hong Kong, though I never leave Hong Kong. I live with a Caucasian and have mostly Caucasian friends."

However, this does not mean that local *tongzhi* completely identify with the so-called Western culture. As will be elucidated in the next section, *tongzhi* actively appropriate Western discourse as a strategy to expand their own personal spaces.

TONGZHI STRATEGIES OF RESISTANCE

Hong Kong *tongzhi* are facing two colonizers—the Chinese culture and Western colonial discourse. By constructing their own hybridized sexual-social identities, Hong Kong *tongzhi* manipulate the limited resources available to denaturalize and destabilize the meanings of "being Chinese" in traditional hegemonic discourses and "being lesbigay" in white Western colonial discourse. Both traditions define Chinese *tongzhi* as failures. Western lesbigay discourse may see Chinese *tongzhi* as closeted and lacking the courage to come out, while Chinese culture condemns them as unfilial for rejecting marriage. Chinese *tongzhi* are locked in a contradictory cultural location: they are seen by Chinese as "hypersexual," but by Western lances as "asexual." "Chinese lesbigay" seems to be a contradictory term. One can choose either one, but not both. Instead of denying these two colonizers, many Hong Kong *tongzhi* actually integrate both the Chinese culture and the Western modern liberal tradition, thus opening up unique cultural-sexual space to handle both cultural expectations that are otherwise impossible to fulfill. Hong Kong *tongzhi* are "Chinese but not really," "*gay* but not really" (Petula Ho, 1997); instead, the meanings of being Chinese and *gay* are challenged, destabilized, and transformed.

The contradictory cultural location of Hong Kong *tongzhi* is radicalized by the specific historical context of massive migration during the 1940s and 1950s. Modern Hong Kong is a refugee city, mostly because of the massive influx of Chinese refugees after World War II. For these refugees who left their village and kinship network, the family became a vital source of support. Hong Kong *tongzhi* in the 1960s and 1970s depended upon their families for emotional, economic, and social support, yet found the family deeply oppressive in pushing them to get married. It is under such pressing cultural dislocation that some *tongzhi* resorted to the Westernized discourse as liberation from the severe family pressure they were facing (Ho, 1995).

It is crucial to note how the West is used by *tongzhi* to counteract and subvert those perceived inadequacies in Chinese culture. Hong Kong *tongzhi* use the West to create a new hybrid form of subjectivity and cultural space unavailable in traditional Chinese culture. To be *gay* and, specifically, a potato queen is a way of coping with the cultural, economic, social, and sexual inferiority felt by *tongzhi*. To be *gay* already implies a certain social status, linguistic ability, class position, and cosmopolitan sensibility. It generates a strong sense of superiority contrasting sharply with the experience of growing up in a Chinese cultural predicament that provides them with no language to construct their sexual experience and identity. Even though they cannot become Caucasians themselves, they consume Western commodities, go to Lan Kwai Fong (LKF), speak a Western language and, finally, have Caucasian lovers. To be a potato queen is to imagine, to fantasize, and to attain the glamorous Western world—it is a shortcut to "self-liberation." Racial hierarchy, despite its oppressive power structure, has been used by local *tongzhi* as a powerful tool for resistance and building up desperately needed identity.

Jason, Mas, and Benny all shared their experiences of manipulating Western *gay* discourse to negotiate their space and resolve their contradictory social location. Jason, now forty, was born and grew up in a very poor family in a Lam Tin Estate with more than thirty people sharing one toilet and kitchen. He has a theory that everyone has the potential for bisexuality, depending on what actual personal and social experiences he or she is having. In his case, the most remarkable experience of growing up was the desire to get rich. His parents were too poor to afford anything but the basics. He could have a piece of chicken breast only on his birthday. Jason is deeply touched by his parents' hospitality:

> I would never forget the days when my parents were working day and night. They had no leisure, just work and work. Sometimes when I woke up at midnight, I still found them working. I really felt bad. All their hope and meaning of life were put on me and my two sisters. Since I was young, I have had a dream of traveling the world with them, and letting them enjoy their old age.

From his class background, it is understandable why he chose a Caucasian partner. Jason had his first sexual experience at nineteen when he was working in a factory. The British boss of the factory cruised him and brought him to Repulse Bay, where Jason had the most expensive and extravagant dinner of his life. Jason can still recall the details of that dinner. Then he stayed in the boss's big house on Kennedy Road.

> When we had sex, I vaguely felt that it was something called *tong-xinglian*. But that really did not matter. I was really touched by his classy manner, the extravagant dinner, the big house, and his invitation to me to live in that big house. Indeed, it's better with a man than with a woman, no one would suspect anything. By the same token, I wouldn't mind marrying a millionaire woman. My parents were happy that the boss treated me so well. I am really grateful that I have my own bed and toilet. I began to wear Clark shoes, use Parker pens, and I went to parties full of foreigners. What else could a nineteen-year-old boy expect in the 1970s? When a piece of chicken breast is already a luxury, sexuality is the least important. I am happy and my parents satisfied.

For Jason, to be gay is primarily not about sex, but a classed response to his need to play the role of a filial son, otherwise impossible for him. By virtue of *being gay*, he is almost automatically considered as belonging to a certain social class otherwise impossible to enter. The *gay* identity is a way of coping with the class, racial, and sexual inferiority some Chinese men feel in the overwhelming dominance of Western images in Hong Kong.

The case of Mas (thirty-three) is different. He emphasizes that his English was always the best at school, and he had been sent to various kinds of English competitions. He read English novels since he was nine years old. It was his uncle, an English teacher, who gave him lots of English books to read. "I love English; speaking English is very sexy and it makes me feel unique and high. People would be very surprised by my English ability and they praised me sincerely."

Mas dreamed of going to the English-speaking world. He was introduced to Dateline when he was seventeen by a senior classmate. It was in Dateline that Mas met his American partner, Grant, who finally brought Mas to Chicago for college. Mas said, "I didn't really love him. He was too old, already sixty-three, twenty years older than my father!"

Mas stayed in Grant's house in Chicago, with his tuition fee paid by Grant for five years, until Grant passed away:

> Family is a big problem for me. My siblings are very close to each other. They meet every weekend, for dinner, mah-jongg, and chatting. My grandmum always asks me all these embarrassing ques-

tions, and wants to introduce girlfriends to me. Every New Year, she says this is the last year she will give red-pocket to me. "Next year, bring me a wife!" Being Chinese is so tiring and painful—too many expectations, from your parents, relatives, neighbors and even ancestors who are dead! I felt so free when I went to the United States.

Now Mas has been back in Hong Kong for six years. He is still attracted to Caucasians. "They do not have family problems like Chinese. Once I have a Chinese boyfriend here. Then I realized that I had to take care of his parental issues. He always talked about parents and coming-out anxiety. We finally split."

Mas is very positive about Western culture. He felt grateful to Grant, and stressed that if he had not met Grant, he might have gotten married to a woman. "No matter how patronizing Grant might have been, he appeared at a time when I desperately needed to escape from my problems. Though I didn't love him, it really didn't matter. Both of us got what we needed. Sometimes need is a bigger word than love."

Benny (thirty-two) is the third case. The most significant category used by him is masculinity. He prefers only very masculine men whom he defines as strong, macho, independent, humorous, and professional. His conception of masculinity fits well with the mainstream stereotypes about Caucasian men. Benny is quite skinny and had been teased since primary school by classmates as being short and bony. He said that when fellow students began the game of dating and flirting with girls, he was too shy and ashamed to do anything, only looking at the handsome masculine men. He felt very inferior because of his body shape:

> I like Caucasians because they are bigger. They have bigger size, big organs, and bigger muscles. Chinese are too weak and feeble; the body shape is already inferior. I was rarely turned on by a Chinese, unless he is really macho, not only the physique but also the mental independence and determination, like most Caucasian men. I have never visited any foreign countries. But I am now living with my Caucasian boyfriend.

He later states that he has been to Malaysia and Taiwan. For him, foreign countries means Western countries. When asked about his idols when he grew up, all Benny can recall are Caucasian male stars such as Charles Bronson, Sean Connery, and John Wayne. The point is not whether Caucasian males really are independent, masculine, and humorous, but that Benny has little problem in fantasizing his ideal homoerotic body according to such racial constructs. Benny used a lot of spatial metaphors in his narrative structure. His spatial narrative extended from body shape to class structure:

> When I was small, we lived in a tiny little room, five people in a ninety-square-foot room. I moved to a bigger house when I was around twelve, but that was only 180 square feet. So you can understand why I was so impressed when my first Caucasian lover invited me to stay in his house. Oh, it was huge! The bathroom was already bigger than my previous house. How can I resist the temptation?

Benny is living with his sixty-one-year-old British boyfriend. Benny said that he is happy:

> I feel secure. I never felt so free, so independent and empowered. You know what, he recently put my name on this 1,500-square-foot apartment. So we own this apartment together. It is not just the money, but the sentiment that matters.

Jason, Mas, and Benny have all created their own sexual-social space by affiliating with Caucasians at a time when there seemed to be little prospect to be a Chinese man who loves men. Their identification with Western *gay* discourse is more strategic than a wholehearted acceptance. They get what they want: Jason becomes rich, Mas feels free, and Benny acquires a sense of security and potency. Ironically, the Western discourses they resort to as liberation are also the sources that generate their sense of inferiority in the first place. The choice of the partner's race is indicative of one's strategy to develop one's sexual identity and space.

Postwar Hong Kong *tongzhi* are faced with an unprecedented dilemma. The traditional Chinese cultural space of tolerating homosexuality has faded; people are now very homophobic and conscious about the homo-hetero divide. The modern Western discourse of romantic love has prevailed in Hong Kong, yet *tongzhi* are still pressured to get married. It is under such contradictions that many *nan tongzhi* resort to the newly imported Western *gay* discourse, either to leave Hong Kong, live with a Caucasian gay, read Western *gay* magazines, see Western movies, or simply to go to Lan Kwai Fong frequently to feel the mood of liberation. As one interviewee (Albert) said earlier in this chapter: "the only way to be *gay* is to live with a Caucasian." While some *tongzhi* genuinely believe in the superiority of Western culture, some merely take it as a tool for their own empowerment and have indigenized the Western gay discourses. In the complex layers of cultural contextualization the terms rice queen and potato queen are deeply inadequate to contain the complexities and diversities of local interracial *tongzhi* dynamics.

Chapter 6

The Cultural Politics of TB/G (Tomboy/Girl) in Hong Kong

The contemporary Western tradition of lesbian studies, be it butch-femme role-playing (Davies and Kennedy, 1991), romantic friendship (Faderman, 1991), lesbian continuum (Rich, 1980), political lesbianism (Leeds Revolutionary Feminist Group, 1981), or woman-identified women (Radicalesbians, 1973), has been preoccupied with the search for the subject: "Who is the lesbian?" Such an attempt to define and search for a distinctive lesbian tradition with a core essence has recently been challenged by the post-Foucaultian lesbian discourse of identity (Fuss, 1989; Butler, 1990; Smyth, 1992; Doan, 1994). If identity is not self-contained, but is the product of differences and otherization, we should be warned against the violence of denying the historical diversities and complexities of relationships between women of different races, cultures, and classes. Instead of asking "who is the real lesbian and who is not," which has often presupposed and universalized modern Western sexual discourses, it is more productive to explore the culturally specific categories through which individual women of different cultural backgrounds construct their relationships with other women. The search for "the real lesbian" has the danger of naturalizing and universalizing the division between sexual minority (lesbi-gay) and majority (heterosexual), which is the specific product of Western constructions that may not have the same applicability and resonance in other cultures (Halperin, 1993; Almaguer, 1991; Plummer, 1992). If women's sexuality has historically been marked by its permeability and ambiguities, what we need is perhaps not a single metanarrative but the cultural and class-specific articulations of women's experiences in each specific context.

In this chapter, I will discuss the indigenous identity politics of the *nü* (female) *tongzhi* scene in Hong Kong. The specific practices of TB/G role-play will be singled out because it signifies the most popular and visible icon of local *nü tongzhi*. When I asked about the extent of TB/G role-playing among *nü tongzhi* in Hong Kong, interviewees from different circles gave me similar figures of between 70 and 90 percent. The younger the *nü tongzhi*, especially those around fifteen to twenty, the more likely they would engage in distinctive TB/G role-playing in which interchangeability between TB and TBG is rare. I interviewed twenty Hong Kong Chinese *nü tongzhi* from 1995 to 1996, with each interview lasting at least one and one-half hours, and the results were published in *Stories of Hong Kong Tongzhi* (Chou, 1996b). I interviewed another twenty local *nü tongzhi* in 1997, some of which were published in *Houzhimin Tongzhi*. This chapter is based mainly on the results of these two surveys.

NÜ TONGZHI IN THE 1960s AND 1970s

The most outstanding and visible feature of the contemporary *nü tongzhi* scene in Hong Kong may be TB/G sexual-social role-playing. TB is short for tomboy, and refers to the so-called masculine role in a *nü tongzhi* relationship. TBG is short for tomboy-girl, and refers to the so-called feminine counterpart of the TB. The phrase "so-called" is added because femininity and masculinity are problematic categories, which have historically been collapsed with biological determination to justify the hierarchical duality of male dominance and female submission.

In the 1960s and 1970s when the "homosexual identity" was imported to Hong Kong from the West, it was the male categories "*gay*" and "homosexual" that first appeared. Visible homosexuals in public arenas such as bars or organizations are predominantly male. Although the Ten Percent Club, the first Hong Kong *tongzhi* organization, founded in 1986, claims to be a lesbian and gay organization, most of the meetings and gatherings in the early years were exclusively male. It was not until 1992 that a visible women's group emerged in the Ten Percent Club. Up till now, there has not been any *tongzhi* bar, karaoke, coffee shop, bookshop, or disco in Hong Kong that caters exclusively to women.

In the 1970s, *nü tongzhi* did not even have a name of their own. They could only use male categories such as *gay, tongxinglian,* or homosexual. The term "TB" was first adopted by individual *nü tongzhi* in small circles in the early 1970s and was popularized in the late 1980s. Although the word *tongzhi* is supposedly gender neutral, more often than not it refers to men rather than women. Jennie (thirty-three) said,

> Men and women are different interest groups. There is no need to force us together. *Nü tongzhi* are still struggling for visibility, thus

having a different concern and agenda than that of *nan tongzhi*. The terms homosexual or gay are problematic as they ignore gender, class, race, and other differences. Look at Hong Kong—the *tongzhi* community is obviously divided into female and male. I wonder why sexual preference is more important than gender.

Jennie continues discussing gender differences in terms of social status and power:

> Even among homosexuals in Hong Kong, being gay is better than lesbian. Gay men at least have lots of saunas, bars, and discos to choose. Most *tongzhi* organizations are actually gay male groups. I think in the Chinese society, being a man is already better than being a woman. We are facing not only denigration in terms of sexual discrimination, we are minimized and trivialized simply because we are women. For most *nü tongzhi*, it is difficult to talk about sexuality without talking about gender issues.

In the 1970s and 1980s when *nü tongzhi* had little public recognition, TB became the most distinguished and, indeed, the only identifiable marker for these female PEPS. Most women had no place to go, no groups to contact, and almost no one with whom to confirm her identity. TB/G became the survival strategy for breaking the silence and asserting visibility. As Susan (thirty-nine) observes,

> In the 1970s, you could only know other *nü tongzhi* by luck. Even if you met one at school or in the workplace, how could you confirm that she was? It is so common for *nü tongzhi* to have crushes on straight women. That is really painful for us. After you fall in love many times, and they are all straight women, you will be very frustrated. And when several of your straight friends have been approached by you, it becomes scandalous among your social circle. People gossip behind your back. Most *nü tongzhi* will give in to family pressure and get married, like most women did at that time.

But Susan also worries about TB visibility. She said, "Whenever media portray *nü tongzhi*, they show a macho TB smoking, drinking, speaking dirty words, sitting with her legs open. If I wear dresses and high heels, they simply cannot believe that I am a *nü tongzhi*. TB have visibility and help some potential *nü tongzhi* to identify themselves, but this visibility also creates a bad name for *nü tongzhi*—pervert, man-hater, and rude."

In the 1960s and 1970s, female and male were the only recognized gender/sexual identities; there was no category for those who rejected or transgressed this duality. Many "gay men" at that time treated themselves as women, thus mistaking their sexual orientation for a gender (non-conformist) role, and their homosexual preference as a gender perversity. When the term TB was first created in the early 1970s, it was a gender identity more than a sexual one. The opposite of TB was not heterosexual, but female. Heterosexuality was not even an identifiable sexual identity at the time. Many *nü tongzhi* thought that they had a male soul trapped in a woman's body. Joey (forty) recalls her experiences:

> I remember reading an English psychology book saying that lesbians have a male mind and soul. That made me very sad, thinking that only a sex change could solve my problem. Only later, when I knew that there existed a group of TB who love women, the idea of undergoing a transsexual surgery was dropped. So when I read the novel *The Well of Loneliness*, I completely identified with the heroine Stephanie, though I later realized that I am not the butch type. But Stephanie was the only lesbian role model I could find.

Contact with Western lesbian discourses has also been crucial for Almond (thirty-six). Her parents sent her to the United States in the late 1970s:

> When I came to America, I was prepared for excitement. At the end of the second year, a black woman approached me and I was turned on. We gradually became a couple, a very visible couple, you know, black and yellow. We had genital sex only one year later. If she were a man, I might have settled down and married her, but because of her gender and race, we parted when I graduated and came back to Hong Kong. . . . I was quite feminine in America, but I butch up myself in Hong Kong as a TB, in order to know other *nü tongzhi*. But whenever I am with a girl, people would think I am cruising her, and this girl would also be nervous.

Most TB interviewees said that knowing a self-identified TB had been crucial in helping them to confirm and consolidate their own TB identity. Whether a PEPS takes up a homosexual identity depends on whether she can connect positive associations with the label, and whether she finds some *nü tongzhi* with whom to identify. However, the absence of lesbian identity ironically can generate a rather safe and relaxed space for same-sex eroticism in which PEPS may not be conscious of their "different" eroticism. Winnie (thirty-eight) attained considerable space for tolerance, which has now disappeared. She had a very deep relationship with her classmate in a famous girls' school. At that time, Winnie did not know the words lesbian or homosexual. They loved each other deeply, slept together, and chatted on the phone every day. Winnie said that although *nü tongzhi* have little public recognition, their private space is much greater than that of *nan tongzhi,* as *nü tongzhi* simply go unnoticed:

> In the 1970s there was no problem in being intimate with a woman—it was only a problem when I was with a man. People were very insensitive and ignorant about lesbian sexuality. There was socially nothing disturbing about women loving women. Our parents never realized or suspected that our relationship was sexual; they thought we were just friends. I could do it but could not go public. I was free in the private sphere but severely constrained in the public sphere. It is the issue of gender rather than sexual orientation—all women are severely constrained in the public sphere.

Girls' schools are places where many *nü tongzhi* first explore their homoeroticism. It is a manless context where many interviewees found their first loves. In girls' schools, the headmaster and teachers frequently remind students of the danger of dating, and that they should put all their energy into their schoolwork. Relations with boys are highly sensitive. Thus, intimacy between girls, so far as there is no explicit sexual behavior, can be seen as natural and normal. But girls' schools are far from a haven. Margaret (thirty-seven) shared her experience in a prestigious convent school:

> School is a very desexualized place, no sex, not even the word sex. The whole body is restrained and disciplined. Our hair cannot be four inches below shoulder or two inches higher than the ear, our school dress cannot be two inches higher than the knee, socks can only be white, shoes must be black, and there are many other rules about the scarf, jacket, earrings, necklace, well, literally the whole body.

But Margaret managed to develop strategies of resistance. Margaret dressed as a TB since the age of fourteen: with very short hair in a typical male style, short pants under her dress, along with masculine behavior and dating girls. Her dress was very subversive, yet did not break the school rules at all. She also joined the basketball team and once was the captain. She said that every time she played in a game, many girls shouted her name loudly, which made her feel that she stood out from the crowd. She began dating girls in lower grades when she was thirteen or fourteen. Two of them were her fans who were crazy for her. But Margaret said that she actually learned her *tongxinglian* identity through her teacher:

> I cannot stand the traditional female image, which is weak and stupid, waiting for the prince to rescue her. So I behave in a very strong and masculine way. Someone did criticize me as copying men. I just laughed—men don't deserve it! I just wanted to express myself. But it was hard. I was always the target of school discipline for my deviancy. Actually, I learned *tongxinglian* from my teacher, can you believe it? One day, she called me into the disciplinary room, interrogated me about my relations with the classmate I loved. She asked whether I was *tongxinglian.* I didn't know what exactly the word meant, so I asked her. She was a bit embarrassed and asked whether we had very intimate behavior and she mentioned kissing and caressing. How great! Only then did I realize that women can have sex with women. The night after, I kissed my girlfriend and we had sex for the first time. It was so romantic! So I became *tongxinglian* in 1975.

The term TB/G appeared in Hong Kong in the early 1970s among the young middle class. Joey (forty) admitted that it was class privilege that made the visibility of *nü tongzhi* possible. Joey had been away from Hong Kong from 1980 to 1993, and was shocked to learn that TB/G had become a rigid role-play. She said that the social roles of TB and TBG in the 1970s were determined more by class than gender identification. If the TBG was wealthier, she would always treat her TB partner and take a more active role in their social life. As Joey said:

> It is usually the middle-class professional women who can afford to be lifelong *nü tongzhi.* Most working-class *nü tongzhi* would get married, then disappeared from our *tongzhi* circle. I came across fifty to sixty *nu tongzhi* in the 1970s, but only the several middle-class ones remain. Maybe I should not label them *nü tongzhi,* as they do not use these categories. The circle of *nü tongzhi* is very small, so when a *nü tongzhi* finds her partner, she may be very possessive, or this couple would disappear from the circle. When she goes back to the *tongzhi* circle, it is usually because she has split up with her girlfriend.

Most middle-aged *nü tongzhi* interviewees said that they had not heard of the term TB/G until recent years. They called each other *xiang zhi* (which literally means "mutual knowing") and did not have the concept of sexual role-playing. Even now, we can still find domestic servants who are single by choice for their entire lives. Many were *zishu nü* (see Chapter 1) before they migrated to Hong Kong. Fong-I is now fifty-two. Her aunt was a *zishu nü*. She said,

> When I was fifteen, I started to work in a garment factory where I met A-ming. We were very close and gradually became a couple. I was later pressured by my mother to get married. They introduced me to male partners in whom I had little interest. Then A-ming suggested that I should move in with her. We rented a small room near the factory. I told my parents that I didn't have to walk forty minutes every day from home to work. My mother agreed. Her marriage was not really happy. She sometimes said that my aunt, who is a *zishu nü*, is more relaxed and happier than she is. That, I think, helped my mother to accept the fact that I lived with another woman. We lived together for more than twenty years. For us, there was no such thing as male-female role-playing, we just cared for each other. I think it is better to live with women. You understand and feel for each other. When I hear about all these heterosexual marital problems, divorces, and messy relationships, I think I am lucky.

However, another informant, Jacky (thirty-eight), disagrees with Fong-I and Joey concerning role-play, insisting that rigid TB/G role-playing already existed in the 1970s. Different circles may have very different practices of gender role-playing. *Nü tongzhi* is not monolithic, especially at a time when there was no visible or public *nü tongzhi* culture. Different women have to find their own way and develop their own subcultures. Jacky worked in an advertising company after she graduated from university. She said,

> In the 1970s, role-playing was very distinctive. If the TBG took an active role, her TB would be annoyed and pissed off. I know a couple who split up because the TB was only a factory worker and the TBG was very middle-class. This TB felt very humiliated for financially depending on the TBG. So they parted. But a TB's career was tough, you had to play a very caring and strong role to get the girl, and you needed considerable economic capacity to feed the TBG. That's why working-class TB had to resort to very exaggerated forms of masculinity—it was merely a defense as they had no other weapons. But not all tomboys were *nü tongzhi*. Many tomboys were merely independent women who rejected the traditional femi-

nine role. They had short hair and butch behavior but they were heterosexual. I think only in the 1990s is the term tomboy equated with lesbian.

Ling-xi (sixty-nine) was a *zishu nü* who migrated to Hong Kong in the 1940s. Ling-xi does not have a distinctive sense of role-play with her woman friend. She had not heard the term TB/G until 1995. Although she did not have any concept of sexual identity, Ling-xi said that sex was common among them:

> Of course we had sex; it was just natural. Indeed we would some- times share our sexual experiences, jokes, and gossip. It is funny— you have sex with your lover but won't talk about it; you talk with your friends but would not do it. From 1949 to 1956, I was living in a big house with five other sisters. There was a sister who was really sex-starved. She had sex with every one of us. Of course, some enjoyed it but some didn't. She would simply climb into your bed at night, and start caressing you.

Ling-xi thought that Western sexual categories such as lesbian, dyke, bisexual, or queer were too Western, too sex-oriented and radical. She said, "You should not be too radical. I don't agree with the Western model of parading in public. Chinese people would not accept that. It would have far greater derogatory side effects." This is a common reason offered by local *tongzhi* to explain why Western sexual identities have never been widely used in Hong Kong. Most *nü tongzhi* have little problem accepting their own same-sex eroticism but find it absurd to use Western categories and come out to their parents. Even the activists in the *nü tongzhi* scene have reservations about the coming-out strategy. As early as 1983, Lieh-Mak, after researching lesbianism in Hong Kong, concluded that the reluc- tance of Chinese lesbians to come out of the closet must not be construed as the result of social disapproval of lesbianism in particular, but rather as the result of social constraints on sexual matters in general (Lieh-Mak, O'Hoy, and Luk, 1983). Many *nü tongzhi* simply refuse to amplify their sexual orientation, which for them is merely an integral part of life.

It is also a matter of class and consumption power. As Lisa (forty) told me,

> In the 1960s and 1970s, we simply lacked the necessary financial power to maintain an independent sexual identity like lesbian or TB. When you were poor, relying on your parents, you must get married to settle down. Whether you loved women or men was simply beside the point—heterosexual women also had few choices about their husband and sex life.

Class is still a major issue in the contemporary scene. Many working-class *nü tongzhi* are invisible in the *tongzhi* scene. They interact mostly in an interpersonal context, and have little commitment or sense of belonging to the *tongzhi* community as they do not feel included. Fong (twenty-six) is a working-class *nü tongzhi* who lives with her partner in a small room:

> Both of us are very disciplined about spending. We spend half of our salary in renting this small place. And the rest goes to basic expenditures. I also have to give money to my parents. We don't have much left. We rarely go out for dinner. Watching a movie is already a luxury. So you know why we rarely go to *tongzhi* bars or karaoke—you have to spend at least 150 HK dollars for a night. I prefer to visit friends or to have friends in our house. It is warm and cozy.

It is not just working-class *nü tongzhi* who are invisible in the commercial and organizational scene, but the working class in general. Yet Fong and her partner do make use of heterosexual venues to expand their *tongzhi* space. They always go to straight discos such as China Jump, Hot Gossip, and Manhattan, which have free admission on Wednesday night for women. Fong said, "We are already a couple—both don't want our partner to be cruised by other *nü tongzhi*. It is ironically safer when we go to straight bars. We just dance and enjoy ourselves, and pay no attention to those guys who want to date us."

Many *nü tongzhi* couples have developed a "two against the world" pattern in which they spend most of their time together and disregard the *tongzhi* community, even if their relationship may not be very gratifying. Many *nü tongzhi* said that finding and keeping relationships are their major problems—they are unable to find a partner, and do not know how to cope with a relationship full of problems. This perhaps explains the disturbingly high rate of attempted suicide in the local *nü tongzhi* circle. Among my forty *nü tongzhi* interviewees, eight have attempted suicide, 20 percent of the total population. They all have few problems with their own sexual orientation, but family and social pressure, sour relationships with their lovers, and pessimism about the *nü tongzhi* future frustrate them.

IDENTITY FORMATION OF TB/Gs IN THE 1990s

Since TBs do not identify with the traditional feminine role and rarely use female pronouns to address one another, I will use the Chinese gender-neutral pronoun *ta* or *ta-de* to refer to TBs. The Chinese terms *ta* (s/he) and *ta-de* (her/his) can apply to both female and male.

TB and TBG are mutually constitutive, yet in very different ways. Without a TB, the identity of TBG cannot be sustained. TBGs have the "privilege" of passing as "normal" women and rarely feel the need to adopt a *tongzhi* identity. "TBG" is not a self-identified identity. Not a single interviewee actually referred to herself as a TBG. They are comfortable with being women and would not mind the heterosexual implications of the term TBG—the *girl* of the tom*boy*. I found that all the TBG informants have had relationships with men. Since they are playing a similar feminine role as "girlfriends," they do not feel the need to adopt a new identity when the gender of their partner is different. Their consciousness of being girlfriends seems to overwhelm that of being *tongzhi*. When asked about their sexual orientation, they would say:

- "I am a woman, an ordinary woman."
- "I am *ta-de* (her TB partner's) girlfriend."
- "I am with Ken, a TB."
- "I love a person; gender is not important."
- "Everyone is both yin and yang. If you really want to classify, then I am *tongxinglian*. But I don't like to be classified."

Sexual identity is not a natural or direct result of sexual behavior and desire, but is the outcome of an individual's interpretation of his or her sexual behavior and desire in particular ways. The notion of sexual identity is already culturally specific, as many people from non-Western cultures would not use sexual orientation to classify and divide people. For example, a TBG is a woman who has sex with women but refuses to use the homo-hetero divide to identify herself. None of my TBG informants said she is a *nü tongzhi*, but neither did anyone say that she is heterosexual. Instead, they tend to describe their identity in terms of a social role as a girlfriend ("I am *ta-de* girlfriend"), a concrete relationship ("I am with Ken, a TB"), gender role ("I am a woman, an ordinary woman"), or being beyond gender duality ("I don't like to be classified").

Many TBG take a rather nonessentialist position when they are asked to define and position their sexual identity. They perceive their same-sex eroticism not as "identity" but as specific roles and performances in specific relationships, thus exposing the limitations of the homo-hetero divide. For example, Carly (thirty-one) said,

> I can't say what "is" my sexual identity. I wonder if there is such a thing as sexual identity. Human eroticism is much more complex than any label or identity. I experience my sexuality differently in different roles and relationships. Like my ex-lover Jackie, I think

class and age are more important than gender. She is thirteen years older than I am. What I treasure is the loving relationship.

Many TBGs use the language of love to respond to the identity issue, not necessarily because of homophobia, but because they do not feel the need to use the gender of erotic object choice to classify themselves. Judy (twenty-four) sees no relationship between same-sex eroticism and sexual identity:

> No matter whether I am with a woman or a man, I am the same person and behave the same. I don't shift from homo to hetero just because the sex of my partner is different, do you understand? Why should I use a different label when I am with a different sex? Why don't I use a different name when I am with a person of different height, weight, age, color, ethnicity, surname, or social class?

When asked how they entered this *quan* (circle), all TBGs responded by reporting their first relationship with a TB lover. Not one TBG interviewee stressed that she was born this way. Many of them believed that had they not met their first TB partner, they would probably have continued to date men. The message is clear: there seems to be no choice for a TB, but there does seem to be a choice for a TBG in choosing the gender of her lover. This causes immense tension and anxiety in TB/G relationships. A TB has to face the endless worry of *ta-de* girl leaving her for a man, whereas a TBG faces the accusation of not being a real lesbian or *tongzhi*.

The distinction between a TBG and a heterosexual woman seems to be ambiguous. TBGs dress as most women do, although they sometimes exaggerate their "feminine" features such as their breasts, back, and legs by wearing very tight T-shirts, mini-skirts, or shorts. Many TBGs tend to be quiet in the presence of a TB and let them do the social talking. Put simply, a woman requires the presence of a TB partner to constitute her status as a TBG.

By comparison, TB is a self-inscription, irrespective of whether they have a girlfriend or not. TBs have been defined by the patriarchal society as nonwomen, as they refuse to play the feminine role. Being nonwomen, nonmen, and therefore unidentifiable in the patriarchal language system, they need a clear identity that goes beyond the male-female duality. All TB interviewees stressed that they like women by nature ("I was born this way!"), and elaborated in detail how they exhibited clear signs of erotic interest in women during childhood. They stress that it would be unnatural for them to behave in a "feminine" way. They reported that from an early age they wanted to touch and to be touched intimately by women, they all resented wearing dresses, prefer the so-called masculine traits, such as protecting the weak, are attracted to pretty girls, and finally, all my TB interviewees realized their sexual orientation before they reached the age of fifteen, and most were under twelve. Alex (nineteen), for example, shared the experiences of teasing men about their bodies:

> Since I was twelve, we [three to four female classmates] always talked about the size of the penises of classmates who had passed by, and we would imitate the moaning of women, and have lots of puns and jokes about sex. It was most interesting to notice the embarrassment of these boys—they looked at each other, shocked and helpless, just like a child doesn't know what to do when adults talk about him. It's great fun! In the TV, movies, and everyday lives, it is always the men who comment and stare at the female body. Now, we talk about male bodies and the size of their things, and they are just helplessly embarrassed.

In the TB/G scene, the identity of *nü tongzhi* applies to TBs but not necessarily to TBGs. This may be the result of confusing homosexuality with gender nonconformity—only those who reject the gender conformity of hegemonic femininity are considered to be real TBs or lesbians, whereas TBGs are seen by the mainstream (male) world as normal women, with their same-sex eroticism being ignored, trivialized, and minimized—"She just needs a good fuck by a man!"

"TB" seems to be a membership card for entering the circle. When a new member first joins a *nü tongzhi* gathering, it is usually a TB who checks her identity. Appropriate self-naming, attire, jargon, dress, and manners are the necessary basis for entrance and acceptance by the circle. For example, when Ping (twenty-eight) first entered the scene in 1991, she was shocked by the rigid TB/G distinction. She was asked by a TB she had just met about her identity:

TB: Are you TB or TBG?
Ping: Why should I be categorized?
TB: Everyone has a role.
Ping: What are TB and TBG?
TB: If you are not clear who you are and what you want, you will be assigned a temporary role. Let's assume that you are TBG. OK!

It is interesting that Ping was assumed to be a TBG until proven otherwise. There seems to be a hierarchy of *tongzhi*-ness, as if a TB is one of the real *quan nei ren* (people in the circle) and is supposedly a core member of the *nü tongzhi* circle, whereas a TBG's *tongzhi* status is highly precarious. Unless the new member has a typical TB look and behavior, she may not immediately qualify as a *tongzhi*, and may be classified as TBG for the time being.

Ping complained that a TB even harassed her to inspect her identity, caressed her back to check whether she wore a bra, and touched her thigh suggestively to check her responses. Ping was later classified as a rare species of womanly TB. She was also teased for being a macho TBG who does not know the rules. Ping admitted that there is peer pressure to conform, but said,

> Fortunately, there is now the new trend of the "pure-les" [pure lesbian—no role-playing], that is, woman loving woman and not caring about gender role-play. I am pure-les and self-identified as *nü tongzhi* rather than TB or TBG.

In recent personal ads in *Lui Tong Yuen*, diversity extended beyond the rigid dichotomy between TB and TBG. In issue number 5 (January 1998), for example, a self-identified TB (Wing, twenty-two) stresses that she looks for both TB and TBG women. Another woman (Xiao-Qu, twenty-five) used the Taiwanese *nü tongzhi* term *bu-fen* (beyond categorization) to describe herself as "*bu-fen* but slightly tends toward TB." Again, another self-identified TB used the Chinese name Shirley Ho M. Y. in the personal ads. All these indicate more fluid and diverse identity dynamics within the *nü tongzhi* scene.

Joyce (twenty-two) also had the experience of her TB identity being questioned. Joyce does not drink beer, which is quite rare for a TB. Having a low tolerance for alcohol, Joyce tried very hard and can now drink two bottles of beer in one night. Joyce said, "I passed the examination for TB. You know, you have to smoke and drink, otherwise you can't enter the circle." Joyce has always been criticized for not being TB enough: "One TB even seduced my girlfriend to prove that I am not a real TB, that I should be a TBG." Joyce explained to me that a TB is "obliged" to act aggressively toward other TB when *ta-de* girl is being approached.

To be an accepted member in the circle, one needs a proper name. Joyce admits that her name has caused a lot of suspicion, as it is exceptional for a TB to use a female name. Joyce uses the gender-neutral name "Ah-Joy" in the *tongzhi* circle.

Real Chinese full names are not expected in the circle. Most TB adopt a gender-neutral or male English name, such as Julian, Joe, Ken, Denis, Joey, Billy, Jacky, Wallace, Chris, Leslie, Sidney, Aaron, Peter, or Sam.

Some create a unique masculine name such as He-man, Fai-zai, or Tai-keung. Most Chinese parents give their daughters feminine names such as An-jing (stable-quiet), Ai-mei (love-beauty), or Chun-lai (spring-pretty). There is a Chinese tradition of giving a daughter a male name so that the next child will be a son. Some women have very masculine names such as Dai-nan (make the next child a son) or Ruo-nan (looks/acts like a boy). As one TB said, "My Chinese name is Xiao-Long (little dragon), and my parents really brought me up as a boy. I feel shame for it, so I use the name A-Ming, which is more gender neutral."

In terms of naming, there is an obvious gender difference. All personal ads in *Hong Kong Magazine, Contacts,* and other *nan tongzhi* magazines are anonymous, stressing the objective features of age, outlook, occupation, class, and physical features. On the contrary, the personal ads in *nü tongzhi* newsletters such as *Lui Tung Yuen* include names—indeed, the names are in bold and serve as the title of the personal ads, thus giving a strong sense of personal touch and unique individuality.

Approximately 60 percent of the names in *Lui Tung Yuen* personal ads are Chinese (nicknames). In my research, around 30 percent of local *nü tongzhi* use Chinese nicknames, which contrasts sharply with the *nan tongzhi,* of whom more than 90 percent would use English names for socializing in the *tongzhi* circle. The *nü tongzhi* scene in Hong Kong is marked by racial segregation. Chinese-Caucasian *nu tongzhi* relationships can rarely be found, especially in the bar scene, whereas the male bars and saunas have steady crowds of Caucasian customers. A TB informant who constantly goes to H2O and Circus, two *tongzhi* bars that have mostly women customers, told me that she never sees any Caucasians there; all the customers are Chinese. As the *nü tongzhi* scene in Hong Kong is predominantly Chinese, many of them feel little need to use English names.

TB: THE SEXUAL POLITICS
OF BREAST BINDING

Identity is not self-contained. It is through the constant performance of a TB's toughness, which includes specific forms of attire, social manners, body language, a deep voice, and sexual role-playing, that the TB identity is produced and stabilized. Although *nü tongzhi* are free to adopt different gender roles and behavior, the fact that masculine traits are much more positively valued in mainstream society has encouraged some *nü tongzhi* to take up the TB identity. Many TBs resort to socially masculine roles to attain the sense and space of freedom, status, and autonomy unavailable to women who play the traditional feminine role. Stereotypically, TBs wear male outfits including trousers, business suits, and ties, have very short hair, pay bills, and open doors for TBGs, and TBGs play the traditional role of a wife, who stays at home, and looks pretty and soft.

TB is not only a sexual role, but a social performance in which wearing male or gender-neutral attire is a basic requirement. Leslie (twenty-seven) works in an office and has to wear dresses. She changes to male attire every time she goes to meet *tongzhi* friends at night. Leslie explained, "I like this job very much—I'm well-paid and have great job satisfaction. But I have to wear dresses during work, especially if I go to formal meetings or business lunches. It is really a sacrifice. It is not my real self."

Leslie maintained a strict segregation between work and leisure, private and public, and never let *nü tongzhi* friends enter *ta-de* work world. Once Leslie had an urgent request from a *nü tongzhi* friend, and had to rush to her after work. Leslie then realized that several *nü tongzhi* friends were there. They were shocked to see Leslie in a skirt and wearing makeup. She was very embarrassed: "A TB just stared at me, speechless, as if I was a traitor. That day was the rare day in the year that I put on makeup because I had to meet a big business client. That is why they were so shocked, and all said that I cross-dressed and pretended to be a woman! They tell the joke even now."

This is an antiessentialist idea, where biology fails to be the natural ground for gender identity. A biologically female body by no means guarantees femininity. Womanliness is only a role performance not all females are playing or enjoying. That implies that Leslie's real self is already a self in drag, or indeed, that all gender is drag. Thus, when Leslie wears dresses, she is ironically performing a double drag—a cross-dressed TB now cross-dressed to dress like a woman.[1]

TBs usually go for jobs that allow masculine or gender-neutral attire, and rarely accept a job that requires wearing skirts. Leslie is an exception. A TB's choices in the job market are limited. They rarely work as teachers, nurses, executives, or secretaries because wearing dresses or even makeup would be necessary. In this research, I found that most TBs work in hair salons, factories, advertising companies, television, or the movie industry, none of which require feminine attire and makeup. For example, Ken chose design as *ta-de* lifelong career. Ken stressed that it is a deliberate choice:

There are not many jobs where I can expose my identity without fear. Therefore, I chose design. In this present company, my colleagues knew what kind of person I am right at the start, and I can even bring my girlfriend to the office and let her sit beside me, watching me work. How nice!

Many TBs choose to be self-employed, so they can enjoy the greatest freedom in terms of work attire, and build up unique gender and sexual positions that can resist the traditional feminine role. This does not imply, however, that local TBs are mostly working class. I met two TBs who came from very wealthy family backgrounds. Because of their class background, they can afford to work as a freelance writer and hairstylist respectively and can own comfortable apartments, thus significantly enhancing their *tongzhi* space.

Many TBs, given their male attire and well-trained deep voices, pass as male. Actually, all TBs can tell some personal stories of passing as male: being asked to leave women's public bathrooms, using the men's room without being noticed, being addressed as "sir" (*xian-sheng*), or being approached by gay men. In one case, the chair of the Ten Percent Club (in 1997) and the founder of *Tongzhi* Studio (the first *nü tongzhi* performance group in Hong Kong), Aaron (twenty-four), had the experience that *ta-de* girlfriend did not realize that Aaron was not a man until they had sex for the first time after several weeks of courtship.

Alex (nineteen) was still excited when she recalled her first experiences of passing as a man:

> I was [mis]recognized as male when I went to the ladies' room. This old woman even called the security guard to stop me. That was really embarrassing. From then onward, I never use the ladies' room. That is one inconvenient thing about being a TB. The men's toilet is so dirty, stinky, and unpleasant. Males piss everywhere and have no sense of decency. I have trained myself not to use the public toilet. So when I go out, I drink very little water and can stay on the street for seven or eight hours without going to the toilet. I know some TBs have kidney problems.

Ken (twenty-three) passed as a boyfriend with *ta-de* girlfriend's parents. Ken went to her place to have dinner with her parents. They did not know that their daughter's boyfriend was not a man even after they chatted for three hours. Ken said,

> That was really cool! The idea that I am not a male simply did not come to their minds. I passed and don't have to see them again. Her parents praised me for being caring, sensitive, and career minded. Now she lives with me with her parents' permission. But I will try

not to see them again, to avoid any possibility of my identity and age being disclosed. For me, TB is neither copying or subverting hetero-sexuality, I just find it convenient to have a girlfriend without being noticed. . . . My mother is most clever. Once, a neighbor asked her whether I am her son or not. My mother didn't say whether I am a girl or boy, but that: "I am *ta-de* mother." Chinese language is better here as *ta-de* is a gender-neutral pronoun. There is no need to differentiate for her or him.

Alex and Ken have spent a lot of effort to pass as men. They lower their voices, bind their breasts, and behave in a masculine manner, until they are (mis)taken as male. Speech mannerisms are crucial ways to pass as a TB. Yet, as Alex said, "We act like men but better than men, more sensitive and less bullshit. We behave like men, but with more style and subtlety. TB is male-like, but far better. You need to remember this."

It is well known that some working-class TBs speak very crudely in everyday conversation. During one interview a young working-class TB talked to another TB:

TB1: Your girl is horny! Her body shape is superb.
TB2: It's bloody hard to keep this girl. Lots of competitors. Don't put a finger on her.
TB1: Fuck you, we are brothers. I won't do that.

TBs may swear and publicly fight for their girls They even break glasses and bottles in *tongzhi* venues when there are fights. Although such misconduct is not common, it can easily be amplified and become big news because it is done by women. Indeed, some (male) managers of *tongzhi* venues admitted that they dislike or even reject *nü tongzhi* customers. Yet it is always gay men rather than TBGs that complain about the rudeness of TBs.

Once when I was in H$_2$O with two friends, I suddenly heard a lot of shouting. When I turned around, a TB was breaking a beer bottle on the ground and then hit another TB in the face. They wrestled and pulled each other's hair and clothes. The male manager immediately intervened and asked them to get out. The fight was brief, but the shock remains with me. Violence has traditionally been defined as a male territory, and fighting as a male affair. A young woman who is brutal and aggressive fundamentally challenges and redefines the meaning of women and femininity. This also provokes male anxiety, as these women have taken the supposedly male right and power to be violent and physical. The fight, however unreasonable and inappropriate, demonstrates the power of TBs in refusing to play the feminine role. Some TBs simply refuse to be identified as women.

To pass as male, most TBs conceal their breasts. Women's breasts are a crucial biological marker that have been socially codified and objectified by the male gaze as the feminine erotic symbol. To establish a definite TB identity, TBs need to distinguish themselves from ordinary women. Most TBs never wear a bra. Some wear two tight T-shirts to cover up their breasts. Some others just bind their breasts. Many TBs have gone through a painful struggle with their biological growth:

> **Julian** (nineteen): I will never forget my first menstruation, which came when I was thirteen. It was horrifying. That was a serious blow to my self-esteem. I tried very hard to be masculine and often dreamed of myself as an androgynous person. I have been attracted to girls since I was around ten. I bought men's clothes, I drank beer, pushed my voice down, I thought I was masculine and stronger than men. Then, when the menstruation came, everything was in vain. I had to accept that I am a woman. It caused me great pain and confusion: Can I still love women? Was my sexual fantasy about women abnormal? Should I date boys instead?

> **Ken** (twenty-three): When my breasts grew bigger, I wanted to cover them up. I hated being stared at by men. I hoped to be strong and independent, so that I could have a beautiful girlfriend. Having a pair of big breasts would make me feel like a woman. I started to use Scotch tape to bind my breasts. It was so painful and would even bleed. I got an infection in the first month. But I was willing to pay the cost as I wanted to prove that I was not a traditional little doll. The more pain I experienced, the greater sense of self-esteem and power I attained.

> **Alex** (nineteen): I am really disturbed by my big breasts. Thirty-four-D is really a curse for a TB. So when I watch the bra ads, especially these white lace and sexy black bras, I think it is just for male consumption. I hate the feeling of being objectified by the male gaze. I remember when I first bound my breasts, I felt so proud and empowered. So I told the man who chased me for months: Do you really love women? What a coincidence, I love women too!

It is through breast binding that some TBs defeminize and thus recontextualize the breasts from a conventionally feminine eroticism constructed by the male gaze. Breast binding desexualizes the breasts and simultaneously recategorizes them as proof of a new erotic subject—a TB who is no longer an ordinary woman but a different gender-sexual subject who loves women. Bound breasts have thus resexualized TB in *ta-de* own way. By desexualizing and simultaneously reactivating their breasts in their own way, TBs are able to relocate themselves from the traditional position of sexual object to become self-produced gender-sexual subjects (Chao, 1996).

In the sexual scene, most TBs would not take off their clothes, or let the partner touch their breasts and genitalia, and many would play the role of the top but never the bottom. Rarely would a TB moan during sex. Many said that they would be sexually gratified when their girlfriends had orgasms, which confirms the TB's potency. From a purely biological viewpoint, many TBs are still "virgin," as they may perceive being penetrated as a sign of submission.

Breast binding is a good basis to elucidate the differences among TBs. My TB informants can broadly be divided into three categories: breast binding, nonbinding, and antibinding. The breast-binding TBs make up about 30 percent of the TB population. They identify themselves neither as women nor men but an alternative gender/sexual category, TB. They are highly conscious of their TB-ness and all insist that they were born this way. None of them will undress, moan, or allow themselves to be touched by a TBG during sex. Most of these TBs were younger and came from working-class backgrounds. Finally, none of them have relationships with men.

The second category, which includes around 60 percent of local TBs, is the nonbinding group. They usually maintain a distinctive TB/G role, and would not undress or moan during sex. But they do not bind their breasts, saying that it is natural for them to love women. They need not restrain or harm their breasts. They do not reject their female identity, but stress the limitations of male-female duality, arguing for diversities and differences among women rather than any single definitive discourse on womanhood. In terms of class location, many middle-class TBs find breast binding and passing as men too risky for their professional careers, because exposure of their female sex could ruin their careers. They have enough class and social power to maneuver and do not need radical methods such as breast binding to attain personal space.

The third category, antibinding, includes nearly 10 percent of local TBs. They usually have a weak sense of TB-ness. They would say: "I don't mind being called TB, but I prefer to be just myself," "I am a TB, but people have far more complexity than just a label." Most of them would insist on an egalitarian attitude of mutual respect in intimacy. They would undress during sex and would enjoy the multiplicity of role-playing. They accept their womanhood and the pronoun "she/her." They identify themselves only occasionally as TBs as a subversive strategy and will also emphasize the distinction between TB-ness and masculinity. Even when they play the butch role, they attribute it merely to personal preference. Vin (twenty-five), for example, said that it is her family background that accustomed her to the TB role:

> I am the eldest and grew up with a very working-class background. So I got used to the masculine role. My mother actually kept my hair very short as it is more convenient for doing housework. When I first felt attracted to women, I had already taken a very dominant social role. I just can't imagine myself as a TBG. But it does not mean that I can only like feminine women. Actually, my present girlfriend is very androgynous, sometimes being mistaken for a TB. We have a same-sex love; we don't need male-female heterosexual role-playing. For me, short hair is a symbol of power rather than mimicking men. I am a TB, not a man.

DIFFERENCES AND SIMILARITIES AMONG TBGs

In the TB/G scene, TBs appear to occupy a much more vocal and core position than TBGs. TBs are far more eager than TBGs to maintain the rules and roles of TB/G. This seems to be a direct result of the extent of oppression and denunciation by the mainstream society. If a TB's girlfriend breaks the rules of TB/G role-playing, she may be denounced as not a *tongzhi*, but a *quan wai ren* (people outside the circle). As P-zai (twenty-two), a self-proclaimed TB, complained about her girlfriend Helen,

> Helen is not a *tongzhi* and does not know the rules. I was her first TB boyfriend. You know what—Helen undressed me when I was asleep. So she saw my breasts. I woke up when she tried to touch and caress me. I was so shocked and annoyed. We had a serious fight. The worst thing is that I wore a bra that night. She had begged many times to see my breasts. That night, she asked me again. I conceded and wore a black bra under a thin and tight T-shirt. That is all I could show her. I never thought that she would dare to undress me when I was asleep. I was really angry and simply lost interest in her. We split up the next morning. She breaks all the rules. Everyone must have a position of her own in this world. You cannot be father, mother, son, and daughter at the same time. You can only choose one.

P-zai's anger and disappointment when *ta-de* breasts were seen by Helen is similar to that of a chauvinist straight man who is perceived as campy or effeminate, or when a feminine woman is (mis)taken as macho, aggressive, and rude.

The bra is one of the strongest visual symbols of the embodiment of femaleness. When P-zai's bra and breasts were seen and touched by Helen, P-zai could no longer play the TB role. Instead, P-zai's femaleness was created and amplified by the feminine other (Helen). It is a series of feminine codifications, from bra exposure to the entire process of being stripped, looked at, and touched that defeated what P-zai has tried very hard to resist—a traditional feminine image and position. It further denied and eliminated the sexual tension between TB and TBG, which relies on the recognition of the uniqueness of TB-ness. P-zai is now no different from any ordinary woman. Here lies her frustration and anger. As P-zai said, "I lost interest in her." The sheer presence of Helen reminds P-zai of the failure to transcend the boundaries of male-female duality. Once a TB's breasts are focused on as a feminine and sexual object of desire, the identity of TB-ness is gone. Indeed, a week later, Helen asked to get together again. They had sex. But P-zai said,

> I became "impotent." The idea that she has seen my bra and breasts really turned me off. I simply cannot do it. It is worse than early ejaculation; I am simply impotent. I lost interest in her.

A *nü tongzhi* (Mitchell, seventeen) told me a story about a TB who refused to assume the female identity.

> Once this TB was chatting with us. She kept on saying to me that "You women act too girlish; you women are too gossipy." I was not very comfortable, so I asked her: "Aren't you a woman?" This TB was so angry and behaved in an ultramasculine way. She stared at me and said, "You are a woman and I am the real man, more masculine than men. You can ask all my brothers." Then she tossed back a beer with her "brothers." She didn't talk to me anymore. I know I really hit a nerve and pushed her to face her biological sex, something she would like to forget.

This TB was angry because Mitchell also transgressed the TBG role of quiet and tame listener. In the social scene, most TBGs would let their TB partners dominate the conversation. Mitchell not only refused to play this "feminine" role, she challenged the TB's core identity, that she is a woman, not a (tom)boy.

Likewise, some TBG interviewees have equally rigid expectations of the TB partner. The pressure on TBs to exhibit a potent self is indeed reinforced and perpetuated by a parallel desire among TBGs to seek a masculine body and mind in a TB. One TBG admitted: "Once I had a TB partner whose breasts were bigger than mine. I couldn't accept it. It was so weird." A TBG's sexuality and identity requires an Other who can appreciate, confirm, and glamorize her femininity. Another TBG shared her experiences:

> When Vin undressed that night, I was so surprised. How can a TB take off *ta-de* clothes—aren't you a TB? I have never met any TB who would undress during sex. I did urge my previous partners to undress. They all refused. One finally just pulled *ta-de* T-shirt, showed me the shoulder and told me that is the bottom line—shoulder.

Some TBGs prefer their partners to bind their breasts so as to pass. As Pauline (twenty-seven) said, "I prefer my partner to bind *ta-de* breasts. Hong Kong is too homophobic. If my partner dresses up as a man, we can pass as an ordinary couple. So I like role-playing, and I enjoy my feminine role, Ken enjoys *ta-de* masculine role. It is discreet and simple."

Pauline then mentioned her previous girlfriend in college:

> My previous girlfriend was not a TB and we were very secretive. When we were chatting on the phone, I would avoid letting my parents and siblings know who I was talking to. I spoke in a low voice and avoided any sweet words. And I could not bring her home to see my parents. Even after we broke up, I could not give my parents any hints they could associate with a girlfriend. So I never talked about her age, height, appearance, name, or even personality. My parents just thought that she was a boy. So now I prefer a TB to be my "boyfriend." My parents saw my partner once. They thought that Sidney was a boy. So we pass. And I can talk on the phone with Sidney in soft tones about love and sex, even when my parents are around.

There is indeed a crucial reason why TBs feel the need to amplify their masculinity and toughness. Many TB interviewees have been deeply hurt by their girlfriends' complaints about TB gender identity:

- "Why aren't you a man? It would be so good if you were a man."
- "If you were a man, I could die for you, ten times—a hundred times!"
- "If you had a sex change, I would marry you right away."
- "I want to get married; I want to have children. You can't give me that."

Some TBs therefore resort to the radical device of acting butch in exaggerated forms. As one TB (twenty-six) said,

> We were together for two years. I thought we could be forever. I did everything I could to satisfy her. I even learned plumbing to please her, make her feel that I am better than a man. Just when I began to be slightly relaxed and confident with our relationship, she said one night in a joking way: "You simply cannot give me what I need. I need a man, not a surrogate or fake one!" She thought it was just a joke, but I totally collapsed and went mad. I cried in front of her. It was the first time I cried in front of a woman. I was so frustrated. All along, she appeared to be so liberal and avant-garde. But it was just a facade. If she needs a man, why did she start with me in the beginning? Why?

Age plays an interesting role here. The most visible TB/G scene in contemporary Hong Kong is made up entirely of young women. In H2O and Secret Party, the only two *tongzhi* venues with mostly female customers, more than 90 percent of the customers are under twenty-five, mostly between sixteen and twenty-one. Not every woman can be identified as *nü tongzhi*, even if they have relationships with women. These young women may have relationships with other women for curiosity, for vanity, to show off their avant-garde spirit, or just to try something queer and adventurous. In contemporary Hong Kong, a fourteen- or fifteen-year-old girl has already been tempted and pressured to have romances. Yet many of them find boys their own age too immature, sexist, and insensitive. If a girl is approached by a caring TB who acts like a man—escorts her home, sends her flowers and a teddy bear, writes her love letters—she may be tempted to taste the romance. For a young woman of fifteen or sixteen, having a romance with another woman is not a sin, but a trendy, risky, and subversive deviancy that some would fantasize about. This has been particularly true in the 1990s when gender bending and androgyny have become fashionable.

However, when this young girl reaches her twenties, she may feel the social pressure to date a man. Having a heterosexual relationship would be crucial for her career and social status. Then, when a male with social status and power pursues her, she might find it more beneficial to be with a man. She might quit seeing women. She is not "converted" from a homosexual to heterosexual. She has never identified herself as a lesbian or *tongzhi*. She just changes from one specific relationship to another one, playing very similar roles as a girlfriend. Joanne (nineteen), now in her second year in the university, said:

It is really ironic—in convent [secondary] school it is a fad to date girls, but now [university] everyone dates boys, and it would be weird if I still dated girls. It would be a shame to have no romantic experiences throughout campus life. And romance only means boy-girl relationships. It is especially true as I am living in the student hall. It is so heterosexist. All the boys talk about girls, and girls about boys. Most of the chat and jokes in the hall are like that. It is really hard to resist.

TBGs are not the same as heterosexual women. The major difference between TB/G role-play and heterosexuality is the power dynamics. To begin with, a TB can be noticed simply by her appearance but a TBG cannot be seen and detected unless she lets people know. TBGs can easily recognize TBs, but not vice versa. Most TBs are eager to know who is straight and who is not but need TBGs to confirm them. It is usually the TBG who initiates the social and sexual interaction. This is a difference from heterosexuality: straight men do not have anxiety concerning the sexual orientation of their "target." For heterosexual men, all women they feel attracted to can be potential targets; for TBs, no more than 10 percent of women, if we follow the Kinsey report, can be targets, and they never know who belongs to this 10 percent. It is this anxiety that gives TBGs immense power and space unavailable to straight women. The fact that a TBG has a TB partner changed the dynamics of the relationship—her sense of self-worth is no longer predicated on the presence of a man. It is her partner who has to face the full extent of sexism, misogyny, and lesbophobia. It is usually the TB, not the TBG, who is seen as evil and threatening to society. A TBG appears to be a regular woman, would only be noticed when she is with a TB, and, even so, would sometimes be seen as the victim. On the contrary, a TB passes as a man, and thus directly threatens and challenges the male norm. The pressure on a TB comes not just from society, but also from the fear that a TBG would turn to men and get married. TBs are also insecure about failing to satisfy TBGs' sexual needs. As Peggy (nineteen) said, "Christy always asked me to compare *ta-de* performance with my previous boyfriend. Once I said that *ta-de* sexual performance and potency are better than a man is. Christy was so excited. She kept on asking, 'Is it true? Is it true?' Besides, it is well-known that in Hong Kong, TBs outnumber TBG, making choices more limited. Many TBs complain that in the rare case when two TBGs start a relationship, it simultaneously deprives TBs of two choices.

Indeed, in some *nü tongzhi* gatherings, although there is an admission fee, women who wear dresses are admitted for free. For example, the title of a party organized by Party Factory in November 1997 was "Women

Who Love Women," and the admission fee was 120 Hong Kong dollars. Yet the ads stated clearly: "Wear dress, free admission." The same thing happens in the *nü tongzhi* venue Secret Party, where everyone who wears a dress can have free admission on Wednesday nights. It indicates how much TBs outnumber TBGs and the desire to attract feminine women to a *nü tongzhi* party.

TB is a one-way street. To be a TB is to be denounced by the mainstream culture as not a real woman. What is denied is not just a TB's femininity, but the entire individuality. As Kenis (twenty) said,

> I went through a painful struggle full of pitfalls and hesitations in deciding whether to be a TB or not. I endured much hardship to become a TB—to have relations with a man would destroy my entire world, my social network, circle of friends, social support, and my self-image.

Kenis does not deny the possibility of being attracted to a man, but stressed instead the social implications of having such a relationship. *Tongzhi* identity is established through a process of knowing, accepting, and consolidating the identity. Once the identity is stabilized, it is extremely difficult to reverse and change, as that would imply a serious threat to the entire sense of self. Indeed, Kenis had one sexual encounter with a man:

> That was three years ago, when I first entered this circle. He was rich, studying in college in Canada, and came back to Hong Kong for the summer. He was crazy for me, writing me poems and love letters every day. I was quite touched. But I had already entered this circle, had a bunch of die-hard brothers [TBs], and he was going to leave Hong Kong for his studies. So it was just a one-night stand. Well, I must say I enjoy sex with women more than with men. It is more relaxed and smooth, and you do not have to worry about pregnancy.

Kenis does not reject sex with men. It is the social implications that make such a "heterosexual" relationship unlikely. Homosexuality is not just about same-sex relationships, but neither is heterosexuality only about female-male relationships. Age, class, education, race, and other social considerations are all crucial. In Kenis' narration, it is just not any man but this rich young man, slightly older than Kenis, who studied overseas in Canada who turns Kenis on. Because this man could stay only for a short while, he was the perfect candidate for this experiment. Kenis had made a rational choice about what kind of man and in what social context a "heterosexual experience" would be possible without challenging *ta-de* own TB status and identity. Kenis insists on a TB identity, not because sex with men was unimaginable, but as Kenis said, it "would destroy my entire world, my social network, circle of friends, social support, and my self-image."

This is a crucial reason why all TBs said that even if they find no women partners, they would not consider going with men. It would require finding the rare man who would not feel threatened by a TB. It is not easy for a TB to desire men, partly because men possess the masculine qualities in the socially approved ways that are denied TBs. In the rare case when each finds the other, this couple has to redefine the mode and role of interaction—the man has to drop the heterosexual model of interaction and redefine his maleness, and the TB has to drop the previous mode of interaction with TBGs. Giving up TB-ness means losing the core selfhood that has taken years of hardship and painful struggle to establish.

Throughout the last ten years, when I was rather well-connected with the local *tongzhi* circle, I came across only two women who "turned" from TBs to dating men. Natalie (twenty-one) told me how her role has changed from being a boyfriend to being a girlfriend. Natalie had been a self-identified TB for three years in high school. The first thing she noted was the way people looked at her:

> When I was with my girlfriend before, people stared at me when we were holding hands. They stared at my breasts to check whether I am female or male. They stared at me even if I was alone in the street. People are just curious about my gender. But now when I am always with my boyfriend, people just assume that I am a woman.

The change in the gender of her partner changes the way Natalie comprehends her own breasts. In the past, Natalie wore loose clothes to conceal her breasts, as she hated people gazing at her body. She always hoped that her breasts would become flatter and smaller. She liked winter, as she could put more clothes on to conceal her figure, and she found that flatter breasts made it easier to be accepted by other TBs and TBGs. She said,

> In the past, I wanted my breasts to be smaller. But now, I will be happy if my breasts are bigger and firmer.

Natalie now wears tighter shirts and skirts but still cannot accept tight T-shirts and miniskirts. She worries about her previous TB friends:

> I hate the feeling that I have betrayed the circle. I didn't. But the pressure is heavy. So I won't dress up in really sexy ways, as I don't

want such a sexy Natalie to be seen by my previous friends. They will mock and tease me as traitor. But honestly, I have done many things that I would never do before, like sit-ups, as I want my waist to be slender.

When Natalie was with her girlfriend, she opened the door for her, carried groceries, and paid the check when they dined out. But her boyfriend did not want her to take these roles. The tension is more severe in sex. Natalie continued:

When I was with my girlfriend, we kissed, we fondled with love and sentiment, we made love; it was beautiful. But with Paul [her present boyfriend], he just kisses and fondles in a hurry, no more than three minutes, then he penetrates. All entries are done in a hurry because what he really wants is to "put the thing in." So making love for him is only *yin yu* [eroticism of lust], but with my girlfriend it was *qing yu* [eroticism of sentiment]. And when we have sex, I have always to remind myself that I cannot take the initiative or be too aggressive because Paul once accused me of being sex-starved.

At the time of the interview, Natalie was seriously thinking of splitting up with Paul. Apart from the social and sexual uneasiness, Natalie is also disturbed about losing her TB friends:

I really miss my TB brothers. Don't tell me to choose between female or male. It is not a real choice. I only choose between genuine and egoistic personalities, not between female and male. I think it is bi-phobia that makes people reject TBGs, as if all femmes are straight and all butch are lesbians. How naive!

Because of the severe social pressure on TBs, brotherhood is very important, both for maintaining their TB-ness and disciplining the rules of TB/G role-play. Relationships between TBs are highly desexualized. They treat one another as buddies, stressing the traditional heart-to-heart Chinese male bond. Breasts have very different social connotations in TB relationships. They can see one another's breasts without sexual connotations. TBs usually call one another *xiong-di* (brothers). It is a strategy to desexualize the relations by invoking the incest taboo. One TB even claimed that brotherhood is the definitive feature of being a TB:

You are not a real TB if you have no *yi-qi* [righteousness] for your brothers. I treasured them deeply. Throughout these years all the world has failed me, my girlfriend left me, my family condemned me, my working colleagues gossiped about me. It is only my brothers who stood by me all the way through. We are good brothers; we will not break our brotherhood because of women.

If a TB has sex with another TB, it would destroy one's TB identity. Joe (twenty-five) did have a brief relationship with another TB: "I felt like a gay male couple. All my brothers were disturbed, accusing me of *gao gay* (having gay male sex in a derogatory sense). When I first approached her, she was confused and thought that I had mistaken her for a TBG, and so she butched herself up even more. I did try to present myself in a more feminine way. But the relationship did not last long."

In May 1995 in a radio program on Radio Hong Kong, a TB/G couple who addressed each other as husband and wife shared their experiences. When the host asked the TB, "Can you accept having sex with another TB?" this TB blatantly said, "Impossible! How can a TB have sex with a TB? It would be like two chauvinist males having sex. How disgusting!"

Her statement aroused some controversy among the *nü tongzhi* circle. Some criticized her for internalized homophobia because she insisted on heterosexual role-playing (masculine-feminine) irrespective of their actual biological sexes. However, another TB defended her:

> When a female presents herself in a masculine way to have a relationship with another woman, she exposes the discrepancies between men and masculinity, and also demonstrates the possibility that women can choose a different gender performance. Masculinity, as acted out by a man and by a woman, has very different implications. TB redefines and rewrites the meaning of women, posing a challenge to the essentialist notions of femininity.

Almond (thirty-six) also defends TB/G role-playing:

> For heterosexual couples, they have numerous role models to identify with. They learn from their grandparents, parents, relatives, friends, and their media. And even gay men have some references in the gay magazines. However, we have no one to copy, no way to know how to love and live with a woman. So TB/G at least know how to love a woman and maintain a relation.

Women have different reasons, motives, and purposes to pass as men and wear drag as TBs. The issue of power dynamics in a TB/G relationship will be elaborated in the next section.

WESTERNIZED FEMINIST NÜ TONGZHI
VERSUS LOCAL ROLE-PLAYING TB/Gs

There are clear tensions in contemporary Hong Kong between TB/Gs and the feminist-identified *nü tongzhi*. The former, who dominate the bar scene, reject feminism and queer theory as being too theoretical, Western, academic, and politically correct. On the other hand, TB/G relationships are criticized by some well-educated Westernized *nü tongzhi* as heterosexist and antifeminist. A well-educated *nü tongzhi* (thirty) told me,

> You should see these TBs as men—they are more sexist than men. Many TBGs are heterosexist, insist on addresssing their partners as their boyfriends. I think it is internalized homophobia, i.e., treating all erotic desire as heterosexual. Indeed, the term TBG is heterosexist, as if the only legitimate gender roles for a relationship is boy and girl even for a homosexual couple.

Most feminist *nü tongzhi* insist they are *bu-fen* (unclassified), and challenge the binary classification of TB/G. Ann (twenty-four) said,

> I don't think people can be categorized easily. My appearance is very TB. But in terms of sex, I prefer to be the bottom; and in terms of the social role, I am very independent. I don't think the TB/G duality is rich enough to encompass the diversity and complexity of woman-woman relationships.

Mabel (twenty-nine) comes from a feminist background and she opts for egalitarian relationships. She criticizes TB/G as copying and reproducing heterosexuality. She had a brief sexual encounter with a TB:

> She did not allow me to touch her body. I asked her, if I cannot touch her body, what is the difference between sleeping with a man and a woman? She attains sexual satisfaction when she can make me moan and come—a typical chauvinist mentality. . . . When I decided to cut my hair short, she objected, saying that it was weird, as we would be a TB-TB couple.

The pro-TB/G position is best illustrated by Ting (twenty-five):

> When TBs smoke, drink, or bind their breasts, they are appropriating and imitating, but not identifying with, the male role. What a TB wants is only independence and social power, which in our society

has historically been equated with masculinity. Many critics have confused the two. But rarely would a TB confuse TB-ness and male-ness—what they want is TB subjectivity, not male identity. In a society where feminism is not a choice, TB is one of the limited alternatives where women can attain sexual and social power.

Ting said that she is sometimes disturbed by TB-phobia and the hegemony of *bu-fen:*

> In the present circle, there is a phobia about TBs, as if they are not politically correct. I think we sometimes forget that among *nü tong-zhi,* TBs are most oppressed by the male world. There is also a hegemony of the *bu-fen,* as if the "correct" way to be a *nü tongzhi* is to get rid of role-playing. These *nü tongzhi* always talk about women's choices, that women lack the choice to be queer, wild, single, promiscuous, and so on. But they end up establishing their own formula, which kills a *nü tongzhi*'s choice to be a TB.

It is dangerous to assert a monolithic discourse for TB/G. There are different reasons for a woman to be TB/G; even more diverse dynamics constitute a TB/G relationship. Lenore Norrgard (1990) found that the TBGs in Hong Kong do all the domestic work and the TBs go out to work to earn a living. But I hardly found such a pattern in my research. Instead, there are obvious signs of deviations from the mainstream heterosexist pattern. Many TBs are younger than their TBG partners, a phenomenon which is very unusual in the heterosexual world. Many TBs do not enjoy a higher class position than *ta-de* girlfriends, which is also not the norm in the heterosexual world.

It seems vital to distinguish between TB-ness and maleness. The construction of the TB body usually includes breast-binding, short hair, and male outfits (including underwear), which renders them more TB-like than male-like. Most TBs have a strong and unique sense of TB-ness, which cannot be collapsed with maleness (Chao, 1996). Among all the TB interviewees, no one wants a sex change. They seem to be clear about the distinction between male and masculinity, female and femininity. As He-man (twenty-one) said,

> We behave like men, but we are better than men as we understand and feel with women spontaneously. We know not just the technique and knowledge to please a woman. We don't have the male anxiety of whether we can understand a woman or not.

We should also recall that, earlier in this chapter, Alex (nineteen) insisted that a TB is not copying a man but is indeed more masculine and better than men: "We act like men but better than men, more sensitive and less bullshit. We behave like men, but with more style and subtlety. TB is male-like, but far better."

To equate TB masculinity with (heterosexual) maleness is to collapse the symbolic with the biological, thus dismissing the politics of representation. Binding breasts has no essential or fixed meaning, but is discursively constructed by a complex process of signifying practices. A TB is like a man but quite different, is like a woman but quite different. By performing a nonmale, nonfemale role in the political institution of compulsory heterosexuality, TBs demonstrate the possibility of alternative gender construction for women, that gender is not just binary, either male or female. In a way, everyone is her own gender.

Indeed, to criticize TB as copying men is to presuppose and reinforce a rigid gender duality of either male or female. The eroticism and seductiveness of TBs is their endeavor and capacity to go beyond such duality, and cannot be easily codified and comprehended. TBs both confirm and unsettle the naturalness of gender and the heterosexual norm. In performing the so-called male roles, most TB self-representation seems to echo Lacan's theory of the penis-phallus distinction (Lacan, 1977). When they act out the penetration scene, they simulate the male penis. As Alex said:

> It is fun to use a finger, dildo, or other instrument. I enjoy enacting the penetration scene as if I possess a penis. The feeling that I can get erect and ejaculate for hours makes me high. I can twist the "organ" to please my girlfriend. A man simply cannot come for so long. . . . We are not copying but using the male role for our interest. If penetration is copying heterosexuality, then are kissing and touching also heterosexual?

TB/G also expose the limitations of contemporary Western lesbian studies, which have prioritized butch over femme, with the former postulated as subversive, and the latter apparently an inert counterpart of the transgressive butch. Following Nestle (1987) and Case (1989), Butler (1991) stresses that butch-femme role-play is not a replica of heterosexuality, but a bodily performance that acts out womanliness as a masquerade. Instead of defending homosexuality as a legitimate minority, Butler challenges the naturalness and legitimacy of heterosexuality. Heterosexuality is always and already a "parody of itself," and is always in the process of imitating and appropriating its own phantasmic idealization of itself—and failing (p. 21). Butler (1990) proposes the butch style, where masculinity is set "against a culturally intelligible female body" (p. 123) and therefore denaturalizes the social myth of masculinity and femininity. But she tends to stress the subversiveness only of butch, and has underexplored the subjectivity and the resistant strategies of femme, leaving the femme as a rather passive recipient of butch subversion.

My research found that both TBs and TBGs are autonomous agents actively negotiating and fighting for their own spaces. As the TB has always been seen as the archetypal marker of what a *nü tongzhi* should be, the TBG challenges the monolithic representation of *nü tongzhi*. Exactly because a TBG is with a woman dressed in masculine attire, she denies the naturalness of heterosexuality. That is why she chooses a woman. She also redefines the meaning of femininity and asserts the right of a woman to dress up without necessarily becoming the object of male desire. TBGs question the homo-hetero divide, and neither are they bisexual, as gender simply is not the basis on which they construct their erotic experience and identity. Irene (twenty-eight), for example, comments,

> All women can be *tongxingai*, it is love [*ai*] not sex [*xing*]. If society were more relaxed about sexuality, I think more women would be willing to be with women. . . . Last year, I did have a one-night stand with a man. When we kissed, I touched his breast, and suddenly realized that he does not have puffy breasts like a woman. I decided not to go for men anymore.

Her statement can be read as a powerful refutation of Freud's theory of penis envy. Instead of envying the male penis and feeling inferior for *lacking* it, Irene regretted that her "boyfriend" *lacked* a pair of puffy breasts. Irene also said that "TB = boyfriend - penis + breasts." She explains: "TBs play the social role of a boyfriend, but aren't male chauvinist."

The dominant lesbian studies in the West have privileged the visible masculine butch, the self-proclaimed lesbian, and those women having historical records of romantic friendship. Such insistence on explicitness and visibility has privileged the identity politics of presence over subtleties and ambiguities. "What is lesbian" becomes "what is visibly lesbian," thus confining "lesbian" to those who can afford to be seen as butch or who have the cultural capital to have their same-sex experience historically recorded. In privileging the visible as a sexual sign, we may even have ironically replicated Freud's theory of sexual differences, which is predicated upon the presence of a penis. Early sexologists equally relied on visibility by claiming that the invert could be identified by her enlarged clitoris, excessive body hair, or extreme physical rudeness. In traditional Chinese society when there was no butch culture, the criteria of visibility could either claim too little, that there are no lesbians in China, or too much, that someone must be lesbian because she slept or lived with her close friend.

To conclude, TB/G is a specific Hong Kong phenomenon. It appropriates the Western butch-femme tradition and tomboy terminology, yet transforms and indigenizes it in a local context. Both TBs and TBGs are fighting on multiple battlefields. In terms of culture, they are resisting the severe pressure to get married as well as the entire marital system that would confine them to the domestic. In terms of gender, TBs refuse to play the traditional feminine role and TBGs refuse the presence of men to constitute their "complete womanhood." In terms of *tongzhi* gender politics, they face immensely unsympathetic attitudes from their supposed brothers (*nan tongzhi*), who are generally not very sensitive to sexism and phallocentrism. In terms of role-playing they face criticism from their supposed sisters (feminist-oriented *nü tongzhi*), who always accuse TB/G of being heterosexist, homophobic, and politically incorrect. In terms of colonialism, they face a very potent Western lesbigay discourse that persistently urges them to come out to fight for political visibility and *tongzhi* rights, and may accuse them of being closeted and apolitical. While all these criticisms may be true, it is important to recognize the multiple levels of oppression TB/Gs are facing and the limited resources available to them for maneuvering. TB/Gs actively resist both traditional Chinese cultural imperatives and Western colonial discourse. They are subversive and vocal, not through public discourse or legislative practices, but in terms of the personal politics of self-naming, breastbinding, clothing, and other piecemeal engineering of the body. It is through this active manipulation of their limited social resources in their personal lives that TBs and TBGs are indeed engaging in a highly political process of struggling with the mainstream culture.

SECTION IV:
INDIGENOUS TONGZHI
STRATEGIES OF RESISTANCE

Chapter 7

From Coming Out to Coming Home

This chapter examines Chinese *tongzhi* experiences of "coming home." In the first part, I will argue that the strategy of coming out, which was generated in a specific socioeconomic and cultural context of individualism and the discourse of rights, should not be universalized as the only model of liberation for PEPS. I will examine why Chinese perspectives on the relational conception of self and identity may undermine the applicability of the coming-out model for Chinese *tongzhi*. The second part examines Hong Kong *tongzhi's* reconstruction of their own notions of the closet and coming out. I will explain why coming home can be constructed as one of the alternatives of *tongzhi* empowerment. In the third section, I will discuss successful cases and strategies of *tongzhi* resistance. It is revealed that most successful cases have appropriated mainstream cultural resources for *tongzhi* empowerment. In the last section, I will examine the relevance of confrontational politics in the context of Hong Kong.

COMING OUT IN THE CHINESE CONTEXT

A person's sexual desire can be classified in many different ways. Only in the contemporary Western world do we use the gender of erotic object choice to classify people, thus producing the dual categories "homosexual" and "heterosexual." As Robert Padgug (1990) reminds us, "homosexual and heterosexual behavior may be universal; homosexual and heterosexual identity and consciousness are modern realities" (p. 58). It is therefore neither possible nor desirable to pursue a universal history of homosexuality. The distinction between homo and hetero, defined as persons who possess two distinct kinds of psychosexual subjectivity, is not a fixed and immutable feature of some universal syntax of sexual desire.

Kinsey, in the 1940s, had already stressed that "homo" and "hetero" should only be used as adjectives referring to acts, not nouns for a certain kind of person. There are no such things as "homosexuals" or "heterosexuals" in themselves as they are not transcultural beings applicable to every culture and period, but are value-laden categories peculiar to modern Western society. In an often-cited passage, Foucault (1978) argues: "as defined by the ancient civil or canonical codes, sodomy was a category of forbidden acts; their perpetrator was nothing more than the juridical subject of them. The nineteenth-century homosexual became a personage, a past, a case history, and a childhood, in addition to being a type of life. . . . The sodomite has been a temporary aberration; the homosexual was now a species" (p. 43).

It was only with the development of industrial capitalism in the nineteenth century that sexuality became a discreet and independent domain, separate from the economy, polity, and legal sphere. It is the birth of sexology in the Western context of industrial capitalism that creates "homosexual" as a medical category, transforming same-sex desire into an identity, a different kind of human species. Sexual desire is now regarded as the core of inner selfhood. To quote Sedgwick (1990), "what was new from the turn of the century was the world mapping by which every given person, just as he or she was necessarily assignable to a male or a female gender, was now considered necessarily assignable to a homo- or a hetero-sexuality" (pp. 2-3).

The labeling practices of the sexologist created the possibility for what Foucault called "reverse affirmation," by which the stigmatized could begin to organize around the label and assert the legitimacy of their identity. Identity politics—we share an identity, therefore we form a political alliance—becomes the ground of the lesbigay movement. Coming out, both at the individual and the collective levels, becomes the dominant mode of liberation. The American lesbigay movement prides itself on being out, verbalizing one's identity, and fighting for visibility and legislative protection of legal rights. In *Out of the Closet,* the editors Karla Jay and Allen Young (1992:xxxiii) said that "It is as true today (1991) as it was two decades ago that all lesbians and gay men must come out of the closet if any of us is to be free." Many Western lesbigay academics stress that coming out is a developmental and lifelong process, starting from self-recognition and acceptance to the ultimate goal of becoming a full person in society. Cass (1979) constructs a six-stage "Model of homosexual identity formation," from identity confusion, identity comparison, tolerance, acceptance, and pride to identity synthesis. Coleman (1982) articulates a five-stage coming-out process, including pre-coming out, coming out, exploration, first relationship, and identity integration. Plummer (1981) outlines three stages: coming out to oneself, coming out to the gay world, and coming out to the straight world.

The American concept of coming out is not only a political project of the lesbigay movement, but is often a cultural project of affirming the American value of individualism, the discourse of rights, self-expression, the high level of anonymity in metropolitan areas, and the prioritization of sex as the core of selfhood. The model of coming out is hinged upon notions of the individual as an independent, discrete unit segregated economically, socially, and geographically from the familial-kinship network. In America, individual frankness, the willingness to verbalize one's feelings, and the determination to defend one's right to speak up are treated as the most important aspect of life (Carbaugh, 1988). Honesty with one's parents through verbal communication is seen as vital to a genuine self. The United States also has a political institution marked by parliamentary politics and governed by the principle of one person, one vote. Therefore, turning sexual rights into political rights through coming out is commonly accepted by lesbigays as a major way to defend their interests.

In America, there seems to be a standardized formula of "lesbigay liberation," following the sequence of coming out to oneself; to lesbigay friends, straight friends, colleagues, bosses, parents, media; and finally joining the great parade at the end of June. Coming out becomes the demarcation for the honesty and liberation of a lesbigay person. If one does not complete this sequence of coming out, whether by failing to join the parade or failing to participate in confronting homophobia in the straight world, then one may be accused of not being courageous or liberated enough.

This by no means minimizes the pain of coming out for Americans, nor the diversities of lesbigay strategies in the United States. Many of the white American anthologies of coming out include enormous discussions of bitter negotiations with parents and the emotional difficulty in verbalizing sexual identity. There are also immense debates and controversies among the U.S. lesbigay population concerning the strategies of liberation and coming out. The notion of "U.S. lesbigay movement" is perhaps a misnomer. It is only certain political activists in New York, Los Angeles, and San Francisco that opt for a more confrontational strategy. The vast majority of lesbigays living in the South and Midwest believe and behave otherwise, are generally more quiet, subtle, and even closeted, not the least because of the prevalence of Christian fundamentalism and family values. Indeed, when the metropolitan activists go back to their homes in Oregon, Ohio, or Colorado and live with their parents, they may have to be more subdued. Yet the lesbigay groups advocating confrontational politics, which are indeed a minority within the United States and the United Kingdom, get the most media coverage, especially outrageous presentations of drag queens, ultrasexual lesbians, and gay men in parades, or the confrontational events organized by ACT UP, Queer Nation, and Outrage. Because these images make news, they were always the picture of Western lesbigays as presented in the mainstream media, especially in Asian societies. Many *tongzhi* in Hong Kong and Taiwan, despite the cosmopolitan nature of these two societies, still think that most lesbigays in the United States are living in a "lesbigay paradise" free from homophobic violence and most have come out to their parents, bosses, and their churches.

Zhan chu lai (coming out) has very different cultural and political connotations in Chinese communities. In 1992, a *tongzhi* group in Hong Kong decided to launch a parade, planning to walk from Queen's Pier to Lan Kwai Fong on August 21, yet only about ten expatriates and two Chinese (both overseas Chinese) intended to go. Fearing the event might reinforce the mainstream stereotype of homosexuality as a Western import, the organizers canceled the parade. Meanwhile, local *tongzhi* were being criticized by local Caucasian gay activists for not being sufficiently courageous and liberated (Ma, 1992).

The event reflects the issue of the applicability of the confrontational model of lesbigay politics in a different cultural context where the family-kinship system, rather than personal sexual desire, is counted as the basis of what a "person" is. The confrontational model is more appropriate in a society where individuality and self-affirmation are the basis of personal and cultural identity. The cultural differences in the constitution of self-hood generate a different scenario of issues faced by Chinese *tongzhi*.[1]

Although some American and British lesbigay people feel the need to segregate themselves from family affiliation to assert their sexual identity and the right to their bodies, this strategy is unimaginable for many Chinese *tongzhi*. When we take cultural specificity as the starting point of *tongzhi* studies, we realize that the notions of coming out, the closet, gay liberation, and queer politics are racially and culturally specific categories.

In traditional Chinese culture, an individual exists through and is defined by his or her relationship to others (Hsu, 1953). Everyone is defined as a relational being socially situated within a specific context. Confucian culture begins with the Five Relationships, which lay down the central defining roles for an individual: sovereign-subject, father-son, elder-younger, husband-wife, and friend-friend. Indeed, all human relationships are constructed in hierarchical patterns. The Chinese, or to be precise the Confucian, self is a social and moral self. The modern American concept of the atomic and individuated self is simply alien to the traditional Chinese construct (Scollon and Scollon, 1995).

In contrast with the Western notion of the individualistic self, Francis Hsu suggests the concept of *ren* (person), which includes not only interior (un)consciousness, but also the relationship with the social (Marsella and Hsu, 1985). The self has little meaning outside these social relationships. Ambrose King argues that in the Confucian construct, every human being has the intrinsic capacity to attain excellence (*jun-zi*), which is actualized through compassionate concern for others (King and Bond, 1985:57). Julia Tao argues that the Confucian has an active sense of individuality,

> being a person is something one does, not something one is. It is an achievement rather than a given. . . . In the Confucian human-centered philosophy, there can be no fulfillment for the individual in isolation from others. The moral starting point for Chinese Confucians is mutually constitutive relationships. (Tao and Drover, 1997:11)

Given the Confucian emphasis on the interrelatedness of the sociocentric self in the context of harmony-within-hierarchy, *guanxi* (commonality of shared identification) becomes a crucial reference in social, political, and organizational contexts. It is the proper *guanxi* between self and others that defines and constitutes the sense of selfhood, making it crucial to observe and preserve the correct conduct in maintaining the appropriate *guanxi* in the hierarchical order. The most popular strategy for strengthening *guanxi* is to increase social interaction by giving *ren qing* (favor) to the other. It implies a strategy of *bao* (reciprocity)—every act of receiving means an obligation to return (Yang, 1982).

In this construct, family is perceived as the most basic and profound social institution. It has salience for each individual in terms of emotional support, personal growth, economic bonds, and the entire sense of personal selfhood. Within the family relationship, *xiao* (filial piety) is given central value. Indeed, one of the most important tasks of family members is taking care of the elderly in the family. However, filial acts may sometimes reach an extreme level of masochistic sacrifice and pathological attachment to the parents in which individual needs and personal growth are denied (Tseng and Wu, 1985).

Given the primacy of family status, any conflict inside the family should be kept "backstage" and not be exposed for outsiders to gossip about, as it would cause a loss of face, thus bringing humiliation and social isolation: *bu yao lian* (not wanting face), *mei you lian* (having no face), *diao lian* (loss of face). While the concept of face may have universal applicability, Chinese emphasize not only one's own face but also keeping others', especially the superior's, face (Ho, 1976). Losing face may cause serious emotional disturbance to a person and his or her parents, sometimes to the extreme extent of ending in suicide. Causing others to lose face is seen as rude and inconsiderate, and in the case of a parent, it will be seen as *bu-xiao* (unfilial). Given the cultural preoccupation with maintaining social order, when conflicts arise, the coping strategy is to avoid open conflict and to resort to subtle negotiation, face-saving ploys, and intervention by a third party.

Even in modern cities such as Hong Kong, Taipei, and Singapore, these fundamental Chinese values have been largely retained and modified. S. K. Lau (1982:72-74) describes Hong Kong's culture as utilitarian familism defined as the normative and behavioral tendency of an individual to place familial interests above the interests of society and other individuals and groups.

The Chinese concept of self has generated a very different scenario of *tongzhi* issues from that of their Western counterparts:

1. Whereas the basic tenet of Western lesbigay discourses is to regard the lesbigay subject as an individual with inalienable rights, traditional Chinese culture simply refuses to classify people as homo or hetero because individuals (both women and men, homo- or heterosexually inclined ones) are first and foremost members of the family and wider society.
2. It is inappropriate to treat a *tongzhi* merely as an isolated self seeking personal liberation; instead, a *tongzhi* should be located within his or her context of *guanxi,* especially the family.
3. The major problem for most *tongzhi* is not state oppression, religious fundamentalism, or job discrimination but the family, especially the parents.
4. The problem for parents is not only accepting that their child is a *tongzhi,* but the shame of losing face for having a deviant child who does not get married.
5. In a society where filial piety is of the utmost importance for being a person, hurting the parents could be the most terrible thing for a *tongzhi* to do.
6. The focus of the *tongzhi* movement is not an isolated self called gay, lesbian, or bisexual, but family and social relations that both constitute and oppress *tongzhi.*

Almost all *tongzhi* that I have encountered in Taiwan, mainland China, and Hong Kong agree that the most painful part of coming out is dealing with parents. Just open any local *tongzhi* magazines or books, or start a chat with *tongzhi*, and the headache of coming out to one's parents appears. In the Hong Kong *tongzhi* journal *Satsanga* (September 1996), a mainland Chinese *nan tongzhi* wrote a public letter to his mother:

> Mum, I am really sorry for hurting you, not because I love men, but that I failed to try harder to make you accept and understand me. Last winter when I came back to Shanghai to visit you, you asked me the deepest secret in my heart. Maybe it is the influence of seven years' experience in America, but I feel that I should not lie to you, and so I pulled out everything. To my surprise, your response was so great . . . when I was little, as the only son in the family, when I saw you going to work even when you were ill, I swore to myself, I must earn big money and achieve something in the future, to let you enjoy the remaining years of your life. Now, I have not brought you happiness, instead I give you pain and suffering. I am very sorry. Mum, I failed to serve you as you have served me. I am most willing to fulfill all your expectations, except this thing about marriage.

In *Women Huozhe*, the collected autobiographies of twenty-two mainland Chinese *tongzhi*, the theme of *jia* (home/family) repeatedly becomes the main theme and concern of the authors (Wu and Chou, 1996). You Yun said that she put her relations with her parents in the final part of her chapter, "because it is the most painful and difficult part" (p. 137).

Moving from mainland China to Hong Kong, parents remain the hardest part for most *tongzhi*. The first chapter in *Xianggang Tongzhi Zhanchulai* is written by a *nan tongzhi*, Tang Man-cheung. He explained clearly why he would not tell his parents directly:

> Now the only people left in my family are my mother and myself, and I have never formally confessed to her. But when I was madly in love, my boyfriend was on the phone to me all the time. . . . Whenever I walked in the door, my first words were always to ask if anyone had rung me, so every time he called me, even if I didn't ask, she would take the initiative and tell me. . . . I didn't want to take the risk [of coming out]. I was afraid that if she didn't [accept] it, it would be tantamount to stabbing her in the heart. . . . In fact my mother also had pressure on her. Hers came from the fact that she had to deal with relatives and neighbors asking whether I was dating. If she had never heard my confession, she could pretend and with an easy conscience smooth things. If she heard my confession, then her smoothing things over would become lying. So I left the matter like

a curtain of fine gauze between us, neither of us taking the initiative to pull it aside, and thus neither of us had to confront the issue. (Chou, Mak, and Kwong, 1995:3)

Ben (twenty-seven), an interviewee, is a Taiwanese *tongzhi* who lived in the United States for four years:

I think many Taiwanese *tongzhi* have romanticized the American gay life, thinking that the gay life in San Francisco and New York is so liberating. Well, I think San Francisco is not the real United States but like a big ghetto of enlarged New Park [the major cruising park] in Taiwan. New York is most telling—I can be "out and proud" on Christopher Street, but when I walk several blocks from it, still "out and proud," I will be in trouble. So I always tell my friends in Taiwan: you don't have to feel guilty for being unable to come out to your parents or join a parade. There is no formula of liberation.

It is the anticipation of their parents' deep sense of shame that makes *tongzhi* very reluctant to come out, as it may hurt their parents in an unbearable way. Many *tongzhi* use financial compensation to pacify their parents. As stated by Edwin (forty):

I really feel guilty for not being able to fulfill their wish to have a grandson. All I can do is to gratify them through money. I give them a lot of money, one-third of my salary. All my parents' relatives and friends know that I am very filial and give lots of money to them. They praise me a lot, and that becomes my parents' face.

On the cover of the first *tongzhi* album, *Touch,* produced in Taiwan in early 1997, there is a very striking sentence that deeply touched many *tongzhi* in Taiwan and Hong Kong: "That day, my mother knelt down in front of me, begging me not to be. . . ." For most Chinese, family is the major source of both comfort and pressure, warmth and pain, love and hate. Such a dilemma was strongly felt by Zia (thirty-one):

Mother retired from the restaurant two years ago. She was having a very hard life before retirement—only recently has she begun to be more relaxed. One night, when only mother and I were in the house, she shared her painful struggle during the Second World War, and the hardship she experienced when she first came to Hong Kong. Then she told me that there is only one last worry. There was a long silence, and just when I tried to change the subject, my mother just cried quietly. She said, "Why can't you just marry like everybody else?" That really hurts.

The problem for parents is not just the acceptance of their child as a *tongzhi* but how to "face" the relatives, neighbors, and ancestors. Parents would feel wronged, ashamed, and experience a loss of face. Traditional Chinese parents like to compare their children with other parents' children in terms of social status, achievement, and extent of filial piety. The closer the family ties and the bigger the extended family network, the more pressure and shame would be felt by parents for having a *tongzhi* child. Traditional Chinese parents would sometimes refer to *tongxinglian* as *nie* (curse) and say "How would I be able to face our relatives and ancestors?" *Nie* is a Buddhist concept accepted by most traditional Chinese. It refers to misconduct in a previous life, which has repercussions in later lives and generations. "What is the *nie* I have made?" is a common expression among traditional Chinese. *Nie* is fundamentally different from the Western concept of sin, as there is neither God nor any categorical imperative, but it is the direct ancestral tradition that the parents feel burdened by and accountable for.

For most *tongzhi*, the common strategy is delay: they think that when they are over forty, beyond the so-called age of marriage, then people will not dare bring up the topic of marriage. Tom (thirty-five) expressed such a strategy in a rather horrifying way:

> My mother and father are both in their early seventies. My strategy is to wait—their death will be my relief. My grandmother always urges me to have a girlfriend, saying that she will pass away any time—the only unfulfilled wish is my marriage. She is now ninety-three, still alive. What can I do? I can't kill her, so I can only wait. That is really painful for me—a Chinese son is looking forward to the death of his parents to get relief. How unfilial! . . . I hope to find a lesbian for marriage, or any woman who won't mind a fake marriage, like in *The Wedding Banquet.*

The Wedding Banquet is a Hollywood movie (1993) watched by many *tongzhi* in Hong Kong and Taiwan. The movie is about a Taiwanese *tongzhi* called Wai Tung who is living with his American boyfriend Simon in Manhattan. Wai Tung's parents, who live in Taiwan, are eager to have their son married. Tung decides to arrange a fake marriage with his female friend Wei-Wei. On the night after the big wedding banquet, Wei-Wei initiates sex with Wai Tung and becomes pregnant. When Tung's mother first learns the true story, she accuses Tung of being corrupted by Simon and Western culture. She further blames Tung's previous unsuccessful relationships with women. She then asks Tung not to tell his father, worried that he may not be able to accept it. But Tung's father actually knows that Tung and Simon are lovers. He endorses their relationship by privately giving Simon a gift of money known as a red pocket, asking him to take care of his son. Tung's father says, "I look, I listen, I understand . . . If I don't let them cheat me, I cannot have my grandchild."

In many ways, *The Wedding Banquet* vividly illustrates a Chinese *tongzhi*'s situation:

   a. Wai Tung is pressured to get married, so he arranges a fake marriage with a woman.
   b. Wai Tung's mother regards *tongxinglian* as a Western corruption, and thinks that Wai Tung has turned to *tongxinglian* because of previous unhappy heterosexual relationships.
   c. Wai Tung's parents never accept *tongxinglian* per se but accept their married son having a male partner.
   d. The parents never directly confront or bring up the subject of *tongxinglian*.
   e. The parents endorse the relationship not by words but by the action of giving the red pocket.
   f. The parents do not care much about Tung's "gay" identity so long as he gets married and has a child for them.
   g. The happy ending expresses the collective wish of *tongzhi,* especially male, when Tung pleases his parents and simultaneously retains the relationship with his boyfriend.

REDEFINING THE CULTURAL BOUNDARIES OF "OUT" AND "CLOSET"

Coming out is a race, class, and gender category. Not accidentally, it was Anglo-Saxon gay men who first started and became the strongest advocates for the strategy of coming out. In Asian countries such as China, Japan, Thailand, and India, European countries such as Italy, Poland, or Greece, and in Latino and black culture, PEPS may not have the same "privileged" space to segregate their sexual preference from their family-kinship and cultural identity; neither do they have the cultural tradition of verbalizing their sexuality to constitute "the real self," which is highly valued in the United States.

The lexicon of "coming out" and "out and proud" can be culturally problematic for Chinese, as "out" implies leaving the family, parents, and culture to become lesbian or gay, and "proud" is culturally derogatory, especially for a "deviant" form of sexuality. It seems necessary to articulate indigenous categories and strategies that can reclaim *tongzhi* voices not by denying family-cultural identity but by integrating *tongzhi* into the family and cultural context.

"Coming home" can be proposed as an indigenous lexicon of *tongzhi* self-confirmation. *Jia* (home/family) is a culturally unique category that does not have an equivalent parallel in Western languages. While *jia* condenses the meaning of family and home in the English-speaking world, it is also a mental category that refers to the ultimate home and roots to which a person belongs. *Hui-jia* (coming home) means not only going back home but, more fundamentally, searching the ultimate place to which one belongs. Home refers not only to the biological family that a *tongzhi* has struggled with throughout life, but could also signify the "chosen family" of *tongzhi* friends that is his or her second home of comfort and support. In that sense, *tongzhi* is a process of homecoming and becoming—integrating the sexual with the sociocultural. *Tongzhi* come out not by segregating the sexual from the social and confronting the public, but by coming home. Coming home articulates the visibility of *tongzhi* not as an isolated sexual self abstracted from social relations, but exactly to locate the *tongzhi* mainstream social relations.

It does not, however, imply the romanticization of the notion of *jia*. Indeed, for many *tongzhi*, *jia* is an oppressive institution, not only because of the parental pressure to get married, but also because of the potent capacity of the family to absorb unwanted emotions simply by ignoring the subject. Many *tongzhi* have found it extremely difficult to bring up the subject and talk with their parents. The tension of superficial harmony but tacit speculation becomes anxiety-provoking for many *tongzhi*. The oppressiveness of *jia* is also gendered. Unlike men, who are burdened with carrying the family name, women occupy a much more precarious position in the family. Before marriage, a woman has much less domestic power than her male counterparts, but after marriage, she is seen as leaving her birth home, and yet is always perceived as an outsider in her husband's family. Even worse, a woman is always perceived as a parasite on the family—in her parents' home before marriage and in her husband's after marriage—without which she is seen as rootless and not a complete person.

For most *tongzhi* in Taiwan, Hong Kong, and mainland China, the notion of coming out is not a political category subverting heterosexism but a personal act of negotiating family, social, and personal space. It is common for a local *tongzhi* to ask another *tongzhi*: "Are you out?" "Does your family know?" Usually the question will stir up heated responses, with everyone sharing stories about their families. Yet there is little discussion of the notion of coming out, as if there is a tacit consensus on the meaning of "out" and "closet." In my research, I asked the interviewees to define the meaning of "out" and "closet," and found that their perceptions seem to be rather different from those in the English-speaking world.

What is the "closet" and what constitutes "out"? If one is out only when one is willing to show one's face and real name in the mass media, then fewer than twenty people in Taiwan and Hong Kong together qualified as out. In that case, most Hong Kong and Taiwan *tongzhi* activists would ironically be defined as closeted, which has the implication of hiding in the darkness, being dishonest, and even living in denial. Even if coming out is defined as telling one's parents about one's *tongzhi* identity, more than 90 percent of *tongzhi* in Hong Kong and Taiwan are still in the closet. But this concept may be very misleading in understanding the local *tongzhi* scene. Most *tongzhi*, especially the younger generations, accept their homoerotic desire, have *tongzhi* friends, and have an active *tongzhi* life. Many *tongzhi* say, "My parents should feel or know it. But I won't tell them directly." Obviously, the "out versus closeted" dichotomy is inadequate in understanding local *tongzhi* dynamics.

Hong Kong *tongzhi* seem to have a different notion of being out: *tongzhi* are defined as out when they are active in *tongzhi* venues and organizations even if they do not tell their parents directly; they are seen as very out if they share their *tongzhi* stories with straight friends, colleagues, and family members. The issue of parades and media exposure does not seem to disturb Hong Kong *tongzhi*. Indeed, they were not even mentioned in replies to the question "How would you define out and do you think you are out?" They simply will not consider the possibility of exposing themselves to the media or joining a parade. They seem to be rather comfortable with their own *tongzhi* circle, a kind of ghetto which they insist is different from a closet. Such a ghetto would be highly visible to *tongzhi* but invisible to outsiders. Instead of being self-denying, oppressive, and secretive, the "*tongzhi* ghetto" is seen as nurturing and empowering in terms of building self-confidence, and acting as a support group and social network (Lee, 1994).

Tongzhi in Hong Kong tend to replace the "out versus closet" dichotomy with the expression *chu lai* (to go out there), which is close to "out" but refers to participation in *tongzhi* organizations and venues, rather than self-acceptance, media exposure, or being out to parents. Although the Western concept of the closet has a wide range of connotations, from self-denial, guilt, dishonesty, and staying in the dark to refusal to be publicly known, many Hong Kong interviewees tend to define the closet as "refusing to *chu lai* to join *tongzhi* gatherings or venues." One is most closeted if one refuses to know any other *tongzhi*, but in those cases a person may not be seen as a *tongzhi* at all, at most only a homo/bisexual. In Hong Kong, coming out does not seem to be defined by media exposure or self-acceptance, but by the extent of one's participation in the *tongzhi* scene and relations with the family. The more a *tongzhi* is *in* the circle, the more *out* he or she would be considered by other *tongzhi*.

Coming out is also gendered. All of my informants have come out to at least one straight woman friend, but fewer than 20 percent of them have come out to a straight man. Female and male *tongzhi* seem to have very different dynamics for choosing which sex to come out to. A *nü tongzhi* usually comes out to a woman in whom she has sexual interest, hoping that this woman would accept not only her sexuality, but her love. *Nü tongzhi* find most straight men too rigid, sexist, and homophobic to come out to. *Nan tongzhi* have a very different relationship with straight women, as both of them are oppressed by hegemonic masculinity, which denounces both gay men and straight women as inferior and lesser than men. While straight men may fear sexual tension with their gay male friends, straight women, on the contrary, find these gay men the only kind of males who do not objectify them as sex objects, and thus are most willing to enjoy a rare sense of security with men.

Two *tongzhi* interviewees even criticized the notion of coming out:

> **Andy (thirty-five):** I think coming out is a heterosexist concept. How come all the straights can grow up normally with no pressure to disclose their sexual fantasies, secrets, and sexual experiences, but because I love people of the same gender, I have the obligation to come out as a sexed person and to ask everyone not to discriminate against me? Heterosexuals have not come out yet!

> **Eliza (twenty-six):** It is problematic to demand that all PEPS come out with the same identity. For example, a Filipino domestic servant in Hong Kong may not want to come out as lesbian or *nü tongzhi*, as both identities fail to address her fundamental identity and oppressive experience as a Filipino in Hong Kong. I tend to prioritize Hong Kong Chinese identity (cultural), Buddhism (religion), daughter (family-kin), and vegetarian (ecological-political) no less than my sexuality. So, come out as what?

Local *tongzhi's* reservations about coming out can be clearly detected in the linguistic discourses they use. *Tongzhi* rarely said "come out" in Chinese. In the first anthology of coming-out stories in Hong Kong, Samshasha, the self-identified father of the *gay* movement in Hong Kong, published a story, "Coming Out *Ershinian*" ("Twenty Years of Coming Out"). In this short story of less than 2,000 Chinese words, the English term "coming out" appears approximately twenty times. The second most frequent English words are "gay" and "gay lib," as if these terms cannot be translated into Chinese. In another coming-out story, written by Almond, the only English term she used is "coming out," which appears more than ten times, as if "coming out" is also a Western concept that cannot be expressed in Chinese. Indeed, most authors in that book "automatically" switched to English to write the words "coming out" (Chou, Mak, and Kwong, 1995). Although mixed code is common in Cantonese, it is not coincidental that it is only these "Western concepts" such as "coming out," "*gay*," and "*gay* liberation" that are used by Chinese *tongzhi* in English in a purely Chinese context.

Local *tongzhi*'s reservations about confrontational politics and coming out are shared by some other Asians, blacks, Latinos, and Caucasians in the United States. Indeed, the Chinese emphasis on familial-kinship value is neither essential nor fixed but only a distinctive feature in the historical development of Chinese societies. Many of the above-mentioned experiences and features are not exclusively Chinese but are shared by other Asian and Western societies.[2] Connie Chan (1991) found in her study that only nine out of ninety-five respondents of lesbigay Asian Americans were out to their parents. She comments, "If a daughter or son is lesbian or gay, the implication is that not only is the child rejecting the traditional role of a wife-mother or son-father, but also that the parents have failed in their role and that the child is rejecting the importance of family and Asian culture" (p. 378). Martin Manalansan IV (1996) reports that "many Filipino informants said that they did not have the same kind of issues such as coming out and homophobia . . . they didn't have to come out about being gay because they thought their families knew about their identity without their verbal acknowledgment" (p. 55). Peter Jackson (1995), after studying male homosexuality in Thailand, said, "Western-styled gay politics is also inappropriate in Thailand because homosexuality is not illegal and homophobic violence is not an issue. . . . Gayness in Thailand is thus a cultural movement, not a political one" (p. 267). Peter Tatchell (1991) also comments, "the tactics of the few lesbian and gay activists in Thailand are very different from the confrontational approach of their Western counterparts. This is largely due to Thai cultural tradition, which attaches great value to conciliation and consensus" (p. 41).

TONGZHI EXPERIENCES OF COMING HOME

Despite the immense pressures *tongzhi* face, cases of smoothly integrating a positive *tongzhi* identity into the familial context are not unheard-of. Coming home can be explicated as a negotiative process of bringing one's sexuality into the family-kin network by manipulating mainstream social categories such as *qing, yi, guanxi,* and filial piety. In these "successful" cases, same-sex eroticism has rarely been singled out as a site for conceptual discussion. Instead, it is always the actual same-sex relationship that is drawn into the family, to let the parents understand the *tongzhi* relationship often by bypassing the category of homosexuality or gay. The usual practice is that a *tongzhi* maintains a loving relationship with the parents, then introduces his or her partner into the family as a good friend. The *tongzhi* would deepen the relationship by mundane practices such as shopping or playing mah-jongg together. Dinner has often been cited as a crucial cultural marker for breaking the insider-outsider distinction. The *tongzhi* may then use quasi-kin categories such as half sister/brother to integrate the partner into the family. In particular, three common principles have often been mentioned by my informants.

Establish Guanxi Rather Than Making a Conceptual Argument

In Hong Kong, *tongzhi* activists who can afford to be out to their parents and the media are: economically independent, generally not living with their parents, able to speak fluent English, educated in the Anglo-Saxon world, and male. Even so, many activists have had the experience of a rather indigenous style of "outing"—they are involved so heavily in the movement that their parents "feel" it, sometimes hint at the issue, but never directly ask or mention the term *tongxinglian*. Instead of verbalizing, they use actions in relationships to express themselves. They are not out by Western standards as they have not talked about it directly, yet neither are they closeted or uncomfortable with their sexuality. A local *nan tongzhi* activist (twenty-nine) remarks,

> I never talk about it. No way. But once, in 1993, when I was watching the television news about the Washington Parade, my mum suddenly turned to me and said, "Why don't you people in Hong Kong organize these events here?" She used the "you" in the plural form. I was stunned, replied, "Maybe it's not suitable here." It is my mum who came out, not me. I never told my mum. If she asks, I will admit, but I will not tell her directly—let her decide for herself. She has to face severe pressure from Grandma and Grandpa, relatives,

and friends. She understands, but cannot accept. Even if she accepts, she has to face the outside world.

He continued, talking about the cultural implications:

> It is typical of Chinese parents that they can feel it but would never confront the same-sex sexuality of their children. The parents' tolerance is governed not by a genuine acceptance but the fear of losing face. Though Hong Kong is very Westernized, coming out has never been so important as in the English-speaking world. If you know how deeply I treasure my relationship with my parents, you understand why I never directly come out. Every time I heard about the disastrous stories of coming out from my *tongzhi* friends, I asked myself, is it the only appropriate way of empowerment and liberation? I didn't come out as a sexed category like homosexual or gay, I came out as a son and a decent human being who happens to love people of the same sex. I don't think sex is necessarily more important than family or other parts of me, so why should I segregate them and amplify my sexuality?

In a culture where steady and monogamous relationships are highly valued, many *tongzhi* said that they would not come out to their parents unless they had a stable partner. Most *tongzhi* think that establishing a good relationship between the partner and the parents is much more effective than arguing for the concept of *tongxinglian.* As Richard (thirty) said,

> Theoretical argument is not the Chinese way to win a person. My mother still thinks gay is abnormal, but she accepts her son—me. They simply have no concept of *tongxinglian.* It is counterproductive to argue in concepts. We should just show them what it's like to be a *tongzhi*—healthy and happy, like everybody else.

Richard had a painful experience five years ago of coming out to his parents unexpectedly when his father found his *tongzhi* magazines. They had a big fight. His father condemned *tongxinglian* as pathological and abnormal, saying that he would not have a gay son. Richard left home that night, seriously thinking of suicide as he felt extremely hurt and guilty, and saw no prospect for a *tongzhi* life. It was his *tongzhi* friends who helped him through that painful period. As Richard said,

> That was the most painful stage in my life. The atmosphere at home was really awful—no one talked to me. I could stay at home for

forty-eight hours and not speak one word, as no one talked to me. I felt so bad. Things gradually changed when I met A-Keung. He is a very lively and cheerful person, and helped me to pick up my life energy and hope. One year later, I introduced A-Keung to my parents just as a friend. But it was so obvious. We even slept together once. He became my parents' first encounter with *tongzhi* apart from me. It significantly changed their impression of *tongzhi*. A-Keung's relationship with my father is indeed better than mine! So what can you say—A-Keung simply has the capacity to make my parents forget his sexual orientation. Once, while we were having dinner, my father asked A-Keung whether he has a girlfriend. We all got stuck. I was wondering whether I should explain to him that A-Keung is a *tongzhi*. Then my father suddenly realized something. He just laughed and said, *"Oh, I am sorry, I forgot; I forgot."* Then all of us smiled and changed the subject. *We never mentioned the subject of tongzhi.* Last year when I stayed in Lamma Island for three months with A-Keung, my mother was very caring. She called us every day to ask whether we had enough blankets or food, and would *talk to A-Keung like her son*. My parents never said a word directly. The only exception was one night when my father was very moody and we chatted for almost an hour, which is rare, then he talked about my career future. He suddenly said, "You know your situation. I won't push you for marriage. Even if I push, you will not listen. You are thirty years old already. I know you will not change, even if I object. As a father, I hope you are happy and a decent person. Don't flirt around and bring AIDS back home." That was the only time Father mentioned it. Well, he still does not accept gay, and he has some misunderstanding about AIDS, but his fatherly love embraces me. (emphasis mine)

Break the Insider-Outsider Distinction

In all the successful cases, the insider-outsider distinction between the parents and the *tongzhi*'s partner has been broken down, and the partner is accepted as a member of the in-group. The boundaries of the Chinese familial group are fluid and elastic, including not just parents, siblings, and close relatives, but certain close friends who can be accepted as family members. It is not uncommon for Chinese to take an adopted friend of the same sex, and integrate him or her as a family member. Indeed, the practice of *qi xiong-di* in the province of Fujian in the nineteenth century is the most famous institutional practice of same-sex "marriage." And the relationship among friends is one of the Five Relations. Chinese proverbs such as "rely on parents at home, and on friends outside home" show the importance of friendship. "Within the four seas, all people are brothers" also signifies a unique cultural comprehension of friendship through kin categories such as sister and brother. Given the particularistic ethics of Confucian culture, all strangers need a third party to locate them in the *ren-lun* (family-kin human relationship) to be accepted into the social network. Once located properly in the *ren-lun*, this stranger has immense room to maneuver within the family-kin network. Here lies the strategy through which contemporary *tongzhi* integrate their partners into the family context.

Twenty-five-year-old Ching told me a fascinating story. She has a steady relationship with her partner, Yee, who comes to her place every weekend, sometimes staying overnight in the same bed. They have dinner with Ching's family in the same house. Ching's mother treats Yee almost like her daughter. Does she understand her daughter's *tongzhi* relationship with Yee? Ching replied,

It is so obvious. She understands, of course. But does she accept it? Never! How can a Chinese mother accept her daughter or son being *tongxinglian?* It is suicidal to tell them. You do not confront your parents, you build up a harmonious relationship in order to let things go. My parents are doing their best in the Chinese way—tacit recognition without mentioning it. I want to be their daughter, not a different person called lesbian. And my parents simply do not have the cultural space to support lesbian politics. Why should they?

I did try to tell her. Once, my mum was watching television with me. There was an advertisement on AIDS. Mum said something weird, "You should take good care of yourself. Don't give me trouble. I am too old now; I can't afford too much excitement." I was stunned, thinking that it might be the right time. After all, I have struggled for many years. So I said, "Mum, I have something very serious to tell you." Dead silence. Mum stared at me. Strangely enough, my mother interrupted me and said, "Don't tell me. I don't want to know. You are old enough to decide your road. Nowadays, Mum has no right to say anything. You do what you want. I don't even force you to get married." Well, *she denies the subject, but it is ironically her way of accepting it*. I don't think she wants to know clearly that I am *tongxinglian*. She would have difficulty handling her extended family and friends. I never give up educating her. Last month was Mother's birthday. *She invited Yee to come for the dinner.*

You know, my parents, two brothers, Yee and me as a couple. She passes completely. Isn't that beautiful! (emphasis mine)

It is not easy. For the last two years, Yee always came to visit Ching's mother, shopping and playing mah-jongg with her. Only recently was Yee accepted as "a special friend." After that dinner, Ching's mother told her, "If you live with Yee and don't get married, you will have a hard time. People will gossip about you. Marriage is not necessarily happy, but it is what everyone has done for thousands of years."

Ching once had a serious fight with Yee and they almost split up. One afternoon, Ching was very sad and stayed in her room. Ching's mother opened the door and asked her something. Just before she closed the door, she said in a caring but bitter tone, "Quarrel?" Ching was stunned: "Did my mother know it?" Then Ching overheard her mother tell her father in the living room: "Oh dear, the sweet couple split up!" Her tone sounded as though she thought they should stay together.

It is perhaps crucial that Ching uses food and dinner as cultural markers to break the insider-outsider distinction. Yee's active involvement in shopping and playing mah-jongg with Ching's mother has significantly strengthened the relationship between them. That is why Yee had gradually come to be seen by Ching's parents as their quasi-daughter. Indeed, Ching uses kin categories to express their relationship in three stages: "I think at first my mother treated Yee as my younger sister, then later as her second daughter, and now Yee and me are treated as a couple, like wife and husband." In all the successful cases of coming home, the partner is perceived by the *tongzhi's* parents through quasi-kin categories, which is a crucial indication that the insider-outsider distinction has been broken.

Chinese people have a strong sense of the we-they dichotomy based on family-kinship categories. Yet the definition of family members is not necessarily biological. The boundary and composition of the familial group is forever fluid and undefined (Lau, 1982:81). Sometimes, with the aid of certain family members, an outsider can cross over to become a family member. Yee and Ching are one good case; Roddy and Wah are another.

Roddy (twenty-eight) is a Beijing *tongzhi* who often goes to Tianjin on business. Three years ago, he started a relationship with Wah, who is living with his wife, Ling, a woman from a rural village. Roddy is Wah's first "boyfriend" and is very close to Ling too. Every time Roddy visits Wah, Ling will invite Roddy to sleep with Wah, and she sleeps in the living room to show hospitality to her husband's best friend. Although Roddy is living in a society of severe marital pressure, it is interesting to note how he manages to maneuver within such a limited space of same-sex intimacy:

> Ling knows about my intimate relationship with Wah. For her, marriage and romantic love are different things—romantic love and sex are different again. Marriage is a familial responsibility that need not coincide with romantic love. Even in the West, the concept of romantic love is of recent origin. She takes me positively. Indeed, she has very intimate women friends who are her major source of emotional life. Well, we Chinese treasure friendship more than romantic love.

Once, Ling saw Roddy and Wah caressing each other in bed. Some days later, Ling told Wah, "I know you two are good brothers, like real siblings. But don't do dirty things—you may get AIDS from that. You have a daughter and a family of your own." Some readers may find Ling's responses strange. But in rural areas, where marital responsibility is separated from erotic object choice and where same-sex intimate friendship is highly valued, Ling may treat Wah and Roddy's sexual intimacy as male naughtiness. She would only be really angry and outraged if Roddy were a woman, as that would directly threaten Ling's major identity as a wife. Roddy told me, "Ling and Wah are a very harmonious marital couple, very well matched. In terms of sex, when Ling wants it, Wah does it; he is happy to make Ling happy. He takes it as an obligation, like other obligations. He doesn't mind doing it, and is happy to make everyone happy. If he is really aroused, he will do it with me."

Coming Out By Bypassing Tongxinglian

Most *tongzhi* say that the implicit and subtle way of coming out is more suitable in a Chinese family. They come out by bypassing the discussion of homosexuality. Tat-ming (thirty-six), a typical case, said, "My parents should know it but I never tell them directly":

> I have never dated women, and only men phone me. It is so obvious! Once, when my mother and I were watching a TV program on AIDS, she was so attentive, listening to every word. After the program, she said to me: "A-Ming, you must be careful. AIDS is a fatal disease. You are a doctor and know better than anyone. I never control your private life, but I am too old, don't let me worry." And last month when the TV broadcast Xu You-sheng's marriage, my father said, "I object to these so-called *tongzhi* marriages. I think

everyone should marry. I really don't know what is in your mind, but we are Chinese, so I think you should marry. It is a social obligation for everyone." But the most fascinating experience was last year when I split up with Travis, who had been with me for four years. My mother knew Travis as my best friend. One night, my mother suddenly asked me whether I was very unhappy. I was really depressed at that time, so I didn't say a word. She then asked me, "Is it because of Travis?" I was shocked and didn't know how to respond. She knew that she caught me and said, "Don't think that I am dumb and blind, just that I didn't say it. You two are a good couple, and a good relationship needs lots of effort." I was speechless. Two days later, my mother called Travis to play mah-jongg and now they still meet once or twice a month. I have separated from my boyfriend, but he maintains a good relationship with my mother. Isn't it amazing?

Tat-ming says that his mother accepts him because she does not see him as a gay man, but a whole person in a concrete relationship. Tat-ming stresses that a parent would not reject a *tongzhi* child the way they reject the concept of *tongxinglian*. What his mother accepts is not *tongxinglian* per se but her son's specific relationship with Travis. It is crucial that Travis is someone she knows, likes, and relates to closely. For her, Travis is neither an outsider nor an abstract person called gay; Travis is a special friend of her son. Tat-ming continued,

> The greatest problem in my case is that both of my parents have big families with members really close to one another. All these old aunties always ask me, "Why are you not married yet?" It is very annoying. What can I say? Well, I think the fact that I am a doctor helps a lot. First, these relatives think that I have a successful career, so they dare not push me. You see, status and power. Second, I always provide good medical consultation for them. So they like and respect me. Third, my parents feel honored by my professional status, and they are happy to receive 20,000 dollars every month from me. My father has retired. He depends on me!

Tat-ming has the advantage of being a middle-class professional, but one does not need to be middle-class to negotiate well with one's parents.

Rachel (twenty-nine) came from a working-class background. She got a scholarship when she was eighteen and went to Britain for three years. When she moved out to live with her partner, Wu, her mother asked her: "What if you get old?" Rachel replied: "Wu and I will take care of each other, like ordinary people." After a long chat, her mother said, "You are who you are, but you don't have to tell other people. I would not tell my relatives, friends, or your father; he cannot take it. He is so stubborn. I worry that you will be hurt." Her mother even reminded her that "you should find a Chinese friend, not a *gweilo*!" (a foreigner, especially Caucasian). When Rachel met her present partner, Mandy, Rachel's mother asked, "Is she also this kind of people? I don't want you to waste time with those who are not. And don't let normal people go wrong."

Rachel said that the key point is a warm relationship with her parents. "If the relationship is close, it's easy for the parents to accept one more thing about you. If the relationship is bad, homosexuality becomes a big thing." Rachel has three siblings who have married or emigrated. She is the only one who lives with her parents, and she plays a very filial role:

> My parents always worry that no one will take care of them in their old age. My mother actually invited Mandy to live with us. Mandy is very good at pleasing the elderly—she is now part of my family. For example, she changed her schedule from going to the gym four times a week to having a morning walk with my parents. And she would drive my parents to see the fireworks at Ching-Ma Bridge, and sometimes give my daddy a lift to work as they go in the same direction. My father is very proud of me.

Tat-ming's and Rachel's experiences illustrate a distinctive feature of these integrative strategies—*tongzhi* identity is integrated into the family but it will not be mentioned as such around the family table. The Chinese family, given its hegemonic cultural status, has an immense capacity to absorb certain troublesome and undesirable issues by making them invisible in words but clearly understood by every family member. Rachel, who had an American girlfriend during her three years of study in the United Kingdom, made an interesting remark:

> It seems to be very particular among Chinese when one should or should not say certain things that will be emotionally disturbing, especially to the parents. It is not just about *tongzhi*, but all the sensitive issues. My mother clearly understands my situation, as she said, "Is she also this kind of people? I don't want you to waste time with those who are not. And don't let normal people go wrong." But we never say the word [read *tongxinglian*]. It is too visible and Western. It is ironic that she accepts my relationship with my girlfriend by making it disappear in words but actually permeate the real relationship. I think it is both good and bad: I don't need to emphasize my sexual orientation, but neither can I mention it directly.

These strategies and cases are neither exhaustive nor necessarily Chinese. Many lesbigays in other societies use similar strategies to negotiate acceptance in and integration with the family. This elucidation of *tongzhi* strategies should not be mistaken as an essentialist argument for the so-called Chinese culture. Indeed, the differences among various Chinese societies make any monolithic articulations of Chinese culture highly contestable. *Tongzhi* have different needs and use different strategies to tackle their problems. The situations in Taiwan, Hong Kong, and for the vast population of *tongzhi* in mainland China would require different perspectives and strategies for the empowerment of each. Even in the cases where the parents accept their *tongzhi* children, it does not imply that they understand or accept homo/bisexuality, much less support *tongzhi* rights.

In many cases, family support is rather passive, sometimes superficial. Leo (twenty-seven) shared his experiences:

> Around three years ago, my mother first came to Lantau Island to visit me and Tom. Tom and I were sleeping in the same bed, so we discussed whether we needed to add a bed or not but finally decided not to hide, just let her know naturally. During the visit, my mother asked whether we were sleeping together in the same bed. Well, I just said yes. Indeed, my parents always knew that my relationship with Tom was very close. But only then did they confirm my relationship with Tom. After the visit, my mother was really nice to Tom, treating him like her second son, always inviting him for dinner, boiling nice soup for him and so on. I was very touched, of course. She did not say anything to me, as if nothing had happened. But when I split up with Tom last year, my mother's response was that I should date women, try heterosexuality. She said: "After all, it is not normal. I don't know why you like it, but if you are really filial, you should think of me and get married—then I would be completely relieved." All along she appeared to be open and receptive, but only now do I know that she accepts Tom because she has no better choice, and even if she accepts my relationship with Tom, it doesn't mean she accepts homosexuality.

Leo presents a vivid case revealing the limitations of integrative strategies. They are effective only on a personal level, without challenging the underlying sociopolitical institutions and practices of heterosexism and homophobia. It is necessary to combat heterosexism and oppression on a more structural and institutional level. Although the collective resistant strategy of queering the mainstream will be explained in the next chapter, I will now proceed to illustrate the relevance of confrontational politics in the Hong Kong context.

WHY THE LEGAL DISCOURSES
OF RIGHTS ARE NOT SUFFICIENT

In this section, I will focus on Hong Kong and examine why Hong Kong *tongzhi* are hesitant to engage in confrontational politics in the legal discourse of rights. I contend that reluctance about confrontational politics is part and parcel of the wider sociopolitical conservatism of Hong Kong society. Contrary to the U.S. lesbigay movements, which often focus on legislative protection of lesbigay rights, Hong Kong *tongzhi* adopt a rather nonconfrontational strategy of building the *tongzhi* community. The controversy was most acute during the debate on the Equal Opportunity Bill (EOB) from 1993 to 1995, when the government made an unprecedented move to consult the public about legislative protection of *tongzhi* rights.

The most influential and elaborate sociopolitical discourse of modern Hong Kong is Lau Siu-kai's theory of the minimally integrated sociopolitical system, by which he refers to the harmonious coexistence of two highly autonomous and separate entities—the bureaucratic polity and the Chinese society. The bureaucratic polity, despite its omnipotent political power in Hong Kong, is eager to confine its role to the political, and limit its socioeconomic functions mainly to producing basic infrastructural facilities such as telecommunications and trading services. The government indeed wants to depoliticize society. As Sir Alexander Grantham, the governor of Hong Kong from 1947 to 1958, said in 1950, "We cannot permit Hong Kong to be the battleground for contending political parties or ideologies. We are just simple traders who want to get on with our daily round and common task" (Hong Kong Government, 1950:41).

The Hong Kong Chinese society, on the other side, is marked by *utilitarian familism,* in which the family is the major institution absorbing and resolving the socioeconomic and emotional needs of an individual, thus contributing to the social aloofness and political passivity of the general public. "Given the Chinese abhorrence of conflict and aggression, we find the coexistence of intense emotional attachments among people in small groups, and cold, impersonal postures towards those who are outsiders" Lau, 1982:89). Class consciousness and class antagonism are relatively low, and the feeling of antagonism against the rich is weak. Only 8.3 percent of the population think that the rich have a great responsibility to help the poor, whereas 87.3 percent of the respondents would definitely prefer social stability to economic prosperity, if forced to choose between the two (Lau, 1982:71).

Such an overwhelming concern for order and prosperity has been increased by the refugee nature of Hong Kong society. Chinese migrants, after experiencing the hardships of the Chinese civil war and war with Japan, were desperate for social order. The constant economic growth in the last two decades and the resultant rapid growth of living standards and social services have generated the myth of Hong Kong as an "economic miracle," thus further marginalizing and silencing the voices of the discontented.[3]

With such clear boundaries between polity and society, changes to the sociopolitical system are expected to be gradual and incremental, guided by pragmatic considerations rather than ideological disputes. Although significant democratic progress has been made in the last decade, the value of democracy seems to be as a device to safeguard the existing social order and economic prosperity, more than as a genuine pursuit of political participation and a public voice (Leung, 1996). The sovereign rule of the Chinese Communist Party after 1997 further undermines the popularity of confrontational politics in Hong Kong.

Most *tongzhi* seem to share the public's yearning for order and stability, and are not eager to pursue radical or confrontational politics. The absence of gay-bashing and other homophobic violence have further quieted the *tongzhi* issue in the Hong Kong political agenda. Local *tongzhi* reservations about radical politics are best exemplified by the debate on the EOB.

The EOB was drafted and proposed by Legislative Councilor Anna Wu Hung-yuk in 1993. The bill prohibited discrimination based on gender, marital status, pregnancy, family responsibility, disability, sexuality, race, age, and political and religious conviction. The bill aimed at providing protection against discrimination in areas such as employment, education, housing, and social services. The government criticized Wu's bill as too radical, yet was pressured by the general public to take action against discrimination. Wu's proposals were defeated in the Legislative Council on July 31, 1995.

The government then conducted a public consultation on discrimination concerning age, sexual orientation, and family status. In the consultation paper, "Equal Opportunities: A Study on Discrimination on the Grounds of Sexual Orientation," a questionnaire was included full of discriminatory questions such as, "Would you mind shaking hands with homo/bisexuals?" "Would you mind singing karaoke, dining out, or swimming with homo/bisexuals?" These questions first assume the general public to be heterosexual, and then lead them to believe that it may be a problem to shake hands or generally socialize with homo/bisexuals. During the consultation period, local churches mobilized thousands of Christians to sign petitions against legal protection for *tongzhi*. After three months of consultation, the government reported that 85 percent of the 11,000 respondents strongly rejected legal protection for sexual minorities (Hong Kong Government, 1996). The official document released by the Home Affairs Branch of the Hong Kong government confirms that discrimination based on sexual orientation is a major problem. The surveys found that public acceptance of homosexuality and bisexuality is low; only heterosexuality is regarded as normal. The paper argued that given the strong opposition to positive legal action, the government would resist any positive legal action and would only implement an antidiscrimination agenda in civic education. The government therefore used "social order" and "public opinion" as crucial grounds to refuse any legal actions against sexual discrimination. Although the government did not consult *tongzhi* groups thoroughly and the questionnaire was very biased, the result reflects a crucial cultural attitude toward homosexuality: Hong Kong people in general supported the decriminalization of homosexuality in 1991, yet they are very reluctant to actively grant *tongzhi* the rights of marriage, child adoption, or employment protection. In other words, the general public would not condone violence or discrimination against *tongzhi*, but neither would they condone taking positive action supporting *tongzhi* rights. Finally, another private member's bill against discrimination based on age and sexuality was defeated on June 27, 1997, just before the handover.

In Hong Kong, *tongzhi* have no rights to marry, to adopt children, to apply for public housing, to inherit the property of a deceased partner, or to be protected from job discrimination. Yet local *tongzhi* are not eager to fight for legal protection. Ironically, it is *Contacts Magazine,* which is run by several Caucasian gay men, that was most eager to lobby the government for positive action. Why did the issue of legal protection fail to arouse active participation from the local *tongzhi* community?

According to my research, most *tongzhi* interviewees support the spirit of the EOB but argue that these bills are not practical. Hyman, Jenny, and John represent three typical positions of local *tongzhi*:

> **Hyman (thirty-seven):** I don't think legal reform can solve my problem or other *tongzhi*'s. The major issues for us are not homophobic violence, occupational security, public attack, or religious fundamentalism, but the family and parents. Changing the law does not make your parents accept me. On the contrary, it makes the Chinese government feel threatened, thinking that *tongzhi* are troublemakers, that *tongzhi* ally with Western countries in accusing China of human rights abuses. It would be disastrous for Chinese *tongzhi* if the Chinese

government opened a file on homosexuals. We all know what the Chinese government is capable of. The Chinese government did not bash *tongzhi*, but if we become very confrontational in criticizing Chinese human rights and the oppression of *tongzhi*, it will be a self-fulfilling prophecy.

Jenny (thirty): I don't want to be visible—too many sacrifices of *tongzhi* in terms of exposing their identities are needed. I don't think you can mobilize the *tongzhi* here. And the public would be irritated if *tongzhi* became very confrontational, and they would be pushed by us to take on the label "heterosexual."

John (twenty-six): The EOB is about the protection of *tongzhi* from legal and work discrimination, but it is not the main issue for local *tongzhi*. For the expatriate here, yes, as their privileges are tied up with their jobs in Hong Kong. But for local *tongzhi*, you can get another job, and rarely would a *tongzhi* be fired because of his or her sexuality. The only known media case was an Englishman in an expatriate firm! It was a Caucasian boss who was annoyed by a British gay employee and decided to fire him. There have been no reported cases of local Chinese bosses who fire Chinese employees because of their sexuality. If my boss knew my *tongzhi* identity, she would not fire me, but only gossip about me. The law cannot protect *tongzhi* from being gossiped about, right?

Even *tongzhi* leaders are hesitant to press for legal reforms. Michael Lai (thirty-five), chairperson of the Ten Percent Club in 1994, said that we should learn to walk before we run, and we should take things one step at a time: "We are not trying to confront society. Nor do we aim to challenge the existing system" (Li, J., 1994:17). Among all the *tongzhi* groups, only Queer Sisters has launched an energetic campaign for the EOB. QS stresses that human rights are not a Western value but basic rights of human beings. In 1997, QS issued a pamphlet, "Sexual Rights Are Human Rights," stating, "Human rights are the basic rights that everyone is born with. Anyone should have them, and they should not be defined by the so-called authority." QS also lamented the apathy and conservatism of local *tongzhi* in fighting for their own rights.

Indeed, both the 1991 decriminalization and the EOB were not initiated by *tongzhi* but by the government and straight legislative councillors. In both instances, *tongzhi* groups only reacted. Such political apathy is not just a result of the so-called "Hong Kong mentality," rather, it indicates the specific cultural experiences of *tongzhi*. Ken Chu (thirty-two), the chair of the Ten Percent Club in 1997, said,

> The American model of confrontation is the product of a long history of violent oppression. In the Bible, male homosexuals had to be penalized and stoned to death. In the middle ages, gay people were burned to death. The violence against homosexually inclined people does not disappear in modern society. The massacre of gay people in concentration camps in World War II is just an acute example of such violence. Gay bashing all over America and Britain has never stopped. Even in the 1980s, the neoconservatism of Reagan and Thatcher have produced homophobic policies and discourses against homosexuality. The government apathy, indifference, and stereotypes against the AIDS issue have stirred up the anger of lesbigay people to an unprecedented level which became a crucial context for the birth of queer politics and Queer Nation—a radical and confrontational politics led by the young generation of queers. The problems here in Hong Kong are very different. What we need is self-help and mutual help, to build up a strong *tongzhi* network and upgrade the quality of *tongzhi* ourselves. (Interview, July 11, 1997)

To paraphrase Isaiah Berlin's distinction between "negative liberty," which refers to freedom from interference, and "positive liberty," which refers to the freedom to actualize one's goals, local *tongzhi* are more concerned with the negative liberty of "freedom from" (oppression and interference) than the positive liberty of "freedom to" fight for *tongzhi* rights. Most *tongzhi* are proestablishment (Berlin, 1969). In a commercial city such as Hong Kong where most social energy is invested in money-making, the notion of oppression has little appeal for the Chinese residents.

Economy and class are key factors here. Class location makes a *tongzhi's* situation very different.[4] Contemporary local *tongzhi*, like the rest of Hong Kong, are enjoying the full benefits of Hong Kong's rapid economic development over the past thirty years. Stability and prosperity become the totemic theme shared by most of Hong Kong's people, who are so proud of being a top world finance center. Everyone over thirty years old can still remember the hardships and deprivations in the 1960s and 1970s. Radical confrontational politics are seen by the general public as generating social conflict and economic instability. Such a mentality is so pervasive that most Hong Kong *tongzhi* would find radical politics too threatening.

Such a mainstream *tongzhi* position has been criticized by some Caucasian gay men in Hong Kong, best represented by *Contacts Magazine,* which was started by Barrie Brandon, a British gay man who was the secretary of the Long Yang Club in London before he came to Hong Kong. *Contacts* was very active in lobbying the government for the EOB. Brandon advocates a strong line of coming out and being visible. Indeed, the first article in the first issue of *Contacts* was titled "The High Cost of Life in the Closet," with the opening sentence reading "living in the closet homosexuals confine a large part of personal identity . . . life in the closet is about fear, keeping secrets, feeling split, remaining hidden, telling less than truth" (Rosenbluth, 1993:4). Articles in later issues were very critical of *tongzhi*'s reluctance to come out. An editorial in the April 1994 issue said:

> It seems to me a great pity that in nearly all recent articles, whether radio, TV, newspapers, or magazines, some of our so called "gay activists" are not prepared to challenge homophobia and speak out loudly and clearly for gay rights for the Hong Kong gay community. (p. 3)

In the same issue, the editor also criticized the Ten Percent Club: "It would be great if they could find people who are happy being out to be photographed" (p. 7). Robin Adams (1995a), a core member of *Contacts,* stated that "gay awareness is in its infancy in Hong Kong, not because no one cares, but because we are all so very closeted. Because we have no out gay public figures, we have no strength to come out ourselves" (p. 20). In another article encouraging people to come out, Adams also wrote: "the most significant action we can take is to be visible . . . if every gay man and woman told their families that they were in fact gay, everyone in the world would know a gay person" (1995b:17). However, not everyone has the space to tell the family that they are gay (or lesbian/bisexual), and not every PEPS needs to prioritize sexuality as a master category. The absolutization of the Anglo-American political strategy and rhetoric of coming out may inscribe Chinese *tongzhi* into the hegemonic *gay* discourse, which would define the majority of Chinese *tongzhi* as inferior—closeted and lacking courage. For the Caucasian living in an Asian society, coming out may be liberating and relatively easy; for a *tongzhi* to come out directly to his or her parents may be disastrous instead of liberating.

Adams' optimistic gay politics do not seem to be based on the actual reality in Hong Kong. In a different article, he wrote: "I'll bet it's safe to say that a very large percentage of organizations in Hong Kong already include protection for Gays and Lesbians—it's not such a revolutionary concept" (Adams, 1995b:10). The fact that Adams can neither speak nor understand Cantonese or Mandarin, though he has been in Hong Kong for ten years, may be a reason why he has romanticized lesbigay rights in Hong Kong.

The handful of Chinese writers in *Contacts Magazine* have a very different position on coming out. Columnist Danny Wong said: "Being out is a personal choice and not one that everyone should be required to make. If a person feels that they want to be out, that is their choice. It is their choice if they choose to be in the closet" (1995:10). As a local *tongzhi* said in a Chinese *tongzhi* magazine, "it would not be fair to demand all gays to wear their sexuality like a badge if coming out will jeopardize their personal or public life" (Tsang, 1994:12).

Contacts Magazine was also very critical of the 1996 Chinese *Tongzhi* Conference, a three-day conference in Hong Kong with 200 Chinese participants. The conference published a manifesto arguing that:

> The les-bi-gay movement in Western societies is largely built upon the notion of individualism, confrontational politics, and the discourse of rights. Certain characteristics of confrontational politics, such as through coming out and mass protest and parades, may not be the best way of achieving *tongzhi* liberation in the family-centered, community-oriented Chinese societies which stress the importance of social harmony.

The manifesto was seriously attacked by *Contacts Magazine:* "with an alleged attendance of over 200 people, who met for two and a half days wasn't it remarkable that there weren't any conclusions? That 200 people could meet for that length of time and not reach any conclusions seems to us to be so astonishing that it should be presented to the Guinness book of records as the first Gay conference that didn't achieve anything of note" (*Contacts,* 1997:3). Barrie Brandon also said: "The conference failed to come up with any positive steps that local Chinese *tongzhi* could or ought to take in coming to terms with their sexuality. . . . It seems to some people though that this conference prefers that we all stay in the closet and wait for some divine edict from heaven to bestow equality" (Brandon, 1997:14).

The underlying issue here is not just the relevance of the coming out and confrontational politics, but also the legal discourse of rights. The Western lesbigay movement in the last thirty years has devoted much energy to fighting for lesbigay legal rights in education, work, marriage, the military, social welfare, and the family. But should we transplant the modern Western discourse of rights to protect Chinese *tongzhi?*

Sin Wai-man and Chu Yiu-wai (1997) critically examine the Western legal tradition of rights and the rule of law, which have often been portrayed as culturally neutral and as a major key to Hong Kong's success.

Sin and Chu argued that such a tradition of the rule of law in Hong Kong is actually Western centered and presupposes a notion of "reasonableness" that marginalizes the Chinese concept of *qing*.

> *Qing* is the concept particular to the Chinese, which has no equivalent in the English language. It can be loosely translated as "appeal to other's feeling," "emotions," "sense of humanity," or "common decency." *Li* refers to "discursive reasoning," "rational principle," "logical argument" and the like, and *fa* is almost identical to law. In traditional Chinese culture, *qing*, *li* and *fa* exist in unity. When conflicts arise, "one is well advised to begin with *qing*. . . . Only when all such avenues are exhausted does one turn to *li*. . . . If this too proves unavailing, one then is then forced as a last resort to invoke *fa*." In light of this, the fundamental problem of the Rule of Law is that *qing* is being marginalized while *fa* is represented as the *dao* (way) of a modern society. (p. 6)

In traditional Chinese culture, *fa* is a way to regulate social behavior and to penalize those who act against *li* (ritual, propriety). Yet Chinese tradition stresses that law must be grounded in *qing*, as best revealed in a common saying that "law is nothing more than *ren qing*" (human sentiment or relationship). In view of Chinese cultural practices of the unity of *qing*, *li*, and *fa* and the general cultural concern for integrating *qing* and *li* (*he qing*, *he li*), local *tongzhi's* reservation about Western lesbigay strategies of fighting for legal rights can be seen as questioning the boundary and limitations of legal rights discourse, especially if rights are only confined to *fa*, lacking the elements *qing* and *li*.

The discourse of rights is a powerful impersonal language governing the basic contractual relations between members of the society. It can stop people from infringing on the rights of others, but can generate little genuine concern, respect, and care. As separated from the notion of *qing*, the Western discourse of rights is rather weak in negotiating and resolving interpersonal relationships in the familial context. It would become totalitarianism if we punished those who do not care for and respect our parents, friends, or lovers. Attitudes and manners in interpersonal relationships are the hardest areas to reach with the law. For example, without breaking the law, people can still resent and fear *tongzhi*, a Hong Kong Chinese can stare at a Filipino maid with contempt, and a boss can condemn a female employee in very rude terms.

Rights are impersonally defined, but family relationships, especially in Chinese societies, are highly particularistic and relational. What we expect in the family is not only rights, but more often personal affiliation, warmth, and concern. Even when the parents infringe on the rights of their *tongzhi* child, it is very difficult and often undesirable to use the language of rights to resolve the problem. People will explain, negotiate, and bargain, but will not go to court to prosecute their parents.

The focus of the modern lesbigay movement on visibility (legislative practices, parades, and rights protection) fits an individualistic society where individual rights and freedoms are given the highest social value. To impose the same discourse upon a society where sexuality is never segregated from the wider social relations and is rarely discussed may simply ignore the rather invisible social relations that both constitute and oppress *tongzhi*.

The discourse of rights is actually a minimal ethical thinking of contractual relationships, which sets only the basic protective boundaries for human interaction. Beyond this, there is a huge area to maneuver, within which the language of rights may be neither effective nor desirable. As stated by Rosemarie Tong (1984:203), "the law is a minimalist institution. It punishes only manifest or serious harms. It does not censor or sanction those hidden or less blatant harms that plague society more routinely. Nor does it, as a rule, reward positive behavior that benefits society." Such contractual legal discourses originate in nineteenth-century liberalism and laissez-faire economic theory where the state has the obligation to protect the basic rights of the citizens. Modern Western lesbigay discourse is indeed the product of modernity, tied up with the libertarian notion of an individuated self who is said to be liberated from the constraints of tradition and cultural collectivity to become a free sexual subject (*gay*). Since everyone is said to be an independent and absolute moral sovereign, and is not seen as related to others in inextricable or intrinsic ways, what separates us is epistemologically and morally prior to what connects us (Tao and Drover, 1997). In other words, the rights discourse is predicated upon the modern Western individualist tradition, which assumes that every person is individualistic, egoistic, and atomistic.[5]

Moreover, the libertarian argument for state intervention to protect *tongzhi* rights could be a dangerous invitation to state control and regulation of sexuality. In the context of mainland China, where the government has never felt the need to criminalize same-sex relationships as they are not yet a political issue, the outcry for legal protection could ironically invite the dictatorial government to adopt the homo-hetero duality and to control the activities of "homosexuals." Even in the supposedly libertarian Hong Kong government, the legal intervention in 1991 is notorious for producing the heterosexist definition of private-public separatism in which same-sex sexuality must disappear in the public arena and can only exist in the private, yet a private room with three persons or more is defined as "public." Therefore, the 1991 decriminalization actually invented the category of "civilized, monogamous *tongzhi*" whose rights should be protected only because they strictly confine their homoeroticism to private rooms, whereas the majority of *nan tongzhi* who cruise in toilets, or those having twenty-year-old boy-friends, are the "corrupted ones" who now become the target of criminal punishment. It is a deeply sexist discourse, as *nü tongzhi* sexuality is simply ignored and trivialized. It is also a class issue, as working-class men who have less economic power to own their own private homes, are more vulnerable to police raids in the cruising areas, and once caught are unable to hire the best lawyers and may not be able to command the English language in the legal proceedings. In a word, without challenging the hidden ideologies of the present legal system, the outcry for (PRC) government intervention and protection of *tongzhi* rights may only trap the newly emerged "homosexual bodies" in the complex web of discipline and control of the state apparatus.

However, this does not mean that *tongzhi* rights have not been infringed or that the discourse of rights is redundant. Far from it. Chinese *tongzhi* are oppressed in the Chinese family-kin system where individual rights are often denied. *Tongzhi* are oppressed not only in large-scale sociopolitical institutions, but most acutely by their intimate loved ones—the parents who insist the *tongzhi* child should get married, the mother who feels great shame for losing face, the father who shows contempt, the siblings and close friends who tease and gossip about *tongzhi* behind their backs.

For many Chinese *tongzhi*, family harmony and social order are the most hegemonic and oppressive categories that may torture them for their whole lives. Yet most of the thorny issues faced by Chinese *tongzhi* cannot be solved by the legal discourse of rights. Could a *tongzhi* child use the discourse of rights to sue his or her parents for self-blaming and self-guilt? Could the law stop parents from pressuring their children to get married? Could the law prosecute a mother who begs her son not to be a homosexual? Could a *tongzhi* prosecute a friend who teases her behind her back?

For *tongzhi*, the most beloved ones are exactly those who oppress them most. It is this intricacy that renders confrontational politics inappropriate for most *tongzhi*, whose main enemy is not some impersonal system called religious fundamentalism, the state apparatus, or the capitalist work system. In a culture where same-sex eroticism is not seen as the private property of a minority population, but a practice that everyone can potentially engage in, we can perhaps emphasize everyone's need and rights for intimacy irrespective of gender. It would imply a different strategy for liberation, not just the sexual liberation of homo- and bisexuals, but a *tongzhi* movement that invites everyone to explore their own eroticism beyond the homo-hetero duality. The goal it is striving for ultimately is not a contractual and individualistic society where *tongzhi* rights are observed by the heterosexual world only because of legal restrictions, but a society where it is simply unnecessary to stress one's sexuality, whatever it is. It is the strategy of queering the mainstream that I will turn to in the last chapter.

Chapter 8

Tongzhi Identity Politics
As Queering the Mainstream

Throughout this book, I have argued for the need to explore and develop the specific categories through which individual PEPS construct same-sex eroticism. I have historicized the cultural specificity of identity politics and confrontational politics, which have been especially empowering and successful in the United States. The modern Anglo-American experience of the lesbigay movement has been predicated upon the notion of identity politics. It is a segregational model in which sexual orientation is seen as separable from race, culture, kin, class, and gender. It also dichotomizes and essentializes same-sex and opposite-sex desire, and segregates lesbigay people from the "general public." However, "sexual identity," as historically conferred through multiple layers of economic and sociocultural constructs, is itself highly contestable. As a matter of fact, generic identity based on sexual orientation did not exist in traditional China.

In traditional Chinese culture, same-sex and opposite-sex eroticism were not dichotomous because "sexuality" was not independent of but discursively constituted by the specific kin-class relations in the wider society. The danger of segregational identity politics is that it suspends the social, as if all PEPS shared an essential core *gay*ness irrespective of and uninfluenced by gender, culture, class, and social context. To universalize sexual identity politics is to take class, culture, gender, family-kin, and race as the presupposed but unclarified foundation of sexual identity, thus failing to explore the fundamental sociocultural mechanisms that produce the categories "sex" and "sexual orientation" in the first place.

If sex is a contextualized and constructed experience rather than just an act, we need to explore under what social conditions certain behaviors are constituted as "sexual," and how certain biological bodies are "sexed" and inscribed with discourses of "sexual orientation." In short, we must examine how "sexed subjects" are produced as such in the first place.

"Homosexuals" are not homogenous. The absolutization of sexual identity, defined rigidly by a homo-hetero duality, is often a totalizing project that denies the complexities and diversities of the contradictory locations the "homosexual self" occupies. The totalizing project of "being lesbian" or "being *gay*" is problematic because PEPS of different race, culture, gender, class, and marital status differ from one another in significant aspects. It implies not the denial of identity politics, but a diversity-sensitive framework of "sexual identity" in which identity should be used strategically and critically without "essentializing it" (Scott, 1992). As early as 1985, queer theorist Jeffrey Escoffier argued that "the politics of identity must also be a politics of difference . . . the politics of difference affirms limited, partial being" (p. 2).

Given the traditional Chinese conception of sex as relational and contextual, we need to reorient sexuality by highlighting the interweaving relationships among gender, sex, culture, family, class, and kin. The refusal of many Chinese *tongzhi* to take up the lesbigay identity and come out can be seen as a resistance to accommodating the American lesbigay discourse. It is therefore important not to translate the Chinese term *tongzhi* as "comrade," "gay," or "queer," because *tongzhi* will immediately be subsumed and absorbed into the signification system of the English language and culture and be reduced to an earlier form of the U.S. *gay* movement. *Tongzhi* is irreducible to "lesbigay," "homosexual," or "queer." The insistence on coining the new word *tongzhi* is a strategy to maintain the cultural specificity of *tongzhi*. Adding the cultural label "Chinese" in front of "*gay*" does not help as it presupposes the universality of (American-white) "*gay*ness."

The dichotomy between "being Chinese" and "being *gay*" is most true when *gay* is constructed as a white project. Many *tongzhi* refuse to segregate sexuality from their kin-family and sociocultural identity but strive for expansive and connective forms of identity formation. This is best captured by Rachel (twenty-nine), whose story was discussed in Chapter 7:

> My identity does not stem from a single place nor follow a particular path. I experience the different dimensions of the self every day. Identity expands, grows, develops, overlaps, and fades. But it does not mean that I am *tongzhi* today and straight tomorrow. No, there are boundaries that are both limiting and empowering. As a Chinese daughter living with my parents, I can't just single out my sexuality and think that I am liberated as a lesbian or bisexual. No, I won't be liberated unless my sexuality is integrated into my familial, cultural, and social body.

Rachel also emphasizes the notion of (sexual) identity as a "role":

> I don't see my identity as fixed or definitive, like "I am a lesbian" or "I am a Chinese." Instead, I perceive my identity as a continual process of performing different roles in different situations. It is meaningless to ask me in the abstract, "Am I Chinese?" or "Am I lesbian?" I want to develop rather than define my identities, which are something always in the plural. . . . I like *tongzhi* as it is up to me to explore the *zhi* (goal or spirit) that I share (*tong*). And I think we confuse our "oppressors" by using their sacred terms.

This is perhaps why the category *tongzhi* is popular among Chinese. *Tongzhi* is a discursive practice whose meaning depends on the everyday practices of its participants. *Tongzhi* can be understood as a multiple and fragmented subject, having no unified or ontological essence, thus making the search for any final definition or monolithic strategy of *tongzhi* not only impossible, but undesirable. It opens up an internal space in which no one can monopolize the definition of *tongzhi,* but all PEPS are encouraged to define, enrich, question, and defer the meaning of *tongzhi. Tongzhi* can thus be seen as a site of power struggle that constantly unsettles and challenges the harmony, stability, and hegemony of identity. Although *tongzhi* is also a highly political and empowering symbol to rally social action and collective identification, it is akin to what Gayatri Spivak (1987:205) calls "strategic essentialism" in which *tongzhi* identity is continuously assumed and immediately called into question.

Tongzhi is a self-proclaimed process. Even within the PEPS circle, *tongzhi* has a range of meanings, from narrowly referring to self-identified homosexuals to broadly referring to everyone who identifies with the struggle against heterosexism. In Hong Kong and Taiwan, there are several self-identified "straight-*tongzhi*" (heterosexuals who take the fight against homophobia and heterosexism as their identity) activists who have played crucial roles in *tongzhi* movements. Their overall acceptance by the *tongzhi* community indicates not only rejection of a rigid homo-hetero duality but also the immense space through which *tongzhi* is continually constituted and deferred. This indeterminate and evolving nature of *tongzhi* identity opens up immense potential for a localized politics of coalition building between *tongzhi* and other sociopolitical allies based on gender, race, class, ethnicity, and other marginalized voices.

Tongzhi is not just a sexual category. It is social and cultural, as it stresses the integration of sexuality into the family-cultural context, and also the more inclusive, less dichotomizing orientations. What *tongzhi* reject is not identity politics per se but imposing confrontational and minoritizing identity politics on local contexts. *Tongzhi* insist on the sexual rights of PEPS but would not dichotomize the homosexually inclined ones from the heterosexually inclined ones.

Yet, it is dangerous to romanticize *tongzhi*. When the term *tongzhi* was first appropriated in 1989 by a Hong Kong activist, it strikingly combatted the mainstream homophobic vulgarization of homo/bisexuality. However, as the voices of *tongzhi* become more visible and vocal, *tongzhi* is often perceived merely as male middle-class homosexuals, at the expense of the voices of the minorities within the minorities—those who do not practice monogamous relationships, bisexuals who are seen as traitors, S/Mers who are criticized as "vulgarizing" the *tongzhi* community, *nan tongzhi* who cruise in toilets, and the effeminate *nan tongzhi* and the masculine TBs who reject straight behavior roles. This normalization and mainstreaming of *tongzhi* may erode, pacify, and absorb the marginality, subversiveness, and progressiveness of "sexual minorities." In this regard, the recent emergence of *tongzhi* discourses in Hong Kong and Taiwan is indeed deeply inadequate in subverting both the mainstream culture and the classism, racism, sexism, ageism, and bi-phobia within *tongzhi* communities.

It is therefore crucial and urgent to pluralize and destabilize *tongzhi* and to explore the signification process through which the category *tongzhi* is constituted, activated, and actualized by each individual *tongzhi*. While the signifier *tongzhi* has been very empowering for PEPS who construct a postcolonial identity that blends their sexual identities with their cultural experiences, what is needed is not only a linguistic revolution but political interventions that actually change the sexist and classist power relations in the mainstream world and within *tongzhi* communities.

It is a pressing task to problematize and destabilize any monolithic notion of the *tongzhi* movement, which is actually internally divided by class, gender, ethnicity, culture, language, education, and sexual practices. For example, after the 1998 *Tongzhi* Conference, there were debates on the Internet concerning the directions and strategies of *tongzhi* movement. Dan Tsang, a participant who has been living in the United States for many years, criticized the concept of "Chineseness" and nonconfrontational politics:

> I know Mandarin was the "official" language at the 1998 conference, and will probably be at the next one. John Loo [the Secretariat of the Conference] hopes we would have improved our [Mandarin] language skills by then. But is it necessary to learn Mandarin? Does knowing Cantonese [but not Putonghua] or even English make one less "Chinese"? I know the goal was to make our mainland brothers

and sisters feel welcome, but I still wonder if this is not imposing some kind of colonialism [even if from Beijing] on ourselves. . . . The conference press release repeats the old canard [from the previous conference] that Chinese oppose "confrontational" tactics and favor "social harmony." How utterly regressive and Confucianist! How about the years of protest by students, workers and others in this century? Are we to just dismiss this as "Western" ways not worthy of our second glance? This "essentializing" of Chinese tradition is surprising; a social movement, as the *tongzhi* movement surely is, needs to have more critical self-appraisal. . . . Perhaps there is no unity among Chinese, nor is there unity among *tongzhi*. We cannot paper over our differences, but need to struggle like good comrades. We need to discuss openly what are our common understandings, and our principles of unity, and not expect someone else to summarize our conference. (E-mail, 1998 *Tongzhi* Conference, March 1998)

Given the vast differences and diversities among *tongzhi* in Hong Kong, Taiwan, and mainland China, Tsang offers a crucial warning against "cultural essentialism." Another participant, Tan Chong-kee, who has a highly mixed cultural background and eclectic experiences, responded:

Each country faces different political, social and economic realities and must come up with different strategies to address them. . . . It is time we drop cultural essentialism. If one thing is clear from the many arguments throughout the conference, there is no one Chinese culture. (E-mail, 1998 *Tongzhi* Conference, March 1998)

There were also "harsh" comments from someone who had not attended the conference. In an e-mail to the discussion group, Luv Bangor said,

Dear Sir or Madam: I have read with disgust regarding the so-called conclusion of your Tongzhi Conference in Hong Kong. It is bad enough to use the word Tongzhi in your title, it is worst that the attendance agree on the "anti-American style" gay movement. If anyone of those idiot who attended the conference have ever read any history books, improvement in Human Right only happens after someone get up, shout for it, get put in jail for it, and get shot for it, it is the same anywhere in this world. These so called leader or speakers for the conference are a bunch of coward who want to whine their way to get the society to accept them. . . . Finally, stop using that fucking word "Tongzhi," no one want to be a god dame communist. (E-mail, 1998 *Tongzhi* Conference, March 1998) [sic]

This abrasive e-mail stirred up more debate. Pan Puan, a Malaysian activist, said,

> I don't think we had mentioned that gay movement in Asia is "anti-American style." I don't think anyone of us deny the good influence of American gay movement. We just cannot agree with bringing the whole style of American gay movement to here. Every culture handles things differently. . . . If you believe that in order to get gay movement going, one should get up, get jailed, get burn, why don't you be the first one who do that in China. I am sure that they are more than pleased to burn you if you did what you said, but don't burn all other gay persons who still want to live a tough gay life. . . . Sorry to tell you that the whole Far East region's Chinese communities have accepted the word tongzhi as equal to gay. By the way, my name is Pan Puan from Malaysia and it is also sorry to tell you that gay movement in this country also decided in whole by all gay groups to be non-violent and non-political. We are made out of Malay, Chinese and India gay men and gay women. So it is not only "some idiots" from Hong Kong, Taiwan and China who feel that way about gay movement. (E-mail, 1998 *Tongzhi* Conference, March 1998) [sic]

Given the diversity of the kinds of oppression and social situations faced by *tongzhi*, the pluralities of perspectives and strategies should be celebrated rather than leveled off. Differences are not divisive but the source of inspiration. What divides people is not the differences among PEPS, but the failure to recognize such differences. When the need for unity is mistaken for homogeneity, unity becomes a violence of exclusion. In other words, instead of erecting and glamorizing *tongzhi* as the standard identity for all Chinese PEPS, we should explore the power relations through which the knowledge and subjectivity of *tongzhi* is produced. It is exactly the internal indeterminacy of *tongzhi* that invites the voices of the discontented and the marginalized. It is not coincidental that in the last several years, the strongest voices in Hong Kong to redefine and reconstruct *tongzhi* have come from women, bisexuals, and other marginalized people—most notably the Queer Sisters (QS).

QS speak not only as a queer platform, but also as feminists. QS insists on not being classified as homosexual or *gay* as this only undermines gender specificity, taking phallocentrism as the norm for same-sex eroticism. QS also rejects the label "lesbian," as they insist on going beyond the homo-hetero duality or any oppositional sexual identity that is defined by the gender of erotic object choice. They advocate an inclusive strategy to explore and develop the sexual space and visibility of women, especially non-heterosexual-identified women. The first issue of the QS newsletter in 1997 states clearly that:

> QS is a feminist organization that advocates . . . women's rights to explore, discover, and choose their own sexualities, like choosing the gender of erotic object choice, the gender of clothing, the way to make love, and their own gender (identity and performance). Our insistence on multiple sexualities challenges the homo-hetero duality and the equation between *tongzhi* and *tongxinglian*. (*QS Newsletter,* 1997:1)

It is therefore a strategy to engender sexuality, to queer feminism, and to politicize women's sexual rights. A core QS member, Anson Mak (1998), writes, "for us, *tongzhi* movement refers not only to those who identify themselves as *tongzhi*, but to anyone who has been discriminated [against] in terms of sex" (p. 4). In the sixth issue of *Hong Kong Cultural Studies Bulletin,* organized by some of the core members of QS, there are critical reflections on the relations between feminism and *tongzhi* identity. Another core QS member, Zhou Zhong-di, is disturbed by the way *tongzhi* have always been equated with homosexuals:

> Most Hong Kong people and Chinese from both PRC and Taiwan tend to see *tongzhi* as "tongxinglian," or even as *gay* (male homosexuals). I think it is wrong. There is a *tong (means same/homo)* for both *tongzhi* and tongxinglian. However, if we just take the *tong* and drop the *zhi*, it's not only illogical, but loses the literal meaning of *zhi tong dao he* (sharing the same spirit/goal/orientation). . . . The most disturbing thing in the present *tongzhi* movement is that only tongxinglian are prioritized. Other sexual minorities would be treated according to their numbers and the extent of social acceptance. For example, during the EOB debate, many *tongzhi* groups use the term *gay*—in Hong Kong it means male homosexuals—to include both female and male, and also bisexuals. How is it different from the patriarchal usage of MAN to represent all human beings? (Zhou, 1996:68-69)

It thus exposes the pressing issue of the discrepancy between the vision of *tongzhi* and the common mainstream *tongzhi* representation as "male homosexuals." Many *nü tongzhi*, for example, feel accepted in the *tongzhi* community only if they subscribe to the "male-stream" of *tongzhi*, especially in terms of prioritizing the phallocentric definition of sex. For example, the decriminalization of homosexual acts in 1991 concerns only the freedom and rights of *gay* men. Women are ignored socially, sexually, and legally, and do not have equal discursive power in terms of defining the meaning of *tongzhi*. In the last two years, QS has allied with (heterosexual) women's groups no less than with (male) *tongzhi* groups. In 1996, QS formed the Hong Kong Women's Coalition, together with the Women's Christian Council, the Federation of Women's Centers, the Women's Workers Association, the Federation of Trade Unions, the Hong Kong Christian Institute, the Student Christian Movement, and the Christian Industrial Committee. This is also a resistance to prioritizing sexual identity at the expense of gender.

Indeed, the so-called Chinese tolerance of same-sex eroticism is predicated upon upper-class male status and gender privileges. Woman-woman sexuality is tolerated only because it is ignored, minimized, and trivialized. This explains not only the frustration and anger of *nü tongzhi* but also their insistence on the gender-specific category.

In the context of Hong Kong, the reservations about Western sexual identity are both a gender and a cultural issue. A local Caucasian activist, Robin Adams, said, "What exactly is wrong with the words queer, *gay* . . . aside from the benefits of granting a unique Chinese identity to a group searching for its own, I'm still trying to figure out why people in Hong Kong are so opposed to using these western words" (Web page, Hong Kong Queer, March 1997).

It is crucial that a QS member, Marian K., replied not only from a feminist perspective, but also by integrating her cultural experiences as Hongkongese:

> A name is not just a name, it contains a cultural, [sic] an ideology, a HIStory. Just like I will feel very uneasy while people address woMEN as a HE-human-being. . . . I would not oppose to [sic] anything because it is Western, what I oppose is it's [sic] Western imperialistic superiority. . . . As I talked to my local feMALE friends, many of them do not have a label for themselves, no matter it's *gay*, lesbian or bi or whatever. Some think that they do not need or want any, some are simply lost, they will just say: people like us. I know I am in no position to judge other people's culture, so I believe what people are doing in the West, i.e. identity politics, is their best choice. But this is not the case here. Hong Kong people didn't even have a identity as Hongkongers before the 1997 issue, needless to say, for queer Hong Kong people. (Web page, Hong Kong Queer, March 1997)

Anson Mak (1996), in an interview with *Marie Claire*, emphasized that QS concerns not only *tongzhi* but sexuality and women's subjectivity. She cites the example of S/M:

> In the *tongzhi* discourse in Hong Kong, we find no linguistic catego-
> ries to understand S/M. S/M in Hong Kong only refers to obscene
> video porno, without even a Chinese word for it. Maybe in Hong
> Kong, we should start with women treating their bodies as a sexual
> subject, so as to see how women understand, explore, and develop
> their sexuality, and to explore various forms of sexual expression, so
> unlike the Western world, which treats S/M as a sexual identity to
> resolve the problem. . . . Hong Kong people do not stress identity;
> they are ambiguous about identity as basic as Hongkongese and
> Chinese. How can you ask people to come out and say "I am a
> homosexual" and be proud of it? . . . Although I like the concept
> "queer" . . . the Eastern world has no such concept. I don't think we
> should implant Western categories without digesting them. (p. 73)

It is inspiring that Anson Mak cited S/M, which in Hong Kong (or Taiwan and mainland China) never constitutes as a sexual identity. In a world where those who participate in S/M are not seen as S/Mers, should these participants be asked to reclaim an identity that does not even exist yet? Such a confrontational strategy of identity politics may ironically generate phobia and oppression of this new sexual subject, "S/Mer," created by its own "liberating practices" and "truth claims." Stigmatizing oneself as a targeted minority would antagonize and deprive the majority's potential to explore sexuality beyond hegemonic heterosexuality. In a culture where homosexuality, S/M, and bisexuality are not seen as private properties possessed by definite minorities but as possibilities for every-one, a more fluid and relational conception of identity politics could be more effective and appropriate for *tongzhi* resistance.

It is interesting that both Marian K. and Anson Mak position their reservations about identity politics in the sociocultural context of Hong Kong in which people generally reject any rigid notion of identity, as even the identities Hongkongese or Hong Kong Chinese are only of recent invention. Indeed, the production of *tongzhi* identity is not unrelated to such ambivalence toward Hong Kong identity and so-called Chineseness.

Hong Kong identity is always fluid, marked by its pragmatic flexibility, apolitical utilitarianism, hybrid Chinese-English culture, and unwilling-ness to be tied to any fixed identity. This contradictory hybridity is best captured by a Hong Kong author and critic, Leung Ping-kwan (1989):

Vis-à-vis foreigners, Hong Kong people are of course Chinese, but vis-à-vis the Chinese from mainland or Taiwan, they seem to have the imprints of the West. A Hong Kong person who came from China after 1949 is obviously an outsider or someone coming south; but to those who came south during the 1970s and 1980s, such a person is already a local. A Hong Kong person may speak English or Putong-hua, but it is not the language with which he [*sic*] is familiar since childhood; and yet what he [*sic*] knows best, Cantonese, is not conve-nient for writing. He [*sic*] recites the Chinese classics while at school, but in his [*sic*] eventual employment he [*sic*] would have to acquaint himself [*sic*] with forms of commercial correspondence or the brief and cute wordings of advertising. Such linguistic impurities are also a reflection of the impurities of Hong Kong's cultural identity. (p. 71)

The linguistic and societal impurities are further complicated by politi-cal colonialization, in which Hong Kong is faced with a thorny issue unheard-of in colonial history: "How do we talk about a postcoloniality that is a forced return to a 'mother country,' itself as imperialistic as the previous colonizer?" (Chow, 1992:158).

The Hong Kong identity is a recent invention less than three decades old. Local critic and historian Elizabeth Sinn sarcastically notes that in Hong Kong cemeteries, only recently could we find the first Hong Kong *ren* (people) (quoted in Siu, 1996). Hong Kong used to be only a transient place for its residents, who did not perceive Hong Kong as their home. Since World War II, Hong Kong has gradually developed a unique social and cultural identity of its own, as a modern industrial city exposed to Western acculturation, which resulted in a lifestyle very different from that of the Chinese in mainland China. It is because of such "deviation" from the "original" Chinese culture that Hong Kong is always treated as "inau-thentic" because it has been "contaminated" by the "capitalist West."[1]

Culture is never pure. Like the categories lesbian, bisexual, and *gay*, "Chinese" is a discursive practice that has often been stabilized and natu-ralized as a source of identity for those inscribed as "Chinese." This stabilizing process, which essentializes and ontologizes *gay* or Chinese culture, is also an imperialist process. In recent years, the notion that human beings are naturally divided into different races and cultures has been seriously contested (Phelan, 1997a). It is dangerous to conceive the West and the East, America and China as autonomous and segregated spaces as if they never interact. East and West are relative concepts; without West, there can be no East, and vice versa. Mainland China, Hong Kong, and Taiwan are all historical products that emerged, developed, and transformed in the discursive field of the socioeconomic and political site of power relations without any necessary or fixed essence. (Chinese) Culture, in the transhistorical sense, does not exist. It does not imply the irrelevance of the concept "Chinese culture," but that, like *tongzhi* or any sexual identity, it has to be negotiated.

Given the highly hybridized Hong Kong identity, it is perhaps not coincidental that the category *tongzhi* was first appropriated by a Hong Kong activist. Historically, there was an absence of the notion of "Chinese *gay*": Hong Kong PEPS were trapped by two colonizers in a no-win situation in the 1970s: they were too *gay* to be Chinese, but too Chinese to be liberated *gays*. They had little choice but to create their own identities and strategies of resistance in diverse ways. The rise of *tongzhi* must be located in such a context of ongoing negotiation with colonial Britain, the global hegemony of Americanism, Chinese hegemonic constructs of the family and marriage, and the cultural absence of the homo-hetero duality. Indeed, the category *tongzhi* is by no means purely Chinese. Historically, it originates from communism, which is itself a Western discourse. When it was appropriated by Chinese revolutionaries, this "Western" term was indigenized. Only in recent years have Chinese PEPS appropriated this revolutionary term in the context of sexual politics, thus hybridizing and destabilizing the duality between West and East, sexual and political.

Tongzhi discourses have made a unique contribution to both Chinese culture and Western lesbigay discourse, as they unsettle the essentialist and totalizing conceptions of both sexual identity (*gay*ness) and cultural identity (Chineseness) (Spivak, 1987:205). *Tongzhi* is subversive from within—resources from the Western lesbigay and Chinese culture have been manipulated to negotiate their own space for same-sex eroticism. This, in return, challenges, expands, and redefines the hegemonic construction of Chineseness and *gay*ness. *Tongzhi* discourses challenge the fundamental basis of Chinese culture—the kin-family—not by denying it but by queering it. As elaborated in previous chapters, many *tongzhi* come out not by denying their cultural identity, but actively manipulating the most fundamental cultural ingredients such as non-verbal negotiation, breaking the insider-outsider distinction, using kin categories to construct same-sex relationships, establishing harmonious relationships with parents, and face-saving strategies. Chinese cultural categories are thus transformed by *tongzhi* to become a rich basis on which *tongzhi* negotiate their multiple identities and selfhood.

One contribution of *tongzhi* discourses is to position the heterosexual mainstream not as the enemy, but as allies, friends, and even colleagues that can share the goal of exploring their own sexuality and fight for everybody's rights to love beyond gender. Historically, in China, the line between homo and hetero was fluid, migratory, and fictive, with multiple layers of intersection and crossover. If we take this notion of fluid and contextualized sexuality seriously, then fighting for the right of intimacy beyond gender is not only the agenda of the homo/bisexual minority, it is everyone's concern. It is an insistence on *tongzhi* voices without reproducing the homo-hetero dichotomy. Once the homo-hetero and masculine-feminine dualities are unraveled, sexual and gender identities do not need to be oppositional, fixed, or homogenizing. Indeed, the homophobic heterosexist institution would then be deeply threatened and destabilized as it would lose the necessary "enemy" (homo/bisexual) to sustain and legitimize its imagined stability and hegemony.[2]

The problem with confrontational politics is that it ghettoizes PEPS and antagonizes the majority. This insistence on the *gay*-straight dichotomy may ironically discourage and even deny a more fluid sexuality that straight-identified people may be able to explore. The notion of exclusively *gay*, though empowering to many, can be as constricting and bi-phobic as the notion of exclusively straight. Confrontational and minoritizing identity politics have recently been problematized by U.S. and U.K. queer theorists. As articulated by queer theorist Gary Lehring (1997),

> The dilemma of a *gay* equal rights movement is that in accepting the essentialization of personal identity, they also accept the inferior status that this identity assigns them in the heterosexual/homosexual dichotomy. . . . By simply demanding the same rights as heterosexuals, in requesting integration into the social institutions of marriage and family, nothing is done to change the process by which difference was constructed in the first place, leaving the cultural and social institutions which produce "otherness." . . . Even when successful, the guarantee of equal rights and integration will leave the same bias and hatred towards gays and lesbians operating within the straight/ *gay* dichotomy.

Confrontational politics, while deeply empowering to certain lesbigays, often reenact the homo-hetero duality that produces the lesbigay's stigmatized position in the first place. Chu Wei-cheng (1997a), in his PhD thesis on Taiwanese *tongzhi* discourse, concludes:

> A metropolitan-styled gay movement may after all require a metropolitan-styled homophobic oppression to provoke it. In other words, if the gay activism in question could achieve postcolonial autonomy by devoting meticulous attention to the specificity of local oppression and then devising effective interventionary strategies accord-

ingly, it may well flourish without the local reproduction of an oppression as fierce as that in the metropolitan world. (p. 259)

Indeed, the rigid homo-hetero duality has historically been a strategy used by the straight world to "protect" itself from homoerotic flirtation by externalizing and projecting their own homoerotic anxiety onto the stigmatized minority. Perhaps we should remember the striking statement by Kate Millett twenty-five years ago: "Homosexuality was invented by a straight world dealing with its own bisexuality" (1975, quoted in Wolff, 1977:50).

As succinctly put by a Beijing *tongzhi*, "the question is not how should society help us, but how should we help society. I think we have a unique role to help Chinese people to reexamine our family values, gender roles, and marriage system. It is time for everyone, both *tongzhi* and non-*tongzhi*, to critically reflect: What is a man? What is a woman? I think *tongzhi* can be a catalyst for the progress of Chinese culture. Heterosexuals will benefit from our struggle. We are in the same boat!"

Tongzhi can be a valuable asset both to Chinese culture and even to the Western lesbigay world. They open up spaces by queering the mainstream—by exploring homoeroticism not by segregating the minority but reclaiming the rich homoerotic undercurrent that already exists within mainstream culture. *Tongzhi* both integrates with and subverts mainstream culture by exposing the homoeroticism that has been externalized and projected by the mainstream onto the stigmatized minority. In other words, *tongzhi* seduce and penetrate rather than confront and segregate themselves from the mainstream.

East Palace, West Palace (1998), the so-called first *tongzhi* movie in China, serves as a vivid illustration of this strategy of queering the straight. East Palace and West Palace are the *tongxinglian* slang names for the public toilets on either side of Tiananmen Square. The movie presents two male characters: one young male *tongxinglian* (A-Lan) and a straight policeman who hauls him in for an overnight interrogation. This cop signifies not only the straight world, but is a powerful symbol of dictatorial control in China. The political implications are sharpened by the fact that the filmmaker, Zhang Yuan, had been warned by the Chinese authorities about his five previous "illegal" movies. In the movie, A-Lan is trapped by his own childhood experiences and desperately yearns to be caught and punished to gain satisfaction. He actually entices the cop to catch him and bring him to the police station for interrogation. The movie can be read as proposing the strategy of "queering the straight," in which A-Lan keeps flirting with and seducing the cop and successfully provokes his desire for sadomasochism, transvestism, and homoeroticism. A-Lan is

portrayed as a charming storyteller in sharing his personal story of homoeroticism, which sets the mood of the cop and the movie itself. While the
movie elaborates in detail the sociopsychological grounds for A-Lan's
sadomasochist desire, it is actually the policeman who requests that A-Lan
cross-dress, who enjoys the sadomasochistic "torture" of A-Lan, and finally falls prey to A-Lan's seduction by passionately kissing A-Lan. The final
scene portrays the cop in a situation of "escaping" the police station,
followed by the closing shot, in which A-Lan leaves the station in the most
serene and self-contained elegance. Among the last dialogue in the movie
is a question thrown by A-Lan back to the cop: "You always ask me what
I want, but do you know what you want?"

While the straight world, as represented by this policeman, is being
seduced and challenged by a *tongxinglian,* the film clearly goes beyond
identity politics. When A-Lan first comes out when he is caught, he pro-
claims firmly: *wo shi tongxinglian* (I am homosexuality), instead of *wo shi
tongxinglian zhe* (I am a homosexual person). Though the cop "uncon-
sciously" exhibits his own desire for and pleasure in sadomasochism,
cross-dressing, and homoeroticism, the movie never intends to define his
sexual identity. Indeed, the homoerotic desire of this cop is rather ambiguous—when he kisses A-Lan, A-Lan is wearing women's clothes on his
request. It is unclear whether this cop treats A-Lan as a man, woman,
transvestite, *gay,* or straight. Indeed, the sadomasochism, transvestism,
and same-sex eroticism that appear to be associated with the *tongxinglian*
character A-Lan are fully found in the straight world as represented by the
cop. If same-sex eroticism (and sadomasochism and transvestism) is
something everyone can experience, the homo-hetero duality and any rigid
identity politics seem to be counterproductive in understanding not only
the *tongzhi* world but also the so-called straight world, which is never
immune to the seduction of homoerotic desire.

Although the situations in Taiwan, mainland China, and Hong Kong are
unique and different, I will use the case of the "Ten Great *Tongzhi* Dream
Lovers Election" in Taiwan in 1996 to exemplify the possibility of developing different kinds of strategies for coming out on the public and political level. The event was organized by the Taiwanese *tongzhi* group TF
(*Tongzhi* Front for Space Rights), which set up dozens of polling boxes in
different *tongzhi* venues, listing twenty male and twenty female celebrities, politicians, and social figures for *tongzhi* to select from as their dream
lovers.

By incorporating mainstream celebrities into the *tongzhi* scene, TF no
longer speaks from the outside as a marginalized group. Instead, it penetrates into the mainstream and challenges the apparent straightness of the

straight world by queering celebrities. It is a deliberate move to queer the mainstream and challenge the rigid homo-hetero duality of mass culture by selecting the most popular mainstream celebrities and politicians. Indeed, the mass media turned it into an interesting social event by interviewing the listed celebrities and reporting their responses, ranging from very homophobic to very positive reactions (Li, 1996a:10). Leslie Cheung, a famous movie star and singer, said that he is glad to know that he is admired by everyone irrespective of age, gender, and sexuality. Huang Lu Er, a famous Taiwanese singer, who got the most votes in the election, said, "*tongzhi* are no longer silent or trembling on the dark street corner. *Tongzhi* have come out courageously to say hello to anyone." The most homophobic response among the celebrity candidates came from singer Zhong Han-Liang of Hong Kong. He said: "I am very angry. How can I be picked by *tongzhi?* I think I have to be more macho and masculine." It is culturally significant that the most homophobic response came from a person from Hong Kong, a place of 150 years of colonialism where Western homophobic hostility has become deeply rooted. The Taiwanese *nan tongzhi* were quick to tease Zhong by retorting: "If you were more macho and masculine, we would love you more!"

TF also asked Taiwan *tongzhi* to dress up in rainbow colors from the February 8 to 14. The purpose is obviously not counting the exact numbers of *tongzhi* but exhibiting visibility and collective power. Since thousands of citizens would coincidentally dress in red on the eighth, orange on the ninth, and so on, such an event problematizes the stability of the straight identity by posing and simultaneously challenging the impossible question of who is and who is not *tongzhi*. At that time, it was not the *tongzhi* being put under the spotlight of the mainstream media's voyeurism—instead it was the general public dressing in "rainbow colors" who have to engage with their own sexualities in an unprecedented way. TF broke the rigid boundary between private and public by penetrating into each family through the newspaper, television, and other public media discussions about celebrity responses concerning homoeroticism.

In recent years, the Taiwanese *tongzhi* community has proposed the notion of *Jiti xianshen* (exposing collective identity), which is a kind of coming out as a collective rather than showing individual faces. It is a strategy used in the specific context of Taiwan, where the severe pressure to get married and the dominance of traditional Chinese values have made the model of coming out simply inappropriate for most *tongzhi*.

The "Ten Great *Tongzhi* Dream Lovers Election" was just one small example of pursuing a more indigenous strategy of coming out and exhibiting visibility, not by confronting one's parents, but by creating an event in which it is really homoerotic desires, not any single person, that comes out and seduces the public. Homoeroticism was stirred up, and it became difficult to answer discreetly "who is and who is not." Homoerotic desire, rather than a fixation on some minority persons, becomes a potential and a fantasy to which no one is immune. Homoeroticism goes beyond boundaries, and is not the private property of a definite sexual minority. This event further exposes the absurdity of the rigid homo-hetero duality that is always used by the straight world to "protect" themselves from homoeroticism. In the press conference for the event, a *nan tongzhi* opened the polling boxes, which contained more than 11,000 voting papers, literally throwing them out in front of the reporters. He said, "people always said that they cannot see the existence of *tongzhi*. Now you see it, we are out and visible, by thousands of votes" (Li Man, 1996:9). In this event of collective coming out without personal exposure, Taiwanese *tongzhi* indigenized and redefined the notion of visibility. They managed to go mainstream and seduce the public to engage with their own erotic desire: are you really as straight as you may think you are?

Instead of demanding that the sexual minority come out and face more severe oppression, the Ten Great *Tongzhi* Dream Lovers Election shifted the focus literally to every citizen to face his or her own sexuality. It implies a very different strategy of the *tongzhi* movement; it is no longer minority rights but the majority's rights to reclaim the space to love beyond gender duality. Instead of homo/bisexuals criticizing mainstream heterosexuals, which would then create and antagonize a heterosexually conscious majority, now *tongzhi* invite everyone, irrespective of their sexual orientation, to join them in exploring their own sexual desire. It implies a strategy to go beyond the duality of minority versus majority, *gay* versus straight, homo versus hetero, in order to envisage and attain social harmony for everyone without losing the specificity of the *tongzhi* identity and struggle.

Oppositional identities such as homosexual, *gay*, or lesbian, despite their empowering impact, are produced and implicated in the very homo-hetero binary structure they claims to go beyond. The discourse of "sexual liberation" based on stigmatized "sexual orientation" and "sexual identity" is a culturally specific project that need not be the only way to *tongzhi* liberation. What is also needed is a fluid and contextualized conception of sociosexual identity that empowers PEPS without reproducing the homo-hetero duality or pushing the mainstream majority to take up a sexual identity of "heterosexual" and the homophobic consciousness to counteract the new enemy, *gay*. Although *tongzhi* has a social history of only several years, it has such potential for a new horizon of same-sex eroticism, especially at a time when mainland Chinese are not yet implicated in the straight-*gay* dichotomy or any intense homophobic consciousness. If same-sex eroticism is not a private property of a stigmatized minority but a performance, act, social role, possibility, and potential that anyone can experience, then the imagined us-them dichotomy between gay-straight or homo-hetero and the concomitant homophobic enterprise immediately loses its solid foundation. In this case, same-sex eroticism is no longer a minority issue but a basic human issue that concerns everyone and permeates every aspect of social life.

Notes

Introduction

1. This concept of *tongren* was suggested by my friend, Laurent Long.
2. I use the term "discourse" in the Foucaultian sense of containing both linguistic and nonlinguistic constructions of knowledge and subjectivity. To quote Foucault, "we shall call discourse a group of statements insofar as they belong to the same discursive formation; it does not form a rhetorical or formal unity, endlessly repeatable, whose appearance or use in history might be indicated (and if necessary explained); it is made up of a limited number of statements for which a group of conditions of existence can be defined" (1972:117).

Chapter 1

1. For an excellent historical overview of same-sex eroticism in traditional China, read Samshasha (1997).
2. For an overview of the Chinese historical constructions of the notion of sex, see Van Gulik (1961).
3. Dikotter has offered a critical analysis of the change of paradigm from yin-yang to the scientific model of biological determinism. See Dikotter (1995).
4. For a critical analysis of the Chinese translation of the Western notion of gender into *xing bie*, see Tani Barlow (1993, 1994).
5. For an elaborate exposition of *qing,* see Tsang (1986).
6. For an overview of Buddhist conceptions of social reality and human sexuality, see Conza (1995) and Spiro (1970).
7. Even in the Western world, it is only in the twentieth century that the marital institution has been heterosexualized as a kind of heteroerotic love. Indeed, when the English term heterosexuality was first used by James Kiernan in 1892, heterosexuality was seen as pathological because it signified a sexual instinct not aimed at procreation. Until the 1890s, sexual instinct was identified as procreative desire, and all nonprocreative sexual desire such as heterosexuality, homosexuality, sadomasochism, and masturbation were seen as pathological. The definition of (ab)normality was predicated not on gender of erotic object choice but whether the sexual act was procreative and marital. Even until 1923, *Webster's Dictionary* still defined heterosexuality as a "morbid sexual passion for one of the opposite sex." For the historical and social invention of heterosexuality, see Ned Katz (1995).

8. From the third century *Wei lue* of Hu Huan, in (Liu Yiqing) Liu I-ching (1976:309).

9. Samshasha (1997). Translated by my friend, Angelina Chin.

Chapter 2

1. I find Rey Chow's notion of "two colonizers" and Petula Ho's usage of two colonizers in the "homosexual" context in Hong Kong very inspiring and helpful. In this chapter and Chapter 5, I will employ this notion of "two colonizers" in the context of Hong Kong *tongzhi's* search for their indigenous identity. See Chow (1992) and Petula Ho (1997).

2. Derrida's notion of difference has helped to deconstruct the essentialist notion of identity as fixed and self-constitutive. See Derrida (1981).

3. For the cases of homosexual offenses, read Henry Lethbridge (1976).

4. For a detailed analysis of the MacLennan Incident, see Chou and Chiu (1995) and Petula Ho (1997).

5. Petula Ho has offered a critical analysis of the MacLennan Incident. See Petula Ho (1997).

6. Samshasha argues that what has been imported from the West is not homosexuality but homophobia; see Samshasha (1997 [1984]).

7. But the cry for localization was also strong, even if unconscious. The Ten Percent Club, the largest local *tongzhi* group, has witnessed in recent years the obvious trend of localization, with its core activists mostly Hong Kong-born, having no overseas experience and the majority of members mostly local young people without advanced education.

Chapter 3

1. In the recent survey by Zhang Bei-chuan, 43.2 percent of the interviewees are not prepared to get married, 32.8 percent are undecided, and only 25 percent are prepared to get married. Among those who are still single, 71.6 percent said that their parents strongly pressure them to get married. Yet the high rate of resisting marriage may be biased by the education background of the sample, because 62.7 percent of the interviewees have university degrees. The pressure to get married will be much more severe for those who have less capacity for economic independence and intercity migration. See Zhang (1998).

2. In contemporary China, people tend to address each other as either *xiao* (little) or *lao* (old), rarely as equals, as would be the case if they used first names.

3. Since Liberation (1949), despite the right to choose one's own spouse as guaranteed by the 1950 Marriage Law, matchmakers still play a crucial role in uniting couples with compatible socioeconomic backgrounds. Communist Party Secretary Hu Yao-bang in 1984 encouraged the Party and workers' organizations to assist young people with marriage introductions. In 1984, for example, there were fifty-three Marriage Introduction Bureaus (*hunyin jieshaosuo*) organized by the municipal government, the Communist Youth League, and the Women's Fed-

eration. A survey showed that in 1986, only 30 percent of all marriages were free from family influence. See Xiao-chi (1986).

4. It does not, however, imply the birth of civil society in contemporary China, as the presence of overwhelming state control significantly limits the development and nature of the public sphere. See Yang (1994).

5. Momentum and dynamics come from different sources and move in different directions. For example, in one disco (*Nan Fang Zhi Ye*) in Guangzhou, the name of the bar is in Chinese only, and there is Chinese music and slow cha cha dancing, which can be seen as an indigenous Chinese strategy of using the cultural tolerance of same-sex intimacy in a *tongzhi* context.

Chapter 4

1. In 1997, when I began to write this book, I decided that this chapter should be written by a Taiwanese, and a Taiwanese *tongzhi* scholar agreed to do me the favor. After almost a year of delay, this scholar, because of a personal crisis, was unable to write. So I invited two other Taiwanese scholars, but for personal reasons both turned down the invitation. So I finally wrote the chapter myself. I have to thank Tan Chong-kee, Ryan Wu Jui-yuan, Chu Wei-cheng, June Wang, Josephine Ho and Wang Xiao-shan for their help and comments on my manuscript. To be consistent with the rest of the book, I use pinyin instead of Wade-Giles transliteration system, although it is only in recent years that pinyin has been more popular in Taiwan.

2. From the pamphlet by *Women Zhi Jian* (Between Us) circulated in the first U.S. *Tongzhi* Conference in America in June 1998 in San Francisco.

3. *Awakening* was founded in 1982 and was owned by the Awakening Foundation, which started another feminist journal, *Stir* (Sisters in Revolt) in June 1996.

Chapter 5

1. I would like to thank Rodney Jones for lending me his collections of these two magazines.

2. As Edward Said says, "Orientalism is a style of thought based upon an ontological and epistemological distinction made between the Orient and the Occident (Said, 1978:2).

Chapter 6

1. Here, I am using Judith Butler's (1990) and Marjorie Garber's (1995) conception of gender as performance to analyze the local scene.

Chapter 7

1. For comparative studies of the Chinese and American conception of the self, see Anthony Marsella and Francis Hsu (1985).

2. See Russell Leong (Ed.) (1996) for a comprehensive overview of Chinese American experiences of sexuality.

3. While Lau has been criticized for being conservative and pro-status quo, his analysis seems to be a fair description of Hong Kong's political scene, especially in the 1970s and 1980s. See Leung (1996).

4. Local scholars have observed the emergence of the new middle class in Hong Kong since the 1980s and have pinpointed its common features: Hong Kong-born, grassroots origin, Western-style education in local school, college graduate, liberal-democratic and egalitarian in political orientation. Yet these scholars also stressed that the new middle class is individualistic, disunited, lacking class consciousness, obsessed with social order and economic prosperity, and politically very difficult to mobilize. See Leung (1996).

5. Starting from Gilligan's critique of the male model of Kohlberg's supposedly gender neutral theory of human development, contemporary feminists have critically examined the entire project of modernity and its notion of the egoistic and atomistic self. Feminists such as Seyla Benhabib, Iris Young, and Nancy Fraser have appropriated the insights of communitarian theory to challenge modern liberalism and its ideal of a disengaged and isolated self. See Iris Young (1990).

Chapter 8

1. Tu wei-ming's (1991) notion of Pan-Cultural China is one of the best examples of such a formulation.

2. Jonathan Dollimore (1991) refers to homosexuality as "society's most anxiety-producing 'other.'"

Bibliography

Adams, Robin (1995a). "Letters." *Contacts* (Hong Kong), December, p. 20.

Adams, Robin (1995b). "Outright." *Contacts,* September, p. 10.

Aggleton, Peter (ed.) (1996). *Bisexualities and AIDS: International Perspectives.* New York: Taylor and Francis.

Aldrich, Robert (1993). *Seduction of the Mediterranean: Writing, Arts and Homosexual Fantasy.* London: Routledge.

Almaguer, Tomas (1991). "Chicano men." *Differences,* 5:75-100.

Ames, Roger (1981). "Taoism and the androgynous ideal," in Richard Guisso and Stanley Johannesen (eds.), *Women in China.* New York: Philo Press.

Ang, James (1996). "Prelude." *G/L Magazine,* June, p. 8.

Bai Xian-yong (Kenneth Pai) (1983). *Neizhi* (Crystal Boys). Taipei: Yuan Jian.

Baker, Hugh (1979). *Chinese Family and Kinship.* London: Macmillan.

Ban Gu (1955). *Han Shu* (Standard History of the Former Han). In the Twenty-Five Histories, Vol. I. Taipei: Kai Ming Bookstore.

Bao Ruo-wang (Jean Pasqualini) and Rudolph Chelminski (1993). *Prisoner of Mao.* New York: Coward, McCann, and Geoghan.

Barlow, Tani (ed.) (1993). *Gender Politics in Modern China: Writing and Feminism.* Durham and London: Duke University Press.

Barlow, Tani (1994). "Theorizing women: Funü, guojia, jiating" (Chinese Woman, Chinese State, Chinese Family), in Angela Zito (ed.), *Body, Subjects and Power in China* (pp. 253-289). Chicago: Chicago University Press.

Barlow, Tani (1998). *Formations of Colonial Modernity in East Asia.* Durham: Duke University Press.

Barrow, John (1806). *Travel in China.* London: Cadell and Davies.

Beijing Medical University (1990). *Jinshen Yixue Yu Xiangguan Wenti* (Psychopathology and Related Problems). Beijing: Beijing Medical University.

Beijing Renmin Jingcha (1989). *Renmin Jingcha* (People's Police). Beijing: Beijing Renmin Jingcha.

Benbahib, Seyla (1992). *Situating the Self.* New York: Routledge.

Berlin, Isaiah (1969). *Four Essays on Liberty.* Oxford: Oxford University Press.

Bhabha, Homi (1990). *The Location of Culture.* London: Routledge.

Binion, Gayle (1995). "Human rights: A feminist perspective." *Human Rights Quarterly,* (August):509-526.

Bond, Michael (1984). *Type of Reward As a Factor Affecting Distributive Strategies in Hong Kong.* Unpublished manuscript, The Chinese University of Hong Kong.

Boudieu, Pierre (1984). *Distinction: A Social Critique of the Judgement of Taste.* London: Routledge.

Brady, Anne-Marie (1995). "East meets West: Rewi Alley and changing attitudes towards homosexuality in China." *East Asian History,* 9 (June):97-120.

Brandon, Barrie (1997). "Media watch: Chinese *Tonghzi* Conference." *Contacts,* January, p. 14.

Brownell, Susan (1995). *Training the Body for China.* Chicago: Chicago University Press.

Burdman, Pamela and David Tuller (1997). "Chinese man champions gay rights." *San Francisco Chronicle,* January 11, p. 7.

Burton, Michael (1991). *Western-Sino Intermarriage in Hong Kong.* MPhil Thesis, University of Hong Kong.

Butler, Judith (1990). *Gender Trouble.* New York: Routledge.

Butler, Judith (1991). "Imitation and gender insubordination," in Diana Fuss (ed.) *Inside Out: Lesbian Theories, Gay Theories.* London: Routledge.

Butler, Judith and Joan Scott (eds.) (1992). *Feminists Theorize the Political.* London: Routledge.

Campbell, Neil (1987a). "Against gay law revision." *Hong Kong Standard,* July 23, p. 10.

Campbell, Neil (1987b). "Report reveals a number of defects." *Hong Kong Standard,* August 10, p. 16.

Cao Xue-qin (1973). *Hong Lou Meng* (The Dream of the Red Chamber, The Story of the Stone [SS]). David Hawkes trans. Harmondsworth: Penguin.

Carbaugh, Donal (1988). *Talking American.* Norwood, NJ: Ablex.

Case, Sue-Ellen (1989). "Towards a butch-femme aesthetic," in Lynda Hart (ed.) *Making a Spectacle: Feminist Essays on Contemporary Women's Theater.* Ann Arbor, MI: University of Michigan Press.

Cass, V.C. (1979). "Homosexual identity formation." *Journal of Homosexuality,* 4:219-235.

Chamberlain, Heath (1993). "On the search for civil society in China." *Modern China,* 19(2):199-215.

Chan, Ben (1983). "The paradox of gay decriminalization." *South China Morning Post,* July 16, p. 19.

Chan, Connie (1991). "Issues of identity development among Asian-American lesbians, and gay men," in Linda Garnets and Douglas Kimmel, *Psychological Perspective on Lesbian and Gay Male Experiences* (pp. 376-388). New York: Columbia University Press.

Chan, Julian (1997). "1997, PLA liberating *tongzhi?*" *G/L Magazine,* February, p. 52.

Chan, Rick (1983). "Gay law report under fire." *Hong Kong Standard,* June 11, p. 9.

Chan, Tonny (1983). "Teachers Association against homosexuality." *Hong Kong Standard,* June 9, p. 21.

Chang Jing-sheng (1926). *Xing Shi* (Sex Histories: China's First Modern Treatise on Sex Education). H.S. Levy trans. (1968). Yokohama: Bai Yuan Society.

Chao Yeng-ning (1996). *Embodying the Invisible: Body Politics in Constructing Contemporary Taiwanese Lesbian Identity.* PhD thesis, Cornell University, Ithaca, NY.

Chatterjee, Pratha (1993). *The Nation and Its Fragments: Colonial and Postcolonial Histories.* Princeton, NJ: Princeton University Press.

Chen, Chapman (1992). *An English Translation of Yu Da-fu's* Obscure Night: A Superfluous Man and the Birth of a Tragedy, *with a General Introduction.* Department of Translation, Chinese University.

Chen, Jerome (1979). *China and the West: Society and Culture, 1815-1937.* London: Hutchinson.

Chen, John (1991). "Comments on homosexuality." *Daily Information Bulletin,* Government Information Services, August, p. 13.

Chen, Louis (1984). "Quizzed over gay policy." *Hong Kong Standard,* February 27, p. 15.

Chen Chi-li (1973). "Homosexual scandal." *Express Press,* July 11, p. 7.

Chen Ruo-xi (1986). *Zhi Hun* (Paper Marriage). Hong Kong: San Lian.

Chen Sen (1962). *Pinhua Baojian* (Prized Guidebook for Appraising Flowers). In Kong Ling-jing (ed.), *Zhongguo Xiaoshuo Shiliao* (History of Chinese Novels). Beijing: Zhong Hua Bookstore.

Chen Tang-yuan (1928). *Zhongguo Funü Shenghuoshi* (The Story of Chinese Women). Shanghai: Commercial Press.

Chen Xiao-mei (1995). *Occidentalism.* New York: Oxford University Press.

Cheng, Christy (1982). *The Chinese Conception of Face: A Conception and Empirical Study.* Master's Thesis, National Taiwan University.

Cheng, Daphne (1987). "Call for gay law amendment." *South China Morning Post,* March 5, p. 7.

Cheng, Daphne (1990). "Homosexuality unaccepted." *South China Morning Post,* June 13, p. 18.

Cheng, Fonnie (1990). "Gays against Asian values." *Daily Information Bulletin,* July 11, p. 18.

Cheng Ai-ling (1997). "Reclaiming the history." *China Times,* February 5, p. 11.

Cheng, Terry (1980). "MacLennan inquiry: Possible for intruder to enter flat—manageress." *Hong Kong Standard,* July 12, p. 12.

Cheng Hao (1934). *Renlai De Shenghuo* (The Sexual Life of Human Beings). Shanghai: Yadong Shuju.

Cheng Sea-ling (1997). *Consuming Places in Hong Kong: Experiencing Lan Kwai Fong.* Unpublished Manuscript.

Chew, Linda (1989). *Female Homosexuality in Hong Kong: A Psycho Sexual Investigation.* MSocSci Dissertation, Hong Kong University.

Ching Hsia-ko (ed.) (1931). *Ma Jen Te Chieh-ching.* Shanghai: Chunyang Shuchu.

Chi Ta-wei (1995). "We are still cleaning the stage floor." *Awakening,* July, pp. 23-24.

Chi Ta-wei (ed.) (1997). *Queer Archipelago.* Taipei: Meta Media International Co.

Choi, Ben (1987). "Gays destroy family structure." *Hong Kong Standard,* July 23, p. 19.

Chou Wah-shan (1994). *Tongzhi Shenxue* (*Tongzhi* Christian Theology). Hong Kong: Hong Kong Queer Studies Forum.

Chou Wah-shan (1995). *Tongzhi Lun* (Theories of *Tongzhi*). Hong Kong: Hong Kong Queer Studies Forum.

Chou Wah-shan (1996a). *Beijing Tongzhi Gushi* (Stories of Beijing *Tongzhi*). Hong Kong: Hong Kong Queer Studies Forum.

Chou Wah-shan (1996b). *Xianggang Tongzhi Gushi* (Stories of Hong Kong *Tongzhi*). Hong Kong: Hong Kong Queer Studies Forum.

Chou Wah-shan (1997). *Houzhimin Tongzhi* (Postcolonial *Tongzhi*). Hong Kong: Hong Kong Queer Studies Forum.

Chou Wah-shan and Andy Chiu (1995). *Yigui Xingshi* (History of the Closet). Hong Kong: Hong Kong Queer Studies Forum.

Chou Wah-shan, Anson Mak, and Daniel Kwong (eds.) (1995). *Xianggang Tongzhi Zhanchulai* (Coming Out Stories of Hong Kong *Tongzhi*). Hong Kong: Hong Kong Queer Studies Forum.

Chow, Rey (1991). *Women and China Modernity: The Politics of Reading Between West and East.* Minneapolis, MN: University of Minnesota Press.

Chow, Rey (1992). "Between Colonisers: Hong Kong's Postcolonial Self-Writing in the 1990s." *Diaspora,* 2(2):151-170.

Chow Tse-tsung (1960). *The May Fourth Movement.* Cambridge, MA: Harvard University Press.

Chu, Julian (1973). "On the shame orientation of the Chinese," in Li I-yuan (ed.) *Symposium on the Character of the Chinese: An Interdisciplinary Approach.* Taipei: Institute of Ethnology, Academia Sinica.

Chu Tzu-ching (1928). "Na-li Tsou," *I Pan* 4(3):21-55.

Chu Wei-cheng (1997a). *Homo and Other: Articulates Postcolonial Queer Subjectivity.* PhD Thesis, Sussex University.

Chu Wei-cheng. (1997b) "Post-colonial reflections on Taiwan *tonghzi* movements/culture," in Josephine Ho (ed.) *Proceedings of the Second International Conference on Sexuality Education, Sexology, Gender Studies and Lesbigay Studies.* Taipei: National Central University.

Chung, Cristy, Aly Kim, Zoon Nguyen, and Trinity Ordona, with Arlene Stein, (1996). "In our own way," in Russell Leong (ed.) *Asian American Sexualities.* London: Routledge, pp. 95-96.

Coleman, Eli (1982). "Developmental stages of the coming out process." *Journal of Homosexuality,* 7:31-43.

Collins, Patricia (1991). *Black Feminist Thought.* London: Routledge.

Contacts (1994). "Editorial." April, p. 3.

Contacts (1997). "Editorial." January, p. 3.

Conza, Edward (1995). *Buddhism: Its Essence and Development.* Oxford: Cassirer.

Coupland, Justine (1996). "Dating advertising: Discourses of the commodified self." *Discourses and Society,* 7(2):187-207.

Course, Linda (1983). "Gay law reform will deform social morality." *South China Morning Post,* July 16, p. 14.

Croll, Elizabeth (1981). *The Politics of Marriage in Contemporary China.* Cambridge: Cambridge University Press.

Croll, Elizabeth (1995). *Changing Identities of Chinese Women.* London and Hong Kong: Zed Books and Hong Kong University Press.

Daryanani, Renu (1980). "A G silent on row over MacLennan verdict." *South China Morning Post,* January 18, p. 36.

Davies, Madeline and Elizabeth Kennedy (1991). "Oral history and the study of sexuality and the lesbian community: Buffalo, New York, 1940-1960," in Martin Duberman, Martha Vicinus, and George Chauncey Jr. (eds.) *Hidden from History: Reclaiming the Gay and Lesbian Past* (pp. 246-440). London: Penguin.

de Certeau, Michael (1995). *The Practice of Everyday Life.* Berkeley, CA: University of California Press.

D'Emilio, John (1993). "Capitalism and gay identity," in Henry Abelove, Michele Barale, and David Halperin (eds.) *The Lesbian and Gay Studies Reader* (pp. 467-478). London: Routledge.

Derrida, Jacques (1981). *Positions.* London: Athlone Press.

Derrida, Jacques (1982). *Margins of Philosophy.* A. Bass (trans.) Chicago: University of Chicago Press.

Dikotter, Frank (1995). *Sex, Culture and Modernity in China.* Hong Kong: Hong Kong University Press.

Doan, Laura (1994). *The Lesbian Postmodern.* New York: Columbia University Press.

Dobson, Chris (1983). "Anti-homosexuality laws blasted as 'wicked.'" *South China Morning Post,* November 18, p. 21.

Dolby, William (1976). *A History of Chinese Drama.* London: Paul Elek.

Dollimore, Jonathan (1991). *Sexual Dissidence.* Oxford: Clarendon Press.

Dong Ling (1994). "*Tongxinglian.*" *Eslite Book Review Journal,* 17 (September 13):17-51.

Eastern Flower (1994). "Running out of the closet." *Eslite Book Review Journal,* 17 (September 13):18.

Ebert, Alan (1976). *The Homosexuals.* New York: Macmillan.

England, Vaudine (1983). "Review of gay laws: More data sought." *Hong Kong Standard,* June 9, p. 15.

Escoffier, Jeffrey (1985). "Sexual revolutions and the politics of gay identity." *Socialist Review* (US), 12(3):38-51.

Evans, Harriet (1997). *Women and Sexuality in China.* UK: Polity Press.

Faderman, Lillian (1991). *Odd Girls and Twilight Lovers: A History of Lesbian Life in Twentieth-Century America.* New York: Penguin.

Fairbank, John King (ed.) (1957). *Chinese Thought and Institute.* Chicago: Chicago University Press.

Fang Gang (1995). *Tongxinglian Zai Zhongguo* (Homosexuality in China). Changchun: Jilin People's Press. Hong Kong edition (1995), Tiandi Tushu Gongsi (Cosmos Books).

Fanon, Frantz (1967). *Black Skin, White Masks.* Charles Lam Markmann (trans). New York: Grove Press.

Fisher, Stephen (1975). *Eurasians in Hong Kong: A Sociological Study of the Marginal Group.* PhD Thesis, University of Hong Kong.

Foucault, Michel (1972). *The Archaeology of Knowledge*. trans. A. M. Sheridan Smith. London: Tavistock.

Foucault, Michel (1978). *The History of Sexuality*, Vol. 1. Robert Hurley (trans.) London: Penguin Press.

Fraser, Nancy (1989). *Unruly Presentations*. Cambridge: Polity Press.

Furth, Charlotte (1988). "Androgynous males and deficient females: Biology and gender boundaries in sixteenth and seventeenth century China." *Late Imperial China*, 9(2):1-30.

Furth, Charlotte (1994). "Rethinking Van Gulik: Sexuality and reproduction in traditional Chinese medicine," in Christina Gilmartin, Gail Hershatter, Lisa Rofel, and Tyrene White (eds.) *Engendering China: Women, Culture, and the State* (pp. 125-146). Cambridge, MA: Harvard University Press.

Furth, Charlotte (1998). *A Flourishing Yin: Gender in China's Medical History*. Berkeley, CA: University of California Press.

Fuss, Diana (1989). *Essentially Speaking*. New York: Routledge.

Gan Lin (1993). *Jinye Bu Shefang* (No Defense Tonight). Nanjing: Nanjing People's Press.

Gao Cai-qin (1989). *Xing Yu Rensheng* (Sex and Human Life). Beijing: The Commercial Press.

Garber, Margorie (1995). *Vested Interests: Cross-Dressing and Cultural Anxiety*. New York: Routledge.

Gate, Henry Louis (1986). *Race, Writing and Difference*. Chicago: Chicago University Press.

Gay Asians Toronto (1996). *CelebrAsian: Shared Lives*. Toronto: Gay Asians Toronto.

Gian Jia-xin (1996). *Bring Out Taiwan Lesbians—Lesbian Discourses and Movements in Taiwan (1990-1996)*. MPhil Thesis, National Taiwan University.

Gilmartin, Christina, Gail Hershatter, Lisa Rofel, and Tyrene White (eds.) (1994). *Engendering China: Women, Culture, and the State*. Cambridge, MA: Harvard University Press.

Gledhill, Christine (ed.) (1987). *Studies in Melodrama and the Women's Films*. London: British Film Institute.

Gu Ming-jun (1995). "What can feminists do besides seeing and cross-dressing?" *Awakening*, (159, August):10-11.

Guang Tai (1995). *Taobi Hunyin De Ren* (A Person Who Shuns Marriage). Taipei: China Times.

Gui Zhi-liang (1936). *Nüren Zhi Yisheng* (A Woman's Life). Beijing: Zheng Zhong Shuju.

Guisso, Richard and Stanley Johannesen (1981). *Women in China*. New York: Philo Press.

Hadfield, David (1981). "Publish statements, demands jury foreman." *South China Morning Post*, October 7, p. 25.

Halperin, David (1993). "Is there a History of Sexuality?" in Henry Abelove, Michele Barale, and David Halperin (eds.) *The Lesbian and Gay Studies Reader* (pp. 416-431). London: Routledge.

Hamlett, Tim (1983). "Decriminalization will promote homosexuality." *Hong Kong Standard*, June 9, p. 17.

Hamlett, Tim (1987). "Inquiry should last much longer." *Hong Kong Standard*, July 23, p. 9.

Hamlett, Tim (1988). "Interesting insights into the Yang Report." *Hong Kong Standard*, May 21, p. 18.

Hamlett, Tim (1989). "Violation of human rights." *Hong Kong Standard*, November 15, p. 15.

Hanawa, Yukiko (1996). "Inciting sites of political interventions: Queer 'n' Asian." *Positions*, 4(3):123-140.

Hao Xiu-zhu (1993). "China no longer ignores homosexuals." *Beijing Review*, 36 (January 18):45-46.

Hart, John and Diane Richardson (ed.) (1981). *The Theory and Practice of Homosexuality*. London: Routledge and Kegan Paul.

Harte, Sani (1988). "Social workers shun gay law poll." *South China Morning Post*, July 23, p. 18.

Hawksley, Humphrey (1983). "Corruption of the youth." *Hong Kong Standard*, September 11, p. 23.

Henderson, John (1984). *Development and Decline of Chinese Cosmology*. London: RKP.

Hinsch, Bret (1992). *Passions of the Cut Sleeve*. Berkeley, CA: University of California Press.

HK Clipping (1980-1992). Special collection. Hong Kong: University of Hong Kong.

Ho, Alan (1977). "Pastoral care for homosexuals?" *South China Morning Post*, January 31, p. 10.

Ho, David Yau-fai (1976). "On the concept of face." *American Journal of Sociology*, 2(18):867-884.

Ho, Josephine (ed.) (1997a). *Visionary Essays in Sexuality/Gender Studies: Proceedings of the First International Conference on Sexuality Education, Sexology, Gender Studies and Lesbigay Studies*. Taiwan: Meta Media.

Ho, Josephine (ed.) (1997b). *Proceedings of the Second International Conference on Sexuality Education, Sexology, Gender Studies and Lesbigay Studies*. Taipei: National Taiwan University.

Ho, Petula Sik-ying (1990). *A Study of Interpersonal Relationships in Male Homosexuality*. MSocSci Dissertation, Hong Kong University.

Ho, Petula Sik-ying (1995). "Male homosexual identity in Hong Kong: A social construction." *Journal of Homosexuality*, 29(1):71-88.

Ho, Petula Sik-ying (1997). *Politicising Identity: Decriminalization of Homosexuality and the Emergence of Gay Identity in Hong Kong*. PhD thesis, Essex University.

Holland, Mary (1988). "Everybody's duty to strive for justice." *South China Morning Post*, August 29, p. 13.

Hong Kong Government (1950). *Hong Kong Hansard*. Hong Kong: The Government Printer.

Hong Kong Government (1996). *Equal Opportunities: A Study on Discrimination on the Grounds of Sexual Orientation, a Consultation Paper.* Hong Kong: The Government Printer.

Hong Kong Homosexual Representatives (1988). *Hong Kong Homosexual Political Manifesto.* Hong Kong: Author.

Honig, Emily and Gail Hershatter (1988). *Personal Voices: Chinese Women in 1980s.* Stanford, CA: Stanford University Press.

Hou Li-chao (1986). *Zhongguo Meinanzi Zhuan* (Biographies of Beautiful Chinese men). Taipei: Yuen Liu Press.

Hsu, Francis (ed.) (1953). *Americans and Chinese: Two Ways of Life.* New York: Abelard-Schuman.

Hsu You-sheng (1997). *Danai Wufang* (It's Alright to Love). Taipei: Sunshine Press.

Hu Shu-wen (1995). "The subjectivity already existed, it's you that fail to see it." *Awakening,* (163, December):14.

Hui Yin-fat (1990). "On homosexuality." *Hui Yin-fat's Newsletter*, No. 29 (September):3-4.

Hung, Jean (1995). "The family status of Chinese women in the 1990s," *China Review.* Hong Kong: Chinese University Press.

Innis, Michelle (1990). "More objections on gays." June 17, p. 15.

Jackson, Peter (1995). *Dear Uncle Go: Male Homosexuality in Thailand.* Bangkok, Thailand: Bua Luang Book.

Jay, Karla and Allen Young (1992). *Out of the Closet.* London: GMP.

Jiang Yi-hui (ed.) (1995). *We Are Lesbians.* Taipei: Shi Ren Press.

Jones, Rodney (1997). *Potato Seeking Rice—Language, Culture and Identity in Gay Personal Ads in Hong Kong.* Unpublished Manuscript.

Kapac, Jack (1991). *Gender Meanings and Chinese Male Homosexual Behaviour in the Late Qing Period.* Unpublished Manuscript.

Katz, Jonathan Ned (1995). *The Invention of Heterosexuality.* London: Dutton Books.

Ke Rui-ming (1991). *Taiwan Fungyue* (Erotic Practices in Taiwan). Taiwan: Independent Press.

King, Ambrose and John Mayers (1977). *Shame as an Incomplete Conception of Chinese Culture: A Study of Face.* Unpublished Manuscript.

King, Ambrose and Michael H. Bond (1985). "The Confucian paradigm of man: A sociological view," in Tseng Wen-shing and David Wu (eds.) *Chinese Culture and Mental Health* (pp. 29-45). New York: Academic Press.

Kristof, Dan (1990). "Curing homosexuals in China." *San Francisco Chronicle,* January 31, pp. 7-8.

Kuhn, Franz (ed.) (1967). *Femmes derrière un voile* (Women Behind a Veil), R. Martin trans. Paris: Calman-Levy.

Kwok Nai-wang (1997). *A Church in Transition.* Hong Kong: Hong Kong Christian Institute.

Lacan, Jacques (1977). *Ecrits: A Selection.* A. Sheridan (trans.) London: Tavistock.

Lam, Lydia (1983). "Social breakdown feared if homosexuality made legal." *Hong Kong Standard,* June 15, p. 13.

Lambda (1995). *Women Shi Nü Tongxinglian* (We are lesbians). Taipei: Shuoren.

Lan-ling Xiao-xiao-sheng (The Joker of Lan-ling) (1975). *Jin-ping mei* (Plums in a Golden Vase). Taipei: Wen Hua Publications.

Laqueur, Thomas (1990). *Making Sex: Body and Gender from the Greeks to Freud.* Cambridge: Harvard University Press.

Laris, Michael (1996). "Out of the shadows." *Newsweek,* April 15, p. 12.

Lau, Ricky (1987). "Deviance but not disease." *Hong Kong Standard,* July 3, p. 19.

Lau Man-pang and Ng Man-lun (1989). "Homosexuality in Chinese culture." *Culture, Medicine and Society,* 2(13):465-488.

Lau Siu-kai (1982). *Society and Politics in Hong Kong.* Hong Kong: Chinese University Press.

Law Reform Commission of Hong Kong (1983). *Report on Laws Governing Homosexual Conduct.* Hong Kong: The Government Printer.

Law Reform Commission of Hong Kong (1988). *Homosexual Offenses: Should the Law Be Changed? A Consultation Paper.* Hong Kong: The Government Printer.

Lee, Mary (1982). "Homosexuals should speak out." *Hong Kong Standard,* August 7, p. 23.

Lee, Mary (1983). "Unanswered questions." *South China Morning Post,* June 21, p. 15.

Lee, Quentin (1994). "From the backroom of 64." *Hong Kong 10 Percent Journal,* June, pp. 18-20.

Lee Ou-fan (1973). *The Romantic Generation of Modern Chinese Writers.* Cambridge: Harvard University Press.

Leeds Revolutionary Feminist Group (1981). "Political lesbianism: The case against heterosexuality," in Onlywomen Press (ed.) *Love Your Enemy? The Debate Between Homosexual Feminism and Political Lesbianism* (pp. 51-62). London: Onlywomen Press.

Legge, James (1949). *The Four Books.* Shanghai: The International Press.

Lehring, Gary (1997). "Essentialism and the political articulation of identity," in Shane Phelan (ed.) *Playing with Fire: Queer Politics, Queer Theories* (pp. 173-198). New York: Routledge.

Leong, Russell (ed.) (1996). *Asian American Sexualities.* London: Routledge.

Lethbridge, Henry (1976). "The quare fellow: Homosexuality and the law in Hong Kong." *Homosexuality and the Law,* 6(3):292-326.

Leung, Benjamin K.P. (1996). *Perspectives on Hong Kong Society.* Hong Kong: University of Hong Kong Press.

Leung Ping-kwan (1989). *"Doushi wenhua yu zianggang wenxue,"* Dangdai, 38 (June 1):14-23. Translation quoted in Rey Chow, 1992.

Li, James (1994). "Gay strategy in Hong Kong." *South China Morning Post,* August 15, p. 17.

Li, Thomas (1983). "Gay law should be changed." *The Star,* November 18, p. 8.

Li Man (1996). "Media stars discussing *tonghzi.*" *China Times,* February 10, p. 10.

Li Yin-he (1998). *Tongxinglian Ya Wenhua* (Homosexual Subculture). Beijing: Beijing Jinri Zhongguo Chubanshe.

Li Yin-he and Wang Xiao-bo (1992). *Tamen De Shijie* (Their World). Taiyuan: Shanxi People's Press.

Li Yu (1967). *Rou Pu Tuan* (Prayer Cushion for the Flesh), in Kuhn, Franz (ed.) *Femmes derrière un voile* (Women Behind a Veil), R. Martin trans. (pp. 33-97). Paris: Calman-Levy.

Li Yu (1970). *Liang Xiang Ban* (The Loving Fragrant Companion), in Ma Han-mao (ed.) *Li Yu quan-ji* (Complete Works of Li Yu) (pp. 55-86). Taipei: Cheng Wen Press.

Li Zhi-sui (1994). *The Private Life of Chairman Mao.* Tai Hung-chao trans. London: Chatto and Windus.

Lieh-Mak, Fei, Julian O'Hoy, and Siu Lun Luk (1983). "Lesbianism in the Chinese of Hong Kong." *Archives of Sexual Behaviour,* 12(1):1-20.

Li-fong (1985). "AIDS and homosexuality." *Zhong Hua Daily Post,* July 5, p. 10.

Likosky, Stephen (1994). *Coming Out.* New York: Pantheon Books.

Lin, Angel (1996). "Bilingualism or linguistic segregation? Symbolic domination, resistance and code switching in Hong Kong schools." *Linguistics and Education,* 8, 49-84.

Lin, Julian (1953). "A study of the incidence of mental disorder in Chinese and other cultures." *Psychiatry,* 16, 313-336.

Lin Jian-zhong (1995). *Zhe Tiao Lu Shang* (On this Road). Taipei: Xinglin Wenhua.

Lin Xian-xiu (1997). *Kanjian Tongxinglian* (Seeing Homosexuality). Taipei: Sunshine Press.

Lui, Linda (1991). "Councillors oppose gay reform." *South China Morning Post,* July 12, p. 28.

Liu, Thomas (1988). "Lecturer supports gay law changes." *Hong Kong Standard,* September 24, p. 16.

Liu Da-lin (1988). *Xing Ziyou Pipan* (Critique of Sexual Freedom). Beijing: Social Science Press.

Liu Da-lin (1989). *Xing Shehuixue* (Sociology of Sex). Beijing: Light Press.

Liu Da-lin (ed.) (1992). *Sexual Behavior in Modern China.* Shanghai: Shanghai Shan Lian Press.

Liu Da-lin (1994-1995). "The development of sex education in China." *Chinese Sociology and Anthropology,* 27(2):101-132.

Liu I-ching (1976). *Shishuo Xinyu* (A New Tale of the World). Richard Mather trans. Minneapolis, MN: Minneapolis Press.

Liu Tsun-yan (ed.) (1984). *China Middlebrow Fiction for the Ching and Early Republican Eras.* Hong Kong: Chinese University Press.

Liu Yan-ming (ed.) (1989). *Xing Pianli Jiqi Fangzhi* (Sexual Deviancy and Its Cure). Beijing: People's Press.

Liu Yi-da (1994-1995). "The latest report for the homosexual community in the mainland." *Chinese Sociology and Anthropology,* 27(2):62-71.

Liu Zhi-zhou (ed.) (1994). *Jingshen Bingxue* (Psychopathology). Nanjing: Nanjing Medical School.

Lynn, Richard (1994). *The Classic of Change: A New Translation of the I Ching.* New York: Columbia University Press.

Ma, John (1992). "Gay parade: Failure?" *Eastern Express,* August 22, p. 13.

Ma Han-mao (ed.) (1970). *Li Yu Quan-ji* (Complete Works of Li Yu). Taipei: Cheng Wen Press.

Mackerras, Colin (1972). *The Rise of the Peking Opera 1770-1870.* Oxford: Clarendon Press.

Mak, Anson (1996). "About Queer Sisters." Interview by *Marie Claire* (Hong Kong), (June): 73.

Mak, Anson (1998). "Gender politics and *tonghzi* movement." *Queer Sisters Newsletter,* (3):4.

Malcolm, Dave (1977). "The case of homosexuality." *The Star,* August 3, p. 23.

Man, David (1983). "Breakthrough: Abnormality banned." *South China Morning Post,* September 11, p. 20.

Manalansan IV, Martin (1996). "Searching for community: Filipino gay men in New York City," in Russell Leong (ed.) *Asian American Sexualities* (pp. 51-64). London: Routledge.

Marsella, Anthony and Francis Hsu (eds.) (1985). *Culture and Self: Asian and Western Perspective.* New York: Tavistock Publication.

Martin, Chris (1983). "Homosexuals call for equal rights." *South China Morning Post,* February 7, p. 19.

Matignon, Jean Jacques (1899). *Superstitions, Crime, Misère en Chine.* Lyon: Storck.

McGough, James P. (1981). "Deviant marriage patterns in Chinese society," in Arthur Kleinman and Lin Tsang-yi (eds.) *Normal and Abnormal Behaviour in Chinese Culture* (pp. 171-202). Holland: D. Reidel.

McMahon, Keith (1988). *Causality and Containment in Seventeenth-Century Chinese Fiction.* London: Leiden.

Mohammed, Abdul (1986). "The economy of Manichaean allegory: The function of racial difference in colonialist literature," in Henry Louis Gate, *Race, Writing, and Difference* (pp. 78-106). Chicago: Chicago University Press.

Morris, Brian (1991). *Western Conceptions of the Individual.* Oxford: Berg.

Murray, Stephen and Hong Keelung (1991). "American anthropologists looking through Taiwanese Culture." *Dialectic Anthropology,* 3(6):273-299.

Nardi, Peter (1994). *Men's Friendship.* London: Sage.

Nestle, Joan (1987). *A Restricted Country.* Ithaca, NY: Firebrand.

Ng, Vivien (1987). Ideology and sexuality: Rape laws in Qing China. *Journal of Asian Studies,* 46(1):57-70.

Ng, Vivien (1991). "Homosexuality and the state in late imperial China," in Martin Duberman, Martha Vicinus, and George Chauncey Jr. (eds.) *Hidden from History: Reclaiming the Gay and Lesbian Past* (pp. 76-89). London: Penguin.

Ng Man-lung and Lau Man-pang (1990). "Sexual attitudes in the Chinese," *Archives of Sexual Behaviour,* 19(4):373-388.

Norrgard, Lenore (1990). "Opening the Hong Kong closet." *Outlook,* 7(Winter):56-61.

Norton-Kyshe, James William (1898). *The History of the Laws and Courts of Hong Kong.* Hong Kong: Kelly and Walsh.

Onlywomen Press (ed.) (1981). *Love Your Enemy? The Debate Between Homosexual Feminism and Political Lesbianism.* London: Onlywomen Press.

Padgug, Robert (1990). "Sexual matters: On conceptualizing sexuality in history," in Edward Stein (ed.) *Forms of Desire* (pp. 43-68). London: Routledge.

Pan Kwong-tan (1947). "Cases of homosexuality in Chinese literature," in Pan K.T. trans. (reprint, 1970) Havelock Ellis, *Psychology of Sex.* Taipei: Cactus Publication Company.

Pan Sui-ming and Peter Aggleton (1996). "Male homosexual behavior and HIV-related risk in China," in Peter Aggleton (ed.) *Bisexualities and AIDS: International Perspectives* (pp. 191-217). New York: Taylor and Francis.

Patrikeeff, Felix (1989). *Mouldering Pearl: Hong Kong at the Crossroad.* London: George Philip.

Peng Huai-zhen (1983). *Tongxinglian, Zisha, Jingshenbing* (Homosexuality, Suicide, Mental Illness). Taipei: Olive Culture Press.

Penuel, Williams and James Wertsch (1995). "Dynamics of negations in identity politics of cultural other and cultural self." *Culture and Psychology,* 1:343-359.

People's Daily (1998). "German state passed law to cancel all unjust laws in Nazi court." May 30.

Petersen, Carole (1997). "Values in transition: The development of the gay and lesbian right movement in Hong Kong." *International Comparative Law Journal,* 19(2):337-362.

Phelan, Shane (1997a). "Lesbians and Mestizas," in Shane Phelan, *Playing with Fire: Queer Politics, Queer Theories* (pp. 75-98). New York: Routledge.

Phelan, Shane (ed.) (1997b). *Playing with Fire: Queer Politics, Queer Theories.* New York: Routledge.

Plummer, Kenneth (1981). "Going gay: Identities, life cycles and lifestyles in the male gay world," in John Hart and Diane Richardson (eds.) *The Theory and Practice of Homosexuality.* London, Routledge and Kegan Paul.

Plummer, Kenneth (ed.) (1992). *Modern Homosexualities.* London: Routledge.

Pu Song-ling (1969). *Liao-zhai zhi-yi* (Strange Stories from a Gossip Parlour). Hong Kong: Nan Tian Book Company.

Qiu Ren-zong (1997). *Aizibing Xing He Lunlixue* (AIDS: Sex and Ethics). Beijing: Capital Teaching University Press.

QS Newsletter (1997). "Editorial." No. 1, p. 1.

Queer Sisters (1997). *Sexual Rights Are Human Rights* (pamphlet). Hong Kong: Queer Sisters.

Radicalesbians (1973). "The woman identified woman," in Anne Koedt, Ellen Levine, and Anita Rapone (eds.) *Radical Feminism* (pp. 240-245). New York: Quadrangle.

Rayner, Leonard (1981). "MacLennan Case puts the legal system on trial." *South China Morning Post,* August 9, p. 17.

Rich, Adrienne (1980). "Compulsory heterosexuality and lesbian existence." *Signs,* 5:631-660.

Rickett, Allyn, trans. (1985). *Guanzi: Political, Economic, and Philosophical Essays from Early China,* Volume 1. Princeton, NJ: Princeton University Press.

Ropp, Paul (1981). *Dissent in Early Modern China.* Ann Arbor, MI: University of Michigan Press.

Rosenbluth, Linda (1993). "The high cost of life in the closet." *Contacts,* February, p. 4.

Rotello, Gabriel (1995). Let's talk about sex. *The Advocate,* Vol. 687/688:28.

Ruan Fang-fu (1985). *Xing Zhishi Shouce* (Handbook of Sex Knowledge). Beijing: Beijing Science and Technology Literature Press.

Ruan Fang-fu (1991). *Sex in China.* New York: Plenum.

Ruan Fang-fu and Tsui Yung-mei (1988). "Male homosexuality in contemporary mainland China." *Archives of Sexual Behaviour,* 17(2):189-199.

Said, Edward (1978). *Orientalism: Western Conceptions of the Orient.* London: Routledge and Kegan Paul.

Sampson, Edward (1993). "Identity politics: Challenges to psychology's understanding." *American Psychologist,* 48(12):1219-1230.

Samshasha (Xiaomingxiong) (1997). *Zhongguo Tongxingai Shilu* (History of Homosexuality in China). Hong Kong: Pink Triangle (First Edition 1984).

Sang Tze-lan (1996). *The Emerging Lesbian: Female Same-Sex Desire in Modern Chinese Literature and Culture.* PhD Thesis, University of California–Berkeley.

Sankar, Andrea (1986). "Spinster sisterhoods," in Mary Sheridan and Janet Salaff (eds.) *Lives: Chinese Working Women* (pp. 51-70). Bloomington, IN: Indiana University Press.

Scollon, Ronald (1998). *Mediated Discourse As Social Interaction.* New York: Longman.

Scollon, Ronald and Suzanne Scollon (1995). *Intercultural Communication.* London: Basil Blackwell.

Scott, Ian and John Barnes (1980). *The Hong Kong Civil Services and Its Future.* Hong Kong: Oxford University Press.

Scott, Joan (1992). "Experience," in Judith Butler and Joan Scott (eds.), *Feminists Theorize the Political* (pp. 22-40). London: Routledge.

Sedgwick, Eve (1990). *Epistemology of the Closet.* Berkeley, CA: University of California Press.

Seidman, Steven (1993). "Identity and politics in a postmodern gay culture," in Michael Warner (ed.) *Fear of Queer Planet: Queer Politics and Social Theory* (pp. 105-142). Minneapolis, MN: University of Minnesota Press.

Selfa, Lance (1997). "What's wrong with identity politics," in Donald Morton (ed.) *The Material Queer* (pp. 46-48). New York: Westview Press.

Shanghai Medical University (1984). *Linchuang Jingshen Bingxue* (Clinical Psychopathology). Shanghai: Shanghai Medical University.

Sin Wai-man and Chu Yiu-wai (1997). *Whose Rule of Law? Rethinking (Post) Colonial Legal Culture in Hong Kong.* Unpublished Manuscript.

Sinha, Mrinalin (1995). *Colonial Masculinity.* New York: Manchester University Press.

Siqiao Qushi [anon., pseudo.] (1987). *Ge Lian Hua Ying* (The Flower's Shadow Behind the Curtain). Originally published ca. 1691, a Qing Dynasty block-printed edition from Hunan Province, reprinted 1987, 2 volumes. Taipei: Tan-Ching Book Company.

Siu, Helen (1990). "Where were the women? Rethinking marriage resistance and regional culture in south China." *Late Imperial China*, 11(2):32-62.

Siu, Helen (1996). "Remade in Hong Kong," in Tao Tao-liu and David Faure (eds.) *Unity and Diversity: Local Cultures and Identities in China* (p. 177). Hong Kong: Hong Kong University Press.

Smith, Richard and Daniel W.Y. Kwok (eds.) (1993). *Cosmology, Ontology and Human Efficacy: Essays in Chinese Thought.* Honolulu: University of Hawaii Press.

Smyth, Cherry (1992). *Lesbian Talks Queer Notions.* London: Scarlet Press.

Spence, Jonathan (1984). *The Memory Palace of Matteo Ricci.* New York: Viking Press.

Spiro, Melford (1970). *Buddhism and Society.* New York: Harper and Row.

Spivak, Gayatri Chakravorty (1987). *In Other Worlds.* London: Routledge.

Stein, Edward (ed.) (1992). *Forms of Desire.* London: Routledge.

Supreme People's Protectorate (1984). *Answers to Questions Regarding the Specific Application of Law in the Campaign of Severely Punishing Criminal Offenses*, s. 13. Beijing: Beijing People's Press.

Tan Chong-kee (1997). "Are you *kuer, tongzhi* or gay," in Josephine Ho (ed.) *Proceedings of the Second International Conference on Sexology Education, Sexology, Gender Studies and Lesbigay Studies* (p. 8). Taipei: National Central University.

Tan Chong-kee (1998). *Renegotiating Transcultural Sexuality: The Deployment of Homosexual Eroticism and Prejudices in Taiwanese Fiction, 1960-1997.* PhD Dissertation, Stanford University.

Tan Guo (1994). "Uplifting rainbow." *Eslite Book Review Journal*, 17 (September 13):19-21.

Tao, Julia and Glenn Drover (1997). "Chinese and Western notions of needs." *Critical Social Policy*, 17(1):5-25.

Tao Tao-liu and David Faure (eds.) (1996). *Unity and Diversity: Local Cultures and Identities in China.* Hong Kong: Hong Kong University Press.

Tatchell, Peter (1991). "Thailand, behind the bars." *Outrage* (Melbourne), December: 40-43.

To Chung (1990). *The Attitudes of Traditional Chinese Culture Towards Male Homosexuality*, paper presented at the Fourth Annual Lesbian, Bisexual and Gay Studies Conference. Harvard University. Unpublished Manuscript.

Tong, Rosemarie (1984). *Women, Sex and the Law.* New York: Rowman and Littlefield Press.

Topley, Marjorie (1967). "Marriage resistance in rural Kwangtung," in Margery Wolf and Roxane Witke (eds.) *Women in Chinese Society* (pp. 67-88). Stanford University Press.

Trevor-Roper, Hugh (1973). *Hermit of Peking: The Hidden Life of Sir Edmund Backhouse.* New York: Penguin.

Trumbach, Randolph (1989). "Gender and the homosexual role in modern Western culture," in Dennis Altman, Carole Vance, Martha Vicinus, Jeffrey Weeks, et al. (eds.) *Homosexuality, Which Homosexuality?* Amsterdam: Schover.

Tsang, Adolf (1986). *Sexuality: The Chinese and the Judeo-Christian Tradition in Hong Kong.* Paper presented at the Conference of the Hong Kong Psychology Society, Hong Kong, July.

Tsang, Edward (1994). "Stay tuned." *Hong Kong 10 Percent Journal,* June.

Tseng Wen-shing and David Wu (eds.) (1985). *Chinese Culture and Mental Health.* New York: Academic Press.

Tu Wei-ming (1991). "Cultural China: The periphery as the centre." *Daedalus,* 122(2):135-164.

Van Gulik, Robert Hans (1961). *Sexual Life in Ancient China.* Leiden: E.J. Brill.

Vitiello, Giovanni (1996). "The fantastic journey of an ugly boy: Homosexual and salvation in late Ming pornography." *Positions,* 4(2):291-320.

Volpp, Sophie (1994). "Discourse on male marriage: Li Yu's a male Mencius's mother." *Positions,* 2(1):115-132.

Wan Rui-xiong (1990). *"Xingai de bianzou"* (The bigger variations of sex and love) in Wen Bo (ed.), *Nüshi Rentan* (The Ten Women's Tales). Beijing: China Social Science Press.

Wang Cheng-pin (1939). *Qingchun de Xingjiaoyu* (Sex Education for Youth). Shanghai: Xiongdi Chubanshe.

Wang Ling (1993). "Public hearing on gay rights." *China Times,* December 29, p. 16.

Watson, Burton (trans.) (1961). *Ssu-ma Chien, Shih Chi* (Records of the Grand Historian of China), Vol. 2. New York: Columbia University Press.

Watson, Burton (trans.) (1964). *Han Fei Tzu: Basic Writings.* New York.

Watson, Rubie, and Patricia Ebrey (eds.) (1991). *Marriage and Inequality in Chinese Society.* Berkeley: University of California Press.

Weixing Shiguan Zhaizhu (Owner of a Sexology Library) (1964). *Zhongguo Tongxinglian Mishi* (A Secret History of Homosexuality in China). Hong Kong: Universe Press.

Wen Bo (ed.) (1990). *Nüshi Rentan* (The Ten Women's Tales). Beijing: China Social Science Press.

Wen Jung-kwang (1978). "Sexual attitudes of college students." *Green Apricot,* 46:106-107.

Wen Jung-kwang and Chen Chu-cheng (1980). "Male homosexuals in Taiwan: A clinical study of 35 cases." *Journal of Formosan Medical Association,* December, pp. 82-92.

Wen Yi-duo (1944). *Shenhua Yu Shi* (Myth and Poems). Beijing: Old Classic Press.

Williams, Walter (1994). "The relations between male-male friendship and male-female marriage," in Peter Nardi (ed.), *Men's Friendship* (pp. 186-200). London: Sage.

Wilson, Richard (1981). "Moral behavior in Chinese society: A theoretical perspective," in Richard Wilson, Sidney Greenblatt, and Amy Wilson (eds.), *Moral Behavior in Chinese Society* (pp. 1-37). New York: Praeger.

Wolff, Charlotte (1977). *Bisexuality.* London: Quartetbook.

Wong, Danny (1995). "Do it your way." *Contacts,* December, p. 10.

Wong, Iris (1987). "Sexism in gay law." *Hong Kong Standard,* October 4, p. 20.

Wong, John (1982). "90% objection against gay law reform." *Hong Kong Standard,* March 3, p. 11.

Wood, Christopher (1984a). "Expertise fighting for gay rights." *South China Morning Post,* February 15, p. 18.

Wood, Christopher (1984b). "Gay law reform needed." *South China Morning Post,* May 5, p. 31.

Wu, Gary and Chou Wah-shan (eds.) (1996). *Women Huozhe* (We Are Alive). Hong Kong: Hong Kong Queer Studies Forum.

Wu Jui-yuan (1998). *As a "Bad" Son: The Emergence of Modern "Homosexuals" in Taiwan.* MPhil Thesis, Taiwan Central University, Taipei.

Wu-xia A-meng (1912). "Duan-xiu Pian" (Essays on Cut Sleeves), in The Classics Co-operative (eds.), *Xiangyan Congshu* (A Collection of Love Stories). Part 9, Chap. 2. Shanghai: The Classic Co-operative.

Xiao-chi (1986). "Changes in marriage." *Renmin Wanbao,* January 27, p. 4.

Xiao Quan (1996). "Ai, tongxinglian" (Oh, Homosexuality). *MingPao Monthly,* April, pp. 79-81.

Xu Ji-min (ed.) (1983). *Xing Kexue* (The Science of Sex). Nanjing: Jiangsu People's Press.

Xu You-sheng (1997). *It's All Right to Love.* Taipei: Happy Sunshine Press.

Yang, Chris (1982). "Yuan and its functions in modern Chinese life," in *Proceedings of the Conference on Traditional Culture and Modern Life* (pp. 103-128). Taipei: Committee on the Renaissance of Chinese Culture.

Yang, Mayfair Mei-Hui (1994). "Film discussion groups in China." *Anthropological Review,* 10(1): 112-125.

Yang Cui Xiao, et al. (1990). *Encyclopedia of Criminal Science.* Nanjing: Nanjing University Press.

Yang Ti-liang. Report of the Commission of Inquiry into Inspector MacLennan's Case. Appendix 19, pp. 236-242.

Yi Jia-yue (1923). "Zhongguo de xingyu jiaoyu wenti" (The problem of sex education in China). *Jiaoyu Zazhi,* 15(8, August): 22149-22170.

Young, Iris (1990). *Justice and the Politics of Difference.* Princeton, NJ: University Press of Princeton.

Young, Rhett and Roger Ames (1977). *Lao Tze: Text, Notes and Comments.* San Francisco: Chinese Material Center.

Yu Da-fu (1947). *Chen Lun* (Sinking). Shanghai: People Knowledge Press.

Yuxuan Aji (1995a). "Before holding hands, it is necessary to split up." *Awakening,* (161, September 5):16-18.

Yuxuan Aji (1995b). "The right of marriage and the right not to marry." *Girlfriends,* 3(February):16-17. Also published in *Awakening,* February 1995.

Zhang Bei-chuan (1994). *Tongxingai* (Homosexuality). Shandong: Shandong Science and Technology Press.

Zhang Bei-chuan (1998a). "Concerning for people." *Friend Exchanging,* (1): 4-5.

Zhang Bei-chuan (1998b). *Research on Male Homosexuals in China.* Unpublished Manuscript.

Zheng Mei-li (1997). *Nüer Quan* (The Circle of Women). Taipei: Fem Books.

Zhong-fong (1971). "Ren-yao crisis." *Public Daily Post,* August 14, p. 8.

Zhou Jian-ren (1931). *Xingjiaoyu* (Sex Education). Shanghai: Shangwu Yinshuguan.

Zhou Qian-yi (1997). "*Tongzhi* partner relationship, construction of subjectivity and thinking or movement." *Stir,* (3, January):39-40.

Zhou Zhong-di (1996). "*Tonghzi,* equal rights, movement." *Hong Kong Cultural Studies Bulletin,* (6):63-69.

Zhou-wai (1983). "Foreign corruption causing *long yang.*" *Sing Pao,* December 25, p. 13.

Zhuang Wei-qiu (ed.) (1990). *Zhongguoren De Tongxinglian* (Chinese Homosexuality). Taipei: Zhang Laoshi Chunbanshe.

Zito, Angela and Tani Barlow (1994). *Body, Subjects and Power in China.* Chicago: University of Chicago Press.

TONGZHI JOURNALS AND NEWSLETTERS QUOTED IN THIS BOOK

Hong Kong

Contacts Magazine
Hong Kong Magazine
Hong Kong 10 Percent Journal
Queer Sisters Newsletter
Satsanga

Taiwan

Awakening (feminist magazine)
Girlfriends
G/L
Stir (feminist magazine)
Tongyan Wuji

Index

Macartney, Lord George, 43
Mackerras, Colin, 36
MacLehose, Sir Murray, 68
MacLennan, John, 66-67, 80
MacLennan Incident, 60, 63, 66-67,
    79, 80
Malaysia, gay movement in, 288
Male, idea representation of, 35
Male brothels, Qing Dynasty, 35, 50
Male favorites, in homoerotic
    literature, 32
Male gaze, 47, 230
Male homosexuals, poetic
    euphemisms for, 27
Male masturbation, 18
Male prostitution, in traditional
    Chinese culture, 26
Male same-sex marriage (*Qi
    xiong-di*), 36-38
Male-female binaries, in
    Anglo-American culture, 21
Males, portrayal of, 33-34
Man, Anthony, activist, 82
Manalansan, Martin, IV, 262
Mandarin
    interracial *tongzhi* relationships,
        201-202
    tongzhi conference, 286-287
Mandate of Heaven, 14
Mao Tse-tung, 55
Marital system, traditional Chinese,
    15, 23-25
Marriage
    Hong Kong, 89
    interracial, 199
    law
        PRC, 105
        Taiwan, 155
    PRC, 101, 103-105
    resistance, 40-41, 122, 127, 245
    same-sex in PRC, 109
Martial arts family, 151
Masculinity (*nanzi qi*)
    British construction of, 61
    Chinese construction of, 34-35
    Westernized construction, 210

Masturbation
    Chinese medical literature, 50
    Chinese view of, 18
    modernity discourse, 45
Matignon, J. J., 50
Matrimonial Ordinance, Hong Kong,
    86
May Fourth Movement, intellectual
    trends, 15, 22, 44
Media
    confrontational coverage, 5-6, 252
    demedicalization of *tongxinglian*,
        131, 132-133
    positive coverage, 153, 159-164
    sensationalism, 149, 164
    on TB/G, 215
    Western lesbigay world, 106
Medical profession, divided on
    decriminalization, 73
Mem-bah, use in Hong Kong, 80, 90
"Member," use in Hong Kong, 80
Men
    coming out, 261
    interracial relationships, 189-199
    Jia (family/home), 259
    personal ads, 181-186
*Men and Women—The World
    Journey of a Sexologist,* 51
Mencius, on sex, 14
Meng Huan Kuai Che (Dreamland
    Express), 149
Men's World (forum), 137
Mental disease model
    in PRC, 108
    in Taiwan, 147-149
Meridians (*jingluo*), yin-yang
    system, 20
"Middle class," 85
Middle Kingdom, impact of West,
    43-44
Midnight Cowboy, 149
Migration plans, 199, 206
Millett, Kate, 295
Minan language, Taiwan, 142, 143

Order Your Own Copy of
This Important Book for Your Personal Library!

TONGZHI
Politics of Same-Sex Eroticism in Chinese Societies

_____ in hardbound at $69.95 (ISBN: 1-56023-153-X)

_____ in softbound at $27.95 (ISBN: 1-56023-154-8)

COST OF BOOKS_____

OUTSIDE USA/CANADA/
MEXICO: ADD 20%_____

POSTAGE & HANDLING_____
(US: $4.00 for first book & $1.50
for each additional book
Outside US: $5.00 for first book
& $2.00 for each additional book)

SUBTOTAL_____

IN CANADA: ADD 7% GST_____

STATE TAX_____
(NY, OH & MN residents, please
add appropriate local sales tax)

FINAL TOTAL_____
(If paying in Canadian funds,
convert using the current
exchange rate. UNESCO
coupons welcome.)

☐ **BILL ME LATER:** ($5 service charge will be added)
(Bill-me option is good on US/Canada/Mexico orders only;
not good to jobbers, wholesalers, or subscription agencies.)

☐ Check here if billing address is different from
shipping address and attach purchase order and
billing address information.

Signature_____

☐ **PAYMENT ENCLOSED: $**_____

☐ **PLEASE CHARGE TO MY CREDIT CARD.**

☐ Visa   ☐ MasterCard   ☐ AmEx   ☐ Discover
☐ Diner's Club   ☐ Eurocard   ☐ JCB

Account # _____

Exp. Date _____

Signature _____

Prices in US dollars and subject to change without notice.

NAME _____

INSTITUTION _____

ADDRESS _____

CITY _____

STATE/ZIP _____

COUNTRY _____ COUNTY (NY residents only) _____

TEL _____ FAX _____

E-MAIL_____

May we use your e-mail address for confirmations and other types of information? ☐ Yes   ☐ No
We appreciate receiving your e-mail address and fax number. Haworth would like to e-mail or fax special
discount offers to you, as a preferred customer. **We will never share, rent, or exchange your e-mail
address or fax number.** We regard such actions as an invasion of your privacy.

Order From Your Local Bookstore or Directly From
The Haworth Press, Inc.
10 Alice Street, Binghamton, New York 13904-1580 • USA
TELEPHONE: 1-800-HAWORTH (1-800-429-6784) / Outside US/Canada: (607) 722-5857
FAX: 1-800-895-0582 / Outside US/Canada: (607) 772-6362
E-mail: getinfo@haworthpressinc.com
PLEASE PHOTOCOPY THIS FORM FOR YOUR PERSONAL USE.
www.HaworthPress.com

BOF00